HOUSING THE HOMELESS

HOUSING THE HOMELESS

Edited by Jon Erickson and Charles Wilhelm

With a new introduction by Jon Erickson

TRANSACTION PUBLISHERS
New Brunswick (U.S.A.) and London (U.K.)
A Center for Urban Policy Research Book

Library of Congress Catalog Number: 2011040715
ISBN: 978-1-4128-4768-1
Printed in the United States of America

Library of Congress Cataloging-in-Publication Data

Housing the homeless / Jon Erickson and Charles Wilhelm, editors ; with a new introduction by Jon Erickson.
    p. cm.
Reprint. Originally published in 1986.
ISBN 978-1-4128-4768-1
    1. Homelessness--United States. 2. Homeless persons--Services for--United States. 3. Housing policy--United States. 4. Shelters for the homeless--United States. I. Erickson, Jon Karl. II. Wilhelm, Charles, 1948-
HV4505.H68 2012
363.50973--dc23
                                                              2011040715

**To Paul Davidoff
(1930-1984)**

Contents

I.   Images of the Homeless

II.   Background and Politics

III. The Importance of Numbers

IV. Who Are the Homeless and Why?

V. Solutions to the Problem

VI. Resources

List of Exhibits

Acknowledgments

The preparation of this reader would have been impossible without the assistance and cooperation of many individuals. Dr. George Sternlieb, Director of the Center for Urban Policy Research, encouraged and supported the development of this project. Dr. Robert Burchell provided many helpful criticisms and suggestions on the reader's contents and organization, as did Dr. Robert Lake and Dr. David Listokin. A special "thank you" goes to Brother David Fitzgerald, of the Ozanan Shelter in New Brunswick, New Jersey, for allowing us to work on this project at the shelter.

In addition, our sincere appreciation goes to Lydia Lombardi and Arlene Pashman for their invaluable assistance in manuscript preparation, and Mary Picarella for guiding the reader through the publication process.

We are most grateful to the contributing authors and publishers for their kind permission to reprint these articles.

Jon Erickson
Charles Wilhelm

About the Contributors

Jonathan Alter, Alexander Stille, Shawn Doherty, Nikki Finke Greenberg, Susan Agrest, Vern E. Smith, George Raine, Darby Junkin, Jerry Buckley, Marilyn Taylor and Patricia King are journalists with Newsweek, Inc.

Rose Anello and Tillie Shuster are with the Community Service Society of New York.

Richard P. Appelbaum is Associate Professor of Sociology at the University of California at Santa Barbara.

Ellen L. Bassuk, M.D., is Associate Professor of Psychiatry at the Harvard Medical School.

Donald J. Bogue is Professor of Sociology at the University of Chicago.

Alice Callahan, Jeff Dietrich, and Gary Blaise are with the Los Angeles Catholic Worker.

John R. Coleman is President of the Edna McConnell Clark Foundation.

Jon Erickson is a Research Associate at the Center for Urban Policy Research.

Chester Hartman is Chair of the Planners Network, 1901 Que Street, N.W., Washington, D.C.

Marjorie Hope and James Young teach Sociology at Wilmington College, Ohio.

Kim Hopper and L. Stuart Cox are on the research staff of the Community Service Society and the New York Coalition for the Homeless Board of Directors.

Philip Kasinitz is a graduate student of New York University.

Nancy K. Kaufman is Deputy Director of the Governor's Office of Human Resources in Boston, Massachusetts.

S. Anna Kondratas is a Schultz Fellow at the Heritage Foundation.

H. Richard Lamb, M.D., is Professor of Psychiatry at the University of Southern California School of Medicine and Chairperson of the American Psychiatric Association Task Force on the Homeless Mentally Ill.

Thomas J. Main is program officer with the Smith Richardson Foundation.

Harry Murray is a member of the Department of Sociology at Syracuse University.

Marcia Z. Nelson is a journalist in suburban Chicago.

Michael H. Phillips is a professor at the Department of Social Service at Fordham University, Daniel Kronenfeld is Director of the Henry Street Settlement and Verona Jeter is Director of the Urban Family Center.

Tom Robbins is the editor of *City Limits*, a magazine about New York's housing and neighborhoods.

Roger Sanjek is Associate Professor of Anthropology at Queens College, New York and is Chairperson of the National Gray Panthers Housing Committee.

John C. Schneider was an Associate Professor of History at the University of Nebraska and is now with Robert Jameson Associates of Burlington, Massachusetts.

Patricia Cayo Sexton is Professor of Sociology at New York University.

Harvey A. Siegal is Associate Professor in the Department of Medicine in Society at Wright State University.

Mark J. Stern teaches at the University of Pennsylvania School of Social Work.

Lorene Hemphill Stone is an Assistant Professor of Sociology at Lamar University, Texas.

Madeleine R. Stoner is Assistant Dean of the University of Southern California School of Social Work.

Charles Wilhelm is a project coordinator at the Capital Budget Homeless Housing Program in New York.

Introduction

Jon Erickson and Charles Wilhelm

HOMELESSNESS has become a social issue of vital national concern. As the number of the homeless has grown, the complexity of the issue has become increasingly clear to researchers and private and public service providers. The plight of the homeless raises many ethical, anthropological, political, sociological and public health questions and concerns for everyone. Perhaps the most serious and perplexing of these questions is what steps private charitable and public organizations can take to alleviate and eventually solve the problem at a time of fiscal restraint.

The concept of homelessness is difficult to define and measure. Generally, persons are thought to be homeless if they have no permanent residence and seek security, rest, and protection from the elements. The homeless typically live in areas that are not designed to be shelters (e.g., parks, bus terminals, under bridges, in cars), occupy structures without permission (e.g., squatters), or are provided emergency shelter by a public or private agency. Some definitions of homelessness also include persons living on a short-term basis in single-room-occupancy hotels or motels or temporarily residing in social or health-service facilities and having no permanent address. With estimates of the homeless population ranging from 250,000 to 3,000,000 (or over one percent of the total population), the magnitude and causes of the problem are unclear and the subject of much debate.[1] What is clear is that in most of our central cities the homeless have become a visible and disturbing fact of life.

This collection of articles, reports, and case studies brings together a wide variety of perspectives to help develop a clearer understanding of the homelessness problem. The objective in presenting this diversity of views is to illustrate the complexity of the problem. In fact, homelessness is not one problem but is the result of many separate and distinguishable social parameters.

In this introduction, the history and major sources of homelessness are reviewed. Secondly, past attempts to enumerate the homeless population are presented. Next, existing and possible policies and programs for the various elements of the homeless population are catalogued. Lastly, the introduction contains a review of the readings selected for this text. The object is to give the reader the background necessary to understand the approaches various authors have used. The editors recognize the limitation of any collection of articles to describe adequately this or any other complex phenomenon.

The History and Sources of the Homeless

America's first European settlers included the homeless. The homeless problem had long existed in England, at least since the fourth century A.D. when the Picts, the Attacotti and the Scots revolted against their Roman lords because of high rents and slave conditions.[2] With the opening of the colonies to settlement, the English developed an effective method for dealing with the homeless: ship the vagabonds and sturdy beggars to the colonies. In the county of Dublin, the homeless were ordered to prison to remain until "they shall be sent on board His Majesty's [George II] fleet, or to some of the plantations in America for any term not exceeding seven years."[3] With compassion that equalled England's, the colonies reacted by enacting a series of legal residency laws. By 1650, vagrancy was against the law in all the colonies. New York City was the only political subdivision in the budding colonies to offer assistance to the homeless with the opening of the first almshouse.[4]

Homelessness in America After the Civil War

Modern American homelessness originated in the industrial revolution during the second half of the nineteenth century. This period's major homeless group was laid-off laborers who inhabited the work camps and performed the massive amounts of manual labor required to build the railroads and economic infrastructure needed to initiate an industrial economy. The growth of railroad mileage in the United States from 9,021 in 1847 to 30,265 in 1861, suggests the size of the contribution to the American economy of these Low-status males.[5]

In the lineage of the homeless in America the hobo has the most glamorous reputation and at the same time the most tragic lifestyle. Among the earliest hoboes were jobless Civil War veterans, railroad workers and factory workers unemployed by the depression that followed the Panic of 1873. The period 1873-1879 was one of the most prolonged depressions in American history with an estimated two million unemployed workers (approximately 13 percent of the labor force).[6] Although no precise accounting of the homeless existed then or does now, the indirect evidence for this period suggests the homelessness problem was significant. For example, in 1874, over 60,000 transients (more than 5 percent of the city's total population) were lodged in Philadelphia. The homeless actually outnumbered the residents of its most densely populated ward. In response to the rise in homelessness in New York, in 1873 the YMCA opened a branch in the Bowery, and by 1874 several additional charitable shelters were opened.[7]

Beginning in the 1870s, skid row or the mainstem, a specific low-class residential-commercial enclave, evolved to fulfill the needs of the hobo or transient worker population. Skid rows formed to provide the lodging houses, saloons, and other services used by single, transient workers. The early skid row functioned as an active labor marketplace for transient workers seeking their next jobs. In this marketplace laborers and prospective employers could meet and arrange future employment. Throughout the nation skid rows provided working men temporary residences between jobs. During economic boom periods skid row seems to have been a thriving, if marginal, neighborhood.[8]

However, the periodic downturns in the economy, especially the Panic of 1893 and the resulting depression with six years of over 10 percent unemployment, placed a severe burden on the skid rows. Although precise numbers are not available, the size of the transient population appears to have grown significantly. In 1896, the first publicly owned emergency housing opened with New York's remodeling of a waterfront barge to house 1,300 people.[9]

The number of homeless transient men rose and fell with the business cycle and the seasonal nature of industries such as harvesting, lumber, and construction. As a result, homelessness was for many tied to the industrial conditions of the period. The poor working conditions of this period and the cohesion of many transient workers helped produce one of the most radical union movements in the United States, the Industrial Workers of the World. Many hoboes and day workers were involved in the I.W.W. The I.W.W. publications, *The Industrial Worker* and *Solidarity*, became the chroniclers of the plight of the homeless. Ralph Chaplin, a hobo songster and poet, captures the essence of this hope for cohesion of the homeless in his song, *Solidarity Forever*:

It is we who plowed the prairies; built the cities
  where they trade.
Dug the mines and built the workshops; endless miles of
  railroad laid.
Now we stand, outcast and starving, mid the wonders we
  have made;
But the union makes us strong.[10]

During the early 1900s, another shift in the labor market resulted in the gradual reduction in the demand for seasonal workers. Mechanization of farms and industry and the decline in railroad construction reduced the need for unskilled and semi-skilled migrant labor. Aside from the recession of 1921-22 when municipal lodging houses were filled to capacity, the population of skid row areas was on the decline. Gone were the robust, migrant hoboes. In their place was a smaller population of men who were long-term residents, the homeguard. The homeguard was a combination of odd-jobbers, day workers, the handicapped, and societal misfits.[11]

The Great Depression

The next major period of homelessness in the United States was the Great Depression of the 1930s. During this period, hundreds of thousands of unemployed workers and tens of thousands of foreclosed and evicted families formed a large homeless population throughout the country. An example, as seen in John Dos Passos's description, was the masses of squatters living in caves dug in sandpiles on the outskirts of Detroit.[12] The U.S. Congress held hearings in response to the 1932 publication by the Department of Labor's Children's Bureau of the "Memorandum on the Transient Boy." The Children's Bureau study was a survey of 158 emergency relief agencies in 60 cities of 50,000 or more population. The survey showed that by November 1932, various agencies were providing almost 400,000 lodgings for the homeless. As a result of the study, Congress established in 1932 the Committee on the Care of the Transient and Homeless. The Labor Department study and the hearings that followed resulted in the creation of the Federal Transient Program by the Federal Emergency Relief Administration on July 26, 1933. By 1935, the program was assisting 373,600 homeless a month.[13] But with the advent of World War II and the resulting economic boom, homelessness almost disappeared as a social problem.

Homelessness Since World War II

After the Depression and continuing to the 1960s, the skid row continued to provide shelter for the relatively small number of homeless in a unique setting of missions, bars, social-service agencies, and single-room-occupancy or welfare hotels. As John C. Schneider notes in one of the readings, the function and residents of skid row evolved from a transient labor residential area that by 1960 was just a remnant of its past.[14] Skid row areas had declined in size and were now dominated by a smaller, older, often alcoholic, and welfare-dependent population.

The Single Male Transient

The single, older male transient population is perhaps the most visible of all homeless groups. As noted in the section on skid row and the single-room occupancy hotel, the size and composition of this population has grown and declined in response to the overall economic climate. Although this population probably peaked in size during the Great Depression with Hoovervilles, skid rows, and makeshift shantytowns located in nearly every city, remnants of the older, transient male population have continued until the present day. Although the skid row areas almost disappeared as a result of private and public urban renewal efforts, with the recession of 1980-82 this population began to reappear in depth.[15]

Traditional, economically based homelessness grew during the economic downturn of the early 1980s. The subsequent loss of many jobs left those who were undereducated and unskilled—some of whom were Vietnam veterans— in the difficult, if not impossible, position of meeting food and conventional shelter costs. The unemployment rate rose above 10 percent during part of 1982 for the first time since the Depression, and although it has declined closer to 7 percent, the unemployment rate continues to be a historically high percentage of the labor force for a period of economic growth.[16] For many the combination of lowered incomes at a time of high or unchanging housing costs has resulted in evictions or mortgage foreclosures. According to the HUD *Homelessness Report*, 35 to 40 percent of the homeless continue unhoused due to economic conditions that resulted in loss of their homes.[17]

In summary, historically the rise and fall in the number of homeless appears to be directly related to the structure of the labor market and overall economic conditions. Beginning in the late 1970s there have been some large shifts in the composition of the homeless. Joining economic conditions as a cause of homelessness are two new factors that can broadly be grouped into

(1) significant shifts in social welfare policy, and (2) the decline of the intact and extended family.

The major changes in social welfare policy that have contributed to homelessness are deinstitutionalization, reductions in subsidized housing, and the recent eligibility reviews for Social Security Disability Insurance. The reduction of the percent of intact families is related to increased homelessness through the rise of low-income, single-parent families. These three primary factors in the rise of homelessness are interrelated. Mental illness, cutbacks in social-welfare programs, and the feminization of poverty all are related in part to economic instability and governmental policies designed to promote economic growth. However, whereas in the past homelessness has declined at the end of an economic downturn, homelessness in the 1980s may not be solved by the current economic recovery due to permanent changes in social-welfare policies and the family structure.

Shifts in Social-Welfare Policy

A combination of drug therapy, fiscal restraint, and legal advocacy for the mentally ill during the 1960s created a new population of the homeless—the mentally ill. Beginning in the late 1950s, large numbers of persons previously confined to mental institutions were released into the general population. The number of confined mental patients peaked in the 1950s at roughly 650,000. By 1978 the number had declined to 150,000.[18] Although many deinstitutionalized persons have been well served by community mental health facilities and services, the demand for services has greatly outstripped their availability. Additionally, whereas the actual "deinstitutionalized" population is probably decreasing, the number of homeless persons with psychological disorders is increasing, since along with deinstitutionalization came tighter admission criteria for mental institutions. The mentally troubled homeless individual is now likely never to have been eligible for, or a patient in, a mental health institution. Recent estimates suggest that between 20 and 50 percent of the current homeless population are suffering from some form of mental illness.[19] The ex-mental patients have joined the alcoholics and transients in a changing housing world.

As public urban renewal and private revitalization reduced the size of skid row and the single-room-occupancy (SRO) housing stock, the 1980s also have witnessed a decrease in the number of new or rehabilitated, federally subsidized housing units. Federally subsidized housing production reached a peak in 1971 of over 480,000 units. By 1983, the figure was less than 70,000 units. The relative cost of renting has also increased substantially since 1975.

In 1975, 14.7 percent of all renters paid more than 50 percent of their income for rent. In 1983 this figure had increased to 21.5 percent. As the cost of housing has gone up, and the production of subsidized units has decreased, the cumulative effect is that many households find it increasingly difficult, and in some cases impossible, to find or keep affordable rental housing.[20]

Added to the problems of an inadequate supply of low-cost housing and high unemployment are changes in support programs. In March 1981, the Reagan administration initiated a review of persons who were considered to be possibly ineligible but who were receiving Social Security Disability Insurance for either a physical or mental disability. Estimates are that as many as 200,000 persons lost their benefits before the Administration (in April 1984) stopped benefit cutoffs to additional recipients in response to reports that many truly eligible persons were suffering undue hardships by losing their benefits. As a result of this loss of income many households reportedly experienced eviction for non-payment of rent and found themselves on the streets.[21]

Changes in the Family Structure

Another recent major source of homelessness is related to the reduction of the percent of intact families in America. Increasingly, women, with or without children, are joining the ranks of the homeless as a result of the much discussed feminization of poverty and domestic violence. This new and growing group, with more than 3.5 million female-headed families and seven million children in poverty in 1983, now represents as much as 30 percent of the SRO resident population and often is untouched by the few programs operating to serve the homeless.[22] In New York City during 1984 over one-half of the total homeless were in family units, not the traditional single, male adult. Peter Smith, President of New York's Partnership for the Homeless, has suggested that the number of homeless families could double by the winter of 1985.[23]

Lastly, there are a number of homeless groups or seasonally homeless groups that stand out. Often considered part of the homeless population is the youth runaway. This population alone may be over one million.[24] Consideration of this major social issue is beyond the scope of the present work. Also not examined in this reader are illegal immigrants, seasonal farm workers, and the victims of natural and human-made disasters who are temporarily or seasonally homeless. All these people become homeless, even if for relatively short periods of time, and seek assistance from social and housing programs that are already severely overburdened.

How Many Homeless?

Empirical social science has not been used to determine the extent of homelessness. However, this lack of formal measurement has not prevented many agencies and service advocates from suggesting a variety of estimates. These estimates of the homeless vary from a low of 250,000 to a high of 3,000,000.[25] This range not only signals how little is known about the problem, but unfortunately has become an indication of how various groups judge the seriousness and policy ramifications of homelessness. The value/fact debate over the number of homeless represents the political use and reuse of social science.[26] To present a low numerical estimate of homelessness suggests that the problem is not a national issue but a problem that can be effectively handled at the local level. To present a high numerical estimate suggests the failure of the Reagan administration's social and economic policy and the urgent need for massive federal funding.

In response to the need for information about the homeless, the U.S. Department of Housing and Urban Development prepared a report (see Section III for an excerpt from the report and comments and criticisms of it) which established an official number of homeless at 250,000 to 300,000. This estimate was much lower than the 1 to 3 million estimate commonly used in the press and by homeless advocates and service providers, including the Department of Health and Human Services. The accuracy and political motivation of those involved in preparing the report were questioned. Reagan administration supporters found comfort in the lower estimate and suggested that the problem was relatively small. The homelessness problem, disturbing as it was, for this group was not the result of administration policies, nor was the problem beyond the means of state and local governments' ability to address. On the other hand, those persons seeking a commitment of federal funds to address homelessness were outraged by the report's findings.[27]

Perhaps the most important insight from this debate over numbers and appropriate policy responses is that there is a growing number of homeless persons in our major cities that require emergency shelter. For example, in New York City on January 15, 1985, the city alone provided temporary shelter for 19,000 people. This number is the largest since the Depression, and is not comprised exclusively of single men and women. The number of homeless families in New York City shelters has risen from 1,400 in January 1983, to 2,400 in January 1984, and to 3,300 in December 1984. This represents a staggering annual rate of increase of more than 67 percent in the number of homeless families being served. And this increase is not occurring just in large cities. After a court ruling mandating the provision of assistance to the homeless, Atlantic City witnessed a more than doubling of persons on the local welfare rolls from 374 in January 1984 to 859 in February 1985.[28]

Policies for the Homeless

The nine primary groups that comprise the homeless population seem to share little in common but the lack of permanent shelter. The groups are: (1) the traditional single, older-male transient, (2) the deinstitutionalized mental patient, (3) youth runaways, (4) foreclosed or evicted families and individuals, (5) mentally and physically disabled persons with low incomes, (6) abused or battered women with or without children, (7) victims of natural and man-made disasters, (8) illegal immigrants, and (9) victims of alcoholism. Although the homeless population is quite diverse, there are essentially four policy or program options upon which most researchers who have studied the problem agree.

The Prevention of Homelessness

First, but not always obvious from policy discussions or news stories, is a set of policies that would prevent homelessness. Homeless individuals and families were not always on the street. Timely intervention and the availability of suitable housing options may be the best homeless program of all.

Researchers and advocates often refer to the "hidden homeless"—the thousands, maybe millions, of persons who, for whatever reason, lost their own homes and now are doubled or tripled up with friends, relatives, or in other temporary housing arrangements. Governor Cuomo of New York has estimated that there are more than 500,000 hidden homeless persons in his state alone. Any small, overall change in the ability of these individuals or households to find temporary housing at a time of a tight housing market could result in a dramatic increase in the number of the homeless.[29]

Included in homeless prevention policies are a number of differing programs. The most obvious programs would be efforts to greatly expand the nation's low-income housing stock either through expanding housing construction and rehabilitation programs, or through Section 8-type rental supplements. Roger Sanjek, in Section V, strongly endorses this specific approach. Another program to address this issue would be to expand the number and increase the quality of residential community mental health programs and insure a better linkage between mental institutions and community services. The expansion of private and public community facilities (such as halfway houses) that provide services to alcoholics, drug abusers, and ex-prisoners, would all serve to prevent future and reduce existing homelessness. All these efforts would require additional private sector and government funding. There is no way to avoid this fiscal strain.

However, at a time of federal cutbacks, small local and state efforts can begin to address this policy approach. A New Jersey homelessness prevention program (see Section VI for a program description) is an example of a relatively inexpensive attempt to intervene with landlords or others to prevent eviction or foreclosure and use Section 8 to house the evicted before they reach the streets.

Emergency, Short-Term Shelters

Once an individual or family is homeless, the need for short-term emergency accommodations is paramount. The ideal purpose of the emergency shelter is to get the homeless off the streets and into a safe and healthy environment. The emergency shelter is not a solution to homelessness, but a short-term service facility in which longer-term needs (e.g., income support, job training, mental health services and permanent housing) can be identified. Once the service needs are identified, individuals and families would be transferred or referred to the appropriate facility or services. Although there is no agreement on the appropriate size for such shelters, the trend is toward smaller shelters (fewer than 100 beds) and toward providing ongoing albeit short-term accommodations as opposed to forcing persons into wandering from shelter to shelter each night in search of a bed (see Kaufman article in Section V).

Transitional Phase

After the needs of the homeless person or family have been identified, referral should be made to an appropriate longer-term residence. Such facilities would be designed to fit specific population subgroups and their needs. At the transitional shelter, the provision of health, mental health, employment, and social-service programs are key components. The search for permanent shelter should occur once the basic needs and future services are provided or initiated. See the Henry Street Settlement House description in Section V for an example of an existing operation of this type.

Permanent Housing

In many cases, the provision of permanent subsidized housing may be all that a homeless person or family requires. But for many, a package of social services and specialized facilities may be necessary to insure that homelessness does not reoccur. Permanent housing for some may mean a family-care home, congregate housing, or specialized medical or mental-health-care facilities. The necessity of integrating the homeless into existing social programs while appropriate permanent housing is found may be central to the long-term solution of homlessness.[30]

In summary, homelessness is a complex multi-dimensional problem that cannot be addressed simply through providing shelter to people on cold nights. Many localities have unfortunately opted either to do nothing or to provide only emergency shelters. The short-term emergency shelter may appear to be the cheapest solution, but unless the cycle of homelessness is broken, the need for more shelters can only grow. To break the cycle of homelessness through the development of comprehensive and coordinated programs may in fact be less expensive in the long run. As Ellen L. Bassuk notes, the key question is:

Are Americans willing to consign a broad class of disabled people to a life of degradation, or will they make the commitment to give such people the care they need? In a civilized society, the answer should be clear.[31]

Organization of Readings

This text is divided into six general topic areas. Beginning with portraits of the homeless problem, it includes sections on the background and politics of the issue, the numerical estimates of the people affected, description of three selected sub-groups of the homeless population, and strategies to solve or alleviate the problem. Lastly case studies, resources, and proposals are included to provide examples of what specifically can be done at the state and local levels.

Section I: Images of the Homeless

The mass media have played a major role in educating the public about the growing crisis of homelessness. In the first section of this reader, five portraits of homeless people are presented to demonstrate the seriousness of the problem and the manner in which the popular press has covered the issue.

Jonathan Alter et al., in a *Newsweek* cover story, address the nationwide scope of the problem at a time of overall economic recovery. The article also demonstrates a change in the way the media and the public view the homeless. The homeless are increasingly portrayed as victims in need of assistance, as opposed to undeserving alcoholic bums on skid rows. This overview provides a good introduction to issues and initial policy responses of cities and the federal government.

Whereas *Newsweek* addresses the homeless as a social problem requiring government, religious, private, and social-service agency responses, the Marcia Z. Nelson article reviews the problem and suggests the political potential of the homeless as a progressive political force. To Nelson the homeless are a group that, if organized, could be a source of creative solutions to their individual situations and to changing the overall political and economic structure that has given rise to the problem. Recent organizing efforts in Philadelphia, resulting in over 4,000 homeless union members, suggest the potential of this strategy.[32]

Tom Robbins provides a strongly written portrait of New York City's homeless families. He observes the terrible conditions in welfare hotels and the inadequate response of the City to the problem. John R. Coleman, president of the Edna McConnell Clark foundation, examines the physical and psychological harshness of life on the streets through a diary of his ten-day experience. Whether on the streets or in the shelters of New York City, his encounter with homelessness provides a vivid picture of the abusive manner in which the homeless have been treated.

Harry Murray provides a study of day-to-day life of homeless shelter users. Murray finds the homeless shelter-user experiences a daily routine that has as its primary goal simply survival, as opposed to the longer-term goals and aspirations of the general populace.

Section II: Background and Politics

Patricia Cayo Sexton opens this section by addressing the history of homelessness and current nature of homelessness from the critical perspective of Marxist analysis. She finds that there is an historic dialectic of compassion and contempt for the poor, and that America's homeless are witnesses both to the conservative tendency to label them unworthy and undeserving, and to the public's attempts at compassion and charity. Sexton concludes that the active involvement of citizens with the homeless can be a viable part of a political strategy to encourage the development of adequate social-welfare policies.

Marjorie Hope and James Young argue that compassionate, humane treatment for the homeless is an urgent necessity. They go further to push for programs to provide the housing and services necessary to prevent homelessness. Although they call for increased church involvement, they note that the religious community cannot possibly do the job alone.

Thomas J. Main views the issue from a more conservative perspective. He critiques the approach of homeless advocates for not distinguishing between the deserving and undeserving homeless. Main finds from his review of New York shelter statistics that many homeless are able-bodied men who may in fact have other housing options. This subgroup of the homeless may choose shelters to get something for nothing and should be required to participate in some sort of work requirement. For Main the homeless advocates are so busy blaming the system that they miss the question of individual responsibility.

Mark J. Stern addresses the emergence of homelessness as a public issue. His primary concern is not with the facts or characteristics of the homeless, but with the manner in which the issue is conceptualized. Stern suggests that the politics of poverty have changed with the Reagan administration's reestablishment of the symbolic importance of the gift relationship between the well-to-do and the docile, appreciative, and deserving poor. In his view, this is a change from the liberal view of preceding administrations that overall structural conditions resulted in poverty and the poor were entitled to a decent life.

Section III: The Importance of Numbers

In April 1984 the U.S. Department of Housing and Urban Development (HUD) released a report on homelessness. The report was immediately attacked by many who had been working on the homeless issue as seriously flawed. Included here are the chapter in the HUD report that estimates the number of the homeless and three reviews of the report.

The HUD report excerpt begins with a review of past estimates of the number of homeless which run as high as 3 million persons, and states the need to have a more precise numerical estimate. The more precise estimate that HUD attempted to achieve is based on four methods, each of which relies on research or expert opinion of other individuals or groups. The article excerpt by S. Anna Kondratas of the Heritage Foundation strongly defends the HUD report and its methodology. She concludes by noting that if the problem is as small as suggested by HUD, then responsibility for the problem rests primarily with state and local governments and private charities.

Chester Hartman, in his review of the report, notes that "systematically aggregating lots of guesswork does not produce a reliable number, no matter how scientific the procedure. . . ." Hartman concludes that new, more systematic studies should be undertaken. Richard Appelbaum critiques each of the four HUD report estimation procedures. He finds much fault in the report and suggests that the methodological problems all biased the estimates in a downward direction.

Section IV: Who Are the Homeless and Why?

As noted earlier and in many of the readings, the homeless are not an undifferentiated mass of people. As the numbers of the homeless have grown, the diversity of the causes, people, and appropriate policy instruments has become increasingly clear. As noted earlier, there are at least nine types of groups of homeless persons. Here we examine three of these groups in some depth. The three groups are: (1) the traditional skid row/SRO resident, (2) the emotionally troubled homeless, and (3) the growing number of homeless women.

John C. Schneider addresses the history of skid row from 1880 to 1960. He traces the evolution of skid row from primarily a single workingman's residential district to a depressed and rapidly disappearing residential area for primarily older, social-service-dependent persons. He attributes the decline of skid row to the changes in the labor market for unskilled and semiskilled laborers.

Donald Bogue provides an in-depth analysis of the skid row resident in the Chicago of 1957-58. Bogue presents a complex picture of the many reasons for persons becoming skid-row residents. Just as there is no typical homeless person, there is no typical skid-row resident. The Bogue piece, although somewhat dated, provides a clear rationale for including the skid-row resident in the homeless category, and presents a detailed and successful methodology for studying the spatially concentrated homeless population.

Harvey A. Siegal describes the present world of the single-room-occupancy (SRO) hotel or welfare hotel. He painstakingly describes the physical social settings in which the New York SRO residents live. Like Bogue, Siegal finds the resident population to be older, poor, and unhealthy; Siegal, however, finds the SRO population to be predominantly non-white.

Philip Kasinitz traces the recent decline in the number of SROs in New York City. He describes the processes of gentrification, redevelopment and conversion that have eliminated SRO hotels from the low-income housing stock. He also notes the rise in the number of psychiatric patients and women residents. He concludes with a plea that either the SRO housing stock be preserved or alternatives provided.

The emotionally troubled adult is a major new source of homelessness. Ellen L. Bassuk explores the rise of this population and the problems it faces in coping with the harsh environment in which it finds itself. She reviews her study of the psychological problems of the homeless which found that 40 percent of those interviewed in a Boston shelter suffered from some form of psychosis.

H. Richard Lamb, Chairperson of the American Psychiatric Association's Task Force on the Homeless Mentally Ill, reviews the history of deinstitutionalization of the mentally ill. He finds that a minority of the chronically mentally ill are homeless; for those who are, however, the problem is not deinstitutionalization, but the manner in which deinstitutionalization is implemented. He also suggests a number of recommendations to address the needs of the homeless mentally ill.

Another growing part of the homeless population is women. Madeleine K. Stoner notes the growth of this population and the reality that homeless women typically suffer harsher conditions than homeless men. The causes of homelessness among women vary greatly, with lack of housing and income, deinstitutionalization, and domestic violence and abuse prime contributing factors. She also examines the almost total lack of services directed at the needs of homeless women and concludes by suggesting a comprehensive service system for the homeless woman.

Lorene Hemphill Stone provides a study of 133 abused women who came to a women's shelter in Michigan. Although Stone does not directly address the issue of homelessness, she does provide a vivid overview of domestic violence that for some results in homelessness. The critics of women's shelters suggest shelters should not be established since they may encourage family dissolution. Stone argues that this is not the case, but that many women have no other option since many cannot qualify for income support or social services until they are divorced. Once out of the home the victims of abuse, especially in areas without shelters, may find themselves on the street.

Section V: Solutions to the Problem

Three different strategies, other than providing short-term emergency shelter, have emerged to deal with homelessness. These strategies are not necessarily in conflict with one another, but rather are complementary approaches.

Kim Hopper and L. Stuart Cox trace the role of litigation in securing the
provision of shelter. They stress the right all people have to adequate, health-
ful accommodations. They further suggest that the homeless have been, and
probably will continue to be, an ineffective political constituency, and that
legal channels have become the best available method to address the
problem.[33]

Roger Sanjek provides a brief review of the impact on homelessness
resulting from the cutbacks in federal housing programs. He finds a great and
growing housing shortage exists for the poor. Sanjek concludes that this
problem can and should be addressed by the federal government.

Michael H. Phillips et al. provide a detailed description of the often-praised
Henry Street Settlement House Urban Family Center. This program is both a
transitional shelter for families and concentrated service-delivery center.
Phillips describes the problems of homeless families, the services offered, and
the costs of operating the Center.

Nancy K. Kaufman describes a comprehensive program to assist the homeless. Based on the Commonwealth of Massachusetts model, she suggests a
three-phase continuum of public-and private-sector services. The first phase
is the emergency response of temporary shelter, food, and financial assistance. Phase two is the provision of a comprehensive social-service program
and transitional housing. Stabilization—with permanent housing, employment, and ongoing social services—is the final phase. Kaufman concludes by
noting that only by moving beyond the provision of temporary shelter facilities can the cycle of homelessness be broken.

Section VI: Resources

In this section six readings concerning policies and programs are presented.
The readings each are or describe an existing or past effort to address the
problems of the homeless.

The first reading is a program description of the State of New Jersey's
recently enacted Pilot Homeless Prevention Program. The state legislature
approved $1.65 million for use in loans and grants to assist persons who are
homeless or unable to make rent or mortgage payments. The major focus of
the program is to keep people in their existing housing or find a suitable
alternative before they reach the street.[34]

The excerpt from *Homelessness in Chicago* is a summary of the zoning and
building code modifications and provisions that have been adopted in that
city to guide shelter location and development. Many cities do not have any
zoning provision for shelters, or have requirements so restrictive as to make it

difficult for shelters to open. This selection illustrates how one city has attempted to deal with the demand for shelters.

The Los Angeles Catholic Worker excerpt presents a review of the estimated costs involved in either building or rehabilitating and operating a structure for use as a homeless shelter. The cost comparisons are for the conversion of an existing building and for a factory-constructed new structure. Although construction and operation costs vary by locality and management goals, this piece covers the approximate cost of establishing and operating a shelter. Recent efforts in New York City to rehabilitate city-owned, vacant apartments, and the purchase of mobile homes for the homeless, suggest that cost of construction may be of secondary importance compared to the time lag involved in rehabilitation versus community opposition to mobile homes.[35]

The Community Service Society of New York provides an overview of community-relations strategies that have proved useful in obtaining community acceptance of a shelter in New York City. Community resistance is often the most difficult hurdle for any potential shelter provider. The experience of the Community Service Society suggests that community concerns and fear can be dealt with successfully.

Included from the Department of Health and Human Services report, *Helping the Homeless*, is a review of the requirements for designing and managing a homeless facility. The report discusses the strategies that have been used for a number of shelters throughout the country. In addition, a brief discussion of potential funding sources is included.

Lastly, reprinted from the U.S. General Accounting Office report, *Homelessness: A Complex Problem and the Federal Response*, is a listing of the major federal programs that are being used to assist the homeless. The summary includes the participating agency, specific program, objectives, and level of funding.

In conclusion, this reader brings together a wide variety of selections in order to present the complexity of the issue, and the diversity of approaches that have been used to describe and address the problem of homelessness. However, the collection is only an attempt to provide an introduction to the topic and not a comprehensive treatment. The recent rise in homelessness has yet to be thoroughly examined by social scientists or addressed by policymakers. With time, more mature and sophisticated research and policy interventions should develop. Perhaps this volume will inspire such efforts.

NOTES

[1] *See*, for example, the numerical references in S. Anna Kondratas, "A Strategy for Helping America's Homeless" in this volume, and United States House of Representatives, Committee on Banking, Finance and Urban Affairs, Subcommittee on Housing and Community Development, *HUD Report on Homelessness* (Washington, D.C.: U.S. Government Printing Office, May 24, 1984).

[2] C.J. Ribton-Turner, *A History of Vagrants and Vagrancy* (Montclair, NJ: Patterson-Smith, 1972).

[3] Ibid., p. 406.

[4] S.E. Wallace, *Skid Row as a Way of Life* (Totawa, NJ: Bedminster Press, 1965). *See also* Nels Anderson, *The Hobo* (Chicago: University of Chicago Press, 1923).

[5] J.F. Rooney, "Societal Forces and the Unattached Male: An Historical Review," in H.M. Bahr (ed.), *Skid Row: An Introduction to Disaffiliation* (New York: Oxford University Press, 1973).

[6] Stanley Lebergott, *Manpower in Economic Growth: The American Record Since 1800* (New York: McGraw-Hill, 1964), pp.164-90.

[7] H.M. Bahr (ed.), *Skid Row: An Introduction to Disaffiliation*; R.A. Bruns, *Knights of the Road* (New York: Methuen, 1980); J.C. Schneider in Section IV of this volume; and Susan Coolidge, *A Short History of Philadelphia* (Boston: Robert Brothers, 1887).

[8] *See* John C. Schneider in Section IV of this volume.

[9] S.E. Wallace, *Skid Row as a Way of Life. See also* Stanley Lebergott, *Manpower in Economic Growth: The American Record Since 1800.*

[10] R.A. Bruns, *Knights of the Road* (New York: Methuen, 1980), pp.161.

[11] See John C. Schneider in Section IV of this volume.

[12] R.A. Bruns, *Knights of the Road.*

[13] The relevant pieces of research produced at this time include "Migrant Families" by John Webb and Malcolm Brown; "The Transient Unemployed" by John Webb; "The Federal Transient Program, An Evaluative Study, Committee on the Care of the Transient and Homeless" by Ellery F. Reed; and "A Survey of the Transient and Homeless Population in 12 Cities" also by John Webb. These works were published by the Works Progress Administration from 1933 to 1935.

[14] *See* J.C. Schneider in Section IV of this volume. *See also* Donald Bogue in Section IV for a detailed description of Chicago's Skid Row in the 1950s.

[15] *See* Kim Hopper and Jill Hamberg, *The Making of America's Homeless: From Skid Row to New Poor, 1945-1984* (New York: Community Service Society, 1984; John C. Schneider in this volume; Harvey A. Siegal and James A. Inciardi, "The Demise of Skid Row," *Society* 19 (January-February 1982), pp. 39-45; and U.S. Department of Housing and Urban Development, *A Report to the Secretary on Homelessness and Emergency Shelter* (Washington, D.C.: U.S. Government Printing Office, May 1984).

[16] *See 1984 Employment and Earnings* (Washington, D.C.: U.S. Department of Labor, 1984).

[17] U.S. Department of Housing and Urban Development, *A Report to the Secretary on Homelessness and Emergency Shelter.*

[18] *See* M. Leepson, "The Homeless: A Growing National Problem." *Editorial Research Reports.* II:16, pp. 794-812.

[19] Ibid. *See also* E.L. Bassuk and H.R. Lamb in Section IV of this volume.

[20] *See* the introduction to David Listokin (ed.), *Housing Rehabilitation* (New

Brunswick, NJ: Center for Urban Policy Research, 1983), p. 4. *See also* 1975-1983 *Annual Housing Survey, Part A: General Housing Characteristics* (Washington, D.C.: U.S. Department of Commerce).

[21] M. Leepson, "The Homeless: A Growing National Problem." It is important to note that since April 1984, many appeals to reinstate benefits by former recipients have been challenged by the Department of Health and Human Services.

[22] *See* Philip Kasinitz and Madeleine K. Stoner in Section IV of this volume; and Michael Novak and Leslie Lenkowsky, "Economic Growth Won't End Poverty," *The New York Times*, July 24, 1985, p. A19.

[23] Deirdre Carmody, "Anguish of the Homeless Outlasts Winter's Cold," *The New York Times*, April 14, 1985, p. 6E.

[24] The causes of homelessness among youth are also related in part to the breakdown of the nuclear family. But whereas homeless adults and families typically have no home to which to return, homeless youth have either chosen or been forced by circumstances beyond their control to leave an existing home. The problem thus is significantly different from the focus of this reader. See U.S. House, Committee on Education and Labor, Subcommittee on Human Resources. *Juvenile Justice, Runaway Youth, and Missing Children's Act Amendments of 1984: Hearing* (Washington, D.C.: U.S. Government Printing Office, March 7, 1984).

[25] *See* U.S. Department of Housing and Urban Development, *A Report to the Secretary on the Homeless and Emergency Shelter*; S. Anna Kondratas in this volume; and Frances Werner, "Homelessness: A Litigation Roundup," *Housing Law Bulletin*, vol. 14 (November-December 1984), pp. 1-14.

[26] The debate over the magnitude of homelessness provides an example of the dictum that social science needs to be anchored to a pragmatic model of decisionmaking that governs the practical discourse among experts, policymakers, and the public. See Frank Fischer, "Science and Critique in Political Discourse: Elements of a Postpositivistic Methodology," *New Political Science*, 9-10 (Summer-Fall 1982), pp. 9-32.

[27] *See* the Housing and Development Reporter issues of August 13, 1984 and September 10, 1984. Also see United States House of Representatives, Committee on Banking, Finance and Urban Affairs, Subcommittee on Housing and Community Development, *HUD Report on Homelessness* (Washington, D.C.: U.S. Government Printing Office, May 24, 1984).

[28] Deirdre Carmody, "Anguish of the Homeless Outlasts Winter's Cold," *New York Times*, April 14, 1985, p. 6E; "Atlantic City Homeless Rolls Double," Newark, *The Star Ledger*, March 25, 1985, p. 9.

[29] Carmody, "Anguish of the Homeless Outlasts Winter's Cold."

[30] *See* Kaufman in Section V and Lamb in Section IV of this volume.

[31] Ellen Bassuk, "The Homelessness Problem," *Scientific American*, vol. 251 (July 1984), pp. 45.

[32] Cecilio J. Morales, Jr., "The Making of a New Union," *In These Times*, May 15-21, 1985, p. 6.

[33] *See* Frances Werner, "Homelessness: A Litigation Roundup" for a review of litigation around the nation as of November 1984.

[34] The New York City program to rehabilitate over 4,500 vacant, city-owned housing units uses a combination of funds from general obligation bonds and Community Development Block Grants. *See* "New York City Undertakes Wide Range of Rehab Projects to House Homeless Families," *Housing and Development Reporter*, March 12, 1984, pp. 900-01, and Peter P. Smith, "Housing the Homeless," *The New York Times*, June 1, 1985, p. 23.

[35] Ibid.

Introduction to the Transaction Edition

I T HAS BEEN twenty-five years since *Housing the Homeless* was first published. In that time, our understanding of homelessness has increased substantially. We know more about who is homeless and why. We have a better method of counting how many persons are homeless. And, federal and local governments have developed a number of programs to address homelessness. The number of homeless appears to have decreased from 1986 to 2007. The current economic downturn may have increased the number of homeless. The reemergence of homelessness as a social problem in the last two years underlines the importance of the efforts that advocates, academics, and professions made in understanding and addressing the issue in the 1980s.

In the 1980s homelessness became a major social issue policymakers all across the United States were trying to address. *Housing the Homeless*, published in 1986, was an early attempt to provide information to planners and other policymakers about the issue and to give some direction about what steps could be taken to address the problem. But in 1986 the problem had not been clearly defined. Homelessness was the subject of much debate. Who are the homeless? Why are some people homeless? How many homeless people are in our cities? What should be done?

None of these questions had been settled. The book reflected various ways people viewed homelessness. Homelessness was a new part of urban life that was disturbing and reflected the inability of all layers of government to solve a very visible social problem. Since the 1980s the homeless have not received much attention except as a side issue related to more pressing topics—for example, when the press focuses on the presence of homeless persons at Occupy Wall Street or other demonstrations or as a possible outcome for families affected by the foreclosure crisis. What was once shocking is now accepted as part of American daily life. This tolerance of homelessness may reflect the relative lack of compassion Americans have toward the homeless compared to our European counterparts (Paul Toro, 2007).

As homelessness became a recognized social problem, researchers in many fields initiated work to examine the many facets of this new phenomenon. In the 1950s and 1960s the study of individuals who now would be called homeless was dominated by a relatively small number of sociologists and ethnographers. Beginning in the 1980s, researchers in many fields have looked at the problems related to homelessness. The result is that homelessness as a field of study is not dominated by any single discipline or profession and has given rise to a rich and complex level of research.

How Many People Are Homeless?

In 1982 Mary Ellen Hombs and Mitch Snyder estimated that 2.2 million persons or approximately 1 percent of the total population of the United States were homeless (See Section Three). This was perceived as a big number and inspired the general media to explore homelessness as a major social problem (see Jonathan Alter, et.al., *Newsweek).* In response to the population estimates developed by social activists, the Reagan Administration's Department of Housing and Urban Development conducted a study estimating the number of homeless at 250,000 to 350,000. Both Hombs and Snyder and HUD conducted surveys of shelter providers. The higher number suggested a national problem and lower number suggested a problem that could be handled at the local level.

Determining exactly how many Americans are homeless has been an ongoing challenge. A number of researchers have tried to measure the extent of homelessness. Three general approaches have been used. The first is the method developed for the Chicago Homeless Study (Rossi, 1989). In that study, an effort was made to count all the persons sleeping at shelter and also do a sample of selected small areas in the city. This combined count could be used to provide a point-in-time estimate of the number of homeless. This is the basic method that is still used by the United States Interagency Council on Homeless annual homeless count (United States Interagency Council on Homelessness, 2011).

The second method is to conduct a shelter count and survey those persons staying at the shelter and the proportion of nights they stayed at the shelter versus on the street. This proportion can be used to develop an overall homeless count. A variation of this approach is to develop a measure of annual homelessness based the turnover in shelter use. This approach has led to results ranging from 2:1 to 4:1, which means that the number of persons homeless over the course of a year would be two to four times the number of people homeless on any given night (Wright, 2009).

The third method is a random sample of the general population that includes asking individuals if they have been homeless in past five years or in their lifetime. This approach results in higher numbers, but may provide a more accurate breakdown of demographic groups given the difficulty of identifying all homeless persons (Bruce Link, 1994). This method has been used to make international comparisons of the number of persons who have experienced homelessness (Paul Toro, 2007).

Who Are the Homeless?

"Home is the place where, when you have to go there. /they have to take you in."
—Robert Frost

Before the 1970s homelessness was not a widely used word. Social scientists and others had written about skid row and single room occupancy hotels (SRO's) for many years. The skid row sections of cities tended to be concentrated area of SRO's, missions, boarding houses that catered to mostly white men who were between jobs, held temporary positions or were old-age pensioners. These areas were specialized neighborhoods with facilities such as bars, hiring halls, inexpensive clothing stores, and welfare services.

In the 1950s, skid rows began to shrink in size. The causes of this decline are numerous but include an increased demand for surface parking lots near the central downtown area, the decline in the demand for casual labor, the reduction in elderly poverty, and urban renewal. The residents of these neighborhoods have been labeled the "old homeless" (Rossi, 1989). The residents of old skid rows were less visible than the new homeless of the 1980s because they segregated into separate neighborhoods and were more likely to find shelter at night.

In the 1970s the growth of new groups of homeless persons occurred. These groups tended to be younger and, as the years progressed, grew include larger numbers of women and children and members of minority groups. The Chicago Homeless Study conducted in 1985 and 1986 found that 75.5 percent of the homeless surveyed were male, 69.3 percent were minority group members, and 55.3 percent were high school graduates. Additionally, 23.1 percent had been hospitalized for psychiatric conditions, 41.8 percent had been incarcerated, and 33.2 percent had gone through detoxification. In 1987 Burt and Cohen did a study of the homeless in twenty cities and found very similar results using the point-in-time method. Phelan and Link, in their 1999 study of persons who previously had been homeless, found that 58.5 percent were male, 15.0 percent were members of a minority group, and 71.8 percent were high school graduates. Only 1.7 percent had a history of psychiatric hospitalization, 22.4 percent had been incarcerated, and 2.5 percent had gone through detoxification (Link, 1999). Phelan and Link's finding suggest point-of-time studies over count persons with criminal, mental, and substance abuse issues. One possible factor is that point-of-time studies are more likely to interview persons who are chronically homeless.

What Are the Causes of Homelessness?

In and around 1986 a number studies were conducted in the United States at the municipal level (See Rossi, 1989, p. 213-22). Most of the studies were exploratory and did not develop estimates of the total homeless population in a given city. But the surveys provided information about who the home-less were and why they were homeless. Christopher Jencks (Jencks, 1994) provides an excellent summary of what is known about the causes and de-mographics of the homelessness in the 1980s. He notes the most promising explanations of homelessness are the decline of beds in mental hospitals and related facilities, drug abuse (especially crack cocaine), changes in long-term joblessness and family structure with the rise of female-headed households and the relative welfare recipient's purchasing power, and the destruction of skid rows and many SRO's. He also suggests that less promising expla-nations include a weakening of social skills and family ties, changes in the housing market, and rent control. Rossi adds alcoholism and persons with physical disabilities as common sources of homelessness.

Jencks (1994) explored the role of the 1980s recession as source of homelessness and found that although the recession may have resulted in an increase in homelessness, homelessness did not appear to decline in following economic recovery. Recent increases the homeless could be the result of foreclosures and high unemployment rates (USICH, 2011)

The Federal Response

A year after the publication of *Housing the Homeless* federal legisla-tion and funding was adopted to address the problem of homelessness (the Stewart B. McKinney Homeless Assistance Act later amended to be the

McKinney-Vento Homeless Assistance Act). This act established a legal definition of homelessness and provides for a yearly one-day count of the homeless. The first definition of homelessness includes people living in places not meant for human habitation (the streets, abandoned buildings, bus and train stations, etc.) and those living in an emergency shelter or transitional housing facility (42 USC Section 11302).

The 2009 Homeless Emergency Assistance and Rapid Transition Housing (HEARTH) Act adds to this definition situations where a person is at imminent risk of homelessness or where a family or unaccompanied youth is living unstably. Imminent risk includes situations where a person must leave his or her current housing within the next fourteem days with no other place to go and no resources or support networks to obtain housing.

Instability includes families with children and unaccompanied youth who: (1) are defined as homeless under other federal programs (such as the Department of Education's Education for Homeless Children and Youth program), (2) have lived for a long period without living independently in permanent housing, (3) have moved frequently, and (4) will continue to experience instability because of disability, history of domestic violence or abuse, or multiple barriers to employment (USICH, 2011)

The Hearth Act also established a planning process known as Opening Doors. The plan's goal is to end veterans and chronic homelessness by 2015 and to end homelessness among children, families, and youth by 2020. The plan presents strategies that build on the philosophy that mainstream housing, health, education, and human service programs must be fully engaged and coordinated to prevent and end homelessness.

The United States Interagency Council on Homelessness (a Federal group established in the 2009 Hearth Act) estimated the number of persons homeless in their one-day January 2010 homeless census as 649,917 and the 2010 Annual Estimate of Individuals Using Shelters as 1.59 million. The disparity between the two figures is a result of the definition including persons in imminent risk of homelessness. In addition, as reflected in the Annual Estimate of Individuals Using Shelters, a one-day count does not reflect the transitory nature of the homeless population.

Of the 649,917 one-day count homeless, 403,543 (62.1 percent) were in shelters. The one-night survey found that 407,966 homeless were individuals (52.0 were in shelters), and 241,951 were persons in families (79, 1 percent were in shelters). Little other information is available from the Annual Homeless Assessment Report aside from the count of persons who either been homeless for longer than a year or homeless four times over the past five years (241,951), and the number of homeless veterans (76,329). The accuracy the data can be questioned, but the data does allow for comparisons over time. The number of homeless persons counted in the one-day survey has declined 14 percent from 759,101 in 2006 to 649,917 in 2010, and the number of chronic homeless has declined by 29 percent from 155,625 to 109,812. It is important to note that between 2009 and 2010 the overall number of homeless increased by 1 percent.

Federal expenditures on the homeless are now calculated by USICH as 3.2 billion dollars. These expenditures cover education for homeless children, health care, services for runaway and homeless youth, veterans' programs, and a wide variety of housing and shelter programs. The number of homeless persons assisted is calculated for each program. It is impossible to get a count of persons benefiting from these programs because many persons may benefit from more than one program. But for individual programs the number of persons assisted is significant. For 2009-2010 in the three largest Federal programs, 920,113 benefitted from HUD Homeless Assistance Grant, 852,881 benefitted from Education for Homeless Children and Youth, and 827,519 benefitted from Health Care for the Homeless (USICH, 2011). The Federal Government has made a commitment but is it really enough to achieve the goals that USICH has set?

What we know now about the homeless is in great part due to the advocacy, research, and policy proposals developed in the 1980s. The readings in this book are as useful and insightful today as they were twenty-five years ago. Homelessness is again an issue before the public. We can build on past research and policy efforts to develop strategies that will address homelessness.

Bibliography

42 USC Section 11302. (n.d.). Title 42 - The Public Health and Welfare, Chapter 119, Subchapter I - General Provisions. Washington, DC: Government Printing Office.

Bruce Link, E. S. "Lifetime and Five-Year Prevalence of Homelessness in the United States," *American Journal of Public Health*, (1994), 1907-1912.

Jencks, C. *The Homeless* (Cambridge, MA: Harvard University Press, 1994).

Link, J. P. "Who Are 'the Homeless'? Reconsidedring the Stability and Composition of the Homeless Population," *American Journal of Public Health,* (1999), 1334-1338.

Paul Toro, C. T. "Homelessness in Europe and the United States: A Comparison of Prevalence and Public Opinion." *Journal of Social Issues*, (2007), 505-524.

Rossi, P. *Down and Out in America* (Chicago: University of Chicago Press, 1989).

United States Interagency Council on Homelessness. *Opening Doors: Federal Strategic Plan to Prevent and End Homelessness: Update 2011.* (Washington, DC: USICH, 2011).

United States Interagency Council on Homelessness. "Consolidated Submissions for Community Planning and Develpment Programs," *Federal Register*, (December 5, 2011), Washington, DC: U.S. Government Printing Office.

Wright, J. D. *Address Unknown: The Homeless in America.* (New Brunswick, NJ: AldineTransaction, 2009).

I

Images of the Homeless

1

Homeless in America

Jonathan Alter, Alexander Stille,
Shawn Doherty, Nikke Finke Greenberg,
Susan Agrest, Vern E. Smith, George Raine

Homelessness is on the Rise . . .

THEY HAVE ALWAYS BEEN WITH US. The same beggar who stretched a suppliant palm toward the passing togas of ancient Rome can be found today on Colfax Avenue in Denver, still thirsty for wine; the bruised and broken woman who slept in the gutters of medieval Paris now beds down in a cardboard box in a vest-pocket park in New York City. They exist on the fringes, taking meals when they find them and shelter where they can. Most have drifted well past the limits of respectability, many deep into alcoholism or mental illness. The public usually views their existence as a shame, a distasteful fact of life met—when it must be faced at all—with averted eyes.

The tattered ranks of America's homeless are swelling, and the economic recovery that made this Christmas merrier than last for most Americans has not brought them even a lump of coal. As subfreezing temperatures settled in last week, scattered anecdotes gave way to chilly facts. Unemployment is at a two-year low of 8.4 percent, but cities and voluntary groups across the country are swamped with thousands more requests for shelter than ever. In Philadelphia, 15,000 received emergency family housing in 1983—five times the number sheltered in 1981. In Detroit, auto sales are stronger but the city estimates homelessness is up 50 percent. In St. Louis, the Salvation Army alone received 4,155 requests, up 47 percent over last year.

From *Newsweek*, January 2, 1984, pp. 20-29. Copyright 1984, by Newsweek, Inc. All Rights Reserved. Reprinted by Permission.

No region has been spared. Atlanta's first overnight shelter opened in 1979; now the city has 27. Salt Lake City's mayor insists his city has become a "blinking light" for wandering homeless, while Phoenix and Tucson complain that hordes of transients have descended on Arizona and must be repulsed. "Our shelters were full in September, long before it turned cold," says Audrey Rowe, commissioner of social services in Washington, D.C. With 100 city beds for about 20,000 homeless, Chicago, like most localities, relies on church and community groups. Sister Carrie Driscoll says she turned away 112 people in one day recently from the Catholic Charities shelter she runs in the city's devastated Woodlawn area. "At night I pray, 'Lord, give me one more bed'."

The bedraggled homeless are walking emblems of poverty and suffering— the only poverty many Americans ever see. But solutions for their plight are not easily found. For one thing, the forces that caused it are longstanding and complex: everything from the disintegration of family ties to significant failures in America's approaches to housing, mental health and welfare for the poorest of the poor. For another, the homeless move outside the ordinary social structures that might help them, and often resist any effort to bring them in. The result is an entire underclass of people who have managed to slide right through the safety nets and into the gutter.

"In the missions you sleep on a folding chair and wake up in the middle of the night with some guy talking weird and drooling all over you," says Billy Collins, a 23-year-old ex-machine-lathe operator who left his family and lit out for Florida and then California. He did not find work—or adventure; instead, he ended up eating scraps out of the dumpsters behind McDonald's and Kentucky Fried Chicken. "The old guys riding the rails will be ready to share what they've got," says Collins. "But people like me will just beat them up and rip them off."

Because they live without addresses, the homeless are unable to receive food stamps and welfare in most states, invisible in unemployment statistics and impossible to count. Estimates range anywhere from 250,000 to 2 million nationwide, tens of thousands of whom hazard the elements every night. The largest private sponsor of shelter, the Salvation Army, provides only 42,000 beds—a drop in the bucket. The largest publicly sponsored shelter system is run by New York, which now houses 6,000. That's double the capacity of two years ago and more than during the Great Depression—but insufficient in a city where officials estimate 20,000 homeless in the under-21 category alone. The chairman of the city's Board of Health says that an average of one homeless person a day is now found dead in the streets.

Like the rich, the homeless judge status by where they sleep. The less chance of interruption by police or other vagrants, the more rest they get. Informal turf arrangements, say skid-row veterans, are beginning to break down under the weight of the new arrivals. But certain distinctions remain. The most successful find refuge in garages or abandoned buildings, over hot air grates or under bridges. The less discriminating settle for phone booths, park benches, trash dumpsters.

The people who pass the night in such accommodations are a much more diverse lot than in the past—and much younger, now averaging in their low 30s. Twenty years ago the homeless consisted almost exclusively of alcoholic skidrow men, mostly older white males. They have been joined by huge numbers of released mental patients, who now make up one-third to one-half of the total, and have added thousands of women to the streets. It's hard to tell who were seriously ill before becoming homeless, and who were driven over the edge by the rigors of street life. Few are dangerous to anyone but themselves.

During the recession there was a sharp increase in younger variations on the traditional hobo—unskilled drifters heading south and west in a futile search for work, many with their families. Recently, however, cities are reporting that the bulk of their homeless aren't transients at all. Many of the locals, says Ed Loring of the Open Door Community in Atlanta, are young men who come out of housing projects and high schools without any marketable skills. Most male homeless have worked at some point, but usually in menial jobs.

The new drifters and dropouts are different from the winos and bag ladies. "You see the embitterment and disillusionment of life in them," says Capt. Cliff Jones of the Grand Junction, Colorado, Salvation Army. Inside New York's Ft. Washington Armory, older men sleep gripping their shoes so they aren't stolen by the newer arrivals. Contrary to myth, most homeless welcome any roof over their heads, but crime in certain urban shelters is so pervasive that some now take the same approach as their psychotic brethren on the street—refusing any offer of shelter.

The paradoxes of homelessness are practically endless. As cities revitalized their downtowns in the 1970s by tearing down dilapidated hotels, they threw thousands who could afford nothing else into the street. As states emptied overcrowded and ill-staffed mental hospitals, they set thousands free to fend for themselves. And now, as local governments and charitable organizations stretch to provide relief, they find, according to some accounts, that the more they do, the more they increase demand. Meanwhile, what they cannot do—from providing underwear (an item, unlike overcoats, that's rarely donated) to finding family backing and permanent housing—is what the homeless often need most.

Some of the denizens of these seedy hotels and abandoned slums go directly into the streets, but many live first with friends and relatives. In fact, the number of American families sharing quarters in 1982 was up 58 percent—the first such increase since 1950. And that has given rise to a curious development. In the past, fire tended to be the most common direct cause of homelessness; now it's often eviction—eviction initiated not only by landlords, but increasingly by friends and relatives. "So many are crammed into already crowded housing with an Aunt Louise," says David Park Smith of the Dallas Coalition for the Homeless. "Pretty soon they wear out their welcome and are out on the streets."

Once the screaming and door slamming subside, the only refuge is emergency shelter. In New York, where especially accurate figures are available, 2,300 families, up from 900 last year, are housed in squalid welfare hotels that charge the city around $1,400 per family per month and boast rats and prostitutes for neighbors. The single-sex shelters for individuals cost the city $24 per "client" per night—most of the money going for personnel. In the East New York shelter, which regularly features an inch of water on a floor where people sleep and two-hour waits for showers, about $3 million a year pays salaries for security officers who are more visible on the payroll than in the shelter.

By contrast, private shelters around the country operate at an average cost of about $3 to $6 a person for smaller, more hospitable quarters often located in church basements or community centers. "There's a psychological effect of being in a church that draws respect from guests," says Luz Martinez, coordinator of a Chicago shelter. Almost all private sponsors argue that while the government does a bad job of running shelters, its funding help is required. Emergency-housing services agrees. In 1983, Seattle, a city sympathetic to the homeless, turned down 4,000 families—about 16,000 people—seeking temporary housing.

> She was called the cellophane lady because of the way she wrapped her legs and feet to protect them from the Philadelphia cold. It didn't work: last winter Lillian Roseborough nearly lost her limbs because of hypothermia. Even so, the 65-year-old woman refused to be removed from the street where she lives—just a block from her daughter's apartment. She insisted that she was ruled by the spirit of "jing-jing," and that if she went inside before the government provided shelter for all street people, she would die.

The immediate reason people are homeless, logically enough, is that they don't have homes, and the primary reason for that is what was once called the low-income-housing crisis but is nowadays more dimly recalled as "something everyone cared a lot about in the 1960s." One reason the issue faded from national view is that the government's housing policies failed. Washington warehoused the poor in dismal high-rise projects, provided loans guaranteed to default and wasted billions in administratively inept programs that ended up subsidizing middle-class renters—and government paper shufflers—instead of the poor. Fewer than half of the 6 million low-income units Lyndon Johnson believed were needed in 1968 ever got built.

But while attention flagged, the problem grew worse. Median rent increased twice as fast as income in the 1970s, and low-income-housing construction came to a virtual standstill. The Department of Housing and Urban Development reports construction and renovation dwindled to 203,113 units in 1979 under Jimmy Carter and to 55,120 in 1983 under Ronald Reagan. Yet census figures show about 2 million Americans living in substandard quarters and hundreds of thousands on mind-numbing waiting lists for public housing: 20 years in Miami, 12 in New York, 4 in Savannah, Georgia.

The Reagan administration's housing policy revolves around $200 million in vouchers for low-income people to use for rent—a plan that assumes there is no shortage of housing, only an inability to pay for it. But a recent Brookings Institution study suggests that the shortage may reach 1.7 million low-income units by 1990. And the total housing subsidy for the poor is small compared to what the middle class and rich receive. Their subsidy comes in the form of a home-mortgage tax deduction that applies even to summer homes and will cost the Treasury about $42.8 billion in 1984.

Those who benefit from this deduction are "gentrifying" the cities; they are helping restore the tax base and quality of life in old neighborhoods. But the side effects are devastating. The first buildings to be abandoned, converted into condominiums or destroyed are often the flophouses called single-room occupancies (SRO's) where many of the very poorest live. About 1 million rooms—nearly half the total—were converted or destroyed nationwide between 1970 and 1980, according to a Columbia-New York University study. New York lost 87 percent of its SRO's in this period. Cities like Denver, Seattle and Rochester have lost more than 50 percent.

It seemed like a good idea at the time. Many state mental hospitals were unspeakably inhumane, and new miracle drugs could control the psychotic without straitjackets. So starting in the mid-1950s, the nation's mental hospitals began releasing inmates in unprecedented numbers. Liberals applauded the new civil rights granted to the nondangerous mentally ill; conservatives were happy to find a seemingly compassionate way to cut state budgets. Between 1955 and 1982 state mental institutions shrank by more than three-quarters—from 558,922 patients to 125,200.

But there is widespread agreement that efforts to "deinstitutionalize" mental patients have backfired. While some do fine, tens of thousands end up homeless—if not right away, then after a few years of bouncing among families, institutions and the street. At the same time, it has become nearly impossible to get the nondangerous mentally ill admitted to state asylums, or to keep them there long enough to get a grip on themselves. In California, for instance, the median stay is now only 16 days.

"If a doctor walked away from an operation for an appendicitis, he would be sued for malpractice," says New York attorney Robert Hayes. "The state has walked away from these patients." Hayes felt so strongly about it that in 1982 he quit the prominent New York law firm of Sullivan & Cromwell and founded the Coalition for the Homeless, which is suing cities for the right to shelter and coordinating the work of 40 groups in states across the country.

Those patients sent back to what the professionals call "independent living" are truly on their own. According to Dr. John Talbott, president-elect of the American Psychiatric Association (APA), fewer than a quarter of the patients discharged from state mental institutions remain in any mental-health program at all. When they crack up, the lucky ones are taken to hospital emergency rooms, where they routinely wait hours—sometimes tied to chairs—for a temporary bed. One out of every five patients at New York City public hospitals is homeless.

Follow-up treatment has been scarce partly because many psychotic street people mistakenly believe they are well, and grow fearful that any contact with authorities will lead to getting locked up again. Large numbers have serious delusions. One woman wandered Hollywood assuring passersby that she was Linda Darnell, a movie star of the 1940s who died in 1965. Another rejected food and water for days because she thought she was a plant and could soak up nourishment from the rain. A man with his possessions in garbage bags told travelers he had seen the Ayatollah Khomeini in the basement of a train station. When wealthier people have mental or drinking problems they often rely on counseling; the poor have it harder. Navigating the byzantine mental-health bureaucracy, says Talbott, "would drive even the normal person insane."

But the main reason mental-health care has left so many homeless is that funding didn't follow the patients out of the hospitals and into the community. A 1963 goal of starting 2,000 community mental-health centers nationwide by 1980 is still 1,283 short. Some community-based care is actually decreasing. Colorado, for instance, has released 1,172 patients since 1981, but the number of halfway houses has fallen from 60 in 1975 to about 10 today. Even the mentally ill themselves recognize the irrationality of the situation. "It's a merry-go-round," says one 48-year-old schizophrenic in New York. "You go to the hospital, then they dump you into those Dante Inferno shelters and then you go back again. This system doesn't make a man go up. It makes him go down."

Some of this results from budget squeezes, but much is the fault of administrators, legislators and civil-service unions. When money is available, it often doesn't go to the homeless mentally ill. In 1979, 43 percent of the $8.8 billion in total mental-health expenditures was spent by state hospitals, and only 17 percent by federal outpatient clinics serving the homeless. Some state officials claim that hospitals have to keep so much of the money in order to maintain specific staffing ratios required by the Joint Commission on Accreditation of Hospitals. But the JCAH says that's untrue.

While homeless psychotics wander the streets without care, most state-employed doctors and staff are back at the nearly empty asylums. In the last 20 years the average patient-staff ratio in state mental hospitals has dropped from 50 to 1 to 1 to 1. And civil-service unions prefer to keep it that way. Efforts to cut or transfer maintenance and support staff in favor of more community efforts are usually straitjacketed. When New York Gov. Mario Cuomo announced budget cuts for the state mental-health system, for instance, the huge Creedmoor Psychiatric Center cut its *community* outreach staff—and protected hospital workers who maintain a 315-acre complex that houses one-fifth as many patients as it once did.

Meanwhile, citing past welfare abuses, the Reagan administration has tightened the review process so that fewer people qualify for benefits. Since 1980 more than 200,000 have been dropped from the rolls of Supplemental Security Income alone, a major source of income for the mentally ill. Many of these people are defined as clinically employable by the government, but in the real world can't possibly get jobs. Among those rejected for benefits in 1982, according to community workers, were an incontinent man who wore seven pairs of pants at once and a woman who thought she was a Vietnam War orphan.

For the nonmentally ill homeless, welfare isn't always much better. In many states it won't pay the rent. A New Mexico family of four is expected to get by on $66 a month in rent allowance. In Indiana, it's $100 a month for rent, regardless of family size. And these states aren't exceptions. Last year Pennsylvania Gov. Richard Thornburgh and the state legislature moved to restrict all able-bodied men to 90 days of welfare a year. Instead of lessening dependency, as conservatives hoped, it simply made many of them homeless and thus still dependent. William Wachob, chairman of the welfare subcommittee of the Pennsylvania State Legislature, charges that "Thornfare," now being revised, is "directly responsible for the increase of homeless."

The counseling service in downtown Houston is called Compass and it's run by a gray-haired woman named Kay White, who helps street people get anchored. The approach avoids "quick fixes and rice-bowl Christianity," she says, and attracts 600 a month. "I listen to them, accept what they have to say and also ask myself if they're trying to rip me off," White says. "Some do and I tell them to leave." Greater numbers don't—and leave with help: a bus token, an apartment lead, a phone number for a job.

Coping with homelessness requires melding public and private efforts in ways that help street people but don't hurt taxpayers. After all, most people take what Jane Malone, an activist on behalf of the homeless in Philadelphia, calls a "minimalist" approach to the problem—essentially, "not in *my* neighborhood." That is understandable; the homeless *do* drive down property values, and it isn't pleasant to find that someone has urinated in your doorway. Some argue that the more that is done on behalf of the homeless, the more comfortable they will be with their plight—and the worse the problem will become.

But if government and the community helped worsen the problem, they can work together to ease it. As George Orwell wrote in "Down and Out in Paris and London," "the 'serve them damned well right' attitude that is normally taken toward tramps is no fairer than it would be toward cripples." Sister Gay of Houston, who has adopted 10 homeless children and tended to their families, believes that. So does a consortium of the U.S. Conference of Mayors and two foundations now sponsoring a $20 million effort to treat the ghastly array of diseases that afflict the homeless.

There are success stories of public-private cooperation: last month a Memphis pilot project opened 10 HUD-owned houses for under $100,000. Still, roadblocks remain. On White House order, the Pentagon has offered 500 locations, mostly unoccupied military-reserve centers, but so far only a few have been put to use—largely because cities and local groups would have to pick up most of the tab needed to make the places inhabitable. The Federal Emergency Management Administration has distributed $140 million over two years in shelter aid, but admits it's a one-time effort. Margaret Heckler, secretary of Health and Human Services, says the Reagan administration is now studying ways to cut the red tape, and *Newsweek* has learned that HUD will decide soon whether to subsidize shelters directly.

Permanent housing is a taller order. One reason it's so expensive for the government to build low-income units is that government contracts usually must pay the so-called prevailing wage—which almost always matches the top union scale in any given region. Andrew Raubeson, director of the Burnside Consortium, which has renovated 450 SRO units for use by poor people in Portland, Oregon, says that his costs are $6,000 to $9,000 a unit, less than a fifth the expense of many government projects.

That's a big difference, and some low-income-housing advocates suggest that waiving the prevailing wage on low-income projects may be the only way to bring the federal government into a partnership to build more housing. Doing so would require amending the Davis-Bacon Act, a sacred cow for most Democrats that even the Reagan administration has not challenged. More flexible wages might also allow unskilled laborers to help in the work of renewing their own neighborhoods. Private tenant organizations around the country have already begun this. Some, in cities like San Francisco, have also won agreement that when developers tear down flophouses, they will help pay for some new low-income housing.

Solutions to the mental-health riddle are following a similar logic of public-private cooperation. Some mental-health professionals and government officials argue that providing community care is prohibitively expensive. But that assumes it is done in what might be called the "prevailing" way—that is, with highly paid psychiatrists and other union-scale mental-health professionals. What homeless mental patients need first, their advocates say, is simply a place to stay and some supervision by compassionate people. Many private halfway houses now provide stable environments for former mental patients for as little as $6,000 per person a year, compared with about $40,000 in state hospitals. With more charitable and government funding, these places could make a major dent in the number of mentally ill homeless without sending them back to asylums.

For mental health, as for shelter and permanent housing, the answer seems to lie in the government's setting aside its inclination to solve the problems itself in favor of helping the community do its natural work. That requires a leap of faith. But it is much the same leap volunteers take as they overcome enough of their nervousness about America's lost souls to pitch in and help.

In Denver, a tattered group of men line a warehouse ramp, waiting in the snowy dusk to enter the Salvation Army Survival Shelter, John Destry, 22, a navy stocking cap rolled on his head, describes his homeless life. "The streets are dangerous," he says. "But, you know, we all do the same things, have the same needs—a hot meal, some warm clothes, someplace to sleep."

Fighting Back

Arizona and Massachusetts Represent the Extremes

Hiking her designer slacks above her ankles, Sandy Cowen crouched, made a face and gnarled her hands in imitation of a man she used to see from the window of her advertising agency in downtown Phoenix, Arizona. This particular gentleman was a bit odd—a street bum who carried around a bucket of soapy water and washed everything in sight, from his feet to the sidewalks. But Cowen is the brains behind "Fight Back"—a campaign by Phoenix leaders to wipe out the "unacceptable behavior" of the area's 1,500 street people—she knew how to handle the nuisance. Police were summoned, and the bum was forced to move on.

The homeless are not welcome in Arizona. Many of them, residents argue, are outsiders looking for a sunny place to sponge off the state. The mayor of Tucson was recently elected to his 13th year in office on a platform that included a vow to get "the transients the hell out of town," and beefed-up patrols of police officers prowl the streets looking for suspicious transient behavior. By contrast, the state of Massachusetts is in the midst of an ambitious effort to help the homeless help themselves. It's more than the difference between Barry Goldwater and Ted Kennedy; Arizona isn't all conservative, and Massachusetts isn't all liberal. But the two states represent the extremes of community attitudes toward the homeless.

"We're tired of it. Tired of feeling guilty about these people," says Cowen, who designed an ad campaign that features a sketch of a man sleeping on a bench with a red line drawn through it (like an international traffic sign). Posted around town, these signs echo the official view of Phoenix, which in 1981 adopted an Anti-Skid Row Ordinance that discourages blood banks, bars, soup kitchens and flophouses. Since 1981 four missions—including two sponsored by the Salvation Army—have closed their doors under pressure. After one of his assistants had her fingers broken by a drunken drifter, newly elected Mayor Terry Goddard, a relative liberal, helped found a task force dedicated to coping with the transient problem and protecting Arizona's image as a sunny paradise.

As homelessness worsens across the Southwest, a game of finger pointing has begun. Skeptics in Phoenix and Tucson believe that Los Angeles, trying to clean up before the 1984 Summer Olympics, will soon send its problem across the desert. Some Arizonians think they should try the same thing themselves.

Tucson residents are divided, but the prevailing attitude seems to be that "Love thy neighbor" should apply not just to the needy but to the family down the street alarmed by the sometimes violent vagrants. Police scour homeless haunts with German shepherd dogs, and one church soup kitchen will be sued as a public nuisance. "These transients are urinating on the sidewalk, sleeping in doorways and frightening shoppers," says Mayor Lewis Murphy, noting that crime by the new arrivals is up. "The last thing we want to do is publicly provide amenities."

That is one of the first things that Massachusetts wants to do. After regaining the governorship last year, Michael Dukakis announced that home-lessness was his No. 1 social-service priority. "Homeless" plays better politi-cally than "poor" as a way to win approval of state social programs, and Dukakis, who lost his bid for re-election in 1978 in part because he alienated liberals, had in recent years grown genuinely alarmed about the growth of the problem. Despite its frigid winters, Massachusetts has roughly the same number of homeless as Arizona—estimated between 5,000 and 10,000.

So far the state has funded 13 shelters on a 75-25 basis with the community groups that run them. It has also opened a 24-hour hot line for referrals, assigned more state caseworkers and changed welfare rules so that people without permanent addresses can receive benefits. Over the objections of real-estate interests, Dukakis rammed through a tough condominium-conversion bill that requires that certain tenants get as much as four years' notice before a building can be converted. In mid-December, the Massachusetts Legislature approved $196 million for low-income housing, which will translate into 2,500 new units and 2,000 renovated ones.

One example of how the public-private cooperation can work is Jessie's House, a new family shelter located in a big white house in Northampton. The city, home of Smith College, has several hundred homeless people—some of them mental patients from a nearby hospital or victims of gentrification downtown. About 20 guests stay at Jessie's House for four to six weeks under strict house rules. Staff members make a determined—and often successful—effort to find them jobs and housing, and friendly neighbors pack the shelter's refrigerators and cupboards with food. A city councilman who opposed the idea was overruled by his constituents.

"Our philosophy," says Priscilla Braman, director of Jessie's House, "is to put a lot of energy into people once and do it right." Arizona's approach, says Tucson's Rev. Dave Innocenti, is often "a traditional Western-cowboy mentality—if you can't pull yourself up by your bootstraps and be a man, get out." There could hardly be clearer proof of the old saw—"cold hands, warm heart"—and vice versa.

The "Street Girls"

They Scrounge for Scraps—and Live in Constant Fear

From a distance, on the snowy streets of Chicago, she could be a coed off to a football game. But get close to the woman called Teddy Bear—her real name is Dolores—and you see that her long woolen coat, preppy sweater, dark pants and sturdy boots have not been donned for a day's outing. She has slept in them. Her black hair hasn't been combed. It is falling over her dark eyes and onto her bruised face.

Teddy Bear's friend Elizabeth also favors pants and sweaters for Chicago's icy weather. She has a quilted coat for the winter but so far has been unable to find boots wide enough for her feet. So she sticks to the Trax running shoes she got during one of her periodic stays at a Veterans Administration hospital. Elizabeth's hair is cut tomboy short—a throwback to her adolescent days.

She can still execute a flying leap, too, the kind she did back in convent school. Sometimes she does one just to try lifting herself out of depression.

The social workers call them homeless women. They call themselves street girls—a motley group scrounging scraps and small change, bag ladies who carry their world around with them or stash it at a friend's home or have nothing left to stash. They sleep in abandoned buildings, overnight shelters, sleazy welfare hotels or with men who take them in for the sake of kindness or sex. They all have one thing in common: fear. Fear of not finding a safe warm place for the night, fear of not getting the meal—or drink—they need, fear of rape or of losing what little they possess. Even the most deranged bag ladies, who just want to be left alone, are vulnerable because of rumors that they keep money in their bags. On the streets, says Elizabeth, "you have to have eyes behind your head and look like you're not scared."

She used to carry a shopping bag with clothes and soap and a toothbrush, but it was "too obvious a target," says Elizabeth, who looks older than her 37 years. Now she keeps clean underwear at the apartment of a divorced woman friend who lets her take a shower now and then. "I haven't carried a purse since I was mugged," she says. "I've had medication prescribed for my depression, but there's no use carrying that around—they'll take it." Teddy Bear, 28, carries nothing; she ends up selling everything for the price of a drink. The hulking body that earned Teddy Bear her name is swollen from wine. "A doctor told me my body is going to give out if I don't stop drinking," she says. "I was doing OK for a few months. I have this friend and she helped me stop drinking and made me think I could get off the streets for good."

But now her welfare check goes for drink again, when her sometime boyfriend doesn't take it from her. She doesn't have the strength to stay away from him when she's drinking, even though it means she'll end up with a black eye. "We fight all the time," says Teddy Bear. So she wanders the streets looking for him—or anyone else who might have liquor.

Like many street people, Teddy Bear's past is hazy. She says she is an orphan, but others say she has a mother *and* four brothers who keep trying to get her off the bottle and the streets. Whatever the truth, Elizabeth says she understands Teddy Bear's drinking problem, because she still carries the scars from her own heavier drinking days—like the one on her wrist from putting it through a saloon window. "I was angry at the bartender for serving me when I'd already had too much," she recalls. "It's the whisky and vodka that makes you so violent you wind up in jail on a drunk-and-disorderly charge. It feels like there's a tornado in your stomach and your head feels like you got hit with a sledgehammer."

It's only since her divorce in 1979 that Elizabeth has had to worry about a roof over her head. "I was married four years to an electrical-engineering student, but he was a Pakistani from a strict Islamic upbringing where they didn't like women going out at night. I've always been a night person, and when he told me that I was the camel and he was the driver, that did it. After the divorce I was too depressed to work, and after four months of not being able to pay the rent, I came home one day to find the locks changed. So I hit the streets. It was cold, but I found an open Datsun to sleep in at night. When the owner saw me one morning he brought out a blanket and apologized for not letting me sleep inside, but five weeks of sleeping in that car landed me in the V.A. hospital with pneumonia."

On a recent evening, Elizabeth sought shelter in the basement of Chicago's Uptown Baptist Church, where Teddy Bear often spends her nights, but she didn't stay long. "I know the shelter is safer than the streets or the subway," Elizabeth admits. "But the smell of dirty bodies is like rotting flesh, and it will get worse by morning. I worry about getting lice from the blankets or sores on my mouth if someone spits in the coffee." So out into the snow she goes, hoping that the Cuban guy who sometimes lets her stay in his room is home and sober. "I'm kind of scared of him since he pulled a knife on me a week ago when he was drinking that crazy rotgut vodka. But at least he's not the type that would make a woman work the streets. How am I going to get married again in this predicament?"

The best resource for the street women of uptown Chicago is Sarah's Circle, a women's drop-in center open five days a week. It's not only the coffee and snacks and the Wednesday-afternoon bingo that draws them. It's the unintimidating, lived-in atmosphere, the tattered sofas and chairs and the old copies of *House and Garden*. There is a kindness at Sarah's, not only from the volunteers but also from other women who have been through whatever you are going through and want to help. They throw their arms around Teddy Bear, tell sympathetic stories about being beaten by their own "old men"— and talk tough about wanting to punch them out. And whereas shelters provide the bare essentials of existence, a place like Sarah's also can permit a homeless woman to reorganize her life and perhaps get on her feet again. A young black woman called Jane is trying to do that—using a sink at the center to wash her clothes regularly and the comfortable lounge to study books from the public library. Unlike the library, where you're asked to leave if you're caught dozing off, Sarah's understands how tired a woman can be after a wary night at a crowded shelter.

For everyone on the street, life is a matter of improvising. After breakfast at the Sally (Salvation Army), Elizabeth stops at a city garage where they let you use the bathroom and just sit in the warmth for a while. Then it's on to the US Submarine Shop, where you can get a large cup of coffe in a Styrofoam cup for 50 cents—a much better deal than at the coffee shop across the street where you get a seat at a table, a cup and saucer, but a lot less coffee. "I don't like to give them my patronage," harrumphs Elizabeth like the greatest of grandes dames.

But then the high-strung, fast-talking extrovert slows down, revealing a flash of the severely depressed woman who still needs medication and periodic hospitalization. The holidays make her introspective. "I never thought it would happen to me," Elizabeth says. "It's all my fault—I can't seem to get my life together. I'm sort of the black sheep of a strict Catholic family. Even if I couldn't be a nun, like I wanted, I figured at least I'd be married with a home. But my family hasn't spoken to me much since I gave my baby daughter up for adoption 10 years ago. Really, she's far better off than I am—living in the suburbs with parents who love her—but my mother always told me that the worst thing you can do is give up your own flesh and blood. I should have been strong enough to get myself out of this predicament."

Teddy Bear, meanwhile, is coming off a binge and hardly notices the holiday season. She wins a Christmas tree in a drawing at Sarah's Circle, and immediately talks about selling it. She's not ready to accept a missionary's offer to sleep off her hangover at an available apartment. "There's too much pressure there not to drink," says Dolores. As for the danger that awaits her in the streets, she says, "The only thing they can do to me is kill me. Everthing else they've done to me. I don't feel it anymore."

2

Street People

Marcia Z. Nelson

S ALVATION, SOUP, AND SOAP.
It smells like laundry in the overheated women's lounge at Pacific Garden Mission, a 108-year-old shelter run by evangelical Christians for some of Chicago's homeless people. Touches of homey elegance gussy up the lounge: an antique bookcase, the coveted sort, with glass doors that lift up; a brass planter that sits atop an antique sewing desk. Christmas cards are stuck to a mirror. In an adjoining dormitory room, the beds covered with patchwork quilts are barracks-neat.

A resident, her hair in pincurls, enters the lounge to do her nails. Two women, one pregnant, loll on a sofa. Another, neatly attired in a coat with a fur collar, ducks in from the vicious Chicago cold. Willing to wait several hours for the Missions dinner, she eases herself into a rocker, takes off her butterscotch-colored knitted cap—she is wearing earrings underneath—and idly studies a small tract.

Other women drift in to rock, sit, study the walls, and wait.

Pacific Garden Mission is Christianity with the sleeves rolled up, a classic example of the traditional way of aiding the homeless. Its old-fashioned compassion comes with its principal concern: saving people's souls while sheltering their bodies.

But there is also a new, secular kind of care: At Cooper's Place, a drop-in center the homeless can use during daytime hours, the bible of choice is *Radical Social Work*, which lies on the desk of Director Abner Cunningham.

Like Pacific Garden Mission, Cooper's building is in the run-down periphery of the city's core. It is the sort of space that could have been a beachhead trendy restaurant in a neighborhood ripe for rehabilitation, but it serves the displaced residents, not the gentrifiers.

One large, bright room, filled with men still dressed for the outdoors, reverberates with the noise of their activities: the snap of playing cards hitting the tables, the incessant drone of television, conversation, raucous laughter. As the day wears on, the decibel level rises steadily.

Cooper's is dedicated to the late Reverend George Thomas Cooper, who operated a shelter and reading room for the last twenty-five years of his life. The center's five staff members try to provide an atmosphere where homeless people can enjoy a respite from the body-numbing cold and psyche-numbing isolation of the streets, and from the intrusive, patronizing "change agents" frequently prescribed by the social service agencies and shelters through which the homeless pass.

Pacific Garden Mission and Cooper's are among the few places where Chicago's estimated 25,000 homeless can find shelter. From New York to Los Angeles, the story is much the same. Two million to three million people have no place to call home, so they sleep in doorways, dumpsters, lean-tos, cars, tents, emergency shelters.

They are white, black, Native American, Hispanic, foreign-born. They are troubled people, vulnerable people: victims of unscrupulous landlords, abusive families, rapacious employers, callous bureaucrats, or of their own addictions or personality disorders. Some have succumbed to just plain bad luck. They are the foot soldiers in the army of today's poor. Many of them might make it in better times, given enough jobs, enough affordable housing, enough social services.

Until recently, they have been silent, pacified with the token turkey of concern at Christmas, ignored by strangers on the street, disfranchised, and insulted by a President who thinks that the homeless members of Washington's "grate society" choose to make their homes on heating vents. But now the homeless are beginning to speak for themselves.

"Within the past five years," says Sue Freeman, who has been homeless off and on since 1983, "like every other group, the homeless have come out of the closet."

Freeman, thirty-nine, is co-chair of the Homeless Caucus in Chicago, which formed last November and testified at the City Council's 1985 budget hearings. Sam Guardino, an organizer who works with the Caucus, terms the Council's final $1.2 million allocation for services for the homeless "essentially a $1 million victory," since the budget originally submitted requested only $200,000 for that purpose.

In New York City, shortly before last year's Presidential election, 410 homeless persons, using such addresses as a sidewalk, a park bench, and post office steps, registered to vote. The registration was permitted after a Federal judge ruled that the homeless had a constitutional right to vote if they met the age and citizenship qualifications.

In Philadelphia last year, the first convention of homeless people drew an attendance of 175. Final conference recommendations included recognition of "the values and rights of all humans regardless of their circumstances," *The New York Times* reported.

In Los Angeles, homeless people helped run an encampment erected late last year by a team of organizers. The day Tent City, which accommodated 300, went down, fourteen homeless people, organizers, and concerned citizens were arrested for civil disobedience at the Los Angeles County Board of Supervisors. The "Tent City 14" were protesting a penalty of sixty-day ineligibility for benefits, imposed whenever a recipient violates the rules governing the county's "workfare" program. At any one time, says Matt Lyons, who works with the Homeless Organizing Team, 5,000 people are on the streets because of the penalty.

"Sixty days on the streets does not rehabilitate anybody," Lyons says.

While some of the homeless have organized to speak collectively, many others are willing to speak individually about the way they live. Their stories make up a giant mural of homelessness in America and a portrait gallery of homeless individuals: single parents, abused wives, confirmed or recovering alcoholics, former offenders, hard-core unemployed, drug abusers, the physically or mentally disabled. Like the unhappy family of Tolstoy's *Anna Karenina*, each homeless individual has a unique tale of misery.

"I am an alcoholic," says Louis Wishman, thirty-eight, who is trying for a second time to stay sober. "It's like a diabetic has to take his insulin every day—I have to stay away from a drink, one day at a time. Every day, twenty-four hours, sometimes two minutes, sometimes ten minutes—whatever it takes."

Louis, sandy-haired, portly, looks like an aging preppy in his argyle sweater vest and gray trousers. He was trained as an accountant and is about to begin an accounting job. Right now he sleeps at an overnight shelter in Chicago's Uptown, an ethnically diverse neighborhood that has served as a dumping ground for deinstitutionalized mental patients. His Christian fundamentalist family relied on welfare when he was growing up. He mentions being institutionalized as a child; his father was an alcoholic, he says. Louis is divorced and has a six-year-old son, whom he watches anxiously for behavioral quirks.

Louis has to struggle to stay on the wagon. "There is no reason for me not to drink," he says. He draws a distinction between sober people—those who are comfortable with themselves when not drinking—and dry people, who are unhappy about not drinking. "I'm dry, very dry," he says.

The Center for Street People, a drop-in shelter for homeless people in the neighborhood, helped Louis. The Center was opened in 1974 for recovering alcoholics. When Louis came to the Center in 1980, he was hired to be a member of its staff, but he couldn't handle it, so he quit.

"I went home and turned on the gas and tried to kill myself," he says, "after a two-week drunk." He was hospitalized for depression, then enrolled in an alcoholism program, got a part-time job at a major Chicago bank, went to school, and cut his ties to the Center. Then he lost the job, finished school, got drunk again, ended up back on the streets, and finally back at the Center. He is again on the staff, as a volunteer "participant," and again seeing a therapist.

"A guy last night asked me what it feels like to be on the streets, and I said, 'It hurts,' " Louis says, " 'because you're not wanted anywhere.' "

Jack, described by people at the Center as "a real street person," says, "If it wasn't for this Center, I'd be dead." He has bad legs, he confides. His speech is slurred but coherent; his chiseled, handsome face, headed toward gauntness, looks a bit vacant. He is perhaps somewhere in his thirties, but seems prematurely slowed down by drink.

"I'm gonna tell you the truth," he begins. "I'm an alcoholic. I drink everything, I even drink rubbing alcohol, I drink beer, I drink anything that's got alcohol." He sniffs periodically as he tells of a recent period of sobriety.

"I did stop for a long time. Six months. And I went to a bar that had some live music. (I like to play the drums.) I went inside that bar. I was sober for six months, and I was doing real good, and—slip of the tongue, instead of ordering a Seven-Up, I said a seven-and-seven."

"You take a match," he says, "and when you strike that match, it's gonna burn."

"You can't get a job around here," Jack says. Chicago's Uptown is filled with day-labor agencies, where lines form at 5:30 a.m. So he picks up aluminum cans, which he can turn in for twenty-two cents a pound. In the summertime, he collects and sells golf balls driven into ponds by unlucky or unskilled golfers. Other homeless people sell blood, food stamps, or prescription drugs they can obtain from unscrupulous doctors who will eventually share in the profits of the street sales.

When Jack has money, he buys wine, not food, because he can get food elsewhere. "I go to McDonald's," he explains, "but I don't go inside. I go in the dumpster, rip open the bags, and eat other people's food, French fries, hamburgers. You don't know what kind of people eat that kind of food, but you're hungry, you just don't care, you're just starving."

Alcoholics fit the traditional image of the homeless person. So do the mentally or physically disabled. Estimates of the proportion of the homeless population who are disabled or disturbed vary too greatly to be meaningful, but the disabled are a visible homeless contingent with special needs.

"It's been a journey, actually, to try to function within mainstream society," says Joletta Wright, thirty-one, who has been staying at Pacific Garden Mission for six weeks since arriving in Chicago from Baltimore, where she had also been homeless. Joletta has difficulty holding a job because of what she describes as a biochemical disorder that requires her to take medication.

"I've had a lot of jobs," she says. "I was a security aide for the housing authority in Baltimore, I worked with the blind and handicapped, I did cashier work." She has also been a seamstress at Catholic Charities in Baltimore, but her real skill is in the graphic arts.

Joletta is extraordinarily tall—six feet, four inches—and dressed in a striped pullover color-coordinated with her skirt. She wears sturdy walking shoes, has large gold hoop earrings. As she talks, articulately but slowly, a fixed stare reveals her state of mind.

"Right now I'm in kind of a daze," she says. "I just have to take it one day at a time. I don't know what tomorrow's going to bring."

Joletta is trying to find a permanent place to live. After being denied Federal Supplemental Security Income (cash aid to the disabled) three times, she recently won approval of her application. Her situation has frayed her family ties—a twelve-year-old daughter remains in Baltimore with the girl's father—and impaired her motivation to keep working.

"I want to work, but, see, you lose incentive," she says. "I'm speaking on behalf of other mental patients, people with disabilities and stuff like that, because that's the way that I came—that's what caused me to be homeless. I had to work toward getting incentive. My incentive is getting low, because I have gotten frustrated with the way the system is."

Homeless people with histories of alcoholism or disability are the most extreme and poignant examples of the dispossessed, but the problems of the homeless stem from something much deeper than individual affliction: Homeless people are poor. There are simply not enough houses or jobs to go around for the country's lowest class, those who long ago fell through the "social safety net."

Many of the people who use Cooper's Place experience some of the problems related to alcoholism, but they suffer even more from chronic unemployment and underemployment. Abner Cunningham estimates that two-thirds of the people at Cooper's Place are willing and able to work.

"My experience here is that if there's a job, Jack or Jill will go to it," he says. "Anything we've had, these guys just jump at it. What's available is short-term day labor. People would love to get that kind of stuff."

Even when day labor is available, though, it won't make ends meet. People become homeless for an immediate reason: simple inability to pay the rent. Inexpensive housing is disappearing, and the demise of that entire housing market is principally responsible for the explosion in the numbers of people on the streets.

"I think folks are beginning to understand that the shame of the old lady on the street corner has something to do with housing in this country," says Robert Hayes, a lawyer for the National Coalition for the Homeless. "The most honest explanation of homelessness is an economic one: supply and demand."

The demand is fierce, and the supply is shrinking. In New York City, for example, 108,000 of the city's single-room-occupancy (SRO) hotel units have given way to the wrecker and the luxury housing rehabilitator. Some Chicago neighborhoods have lost as much as 20 per cent of their housing units over a ten-year period, according to a 1982 report by the U.S. Department of Housing and Urban Development. When Governor Mario Cuomo released a New York state study of homelessness late last year, he said, "Homelessness today is overwhelmingly caused by poverty, not pathology. Our main conclusion is that homelessness is by its nature a crisis of housing."

"We've got nothing that says that housing is a basic human right," says Harvey Saver, executive director of the Chicago Coalition for the Homeless. "This country has no policy, nothing, that really assures that human right: that people are entitled to adequate, affordable, accessible housing."

"An auto has more natural right than a person, and is more protected," asserts Ruth (not her real name), a forty-seven-year-old homeless woman. "For $50 a month, a car can get a heated space. The car has a right to sit on the curb, whereas a poor person can't sit on a park bench without a legal address."

Hayes blames the housing crunch squarely on the Federal Government, arguing that a bipartisan effort begun after World War II to stimulate the construction of public housing in this country was ended by the Reagan Administration. Since 1980, housing construction subsidies have dropped by 78 per cent a year.

Ten or more years ago, the homeless were mostly alcoholic men. But now the population of homeless women is growing as single women and their young children begin to dominate the ranks of the poor.

Bridgette Hawkins, twenty-five, has two daughters and a third child on the way. Bridgette and her family are staying in Dehon House, a transitional shelter in a quiet residential neighborhood on Chicago's North Side. She lost her apartment through roommate difficulties, then lost her money when somebody snatched her wallet.

Bridgette, a large women with a round face, has been on and off Aid to Families with Dependent Children, and currently receives $302 a month in AFDC assistance and $184 in food stamps. She has just returned from apartment hunting—her three-year-old daughter sleeps on her lap—with fresh anger about the stigma attached to public aid.

"The way I figure it is, you need help and they're going to help you," she says. "What happens to me if public aid isn't there? The Government sets up a system for you when you can't help yourself and then terrifies you for being on it." Landlords are reluctant to rent to her, "just because the words 'public aid' are there."

Bridgette has held several of the low-paying jobs to which women are consigned: child-care worker, cashier, waitress, nurse's aide. The experience has taught her that it doesn't pay to work because she can't afford quality child care. "By the time I get through paying the babysitters, I can sit home and get more money from public aid." Once, when she came home from work, her younger daughter had a mysterious black eye, she says.

Though Bridgette is black and lives in the city and Judy Brown (not her real name) is white and lives in the suburbs, their situations are strikingly comparable. Both are single heads of household, too poor to make ends meet.

Judy, with neat short brown hair, kelly green sweater over a black turtleneck, and gold earrings, looks like a young suburban mother. Her story is less typical of the suburbs. Her family has been evicted three times in the past five years, after she divorced an alcoholic who only recently began paying child support. At forty, Judy has three teen-aged children and a five-week-old granddaughter. The lines of her face are tight, her hands are thin. The strain is starting to show.

Judy can't afford suburban apartments, but has chosen to stay in the area where her children have grown up and still attend school. "I just did a lot of things that were best for my children," she says.

Judy and her family are staying in an emergency apartment in Arlington Heights, a northwestern suburb of Chicago. Northwest Community Services, the social services agency which placed her there, received 504 requests for emergency housing in 1984 from people in a suburban area generally thought of as middle- to upper-middle class. Judy sits at the dining table in her apartment, which has been dimmed so her granddaughter can nap. Behind Judy, two painted cupboards with glass doors are completely bare.

"I think the rents are out of line and there's nowhere to go where people will be understanding," she says. "It's hard to find people who will accept a family that's struggling." Judy has obtained a Section 8 certificate—a Federal rent subsidy—in the past, but few suburban landlords were willing to take it, she says.

Judy has had some training as an accountant. The highest-paying job she ever held was at a suburban newspaper, three or four years ago, which gave her take-home pay of $168 a week. "I had to go back to waitressing," she says. "I needed as much cash as I could get."

As a licensed practical nurse, Frances Lahori should not be poor, but she lived—until recently—in the Robert Taylor Homes, one of Chicago's largest low-income housing projects. Now Frances, thirty-one, is homeless, staying at St. Martin de Porres shelter for women on the city's poor south side. She left her abusive alcoholic husband. She has scars on her chest and upper arms where she says he once threw hot grease on her.

"I had been working," Frances says, "but because of all this abuse, I haven't been able to hold a job." Her husband used to call her regularly, and disruptively, at a nursing home where she was the nurse in charge. The abuse has also sent her four times to a state-run mental health institution in Chicago's southern suburbs.

Frances has been on a waiting list for another apartment at the project, since her previous home was broken into four times; she hopes to take her three children to a new place. She is considering getting police protection against her husband, and a divorce.

Sister Connie Driscoll, who opened St. Martin de Porres in 1983 in a neighborhood filled with vacant lots, boarded-up houses, and corner stores hidden behind burglar gates, reports that a rash of wife-abuse over the holidays filled the shelter with battered homeless women. Generally her clients arrive at the shelter after they have been evicted. "They have a choice to make," she says. "Pay the rent or eat."

Smoking slender brown cigarettes, Sister Connie, with her eyepatch and low, husky voice, looks as if she should be running a roulette table rather than a shelter. She sounds tough and angry when describing the problems of her poor, mostly black, female clients.

"You can't even get a rathole for $250," she says indignantly. "I see it as a sexist problem more than a race problem. If we're going to break the cycle of poverty, you can either write them a check for hope or you can write them one for despair, and right now we're writing them a big one for despair."

The check for hope will also have to be big. In mid-1983, the National Low-Income Housing Coalition told Congress that at least 750,000 new units a year were needed. A measure requesting $10 million for shelter and services for California's homeless was passed last year after it was shaved to $3 million. Federal renovation of a shelter for the homeless in Washington, D.C., agreed to by the Government after a protest fast undertaken by members of the Community for Creative Nonviolence, will cost $5 million, according to Mitch Snyder, a spokesman for the group who made headlines during his fifty-one-day fast.

New York City has begun a $43 million program to renovate city-owned apartments into permanent housing for the homeless; Governor Mario Cuomo recently proposed to borrow as much as $1 billion to build 15,000 apartments for the poor in that city.

Two major foundations have also added private money. The Robert Wood Johnson Foundation and the Pew Memorial Trust recently announced a four-year, $25 million program for homeless people in eighteen cities. Under the program, teams of doctors, nurses, and social workers based in clinics at soup kitchens and shelters will provide the homeless with desperately needed health and social services. (Some officials estimate that those who lack permanent shelter for any significant length of time may suffer a decrease in life expectancy of twenty to thirty years. Thousands of homeless people eligible for Federal benefits but not currently receiving them may need special help in applying, according to the recent findings of Representative Ted Weiss, New York Democrat.)

Efforts for the homeless are also being pressed in the courts. The National Coalition for the Homeless has filed suit to require New York City to shelter homeless families; in 1981, that city agreed, as a result of a similar suit, to shelter homeless individuals. The Coalition has also sued over the failure to limit the number of people in a shelter to the maximum of 200 imposed by state law. Los Angeles litigation is attempting to assert the right of homeless individuals to be sent to heated shelters.

But people who live on the streets may be the best source of creative solutions to their problems.

"If I have a job—and I'm looking for a full-time job—I won't be homeless any more," says William Johnson, thirty-two, a former offender who is co-chair of the Homeless Caucus in Chicago. "I'll be able to be self-sufficient, I'll be just like somebody in society—I'll be a citizen. I feel like now, I'm not a citizen of the United States. I feel like I'm an alien."

"All any local government has to do to erase poverty," says Ruth, "is to tax the kicks [recreation] industry. Tax it for the poor, let the proceeds go to the poor. Where's their imagination? Where's their leadership?"

"What we need are overnight shelters that are responsible to the community: based in the community, run by the community," says Sue Freeman. "Secondly, we need efficient drop-in centers staffed by sufficient numbers of people who have been on the street and can relate to street people and give them support and care and just say, 'I understand your isolation.' "

"The only solution to the problem is that street people and homeless people themselves need to be part of their own solution," says Louis Wishman. "It's time that professional organizations hire people from the streets to work with street people. It's time that organizations, instead of hiring middle-class college kids as volunteeers to run their programs, get street people to run them and provide them with some kind of dignity. It's time that older street people, forty-five to sixty-five, who are not going to go back to work in this society, are used as volunteers.

"It's time that the church responds with its mission to care about every human being in this society, not just Ethiopia or Vietnam. It's time that the socialists get off their dead asses and stop worrying about socialism in this country and start dealing with the people who are gonna bring it about."

3

New York's Homeless Families

Tom Robbins

JOSEPHINE CARTER closed the door behind herself and her five children for the last time on December 27, 1983. Behind her she left a one-family house on a leafy street in Cambria Heights in southeastern Queens. Once the property of her common-law husband, they had lived in the home for ten years until they separated and the bank foreclosed on a mortgage she could no longer pay. A local speculator bought it and asked for $350 rent. This was almost a hundred dollars more than the amount she received in her welfare check for shelter. She was soon evicted.

As she and her children came down the stoop they stepped across this city's sharpest dividing line between haves and have-nots, between the merely poor and the desperate. They stepped out of one world and into another. They were now homeless.

A feisty, thirty-eight-year-old, Carter describes herself as "a private person, with my own ways." It was this that made her decide not to grab onto the last rung of the housing ladder by doubling-up with family or friends. At her Income Maintenance Center she was told to get, as best she could, to Roberto Clemente State Park, a gymnasium in The Bronx that has been made over into a mass shelter for families by the city. Her sister and brother-in-law drove her and Simka, who is 15, Obadiah, 13, Emoh, 11, Shoshana, 9, and "the baby," Ketayrah, who is 4, to The Bronx.

There they entered through a balcony overlooking a massive room filled with rows of cots, separated only by the feeble attempts of families to screen themselves off from one another.

From *City Limits*, November 1984, pp. 1, 7-12. Reprinted by permission of *City Limits* (424 West 33rd Street, New York, NY 10001).

"I looked down into the place," recalled Carter, "and saw all those little cots and all those people. There were these state troopers walking around on the balcony and the guards down below. I couldn't believe it. The kids said, 'I feel like I'm in prison, but I didn't do nothing wrong.' "

On that day, Josephine Carter's family joined some 6,000 others who, during the course of the year, had stepped across that same dividing line. And like her, many of them remained there. Last month, hers was one of 3,100 families—nearly 11,000 parents and kids—who were sheltered by the city: enough people to comprise an average-size American town.

It's a population that has already increased by a third over last year and shows every sign of swelling even more. And, although few of those in charge of coping with the families have ventured to say out loud, it's a population for whom the admittedly deficient and stop-gap shelters are becoming permanent housing.

In September, the average stay in the hotels and shelters grew to 7.3 months; 451 families had been there for over a year, 76 of them for more than two years. And it is still climbing.

"The length of the stay has got to grow," said a top official of the city's Human Resources Administration.

The questions of who those families are, and how they managed to stumble into the bottom of New York's housing barrel, have been put aside in favor of the more urgent issue of what to do with them. And meanwhile, the media's erratic but widespread reporting on their dismal plight, with not a little help from the city, has distorted public perceptions. In a classic "blame the victim" scenario, the shorthand explanation for homeless families is that they have somehow created their own misfortune and accelerated their own decline. It's an analysis which forecloses hope for change and solution as much as it lets government and society ease themselves off the hook.

As New York City enters a winter which will once again break post-depression homeless records, the snapshots are being readied of a nameless and homeless mass, filled with misfortune and tragedy to be sure, but nonetheless beyond the reach of effective intervention.

Doubling-Up

As the numbers of the homeless families have grown, the reasons for homelessness have changed as well. When the firestorms of arson were raging across neighborhoods in the South Bronx, the Lower East Side and Browns-ville, and when landlord abandonment was at its height, the breakdown of reasons for homelessness remained fairly steady. Some two-thirds of the population sought relocation because of a catastrophe such as fire or a wintertime burst boiler, and a third of the families had been evicted. As late as 1982, that breakdown held true. But then the proportion began to shift as the numbers started to swell.

"We began to get a new source of families," reported Robert Jorgen, the head of HRA's Crisis Intervention Services unit and a veteran of city efforts on behalf of the homeless. "Many had been evicted by primary tenants, often other family members. A lot were young, new at parenting." Many had never had their own apartment.

Today, the 3,100 families in the shelter system are a direct reverse of two years ago: two-thirds are homeless because they were evicted, while only a third are from fires or building vacate orders. The picture that is slowly coming into focus is one of an enormous number of near-homeless families, clinging tenuously to the last rung of the housing ladder, most of them doubled up with friends or family and living in severely overcrowded conditions.

Last year, based on an analysis of water consumption in its projects, the City Housing Authority estimated that some 17,000 of its 150,000 public housing units are doubled up. That's the only official estimate of the doubling-up phenomenon. But policy makers are beginning to fear that they may be sitting atop a phenomenon of possibly massive proportions. "I wouldn't even hazard a guess on the number of families doubled-up," said Larry Perlman, the Assistant Director of Income Maintenance Operations at HRA who is responsible for the agency's housing activities.

You don't have to look far to see the policy implications of this homeless/next-to-homeless situation. If families who have either lost their own housing (or never had their own) have been able to somehow make do through their own arrangements by living with friends or family, then there's little reason to figure they can't keep doing so.

As Perlman says: "About 30 families every business day show up at the EAU [Emergency Assistance Unit at 241 Church Street in Manhattan] and seem to be eligible for temporary housing. But less than a third of them enter the system because the shelter doesn't appeal to them.... It doesn't stretch my credulity," he adds, "to assume that not everybody in the system is a victim."

It is a very small step from this point to reckoning that the better the homeless remedies offered, the more needy, homeless families will appear. "If you create a system where at the other end of the pipeline you get a better apartment," suggests Perlman, "it's going to draw more people."

Two years ago, said Robert Jorgen, he saw exactly that happen. "When the city was still sending people to New Jersey hotels we got tremendous publicity. We had some fairly nice hotels out there. People saw on TV all the kids splashing around in the swimming pools. Our EAU was packed with people wanting to go to New Jersey who turned around and left when they were told they couldn't."

Since HRA pressured City Hall two years ago for greater access to city-owned property, almost all *in rem* vacancies have been allocated to the homeless. Deputy Housing Commissioner for Property Management Joe Shuldiner is now overseeing a 2,500-unit rehab program aimed exclusively at homeless families. "I wonder whether or not we're dealing with a homeless crisis," he said recently, "or a crisis in bad housing."

But we should also ask, does it make any difference? City officials voicing the "homeless-by-choice" or "good-homeless-solutions-breed-more-homeless" theory are on thin ice and they know it. For one thing, the decision to cross that dividing line between homelessness and its possible alternatives—including unbearable overcrowding amid squalid conditions—is one people are going to make by themselves. No matter what the city's homeless policies, it's hard to see how they can forestall for long the day when families fall off that bottom rung of the housing ladder.

For years, housing activists and others have asked where most of those displaced by the massive abandonment and arson of the late seventies went. Part of the answer may now be emerging.

East 5th St.—Puerto Rico—Newark—the Brooklyn Arms

Sonia Zapata's youngest child was born in the Brooklyn Arms. Jason, who is now eight-months old, arrived about six months after Zapata was shipped out of the Lincoln Motel in Newark in the June '83 New Jersey hotel evacuations. A Lower East Side resident, Zapata, her husband and her two older sons had lived with her sister for several months after returning from Puerto Rico. She was born and raised around Delancey Street and lived for years on East Fifth Street between Avenues C and D. "Now it's all torn down," she says.

She moved with her family to East Eighth Street but there too the landlord abandoned the building. While living with her sister she besieged local housing offices with applications. She had high hopes of getting into Pueblo Nuevo, a new six-story Section 8 project on East Houston Street, but lost out. A friendly social service aide helped her get the Newark hotel placement for which she was grateful.

Her Brooklyn Arms room is larger than many, although there is no furniture other than the three beds, a crib which she fought to get, a bureau and a single table for the food and hot plate which, like all the families, she uses in violation of hotel and health code rules. The second floor room has gotten the hotel's recent partial rehab—a paint job, a new light fixture. The bare cement floor is a dull grey.

"When I first came it was a hell house," she says. "I was robbed in front of my eyes, all my luggage, everything I had, was taken."

Each day her four-year-old boards a minibus for the Nat Turner Daycare Center. Her 18-year-old son is graduating from high school. She worries about the neighborhood she'll end up in, should she be lucky enough to snag one of the city-owned apartments off the "vans" that take families around to see them.

"My kids keep asking me why we have to live here. 'Why can't we live across the street?' they want to know." Out the window, the Brooklyn Academy of Music Local Development Corporation has renovated a large apartment building across the street using a city low-interest loan. She has checked out the rents, however. They are $500 for a two-room apartment, $600 for three rooms.

The Recycled Crisis

Most New Yorkers recollect that the welfare hotel crisis isn't new. In 1972, when the city was sheltering nearly 1,000 families in expensive, barely habitable and dangerous hotels, plucky Department of Social Service caseworkers placed a family in the Waldorf Astoria. And then told the press.

The grisly exposés of the largest welfare hotels compounded the Waldorf outrage and then-Mayor John Lindsay threatened to knock agency heads together unless they came up with a solution. They did, temporarily.

First, the Department of Social Services agreed in emergencies to waive rent levels which exceeded the maximums; second, the Housing Authority, then headed by Simeon Golar, let homeless families cut in front of the waiting list on some of its new, outer-borough, projects.

The Housing Authority also looked for a way to provide decent emergency transitional housing with social services. The result was the Urban Family Center on Baruch Place on the Lower East Side. The 46-unit building, operated in conjunction with the Henry Street Settlement House, opened in 1973 and was able to offer a wide range of services and counseling for the same emergency shelter payments as the hotels.

Meanwhile, Robert Jorgen and his aide, Ed Kopp, were dispatched as HRA troubleshooters to the hotels. What became the Crisis Intervention Services placed workers at each hotel and linked families with apartment application information, the Board of Education and other needs. But while they can answer questions and log complaints, the CIS workers have little ability to affect the day-to-day crisis of homeless living in a rundown hotel.

Back in the Hotels

Having survived the hotel horrors of the 70s, with names like The Hamilton, the Broadway Central and the Greenwich, it was Robert Jorgen's fervent hope that he would be out of the hotel business. Jorgen, who has developed a reputation as a Cassandra of the homeless crisis for his gloomy yet correct predictions about the scope of the problem, pushed for creation of enough family care centers to cover the ebb and flow of homeless clients. They weren't built.

What happened to the aggressive Lindsay-era drive toward solutions? "People lost interest," says Jorgen simply. "When the population went down, the attention went down too."

Today, the City of New York is a better customer of grade-B hotels than ever. At summer's end, the city was farming out families to 50 different hotels and motels in all five boroughs. Payments per room vary, from an average of $50 to a high of $100 per night. Since most hotels charge by the head, packing families into small rooms doesn't affect their volume.

"It's a seller's market," said HRA's Larry Perlman. "The rate is what the traffic will bear."

But no single fact sticks in the public craw as the startling gap between what the city pays in "the welfare hotels" and what it gets for the money. In the fiscal year ended last June 30, the city's hotel tab was a staggering $45 million—nearly twice the amount allocated for low-interest housing rehab loans. Eighty-five percent of the homeless families live in hotels, at a per-head subsidy that (were they somehow able to leap over race and anti-children bias) would comfortably house them in some of the city's choicest rental apartments.

But just like in the early 70s, there's an embarrassing lack of correlation between payment and service.

Some of the worst abuses have been curbed through a vigorous new family hotel inspection program operating out of the Mayor's Office of SRO Housing. Yet the system remains as vulnerable as ever to its more than decade-old bind of paying top dollar for rotten conditions.

The Hotel Carter

Josephine Carter and her kids got out of Roberto Clemente in three days. They were shipped to a hotel on West 43rd Street in Times Square with the same name as hers. She welcomed the prospect of the Hotel Carter as a chance for privacy after her 72 hours of exposure at the wide open barracks-style gym. But the Carter, the most recent large hotel to be brought into the city's system, had perils all its own.

In June 1983, the city was forced to yank over 300 families out of New Jersey hotels after an infuriated Newark City Council denounced it for "dumping" on their city. The city scrambled desperately for local space. A large number of families were taken in by the Hotel Carter which was owned by a Vietnamese businessman, Tran Dinh Truong. Jack Doyle of the American Red Cross Disaster Services unit, which has played the major voluntary role in assisting the homeless, said his agency had recommended that the city tread warily with the Carter. Stories abounded of well-organized drug and prostitution rings operating within the hotel, allegedly with management's knowledge. "We proposed some sort of net lease arrangement," said Doyle, "so that we'd be sure to get some of what we pay for."

But the New Jersey evacuations made it more than ever a seller's market. The city not only gratefully placed hundreds of families in the Carter's rooms, but paid a higher price to boot. Less than a year later, after Carter horror stories outstripped all others, the city reluctantly resolved not to place more families there, and was waiting for hotel management to show up in court to respond to a contempt order for failing to make repairs.

The Carter's management has insisted on a shroud of secrecy around itself. When Steve Banks, a Legal Aid attorney, sought to bring a doctor to Josephine Carter's children, management called the police to have both lawyer and doctor arrested. Through much of 1983-84 the Carter charged *any* guest, including babysitters, $12.50 just to go upstairs. More recently, the hotel has said no guests at all are allowed.

During the eight months Josephine Carter's family lived at the Hotel Carter, the city shelled out $95.10 for every night her six-member family spent in a ten-foot by twelve-foot room with one bed, a single cot and a moldy fungus that started on the bathroom ceiling and grew out into the other room. The monthly rent tab for sheltering families there in April was nearly a half million dollars. During the entire period the Carter remained obstinately out of compliance with the demands of the new beefed-up inspections. Management's sole gesture, when ordered to provide window guards, air conditioners or somehow to secure windows against defenestration of children, was to chain shut windows in a number of rooms. Angry mothers responded by smashing the glass to bring in some air.

Parents And Friends On The Move

Against the gloomy background of growing homelessness, a remarkable demonstration held in late August in City Hall Park burst like a long pent-up storm. As if in defiance of the listlessness and inner fatigue bred by month after month of hotel living, a group calling itself Parents and Friends On the Move shouted, chanted and sang its denunciations of homelessness and the city's hotel and shelter systems. Over a hundred families from hotels in Manhattan, Brooklyn and Queens were joined at the rally by much of the social services and legal network which has emerged to advocate and assist for the homeless.

But for that afternoon at least, homeless families were their own clearest and most articulate advocates. As parents from the hotels who had never before approached a microphone told the noontime crowd over and over, they were there because they needed housing above all else. When the mothers' chorus from the Brooklyn Arms sang their own lyrics of hotel life to gospel tunes and rhythms and a couple of hundred pairs of hands clapped in time along with them, it seemed as if for the first time the unbalance of power vs. powerlessness might well be altered.

To the left of the speaker's platform a tall, four-sided white cardboard construction provided both diversion for the dozens of hotel children as well as an outlet for their own testament about hotel life. With colored felt-tip markers, the kids drew pictures of themselves and their parents, contrasting what life was like in the hotels and what they imagined it could be like outside of them.

When City Council President Carol Bellamy told the families that she also knew that the answer was "Housing, housing, housing," and that no hotel should be paid without a signed contract obligating it to provide decent conditions, she won stormy applause. But as she tried to work her way back to her City Hall office she found herself hemmed in by a crowd of women and men from the hotels who demanded on-the-spot answers to tough questions.

Not surprisingly, this rumble out of the cauldron of the hotels received little press. In the weeks that followed many of those who had worked to organize it felt that their dilemma and needs remained as invisible as ever. Although it remained cohesive and in pursuit of its agenda in Brooklyn where the aid of the settlement house Brooklyn Colony South and the office of Assemblyman Roger Greene had helped to initially organize and launch it, citywide the group groped for ways to bring more families into action. But its impact on individuals was clear. Josephine Carter, who had never addressed a crowd before, described at the rally the harassment she and others underwent at the Carter. She told the crowd that she had been threatened by guards that if she attended the rally her room would burn. A few days later HRA moved her to a hotel in Sheepshead Bay for her protection.

Waiting In Queens

Out on Ditmas Avenue in Queens, across the parkway from the runways of LaGuardia Airport, Jewell Bryant's family is one of 100 similarly non-travelling welfare families housed at the Travellers Inn. Stocky and soft-spoken, Bryant was one of the principal organizers of the City Hall rally although just a couple of weeks afterwards she is questioning its impact. She is quick to point out that this lodging is clean, safe and comfortable compared to her earlier stays. Her single room boasts two neatly made double beds, a collapsible cot in the entranceway, night tables and a bureau. School certificates and awards won by her four children are taped to the four walls. Almost every foot of space is taken by their clothes and belongings. Food is stacked tidily on a shelf, perishables on a ledge outside the second-floor window beyond which airplanes at LaGuradia steadily land and ascend.

In January of 1983, the owner of the two-family home in Bedford-Stuyvesant where she lived told her that the building had been sold and she'd have to leave. For two months she and her children moved in with her sister and her three kids. The only apartments she found affordable were studios.

"It was just too crowded," she says. "Just too much." A caseworker at the Bureau of Child Welfare managed to get her into the Conca D'Oro, a Staten Island hotel. To keep her children in school in Brooklyn she left the hotel with them every morning before six. The hotel was located in a white residential community of single-family homes and there was frequent hostility towards the mostly black and Hispanic hotel families. One night a rock crashed through a window where her youngest son was sitting.

But when she and a friend from the hotel went to the local community board she found a number of sympathetic listeners. "They hadn't known what was going on. When we told them how our [$2.13 per person per day] restaurant allowance couldn't buy us meals in the only restaurant at the hotel, they organized to bring us food." The hotel's management was less pleased with the new local alliance, especially when Bryant brought the leaking roofs and uncleaned rooms to the attention of local papers and politicians. When management harassed her she was able, with the help of Legal Aid, to wrangle a switch to the Hotel Carter, from which she thought it would be easier to get the kids to school.

The Carter was far worse. "The drugs, the pimps, the prostitutes, the robberies. . . . There was nowhere for the kids to play. We were in the middle of Times Square and I didn't want them outside." In June, 1983 she was able to shift once again, this time to Queens where she promptly enrolled her oldest daughter in high school and her three sons in junior high and grade school. When the Parents and Friends group began meeting last spring she joined them. But she fears she has little to show for her efforts. With the kids in local schools she desperately wants a Queens apartment although none she's seen are close to her range.

Meanwhile, the daily hotel grind takes its toll. "We've got no privacy, no way to get away from each other," she laments. "We're always bickering and fighting." Most worrisome is the effect on her kids. Her daughter, once a proud and active student and athlete, is now apathetic and listless. "She comes home and just wants to sleep," said her mother. The hotel stigma has also caught up with them. "One day one of the mothers here overheard my daughter tell some schoolmates on the bus she only got off here to visit her aunt. That's the kind of thing that hurts the most. People have been living in hotels for a lot of years," she notes, "and we're going to have to scream awful loud to be heard."

Battlefronts

Over this winter, as the number of homeless families grows, there will be at least two battlefronts over policy. Last year, the Board of Estimate did not act on a resolution from Carol Bellamy to have the city arrange signed contracts with its larger welfare hotels. Bellamy aide Cindy Friedmutter says the resolution will be reintroduced this fall.

But doubts about the ability of contracts to alter the standoff between the city's emergency shelter needs and recalcitrant owners remain. Vigorously enforced, HRA officials say that contracts could drive more hotels out of the system, recreating the situation which led to farming families out to New Jersey. Adequate enforcement procedures already exist, they say, pointing to fire, building and health codes and the success of the Family Hotel Inspection Program in coordinating them.

Betsy Haggerty, manager of the program, cites the major success the office scored against the Brooklyn Arms, one of the largest welfare hotels with some of the most major repairs to be made. A massive consent agreement has been signed and management has been carrying out a phased repair and moderate rehabilitation program. The hotel, however, has already started the countdown to when it will be demolished or turned into a different use. Owners recently sought and received Board of Estimate approval to demolish the structure.

While the city has been seeking to enforce the consent orders against hotels, it has been less active in the court case brought against it by a group of homeless families last year. Mayor Koch has seized every opportunity to state that the city made a mistake in signing a consent decree concerning provisions for homeless individuals. It has led to far rougher terrain for a similar suit on behalf of homeless families known as *McKean vs. Koch*. Although an interim order handed down by the judge in that suit is somewhat ambiguous, it does hold the city to providing certain minimal necessities in its hotels. But Legal Aid attorney Marcella Silverman, one of the lawyers for the plaintiffs, says that the city has been grossly out of compliance in its placement of families in rooms without adequate space or bedding. "The Corporation Counsel has been fighting this case as though it was World War III," notes Silverman.

Almost as invisible and uncharted as that dividing line crossed by the homeless, is the effect that homelessness is having on families. Josephine Carter says that she explains homelessness to her children thus: "I tell the kids, 'This is a good experience. You're going to learn. This is what happens when you're on welfare and they control your life.'" But, she warns, "What you're doing to these kids you'll be paying for in the end. They'll look on society with hate and shame."

4

Diary of a Homeless Man

John R. Coleman

Wednesday, January 19

SOMEHOW, 12 DEGREES at 6 a.m. was colder than I had counted on. I think of myself as relatively immune to cold, but standing on a deserted sidewalk outside Penn Station with the thought of ten days ahead of me as a homeless man, the immunity vanished. When I pulled my collar closer and my watch cap lower, it wasn't to look the part of a street person; it was to keep the wind out.

My wardrobe wasn't much help. I had bought my "new" clothes—flannel shirt, baggy sweater, torn trousers, the cap and the coat—the day before on Houston Street for $19. "You don't need to buy shoes," the shopkeeper had said. "The ones you have on will pass for bum's." I was hurt; they were shoes I often wore to the office.

Having changed out of my normal clothes in the Penn Station men's room, and stowed them in a locker, I was ready for the street. Or thought so.

Was I imagining it, or were people looking at me in a completely different way? I felt that men, especially the successful-looking ones in their forties and over, saw me and wondered. For the rest, I wasn't there.

At Seventh Avenue and 35th Street, I went into a coffee shop. The counterman looked me over carefully. When I ordered the breakfast special—99 cents plus tax—he told me I'd have to pay in advance. I did (I'd brought $40 to see me through my ten days), but I noticed that the other customers were given checks, and paid only when they left.

From *New York*, Vol. 16, February 21, 1983, pp. 26-35. Copyright by John R. Coleman. Reprinted by permission.

By 9:30, I had read a copy of the *Times* retrieved from a trash basket; I had walked most of the streets around the station; I had watched the construction at the new convention center. There was little else to do.

Later, I sat and watched the drug sales going on in Union Square. Then I went into the Income Maintenance Center on 14th Street and watched the people moving through the welfare lines. I counted the trucks on Houston Street.

I vaguely remembered a quote to the effect that "idleness is only enjoyable when you have a lot to do." It would help to be warm, too.

There was ample time and incentive to stare at the other homeless folk on the street. For the most part, they weren't more interesting than the typical faces on Wall Street or upper Madison Avenue. But the extreme cases caught and held the eye. On Ninth Avenue, there was a man on the sidewalk directing an imaginary (to me) flow of traffic. And another, two blocks away, tracing the flight of planes or birds—or spirits—in the winter sky. And there was a woman with gloves tied to her otherwise bare feet.

Standing outside the Port Authority Bus Terminal was a man named Howard. He was perhaps my age, but the seasons had left deeper marks on his face. "Come summertime, it's all going to be different," he told me. "I'm going to have a car to go to the beach. And I'm going to get six lemons and make me a jug of ice-cold lemonade to go with the car.

"This whole country's gone too far with the idea of one person being at the top. It starts with birthday parties. Who gets to blow out the candles? One person. And it takes off from there. If we're ever going to make things better, we gotta start with those candles."

Was there any chance of people like us finding work?

"Jobs are still out there for the young guys who want them," Howard said. "But there's nothing for us. Never again. No, I stopped dreaming about jobs a long time ago. Now I dream about cars. And lemonade."

Drugs and alcohol are common among the homeless. The damage done by them was evident in almost every street person I saw. But which was cause and which was effect? Does it matter, once this much harm has been done?

My wanderings were all aimless. There was no plan, no goal, no reason to be anywhere at any time. Only hours into this role, I felt a useless part of the city streets. I wasn't even sure why I was doing this.

At about 3:30 in the afternoon, I decided to try to warm up with a few other drifters in Penn Station. An Amtrak police officer came along within minutes and shooed all of us outside.

Only some empty Thunderbird bottles remained behind as evidence that we had been there.

I knew these officers meant business. The week before, while preparing myself for this brief entry into their world, I had observed the homeless around the station through four nights. At about 2 a.m. on the first night, in the men's washroom, I came upon three Amtrak officers who had apparently found two young men having sexual relations in one of the toilet stalls.

The sergeant in the trio said and did little. The second cop was fairly quiet. But the third one—I have his name if Amtrak wants it—was in his element. He called the two cowering men every abusive name he had at his command, threw them up against the wall to frisk them, and then tried to see how close he could come to their outspread fingers with sharp blows of his nightstick. He told one of the pair that they had a big guy named Seymour they saved especially for punks like him and that Seymour was on his way down to do a job on him.

He ordered the man into one of the toilet booths, told him to face the wall, drop his pants, and bend over the toilet. Then he stomped across the washroom floor and in a deep garbled voice said, "I'm Seymour. Where's the guy waiting for a job?"

Noticing that an Allied Maintenance cleaner was in the room and had a plastic spray can hanging from the belt of his orange jumpsuit, the Amtrak cop snatched the can and went into the booth. "Got to lubricate you first, man." He later asked the cleaner what was in the can. When told it was about one-third ammonia and two-thirds water, he grumbled, "Too bad, There should've been more ammonia."

I felt sick and left. But I now knew enough not to fool around with that brand of cop.

A weathered drifter told me about a hideaway down in the bowels of the station, where it was warm and quiet. I found my way there and lay down on some old newspapers to sleep.

How long did I sleep? It didn't seem long at all. I was awakened by a flashlight shining in my eyes, and a voice, not an unkind one, saying, "You can't sleep here. Sorry, but you have to go outside."

I hadn't expected to hear that word "sorry." It was touching.

I left and walked up to 47th Street, between Fifth and Madison Avenues, where I knew there was a warm grate in the sidewalk. (I've been passing it every morning for over five years on my way to work.) One man was asleep there already. But there was room for two, and he moved over.

Thursday, January 20

When you're spending the night on the street, you learn to know morning is coming by the kinds of trucks that roll by. As soon as there are other than garbage trucks—say, milk or bread trucks—you know the night will soon be over.

I went back to Penn Station to clean up in the washroom. The care with which some of the other men with me bathed themselves at the basins would have impressed any public-health officer. And I couldn't guess from the appearance of their clothes who would be the most fastidious.

I bought coffee and settled back to enjoy it out of the main traffic paths in the station. No luck. A cop found me and told me to take it to the street.

After breakfast ($1.31 at Blimpie), I walked around to keep warm until the public library opened. I saw in a salvaged copy of the *Times* that we had just had our coldest night of the year, well below zero with the windchill factor, and that a record 4,635 people had sought shelter in the city's hostels.

The library was a joy. The people there treated me the same as they might have had I been wearing my business suit. To pass the time, I got out the city's welfare reports for 50 years ago. In the winter of 1933, the city had 4,524 beds available for the homeless, and all were said to be filled every night. The parallel to 1983 was uncanny. But, according to the reports, the man in charge of the homeless program in 1933, one Joseph A. Manning, wasn't worried about the future. True, the country was in the midst of a depression. But there had been a slight downturn in the numbers served in the shelters in the two months immediately preceding his report. This meant, wrote Manning, that "the depression, in the parlance of the ring, is K.O.'d."

Already, I notice changes in me. I walk much more slowly. I no longer see a need to beat a traffic light or to be the first through a revolving door. Force of habit still makes me look at my wrist every once in a while. But there's no watch there, and it wouldn't make any difference if there were. The thermometer has become much more important to me now than any timepiece could be.

The best thing about walking Manhattan's streets with so much time on my hands is the chance to stop, look upward, and celebrate what I see. Above the ugly, past the dull, and beyond the pretentious are gems I'd never really looked at before.

Today, I saw the Flatiron Building in a new light. I soaked up the quiet of the Little Church Around the Corner. I studied the ironwork outside a couple of the houses on the west side of Gramercy Park.

No need to hurry on.

The temperature rose during the day. Just as the newspaper headlines seem to change more slowly when you're on the streets all day long, so the temperature seems to change more rapidly and tellingly.

At about 9 p.m., I went back to the heated grate on 47th Street. The man who had been there last night was already in place. He made it clear that there was again room for me.

I asked him how long he had been on the streets.

"Eleven years, going on twelve," he said.

"This is only my second night."

"You may not stick it out. This isn't for every man."

"Do you ever go into the shelters?"

"I couldn't take that. I prefer this anytime."

Friday, January 21

When I left my grate mate—long before dawn—he wished me a good day. I returned the gesture. He meant his, and I meant mine.

In Manhattan's earliest hours, you get the feeling that the manufacture and removal of garbage is the city's main industry. So far, I haven't been lucky or observant enough to rescue much of use from the mounds of trash waiting for the trucks and crews. The best find was a canvas bag that will fit nicely over my feet at night.

I'm slipping into a routine: Washing up at the station. Coffee on the street. Breakfast at Blimpie. A search for the *Times* in the trash baskets. And then a leisurely stretch of reading in the park.

Some days bring more luck than others. Today I found 20 cents in a pay-phone slot, and heard a young flutist playing the music of C.P.E. Bach on Sixth Avenue between 9th and 10th Streets. A lot of people ignored her, even stepped over her flute case as if it were litter on the sidewalk. More often than not, those who put money in the case looked embarrassed. They seemed to be saying, "don't let anyone see me being appreciative."

By nightfall, the streets were cruelly cold once again.

A woman in an expensive fur coat, fur hat, and fur boots was preaching through a loudspeaker in Times Square: "Your cars, your jewelry, your wealth won't get you into heaven without accepting Jesus. Until you call on God to cleanse yourself, you're ordering yourself to hell."

I went up to the woman and asked her if furs would help. She looked at me as if I needed counseling. Or maybe a bath.

I headed for the 47th Street grate again but found my mate gone. There was no heat coming up through it. Do they turn it off on Friday nights? Don't we homeless have any rights?

On the northwest corner of Eighth Avenue and 33rd Street, there was a blocked-off subway entrance undergoing repair. I curled up against the wall there under some cardboard sheets. Rain began to fall, but I stayed reasonably dry and was able to get to sleep.

At some point, I was awakened by a man who had pulled back the upper piece of cardboard.

"You see my partner here. You need to give us some money."

I was still half-asleep. "I don't have any."

"You must have something, man."

"Would I be sleeping here in the rain if I did?"

His partner intervened. "C'mon. Leave the old bastard alone. He's not worth it."

"He's got something. Get up and give it to us."

I climbed to my feet and began fumbling in my pocket. Both men were on my left side. That was my chance. Suddenly I took off and ran along 33rd Street toward Ninth Avenue. They gave no chase. And a good thing, too, because I was too stiff with cold to run a good race.

Saturday, January 22

A man I squatted next to in a doorway on 29th Street said it all: "The onliest thing is to have a warm place to sleep. That and having somebody care about you. That'd be even onlier."

He had what appeared to be rolls of paper toweling wrapped around one leg and tied with red ribbon. But the paper, wet with rain by now, didn't seem to serve any purpose.

I slept little. The forecast was for more rain tomorrow, so why wish the night away?

The morning paper carried news of Mayor Koch's increased concern about the homeless.

But what can he do? He must worry that the more New York does to help, the greater the numbers will grow. At the moment he's berating the synagogues for not doing anything to take street people in.

Watching people come and go at the Volvo tennis tournament at Madison Square Garden, I sensed how uncomfortable they were at the presence of the homeless. Easy to love in the abstract, not so easy face to face.

It's no wonder that the railway police are under orders to chase us out of sight.

Perhaps a saving factor is that we're not individuals. We're not people anybody knows. So far I've had eye contact with only three people who know me in my other life. None showed a hint of recognition. One was a senior auditor at Arthur Andersen & Company, the accounting firm that handles the Clark Foundation, my employer. One was a fellow lieutenant in the Auxiliary Police Force, a man with whom I had trained for many weeks. And one was an owner in the cooperative apartment building where I live.

The soups I've had each night at the Pavillion restaurant, on Eighth Avenue near Madison Square Garden, have been good enough to compete with the fare at some of New York's fancier eateries. The lentil, the clam, and the vegetable taste even better when you consider the price—$1. And there's no problem with slow service during peak hours. Tonight's soup, cream of turkey, wasn't anything special. Still, everyone is allowed an off night.

Early in the evening I fell asleep on the Seventh Avenue steps outside the Garden. Three Amtrak cops shook me awake to ask if two rather good-looking suitcases on the steps were mine. I said that I had never seen them.

One cop insisted that I was lying, but then a black man appeared and said they belonged to a friend of his. The rapid-fire questioning from two of the cops soon made that alibi rather unlikely. The third cop was going through the cases and spreading a few of the joints he found inside on the ground.

As suddenly as it had begun, the incident was over. The cops walked away, and the man retrieved the bags. I fell back to sleep. Some hours later when I woke up again, the black man was still there, selling.

Sunday, January 23

A new discovery of a warm and dry, even scenic, place to sit on a rainy day: the Staten Island Ferry.

For one 25-cent fare, I had four crossings of the harbor, read all I wanted of the copy of the Sunday *Times* I'd found, and finished the crossword puzzle.

When I got back to the Garden, where the tennis tournament was in its last hours, I found the police were being extra diligent in clearing us away from the departing crowds. One older woman was particularly incensed at being moved. "You're ruining my sex life," she shouted. "That's what you're doing. My sex life. Do you hear?"

A younger woman approached me to ask if I was looking for love. "No, ma'am. I'm just trying to stay out of the rain."

That was only the third such approach in five days. My age is telling.

There were moments of special magic late in the afternoon. As darkness fell and fog moved in, the bright lights atop the Empire State and Chrysler Buildings cut through the mist and gave anyone with time to look a picture of their spiky summits floating eerily above the empty streets.

Such building lines as one could see at street level were softened by the fog, and the world didn't seem quite so harsh for a while. Wet, but livable.

So, back to the unused subway entrance, because there was still no heat across town on the 47th Street grate.

The night was very cold. Parts of me ached as I tried to sleep. Turning over was a chore, not only because the partially wet cardboard had to be rearranged with such care, but also because the stiffer parts of my body seemed to belong to someone else. Whatever magic there was in those lights cutting down through the fog was gone by now. All I wanted was to be warm and dry once more. Magic could wait.

Monday, January 24

Early this morning I went to the warren of employment agencies on 14th Street to see if I could get a day's work. There was very little action at most of these last-ditch offices, where minimum wages and sub-minimum conditions are the rule.

But I did get one interview and thought I had a dishwashing job lined up. I'd forgotten one thing. I had no identification with me. No identification, no job.

There was an ageless, shaggy woman in Bryant Park this morning who delivered one of the more interesting monologues I've heard. For a full ten minutes, with no interruption from me beyond an occasional "Uh-huh," she analyzed society's ills without missing a beat.

Beginning with a complaint about the women's and men's toilets in the park being locked ("What's a poor body to do?"), she launched into the strengths of the Irish, who, though strong, still need toilets more than others, and the weaknesses of the English and the Jews, the advantages of raising turkeys over other fowl, and the wickedness of Eleanor Roosevelt in letting the now Queen Mother and that stuttering king of hers rave so much about the hot dogs served at Hyde Park that we had no alternative but to enter World War II on their side. The faulty Russian satellite that fell into the Indian Ocean this morning was another example of shenanigans, she said. It turns out the Russians and Lady Diana, "that so-called Princess of Wales," are in cahoots to keep us so alarmed about such things far away from home that we don't get anything done about prayer in schools or the rest of it. But after all, what would those poor Protestant ministers do for a living if the children got some real religion in school, like the kind we got from the nuns, God bless them?

That at least was the gist of what she said. I know I've missed some of the finer points.

At 3:30 p.m., with more cold ahead, I sought out the Men's Shelter at 8 East 3rd Street. This is the principal entry point for men seeking the city's help. It provides meals for 1,300 or so people every day and beds for some few of those. I had been told that while there was no likelihood of getting a bed in this building I'd be given a meal here and a bed in some other shelter.

I've seen plenty of drawings of London's workhouses and asylums in the times of Charles Dickens. Now I've seen the real thing, in the last years of the twentieth century in the world's greatest city.

The lobby and the adjacent "sitting room" were jammed with men standing, sitting, or stretched out in various positions on the floor. It was as lost a collection of souls as I could have imagined. Old and young, scarred and smooth, stinking and clean, crippled and hale, drunk and sober, ranting and still, parts of another world and parts of this one. The city promises to take in anyone who asks. Those rejected everywhere else find their way to East 3rd Street.

The air was heavy with the odors of Thunderbird wine, urine, sweat, and, above all, nicotine and marijuana. Three or four Human Resources Administration police officers seemed to be keeping the violence down to tolerable levels, but barely so.

After a long delay, I got a meal ticket for dinner and was told to come back later for a lodging ticket.

It was time to get in line to eat. This meant crowding into what I can only compare to a cattle chute in a stockyard. It ran along two walls of the sitting room and was already jammed. A man with a bullhorn kept yelling at us to stand up and stay in line. One very old and decrepit (or drunk?) man couldn't stay on his feet. He was helped to a chair, from which he promptly fell onto the floor. The bullhorn man had some choice obscenities for him, but they didn't seem to have any effect. The old man just lay there, and we turned our thoughts back to the evening meal.

I made a quick, and probably grossly unfair, assessment of the hundreds of men I could see in the room. Judging them solely by appearance, alertness, and body movements, I decided that one-quarter of them were perfectly able to work; they, more likely than not, were among the warriors who helped us win the battle against inflation by the selfless act of joining the jobless ranks. Another quarter might be brought back in time into job-readiness by some counseling and some caring for them as individuals. But the other half seemed so ravaged by illness, addiction, and sheer neglect that I couldn't imagine them being anything but society's wards from here on out to—one hopes—a peaceful end.

At the appointed hour, we were released in groups of 20 or 30 to descend the dark, filthy steps to the basement eating area. The man with the bullhorn was there again, clearly in charge and clearly relishing the extra power given to his voice by electric amplification. He insulted us collectively and separately without pause, but because his vocabulary was limited it tended to be the same four-letter words over and over.

His loudest attack on me came when I didn't move fast enough to pick up my meal from the counter. His analysis of certain flaws in my white ancestry wasn't hard to follow, even for a man in as much of a daze as I was.

The shouting and the obscenities didn't stop once we had our food. Again and again we were told to finish and get out. Eating took perhaps six minutes, but those minutes removed any shred of dignity a man might have brought in with him from the street.

Back upstairs, the people in charge were organizing the people who were to go to a shelter in Brooklyn. Few had volunteered, so there was more haranguing.

In the line next to the one where I was waiting for my lodging ticket a fight suddenly broke out. One man pulled a long knife from his overcoat pocket. The other man ran for cover, and a police officer soon appeared to remove the man with the knife from the scene. The issue, it seems, was one of proper places in the line.

There still weren't enough Brooklyn volunteers to suit the management, so they brought in their big gun: Mr. Bullhorn. "Now, listen up," he barked. "There aren't any buses going to Ft. Washington [another shelter] until 11:30, so if you want to get some sleep, go to Brooklyn. Don't ask me any questions. Just shut up and listen. It's because you don't listen up that you end up in a place like this."

I decided to ask a question anyway, about whether there would still be a chance for me to go to Brooklyn once I got my lodging ticket. He turned on me and let me have the full force of the horn: "Don't ask questions, I said. You're not nobody."

The delays at the ticket-issuing window went on and on. Three staff members there seemed reasonably polite and even efficient. The fourth and heaviest one—I have no idea whether it was a man or woman—could not have moved more slowly without coming to a dead halt. The voice of someone who was apparently a supervisor came over the public-address system from time to time to apologize for the delay in going to the Ft. Washington shelter, which was in an armory, but any good he did from behind the scenes was undone by the staff out front and a "see-no-work, hear-no-work, do-no-work" attendant in the office.

As 11:30 approached, we crowded back into the sitting room to get ready to board the buses. A new martinet had appeared on the scene. He got as much attention through his voice, cane, and heavy body as Mr. Bullhorn had with his amplifying equipment. But this new man was more openly vile and excitable; he loved the power that went with bunching us all close together and then ordering us to stretch out again in a thinner line. We practiced that routine several times.

At one point, the new man jumped up from a card game in which he was a noisy participant and charged across the floor to berate a small, terrified Hispanic who, he claimed, had just defecated on the floor. There was no evidence in sight to confirm that, but who were we to challenge this strutting member of the staff?

Long after the scheduled departure, the lines moved. We sped by school buses to the armory at Ft. Washington Avenue and 168th Street. There we were met, just before 2:30 a.m., by guards. They marched us into showers (very welcome), gave us clean underwear, and sent us upstairs to comfortable cots arranged in long rows in a room as big as a football field.

There were 530 of us there for the night, and we were soon quiet.

Tuesday, January 25

We were wakened at 6 a.m. by whistles and shouting, and ordered to get back onto the buses for the return trip to lower Manhattan as soon as possible. Back at 8 East 3rd Street, the worst of the martinets were off duty. So I thought breakfast might be a bit quieter than dinner had been. Still, by eight, I had seen three incidents a bit out of the ordinary for me.

A man waiting for breakfast immediately ahead of me in the cattle chute suddenly grabbed a chair from the adjoining area and prepared to break it over his neighbor's head. In my haste to get out of the way, I fell over an older man sleeping against the wall. After some shouts about turf, things cooled off between the fighters, and the old man forgave me.

In the stairwell leading down to the eating area, a young man made a sexual advance to me. When I withdrew from him and stupidly reached for my coat pocket, he thought I was going for a weapon. He at once pinned me against the wall and searched my pockets; there was nothing there.

As I came out of the building onto East 3rd Street, two black Human Resources Administration policemen were bringing two young blacks into the building. One officer had his man by the neck. The other officer had his man's hands cuffed behind his back and repeatedly kicked him hard in the buttocks.

My wanderings were still more aimless today. I couldn't get East 3rd Street out of my mind. What could possibly justify some of that conduct? If I were a staff member there, would I become part of the worst in that pattern? Or would I simply do as little, and think as little, as possible?

At day's end I can't recall much of where I went or why I went there.

Only isolated moments remain with me. Like the man on Fifth Avenue caught behind a pretzel vendor who was trying to move her heavy cart through noon-hour traffic. The man, very well and warmly dressed, knew his rightful place in the world, which wasn't behind this lumbering vehicle. "Let's move it," he said. "Let's move it." Late for lunch, I suppose.

Or like staring at the elegant crystal and silver in the shops just north of Madison Square Park and wondering what these windows say to the people I'd spent the night with.

Much too soon it was time to go back to the shelter for dinner and another night. At first I thought I didn't have the guts to do it again. Does one have to do *this* to learn who the needy are? I wanted to say, "Enough! There's only so much I need to see."

But I went back to the shelter anyway, probably because it took more guts to quit than it did to go ahead.

A man beside me in the tense dinner line drove one truth of this place home to me. "I never knew hell came in this color," he said.

I was luckier in my assignment for the night. I drew the Keener Building, on Wards Island, a facility with a capacity of 416 men. The building was old and neglected, and the atmosphere of a mental hospital, which it once was, still hung over it. But the staff was polite, the rooms weren't too crowded (there were only twelve beds in Room 326), the single sheet on each bed was clean, and there was toilet paper in the bathroom.

There were limits and guards and deprivations, but there was also an orderliness about the place. Here, at least, I didn't feel I had surrendered all of my dignity at the door.

Wednesday, January 26

Any thought I had that I could easily get back to Manhattan in the morning for a day in the streets was set aside when I learned that, even before I got breakfast, I had to "see the social worker." That, I assumed, meant counseling about my future. And I'm as interested in my future as the next man.

All nine of us who were new to Wards Island and some who had been there longer were put in a waiting room at 7 a.m. Those of us who had had no breakfast got a plastic bowl of lukewarm farina, a small carton of milk, two slices of bread, and tepid coffee. Not bad.

At one point there were 35 of us in the room waiting to see one staff member or another—23 blacks, six Hispanics, and six whites. That seemed to be about the same ratio I had seen elsewhere in the shelter.

By eleven, few names had been called. I asked if I could leave. "No problem." I was on a Manhattan-bound bus within minutes. I still wonder what the social worker might have told me if he or she had been available.

I tried the mushroom-and-barley soup at the B & H Dairy luncheonette, on Second Avenue between East 7th Street and St. Marks Place. It was expensive, about $2 for soup, bread, and coffee, but worth it. And I didn't have to pay in advance.

A few minutes' walk away, at Cooper Union, I came upon the 9th Street Stompers doing a noon-hour performance in the street. Here were six musicians obviously enjoying themselves and asking us to do the same. When they played "St. James Infirmary," I felt like dancing the day away. Too bad I'm too shy to dance alone.

Back to the shelter on East 3rd Street for dinner.

There is simply no other situation I've seen that is so devoid of any graces at all, so tense at every moment, or so empty of hope. The food isn't bad, and the building is heated; that's all it has going for it.

The only cutlery provided is a frail plastic spoon. With practice you can spread hard oleo onto your bread with the back of one. If there's liver or ham, you don't have to cut it; just put it between the two pieces of bread that go with each meal. Everything else—peas, collard greens, apple pudding, plums—can be managed with the spoon. And talk over dinner or sipping, rather than gulping coffee isn't all that important.

What is hardest to accept is the inevitable jungle scene during the hour you stand in line waiting to eat. Every minute seems to be one that invites an explosion. You know instinctively that men can't come this often to the brink without someone going over. One person too many is going to try to jump ahead in line. One particular set of toes is going to be stepped on by mistake. And the lid is going to blow.

The most frightening people here are the many young, intensely angry blacks. Hatred pours out in all of their speech and some of their actions. I could spend a lot of time imagining how and why they became so completely angry—but if I were the mayor, the counselor, or the man with the bullhorn, I wouldn't know how to divert them from that anger anymore. Hundreds and hundreds of men here have been destroyed by alcohol or drugs. A smaller, but for me more poignant, number are being destroyed by hate.

Their loudest message—and because their voices are so strong it is very loud indeed—is "Respect me, man." The constant theme is that someone or some group is putting them down, stepping on them, asking them to conform to a code they don't accept, getting in their way, writing them off.

So most of the fights begin over turf. A place in line. A corner to control. The have-nots scrapping with the have-nots.

Does the staff at the shelter have any training in dealing with explosions? Those martinets I saw are going to make things worse rather than better if they are on duty and some incident triggers major violence. They equate control with shouting the loudest and banging the hardest. I pray that the staff members I didn't see have a different vision.

Tonight, I chose the Brooklyn shelter because I thought the buses going there would leave soonest. The shelter, a converted school, is on Williams Avenue and has about 400 beds.

We left in fairly good time but learned when we got to the shelter that no new beds would be assigned until after 11 p.m. We were to sit in the auditorium until then.

At about ten, a man herded as many of us newcomers as would listen to him into a corner of the auditorium. There he delivered an abusive diatribe outlining the horror that lay ahead for our possessions and our bodies during the night to come. It made the ranting at East 3rd Street seem tame.

It's illustrative of what the experience of homelessness and helplessness does to people that all of us—regardless of age, race, background, or health—listened so passively.

Only at midnight, when some other officials arrived, did we learn that this man had no standing whatsoever. He was just an underling who strutted for his time on the stage before any audience cowed enough to take what he dished up.

As it turned out, for the 68 or so of us who had been sent to Brooklyn, there were no more than about fifteen beds. Why this was so wasn't discussed. We were just ordered back into the auditorium to await transportation over to Ft. Washington. Losers accept these losses meekly.

It was 3 a.m. when the luckiest of us got to the armory. Still, there was a happy ending: Because we had all been subjected to an ice-cold shower in Brooklyn much earlier, we were allowed to go to bed without another one.

Thursday, January 27

Back on the street this morning, I became conscious of how little time I had left to live this way. There seemed so much still to do, and so little time in which to do it.

One part of me tells me I have been fully a part of this. I know I walk with slower steps and bent shoulders. I know I see the Amtrak cops—but not the city cops—as people to hide from rather than to turn to. I know I worry a lot more about keeping clean.

But then I recall how foolish that is. I'm acting. This will end tomorrow night. I can quit anytime I want to. And unlike my mate from 47th Street, I haven't the slightest idea of what eleven years of sleeping on a grate amount to.

Early this afternoon, I went again to the Pavillion restaurant, where I had eaten five times before. I didn't recognize the man at the cash register.

"Get out," he said.

"But I have money."

"You heard me. Get out." His voice was stronger.

"That man knows me," I said, looking toward the owner in the back of the restaurant.

The owner nodded, and the man at the register said, "Okay, but sit in the back."

If this life in the streets had been real, I'd have gone out the door at the first "Get out." And the assessment of me as not worthy would have been self-fulfilling; I'd have lost so much respect for myself that I wouldn't have been worthy of being served the next time. The downward spiral would have begun.

Until now I haven't understood the extent of nicotine addiction. Depen-

Diary of a Homeless Man 51

dencies on drugs and alcohol have been around me for a long time, but I thought before that smoking was a bad habit rather easy to overcome.

How many times have I, a non-smoker, been begged for a cigarette in these days? Surely hundreds. Cigarettes are central. A few folks give them away, a small number sell them for up to 8 cents apiece, and almost all give that last pathetic end of a butt to the first man who asks for what little bit is left. I know addiction now as I didn't before.

Tonight, after a repeat of the totally degrading dinner-line scene at East 3rd Street, I signed up for Keener once again. No more Brooklyn for me.

Sitting upstairs with the other Keener-bound men, I carelessly put my left foot on the rung of the chair in front of me, occupied by a young black.

"Get your foot off, yo."

("Yo" means "Hey, there," "Watch yourself," "Move along," and much more.)

I took it off. "Sorry," I said.

But it was too late. I had broken a cardinal rule. I had violated the man's turf. As we stood in the stairwell waiting for the buses, he told a much bigger, much louder, much angrier friend what I had done.

The man turned on me.

"Wait till we get you tonight, whitey. You stink. Bad. The worst I've ever smelled. And when you put your foot on that chair, you spread your stink around. You better get yourself a shower as soon as we get there, but it won't save you later on. . . . And don't sit near me or him on the bus. Yo hear, whitey?"

I didn't reply.

The bombardment went on as we mounted the bus. No one spoke up in my defense. Three people waved me away when I tried to sit next to them. The next person, black and close to my age, made no objection when I sat beside him.

The big man continued the tirade for a while, but he soon got interested in finding out from the driver how to go about getting a bus-driver's license. Perhaps he had come down from a high.

I admit I was scared. I wrote my name, address, and office telephone number on a piece of paper and slipped it into my pocket. At least someone would know where to call if the threats were real. I knew I couldn't and wouldn't defend myself in this setting.

While we stood on line on Wards Island waiting for our bed assignments, there were plenty of gripes about the man who was after me. But no one said anything directly to him. Somehow it didn't seem that this was the night when the meek would inherit the earth.

I slept fitfully. I don't like lying with the sheet hiding my face.

Friday, January 28

I was up and out of Keener as early as possible. That meant using some of my little remaining money for a city-bus ride back to Manhattan, but it was worth it to get out of there.

After breakfast on East 3rd Street, I was finished with the public shelters. That was an easy break for me to make, because I had choices and could run.

The day was cold and, for the early hours, clear. I washed the memory of the big man at 3rd Street out of my mind by wandering through the Fulton Fish Market. I walked across the Brooklyn Bridge and even sang as I realized how free I was to relax and enjoy its beauty.

With a cup of coffee and the *Times*, I sat on a cinder block by the river and read. In time, I wandered through the Wall Street district and almost learned the lay of some of the streets.

I walked up to the Quaker Meeting House at Rutherford Place and 15th Street. Standing on the porch outside, I tried hard to think how the doctrine that "there is that of God in every person" applied to that man last night and to some of the others I had encountered in these ten days. I still think it applies, but it isn't always easy to see how.

The morning paper quotes Representative Charles Rangel (Democrat, New York) as saying that the situation with the New York City homeless is "explosive." Has he been on the same trail? Was he one of those I've met in the streets and the shelters?

Darkness came. I got kicked out of both the bus terminal and Grand Central. I got my normal clothes out of the locker at Penn Station, changed in the men's room, and rode the AA train home.

My apartment was warm, and the bed was clean.

That's the onliest thing.

5

Time in the Streets

Harry Murray

"WESTERN MINDS represent time as a straight line upon which we stand with our gaze directed forward; before us we have the future and behind us the past." (Boman 1960:124). I had certainly conceived of time in this manner—all the way through college, graduate school, and my first two years working at a "real job." Then I started working full-time at a free soup kitchen serving primarily those known as "street people." After a year or so of immersion into the subculture of the soup kitchen and its patrons, I became aware that I was thinking of time in an entirely different sense. Time no longer seemed linear, but rather circular—an endless repetition. I began to wonder if this subculture had a different way of experiencing time than did the middle-class suburban subculture in which I had been raised.

The influence of society on the conceptualization of time was noted by Durkheim (1965) when he argued that the very concept of time is social in origin. Later writers depicted social time as a particular type of time, distinct from mathematical time (Sorokin and Merton 1937) or from both physical and biological time (Zerubavel 1981). Social time is characterized by periods which are meaningful (e.g., holidays), separated by periods of no particular meaning (ordinary time, to use Catholic liturgical terminology). Thus, social time is discontinuous, meaningful, and qualitative; whereas mathematical time is continuous, empty, and quantitative (Sorokin and Merton 1937). The very systems of time marking are social in origin:

Reproduced by permission of the Society for Applied Anthropology from *Human Organization*, 43:2, Summer 1984, pp. 154-161. Not for further reproduction.

[S]ystems of time reckoning reflect the social activities of the group. . . .
Agricultural peoples with a social rhythm different from that of hunting or of
pastoral peoples differentiate time intervals in a fashion quite unlike the latter.
. . . [T]ime reckoning is basically dependent upon the organization and
functions of the group. The mode of life determines which phenomena shall
represent the beginning and close of seasons, months, or other time units.
(Sorokin and Merton 1937: 620-621)

A society's conception of time is an essential part of culture, influencing and
being influenced by many other key concepts, including those of the person
and proper conduct (Geertz 1973).

Much of the sociological work on time has concerned means of marking
time (e.g., Zerubavel's (1976, 1981) studies of schedules and calendars), or
styles of time usage (e.g., Calkins' (1970) study of modes of "doing time" of
patients in a physical rehabilitation center). This paper will address neither of
these concerns directly; rather, it will treat an aspect of social time that is of
some importance for a symbolic interactionist approach, namely the images
of time present in a society. I will address this topic by categorizing the images
of time available in the subculture of the homeless, estimating their relative
importance, and discussing the relationship of time image to purpose. Before
doing so, however, it is useful to make a conceptual distinction between time
image and time orientation.

Time images are the symbolic representations (usually spatial)[1] of time
available to persons in a given society. Most common are the circle and the
line, but also available in some societies are the point (Berdyaev 1944) and the
pendulum (Leach 1961). The cyclical image has been associated with traditional societies (Cottle and Klineberg 1974), with sacred time (Zerubavel
1981), and with time in such American subcultures as migrant labor camps
(Nelkin 1970). The linear image has been associated particularly with Western
culture (Boman 1960; Cottle and Klineberg 1974). Zerubavel (1981:113)
argues that both images are present in any culture, although to varying
degrees. Some societies have a predominant image of time that is neither
cyclical nor linear. Geertz noted that in Bali time is "detemporalized," col-
lapsed into the present by linguistic and behavioral conventions that deem-
phasize past and future.

Time orientation is the relative importance of past, present, and future in
decision making. In effect, it could be called the direction in which one faces
time. Time orientation has been strongly associated with time image in the
sociological literature (except where one has been treated and the other
ignored). Past orientations have been linked with cyclical time conceptions,
while future, and even present, orientations have been treated almost entirely

within a linear time conception. There is a certain logic behind these associations. If one believes that time essentially repeats itself, then it is logical to be oriented toward the past, since the past gives an accurate picture of the future. A linear, progressive conception of time, on the other hand, lends itself to a future orientation. Despite the evidence for a correlation between time image and time orientation, it is important to maintain an analytical distinction between the two, not only because the correlation is not exact, but also because they can serve different roles in decision making and action. If the symbolic interactionist approach is accurate, then the symbols one employs for time will affect one's actions. The role of the symbols themselves in action is distinct from the role of the orientation one takes towards those symbols. (If one conceives of time as a line, one can look either backwards or forwards down that line.)

The relationship of time orientation to action has been studied fairly extensively by both psychologists and sociologists, although almost always within the framework of linear time. Present orientation (roughly defined as the tendency to cast purposes within a very short time frame) has been associated with lower social class (Leshan 1952; Banfield 1968), juvenile delinquency (Landau 1976; Barndt and Johnson 1955; Stein et al. 1968), and mental illness (Wallace 1956). Thus, operating within the standard American worldview of linear, future-oriented time, these studies "objectively" demonstrated that non-future time orientations were associated with undesirable characteristics. Deviant behavior is related to deviant time orientation.

When ethnographies of the urban underclass have touched on the concept of time, they too have generally focused on present vs. future orientation. Wiseman (1970:135, 246) speaks of the conflict between the present orientation of alcoholism counselors as a reason for the failure of alcoholism programs. Liebow (1967) argues that the present orientation of street corner men is actually a realistic orientation toward a future that is "loaded with trouble":

> In many instances, it is precisely the street-corner man's orientation to the future—but to a future loaded with "trouble"—which not only leads to a greater emphasis on present concerns ("I want mine right now"), but also contributes importantly to the instability of employment, family and friend relationships, and to the general transient quality of daily life. (1967:68-69)

Within a linear time orientation, then, it has been established that the extent of future orientation is related to behavior. Two observations from the literature indicate that this relationship between orientation and action covers the range of the three possible time orientations. First, time orientation is logically linked to the decision-making process. Past orientation is commonly associated with a concern for means; future orientation, with a concern for ends. For example, Dundes (1980) notes:

> Americans are so future-oriented that they are discontent even with pleasant presents. For the present reality, no matter how good it is, can never be as good as the future might be. (1980:76)

> Americans look into the future in part because they are end-oriented. (1980:72)

In this context of the relationship of past orientation to means and future orientation to ends, I would advance that pure present orientation (as opposed to the short-term future orientations used in the literature above) would be reflected primarily in emotive behavior. The second point that would seem to link time orientation to action is the striking correspondence between the three time orientations and Weber's (1947) three types of authority: traditional authority is past oriented and concerned with means; charismatic authority is present oriented and concerned with emotion; and rational-legal authority is future oriented and concerned with ends. Although this correspondence rests on an extreme simplification, it nonetheless indicates the pervasiveness of the relationship between time orientation and behavior.

The relationship between time image and purposive action has not been investigated as extensively as that between time orientation and action, probably because time image has been associated with total cultural phenomena. However, there is some evidence that time image is also related to behavior. Geertz (1973) gives evidence of this for Bali, where the emphasis on the present is more than just a present orientation, but rather a different image of time:

> . . .[S]ocial activities do not build . . . toward definitive consummations. . . . Issues are not sharpened for decision, they are blunted and softened in the hope that the mere evolution of circumstances will resolve them, or better yet, that they will simply evaporate.

> Balinese social life lacks climax because it takes place in a motionless present, a vectorless now. Or, equally true, Balinese time lacks motion because Balinese social life lacks climax. (1973:403-404)

This paper will address the question of the relationship between time image and purpose by means of an ethnographic study of "street people" in a medium-sized northeastern city. It will argue that the cyclical time image is stronger among the homeless than in "normal" American society and that the strength of the cyclical image is related to the dominance of survival goals and the cyclical schedules of agencies that deal with the homeless.

Methodology

This section describes the participant observation methodology employed, the night shelter which served as the primary site of the research, and the men who patronized the night shelter.

Participant Observation Methodology

The formal data upon which this paper is based were gathered using a participant observation approach at the Cambridge Street Inn—a free, "unstructured," no-questions-asked night shelter which has been operating in a medium-sized northeastern city since 1979. Between September 26, 1980 and April 29, 1981, I worked as a volunteer at the Inn from 8 PM each Wednesday until 7 AM the next morning. Fieldnotes were recorded either during the early morning hours of my shift or the next day.

The total source of data was far more extensive than the formal source. My first contact with the homeless of Salt City was in March 1977, when I began working one night a week in the free dormitory located in a local soup kitchen. From August, 1977 through September, 1979, I worked full-time at this free soup kitchen (six days a week), living in a staff house a few blocks away. It was during this period, when I was fully immersed in the world of street people but was not doing formal observations, that I developed many of the ideas advanced in this paper. In December, 1979, I began working one night a week at the Cambridge Street Inn and have continued to do so, except during summer months, until the present date. In July 1980 I moved into a house in the neighborhood, a situation which allows for numerous contacts with street people. A few ex-patrons of the Inn have resided with us, and many more have come to the house seeking favors or companionship. These contacts have been too numerous to record formally.

The Cambridge Street Inn

The Cambridge Street Inn is a free, unstructured overnight shelter open from 8 PM to 7 AM. There is no admissions procedure—anyone who comes in is welcomed on a "no questions-asked" basis and there is no limit on the number of men who can be accommodated. In social service jargon, one might say that need determination is performed by the applicant. There is neither a "rehabilitation program" nor counselors, although advice is given if requested. There is no limit on length of stay in terms of number of days, months, or years.

The Inn has two official rules: no drinking and no fighting. Violations of these rules are punishable by being barred from the Inn for a set length of time. The "no drinking" rule is interpreted as "no sneaking a bottle into the Inn." The "no fighting" rule is usually applied only to the aggressor if a clear aggressor can be determined.

The Inn is open every night from October through May and three nights a week during the summer. The official nightly schedule is:

8 PM:	The doors are unlocked.
10 PM:	Lights off.
11 PM:	The door is locked; anyone arriving after this time enters only with the worker's permission. If there is a split shift, the new worker arrives between this time and midnight. One staff member goes to sleep; the other remains on watch.
3 AM:	The sleeping staff member is awakened; the other goes to sleep.
6:25 AM:	Lights on.
6:30 AM:	The sleeping staff member is awakened, as are the men who are still asleep.
7 AM:	The men are asked to leave. The doors are locked and the workers leave.

Minor variations in this schedule occur: some staff members will open earlier than 8 PM on very cold nights and/or will let the men stay in a little later than 7 AM on very cold mornings. Also, on Sundays and holidays the Inn stays open until 7:30 AM.

Patrons of the Inn

The Inn serves 30 to 40 men nightly, some staying for one night only, others staying for months or years. The majority of patrons of the Inn had stayed in the soup kitchen dormitory at some point during its existence. In terms of demographic characteristics, roughly 10% are Indian, 45% white, and 45% black, with an occasional Puerto Rican or other nationality. The age range is 18 to late 70's. About half of the men are alcoholics, and somewhat less than half are from mental hospitals, with the balance patronizing the Inn for a variety of other reasons.

The patronage of the Inn changes nightly, although there is a core of a half-dozen men who have been there almost every night since it opened. Of these, all but one are white, and only one has an alcohol problem. Three were former mental hospital patients. Several of these men do maintenance and repair work voluntarily at the Inn.

An additional 30 or so men are "regulars"—not at the Inn every night, but staying for extended periods of time. (The term "regulars" as used by the staff includes the men who are there every night as well.) When not at the Inn, these men have generally acquired a room; gone to another city; are staying at Unity Acres (a refuge for street men located in the country about 60 miles away), the Rescue Mission, the psychiatric center, or a local hospital; or are in jail or prison. Over the years they have regularly reappeared at the kitchen dorm and the Inn. Demographic characteristics for this group are approximately the same as those given above for the patronage as a whole. Most of these men are alcoholics, although a sizeable minority are ex-mental patients, and a few are mildly retarded in addition to having alcohol problems.

There is a large pool of men, well over 100, who show up at irregular intervals for a few nights or weeks. These men generally have a support system of some kind (either personal or institutional) which usually provides them with a home; however, this support system breaks down at times, and they are forced to resort to the Inn for temporary shelter.

Finally, there are those who stay for a night or two and then disappear. Often the workers never even learn their first names. There are two or three new faces every night I work at the Inn. Some of them become regulars, but most move on soon and are not seen again. My impression is that most of those who stay a night or two are younger (late teens or early twenties) than the average regular.

Images of Time in the Streets

There are several images of time available in the street subculture; their adoption by street men depends primarily on the men's situation and purposes. I will focus on the most prominent image, that of cyclical time.

For most of those who are thoroughly enculturated into street life, time has a cyclical quality. This occurs for two reasons. First, one doesn't look to the future in terms of forging ahead, or progressing to new goals. Rather, one's primary goal is survival, a goal which must be re-achieved every day. The overwhelming importance of this goal in street life, and the risks of failing to attain it, contribute to the cyclical quality of time for the street person. The second factor which contributes to time's cyclical quality is the cyclic schedules of the institutions which affect the homeless.

The first important cycle is the daily cycle. For street people, as for most of us, this cycle is largely determined by the schedules of the organizations upon which they depend. The day usually begins early for street men in Salt City—at 5 or 5:30 AM if one is attempting to make it to the slave market (labor pool) by opening time. For those who are not trying to get day labor but are residing at the Inn, the day begins in earnest at 7 AM when they must leave the Inn. The times which are the most essential to street persons in Salt City are:

     6 AM: Labor Pool opens.
     7 AM: Cambridge Street Inn closes.
     8 AM: Rescue Mission day room opens.
     5 PM: Soup kitchen opens for its one meal of the day.
     8 PM: Cambridge Street Inn opens, as does the Rescue Mission Transient Dorm, which costs $1.50 per night.
   11 PM: Cambridge Street Inn locks doors for the night.

The schedules of numerous other institutions—the library, the Jail Ministry Office, the Senior Citizen Center, the skid row bars, the bootleggers—also affect the lives of many street persons.

The detailed daily schedule of the Cambridge Street Inn was presented in the methods section. Some observations about how the patrons adjust to this schedule may be helpful here. Patrons generally react to the Inn schedule in one of two ways. One approach is to adhere to the schedule rigorously, maintaining one's own obligations under the schedule (e.g., being in before 11 PM and leaving promptly at 7 AM) and demanding that the staff adhere to its obligations (ensuring that the door is open at 8 PM, the lights turned off precisely at 10 PM, etc.). An incident which exemplified this approach occurred as a result of my inadvertent neglect of the Inn's traditional policy of closing a half hour later (7:30 AM) on Sundays and holidays. I was working the eve of Lincoln's Birthday and hadn't realized it, so I asked the men to leave at 7 AM as usual. One of the regulars came up to me and said "Today's a holiday, you know. It's Lincoln's Birthday. We should stay in 'til 7:30." I replied "I'm sorry; I forgot about that." He said "The banks are closed today." He went over and sat down in a chair by the table and began reading a newspaper he had brought in with him the night before. His whole demeanor seemed to say "It's my right to be here 'til 7:30 and I'm damn well staying here 'til then." We ended up staying open until 7:30, although most of the men had left at 7:00.

The other approach is to try to negotiate the Inn's schedule. Patrons attempt this particularly with respect to the locking of doors at 11 PM and closing at 7 AM. Generally, one or two men come to the door after 11, at which point they must negotiate their way inside with the worker who answers the door. They are almost always successful in doing so unless they are habitual latecomers, are raucously drunk, or had been in earlier and left to get drunk. Some examples of such negotiations are shown below:

At 1 AM, Willie knocked at the door. He had been late the last two Wednesday nights. I said "It's one o'clock. We close at eleven." He said "But I've been coming in on time the last three nights." I replied "You've been late the last three nights I've worked—you mean you just come in late when I work?" He said "Well, I know it looks like that, but . . ." I said "Well, this is absolutely the last time when I'm working that you'll get in." "If you don't have an empty bed I'll sleep in a chair." I let him in, against my better judgement. He said "Thanks. You want to know the real reason I'm late? I'll tell you. I was at this woman's house and was gonna spend the night with her, but her old man came back. I ran all the way here." (10/29/80)

About 12:30 there was another knock at the door. Art was outside, very drunk. I said "You're too late, Art." He said "I just got out of my taxi." I said "That makes no difference. You're too late." He said "I was at the hospital." "Bullshit, you're drunk." "I am not. You can smell my breath." "I don't need to. I can hear you." (His speech was slurred). "Well, can't you let me in? I'm freezing." "Well, all right," and I opened the door. (11/5/80)

Thus, the 11 PM time is not absolute, but most of the Inn's patrons do abide by it.

Negotiations about the 7 AM leaving rule are less frequent and are generally attempted either by men who are attempting to get a few extra minutes' sleep and refuse to get up until 7:00, or by new patrons (often from mental hospitals) who don't understand or refuse to accept the closing time. One young man went into the toilet stall and refused to come out for about 15 minutes. Another, who had been talking to himself all night, began to slowly roll a couple of cigarettes at 7 o'clock, then spent several minutes looking for his lighter (which he eventually found in his pocket), saying he wasn't leaving until he found his lighter. Then he said, almost to himself but loud enough for the workers to hear, "If someone's gonna tell me to go out there when I've got no place to go there's gonna be trouble. . . .Murder." I told him "Well, it's time to go." He replied "Where am I supposed to go?" My partner answered "That's your decision. Come on, it's after 7 o'clock. You're late already." He said "We're supposed to stay in 'til 12:30." We replied "No, 7 o'clock." He then walked to the door, saying "Hold the door for me." I held the door, and he walked out into the rain. Negotiations about closing time usually net the patron 10 to 15 extra minutes inside (i.e., the duration of the negotiation).

Workers are generally reluctant to use force to eject a patron, preferring that he make the decision to walk out.

The daily cycle is largely determined by the schedules of the institutions with which the homeless men must interact to obtain food and shelter. However, even if the homeless man divorces himself from these institutions, as many do to a greater or lesser extent, he still must find food and shelter every day (or nearly every day). Thus, although the proximate cause of the daily cycle is the schedule of the social service institutions, the ultimate cause is the recurrent necessity of finding food and shelter in order to survive. Of course, for the alcoholic, the recurrent quest for alcohol adds to the cyclic quality of life.

Weekly cycles are of relatively minor importance for most street men. "Weekends" do not exist on the streets. The only day which is differentiated from others is Sunday, because most of the institutions on which street people depend are either closed or have alternate schedules on that day. The labor pools, the library, and the Rescue Mission day room are closed on Sundays.

A weekly recurrence at the Inn is the appearance of the once-a-week volunteers such as myself on a particular night of the week. Certain nights are identified with certain individuals. One of the Inn's regular staff members commented to me on the first night he worked with me in over a year:

> You know, people identify the day with the man. Even though I'm the regular worker here, a lot of the guys come up to you for things because this is your night. (paraphrase)

This comment echoes Zerubavel's (1981:15) observation that "hospital staff members are often associated . . . with the particular 'time slots' they cover."

The monthly cycle is the most prominent in street life in many ways. It was this cycle which first led me to notice the cyclical character of much of street life. The crucial point in the cycle is "mother's day"[2]—the first of the month, when Supplemental Security Income (SSI), Veterans Administration (VA), and welfare checks arrive in the mail. Closely related is the third of the month, when Social Security checks arrive. Many men (mostly the older alcoholics, but also some of the ex-state school or mental hospital residents) receive SSI, VA, or Social Security checks. Few receive welfare, and, when they do, they generally move into their own rooms. Many who do not receive checks still anticipate "mother's day," either because a friend who gets a check promised to "take care" of them, or because they anticipate rolling a drunk who got a check. "Mother's day" nights at the Inn are characterized by a smaller, but more boisterous and intoxicated crowd than usual. In order to understand the monthly cycle and the crucial role of mother's day in this cycle, one must examine in detail what occurs.

Some men receive a check, rent a room, and are not seen again, at least for a while. Often these are men who for some reason lost their room over the course of the month and stayed at the Inn while awaiting their next check in order to get a new room.

For many alcoholics, the arrival of a check is an occasion for a drinking spree. The attitude of "you owe yourself a drunk," described by Spradley (1970) as the reaction of skid row alcoholics to time spent in jail, also applies to the arrival of a monthly check. Often the arrival of the check has been preceded by days or weeks of utter destitution, endurable primarily because of the anticipation that a check is coming. Arrival of the check calls for a celebration of the fact that one is no longer flat broke. There are, however, significant differences in how the men celebrate the arrival of the check. Some will cash the check, rent a room, perhaps make an arrangement for food (e.g., by depositing some cash with the owner of a local restaurant so that one can have meals there throughout the month) and then use the balance for the celebration. Others will give money to a worker at the Kitchen or the Inn to hold for them until they are off the drunk and will then use the money to rent a room. Still others cash the check and immediately go to a bar, get drunk, get rolled, and are broke the same day or within a few days. These men are often back at the Inn within a few days, although they might have had the intention to get a room after a few drinks.

Sometimes alcoholics are a bit more innovative in what they do with their checks. One gay alcoholic regularly buys a used car for $100 or $200, buys some wine and glue, finds a young friend, and hits the road, often heading for Florida. The only variables are how far he gets before wrecking the car (rarely is it farther than the next state) and whether he is arrested at the scene of the accident. He then returns to Salt City to wait for the next check. Another man has been known to pair up with a friend, buy some wine, and rent a room in a Holiday Inn for three or four days, eating, drinking, and watching color TV until his money runs out, and then returning to the streets.

Such actions appear frivolous and irrational from the perspective of the "normal" citizen. However, there is a certain rationale to the actions once one accepts the perspective that, even with money, one is not likely to be able to maintain a "normal" life style. That such a perspective is realistic for many skid row alcoholics has been documented by Wiseman (1970). If one's experience in the past has been one of evictions from rooms for behaviors that one knows will recur, the practicality of using one's money to rent a room is reduced. Granting this, one uses one's money to satisfy other needs and desires.

For an alcoholic who envisions no real hope of returning to "normal" society and who has experienced destitution and powerlessness, the arrival of a check signifies some claim to power. He has little hope that he can regain status in society on a long-term basis, but in the short run he can use the money to briefly experience power and the good things in life. For example, on the first of the month, two regulars stumbled into the Inn dead drunk. In the morning we sat around the table joking. One had gotten his check, and they had gone to a good Italian restaurant for a spaghetti dinner. One said of the other "Unfortunately, he had too much chianti and too little spaghetti." They were broke again, but they had experienced a memorable evening.

Many alcoholics use a good deal of their check money on taxi service. Tired of having to walk everywhere they go, they use part of their money to have a taxi provide them with door-to-door service. This is not pure frivolity, of course; when a "drunk" has money, it is dangerous to walk the streets. Fairly often in the early part of the month a taxi will drop someone off to spend the night at the Inn. There are numerous tales of alcoholics taking a taxi to a city 30 or 40 miles away when they got their checks. At least one alcoholic (not a street man, but someone I saw in a city police court) deposits money with a taxi company at the beginning of the month so that he can call for a ride when he is drunk and broke.

Sometimes men must use part of their check for other practical purposes. Three alcoholics spend a good part of their checks ($75 to $100 per month) on eyeglasses. They have a tendency to break or lose their glasses regularly (about once a month) and so have running accounts with an optometrist, who keeps extra pairs in stock for them. One even has his check mailed to his optometrist, who cashes it for him after withdrawing the amount owed. Medicaid pays for only one pair of glasses every two years, so these men must pay for their glasses out of money that is meant for rent and food.

Some nonalcoholics also spend their checks on matters other than food and shelter. Several ex-mental patients give much of their money away to other street people. Although this practice may seem "crazy," it does have a real element of rationality about it, particularly if one's behaviors are annoying to others. Simply put, the money given away stimulates good feelings toward the giver. Giving money away can forestall reprisals against the person for his behaviors since other street men know that he is a potential source of income to them when he gets another check. Such purchase of good will is a very rational way to spend one's money if one expects to remain on the streets. Further, it reflects a very practical future orientation on the part of the giver.

The whole monthly cycle revolves around "mother's day." Several days thereafter are spent in celebration of receiving the check. These days are often followed by weeks of complete destitution. The last week of the month is characterized by anticipation of the check to come. If the first or third falls on a Sunday or holiday, there is much speculation in the preceding week as to exactly when the checks will come. Usually, SSI, Social Security, and VA checks are received the day before they are due if the due date falls on a day the banks are closed. Welfare arrives the day after. The first part of the month is almost always less crowded than the last week of the month. However, this monthly cycle does not affect all street people. Those who rely on day labor for income and those who have no income whatsoever are often relatively unaffected by the monthly cycle.

There is also a seasonal cycle to street life. The weather is, of course, a major factor in this cycle since the street people are exposed to it to a far greater extent than anyone else in American society. Winter brings great hardship and forces many into constant quest for warmth and shelter in an unfriendly capitalist environment. One street man recounted:

> I was in Consumer's Bank. This guy came up to me and said "We don't want you in here." "Why not?" I asked, and he couldn't give me any answer. I wasn't abusing anything. I was just sitting there trying to do some reading . . . . Sure they want you if you've got money, but if you don't, they've got no compassion. Sure they don't want you unless you're a customer, but where am I supposed to go—in a corner? It's madness downtown. (10/22/80)

Summer, on the other hand, with its long hot days, brings more danger from people. One is in more danger of being rolled or attacked in the summer than in the winter. Interestingly, seasonal changes produce little change in the demand for night shelter. Summer nights can be just as crowded as winter nights. Sleeping out in the winter exposes one to the hazards of freezing weather; sleeping out in the summer, however, exposes one to the equally malignant hazards of one's fellow man. One street man told me that he often must spend 45 minutes watching before crawling into his flop in the weeds because he must be absolutely sure that no one sees him entering for fear of being rolled in his sleep.

A seasonal factor in Salt City is the fact that during the summer the Cambridge Street Inn reduces its schedule to three nights a week rather than seven. This is done because of the difficulty in securing volunteers during the summer and the need to give the winter volunteers a break. This reduction in schedule places real hardships on the men during the summer, for most must sleep "in the weeds," in abandoned houses, or in self-made shacks four nights a week.

A final seasonal factor is farmwork, which begins in April and lasts through the summer. Many of the men are seasonal farm laborers. Some farms send trucks into the city to pick up laborers every day. Others provide lodging for workers at the farms. Planting season marks a temporary end of destitution for many of the men, who work all day, use their earnings to get incredibly drunk at night, and are up and gone before 6 AM the next day to get back to the farm.

The annual cycle has little impact on the streets. The major annual holidays are, on one level, nonevents for the street people (except as they allow them an extra half hour's sleep in the morning at the Inn). The first time I worked a New Year's Eve in the old Kitchen dormitory, I was amazed to find that, by midnight, only myself and one patron were still awake. The other 50 men were sleeping as soundly as they would on any other night. The one patron still awake left about 12:30 saying, "New Year's Eve don't mean shit to me." His comment reveals the level of other major holidays. Thanksgiving, Christmas, and Easter evoke a sadness and bitterness which cannot be assuaged by the hordes or holiday volunteers who descend on the institutions to serve a gala holiday meal. When I asked one Inn patron about Christmas, he replied "No, I didn't see my people—my children. I had nothing to give them. I didn't want them to see how I was living."

The rhythm of time in the streets, then, is largely cyclical. The periods of meaning, the "holidays" of the street, occur monthly, while the homeless are relatively insulated from the annual, irregularly spaced, national holidays (which are, if anything, more empty of meaning than ordinary time in the streets). The fact that the intervals between "street holidays" are uniform (give or take a day or so), while the intervals between traditional national holidays are irregular, adds to the cyclical nature of street life vis-à-vis "normal life."

The twin themes of waiting and repetition, each essential to a cyclical pattern of regularly recurring events separated by "ordinary time," occur fairly often in conversations with the homeless. When one runs into one of the men on the street, one of the most common responses to a friendly "Whatcha doin'?" is "I'm just killin' time 'til____. What else is there to do?" A common theme when men are in a more reflective mood is "How much longer can I endure the sameness day after day?" For the most part, only those new to street life talk of the future as a progression from the past. When concrete goals are spoken of by patrons of the Inn, it is often in the context of plans to travel elsewhere. It often seems unrealistic to plan to accomplish goals in Salt City; past experience gives the lie to any such hopes. Goals become associated with space rather than time; the hope becomes that a new location may make a difference, in the knowledge that a "new time" will never come. Therefore, when patrons speak of goals, it is often in terms of going someplace like Scranton, Erie, New Orleans, or Florida.

Although I have tried to show the importance of the cyclical image in street life, I am by no means contending that this is the only image of time available in the street subculture. This subculture is part of American culture, and, therefore, a linear time image is always available. Homeless men were, for the most part, reared in a linear time culture, and this time image persists to various degrees. Perhaps the diffusion of linear time into the street subculture is best symbolized in Salt City by the digital time and temperature display atop the city's tallest building. Most homeless men don't wear watches; the display is known as "the poor man's wristwatch." It is a primary link to the larger culture's linear time.[3]

Finally, it is important to note that cyclical time is important not only in the street subculture but also in the organizations which were my vantage point into this subculture. Both the soup kitchen and the Cambridge Street Inn have survival-oriented goals: providing food, clothing, and shelter. These survival goals must be reaccomplished every day, and hence emphasize a cyclical sense of time. Most institutions which serve the homeless have the goal of rehabilitation. Rehabilitative goals tend to foster a more linear time sense in that they emphasize a linear movement (off the streets and into conventional society) which is not meant to be repeated regularly but, rather, to be accomplished once-and-for-all. (Calkins, 1970, also links rehabilitation to a linear time image.) Thus a cyclical time image assumes more importance in an organization with purely survival-oriented goals than in one with mixed survival-rehabilitation goals. My perception of a cyclical time image among the homeless may have been facilitated by my presence in an organization with survival-oriented goals.

Conclusion and Discussion

It is important to distinguish between time image (the spatial representation of time) and time orientation (the direction in which one faces time). The most prominent time image in the street subculture is cyclical. The importance of this image is related both to the cyclic schedules of institutions which deal with the homeless and to the cyclic nature of the goal of survival. Daily and monthly cycles are prominent aspects of street life. A linear time image is also available in the street subculture, although it is there primarily by osmosis from the dominant American culture. Linear time is associated with long-range planning and goals other than survival. Image of time is closely linked to purpose. Cyclical time is associated with survival goals; linear time with non-survival goals. It would seem reasonable to hypothesize that a strong linear time image cannot appear until survival is reasonably assured.

The relationship between time image, time orientation, purpose, and behavior is of crucial importance given the current social situation in the United States. In this very linear, future-oriented society, increasing numbers of people are realizing that the nuclear arms race leaves us with no future. This is particularly evident among youth (Lifton and Falk 1982). As our image of time shifts to a line which ends in nothingness rather than extending to infinity, and our time orientation places less emphasis on the future because no future is anticipated, our decision-making processes and our behavior must also change. The destruction of a sense of a future which nuclear weapons have already achieved in some segments of the population will have profound effects on our entire culture. The study of social time can only help point to the problem; the solution lies in working toward the abolition of nuclear weapons.

NOTES

[1] As noted by Bergson. See Boman, p. 126.

[2] "Mother's day" technically refers to the day on which Aid to Families with Dependent Children (AFDC) checks arrive. In this state, this is the first and sixteenth days of the month. The first, however, is generally acknowledged as the major "mother's day" in the street subculture because it is on this day that the Supplemental Security Income (SSI) and Veterans Administration (VA) checks also arrive. Therefore, in the balance of this paper, "mother's day" will refer only to the first, and not to the sixteenth, day of the month.

[3] Other, less common, time images are available on the street. One of particular interest is the image of time as void, sometimes seen among younger street men, who conceive of time as an enemy, as something to be "killed," as an endless void which must be filled with some activity. Each day represents an expanse of time which they must fill with some activity—not necessarily useful activity, just activity. Some youthful patrons have asked me if we could use help at the Inn or soup kitchen, saying something to the effect of "Just so I have something to do. I don't want to spend all day doing nothing again." Some almost seemed to fear the day as a challenge at which they would fail—the simple challenge to find activity to fill up the time. A similar pattern was found by Horton (1967) in his study of young Black street-corner men, for whom: "... yesterday merges into today, and tomorrow is an emptiness to be filled in through the pursuit of bread and excitement." Some street men, particularly those from mental hospitals, fill the void simply by walking. One sees them all over the city, in almost continual motion. Others simply sit. The phenomenon of killing time occurs when survival goals are reasonably assured and one has no other immediate goals. The concept of "killing time," which I found among some of the homeless, presents a paradoxical view of the human condition: one fears time as something which must be filled with action, fears to simply exist in time; and yet one fears above all death, the individual end of time.

REFERENCES

Banfield, Edward. *The Unheavenly City* (Boston: Little, Brown, 1968).
Barndt, R., and D. Johnson. "Time Orientation in Delinquents." *Journal of Abnormal and Social Psychology* 51:343-345 (1955).
Berdyaev, Nikolai. *Slavery and Freedom* (New York: Scribners, 1944).

Boman, Thorleif. *Hebrew Thought Compared with Greek* (New York: Norton, 1960).

Calkins, Kathy. "Time: Perspectives, Marking, and Styles of Usage." *Social Problems* 17:487-501 (1970).

Cottle, T., and S. Klineberg. *The Present of Things Future* (New York: The Free Press, 1974).

Dundes, Alan. *Interpreting Folklore* (Bloomington: University of Indiana Press, 1980).

Durkheim, Emile. *The Elementary Forms of the Religious Life* (New York: The Free Press, 1965).

Geertz, Clifford. *The Interpretation of Cultures* (New York: Harper, 1973).

Horton, John. "Time and Cool People." *Transaction* 4:5-12 (1967).

Landau, Simha. "Delinquency, Institutionalization, and Time Orientation." *Journal of Consulting and Clinical Psychology* 44:745-759 (1976).

Leach, E. R. *Rethinking Anthropology* (London: Athalone, 1961).

Leshan, Lawrence. "Time Orientation and Social Class." *Journal of Abnormal and Social Psychology* 47:589-592 (1952).

Liebow, Elliot. *Talley's Corner* (Boston: Little, Brown, 1967).

Lifton, Robert Jay, and Richard Falk. *Indefensible Weapons* (New York: Harper, 1982).

Nelkin, Dorothy. "Unpredictability and Life Style in a Migrant Labor Camp." *Social Problems* 17:472-487 (1970).

Sorokin, Pitirim, and Robert Merton. "Social Time: A Methodological and Functional Analysis." *American Journal of Sociology* 42:615-629 (1937).

Spradley, James. *You Owe Yourself a Drunk* (Boston: Little, Brown, 1970).

Stein, Kenneth B., Theodore Sarbin, and James Kulik. "Future Time Perspective: Its Relation to the Socialization Process and the Delinquent Role." *Journal of Consulting and Clinical Psychology* 32:257-264 (1968).

Wallace, Melvin. "Future Time Perspective in Schizophrenia." *Journal of Abnormal and Social Psychology* 52:240-245 (1956).

Weber, Max. *The Theory of Social and Economic Organization* (New York: The Free Press, 1947).

Wiseman, Jacqueline. *Stations of the Lost* (Chicago: University of Chicago Press, 1970).

Zerubavel, Eviatar. "Timetables and Scheduling: On the Social Organization of Time." *Sociological Inquiry* 46:87-94 (1976).

____.*Hidden Rhythms* (Chicago: University of Chicago Press, 1981).

II

Background and Politics

6

The Life of the Homeless

Patricia Cayo Sexton

OUTCAST GROUPS vary historically in their composition and in the political meanings and symbols attached to them. What we observe about
one group of outcasts, the homeless in New York City, finds its
reflections on a historical screen of alternating concern and contempt for the
poor.

This group invites political interest because its symbolic associations have
been unexpectedly positive for several reasons, among them:

1. the special characteristics of the group and its growing numbers and
    visibility in front of opulent highrisers and on the steps of elegant
    Manhattan brownstones and everywhere else in the city;
2. the sharply critical response of many New Yorkers to current national
    welfare and economic policies;
3. the creative use of the courts and legal tactics in addition to traditional
    social work and activist approaches;
4. the presence of religiously motivated individuals and groups who have
    assumed a special mission to the homeless; and
5. a good and sympathetic press and, finally, the special qualities of the
    city and its inhabitants—that Big Apple with its fairly big heart and
    (relatively speaking) fairly big pocketbook.

Unfortunately, the extensive literature on social stratification tells us little
about the political and social functions of outcast groups. (The word "outcast" is applied to them because it suggests what is inevitably true: their

From *Dissent*, Vol. 30, Winter 1983. pp.79-84. Reprinted by permission of *Dissent*.

condition results from being cast off, degraded, uprooted, excluded from rewarding work—by other classes, by economic policies, and by a value system that cherishes individual achievement, despises individual failure, and is profoundly suspicious of "misfits.")

In the Marxist view, this class has little political significance because it lacks true revolutionary potential. In the *Manifesto* it is a "lumpenproletariat," a dangerous class:

> [This] passively rotting mass thrown off by the lowest layers of the old society may, here and there, be swept into the movement by a proletarian revolution: its conditions of life, however, prepare it far more for the part of a bribed tool of reactionary intrigue.

In fact, the outcast class has always had political meaning, usually of a passive sort, in that it may move other groups to political acts (often of a punitive sort). And at times it has played an active political role.

After the Protestants closed all Catholic monastaries in Elizabethan England, for example, the realization that the swelling ranks of beggars and vagabonds were joining in religious rebellion finally led to the enactment of the first English poor laws. These laws over time virtually forced the able-bodied poor into workhouse confinement, while providing some meager public assistance to the disabled.

Politically active or not, this outcast class is almost always a political symbol. In the best of medieval times, it was likely to be a cherished symbol—the hapless children of God whose misery was a test of the faith, hope, and charity for the more fortunate. The duty of hospitality to needy strangers was taught by the early Church. An ordinance of the Archbishop of Canterbury in the seventh century, as reported by C.J. Ribton-Turner in *A History of Vagrants and Vagrancy*, published in 1887 (London: Chapman & Hall, p.9), reads:

> Whosoever doth not receive a sojourner into his house, as his Lord ordaineth and promiseth of the Kingdom of Heaven therefore...and hath not washed the feet of the poor, nor done alms, so long let him do, penance on bread and water, if he amend not.

In the 13th century, the wife of the King of Scotland was distinguished for almsgiving:

> During her whole life, wherever she might be, she had twenty-four persons whom she supplied with meat and clothing. Departing from the Church she

used to feed the poor: first three, then nine, then twenty-four; at last three hundred; herself standing by the King and pouring water on their hands. [Ribton-Turner, p. 33.]

In the best of medieval times, of course, people were ordinarily attached to family groupings or communities from which they were seldom totally outcast. The economic and ideological reformations that severed these ties created new groups of outcasts and attached new meanings to them, as can be seen with some clarity in a small volume edited and introduced by Martin Luther in 1528 entitled *Liber Vagatorum*, "Book of Vagabonds and Beggars." This book was published seven years after Luther's formal excommunication from the Catholic Church and four years after his violent denunciation of the Peasant Wars and his break with Erasmus and the Humanists. The book has three parts: the first shows the methods by which mendicants and tramps get their living; the second gives some "notabilia" about these livelihoods; the third presents a "vocabulary of their language or gibberish, commonly called . . . Beggar Lingo."

Luther writes that such a work "should become known everywhere, in order that men can see and understand how mightily the devil rules in this world. . . ." About the vagabond vocabulary he writes, "Truly, such Beggars' Cant has come from the Jews, for many Hebrew words occur in the Vocabulary, as any one who understands that language can perceive." The book's message is essentially that most beggars are frauds and that charity should be given only to those who are known by the givers as honest beggars even when others appear needy and possess official licenses to beg.

The English translator of *Liber Vagatorum* attributes the increase of vagabonds during the 16th century to the begging system of the Catholic friars, religious mendicants who gave to beggars "sundry lessons in hypocrisy, and taught them, in their tales of ficticious distress, how to blend the troubles of the soul with the infirmities of the body." He then contends that poetry became estranged from the nobility, the citizen, and the scholar (who forsook verse and rhyme for more prosaic and mercenary pursuits), and allied itself with beggars and vagrants. Mendicity, he says, became a distinct institution, divided into various branches and provided with a language of its own. Luther sought, he adds, to sweep away two classes of "locusts": the papacy and its members, and "the beggars and vagabonds who imitated the Mendicant Friars in wandering up and down the country, with lying tales of distress, either of mind or body."

Returning to Marx's *Manifesto* for traces of the profounder sources of the shifting historic conditions and meanings attached to the outcasts, we find that early in the industrial revolution the rising bourgeoisie, allied to the religious reformers,

. . . put an end to all feudal, patriarchal, idyllic relations. It has pitilessly torn
asunder the motley feudal ties that bound man to his "natural superiors," and
has left remaining no other bond between man and man than naked self-
interest and callous "cash payment." It has drowned the most heavenly ecsta-
sies of religious fervor, of chivalrous enthusiasm, of philistine sentimentalism,
in the icy water of egotistical calculation. It has resolved personal worth into
exchange value. . . . In one word, for exploitation, veiled by religious and
political illusions, it has substituted naked, shameless, direct, brutal exploitation.

Rather than sweeping out the "locusts" of beggars, the effect of this
"pitiless" upheaval has been to multiply the number of disassociated outcasts
and to diminish the compassionate regard in which they once were held.

Since the Reformation and the rise of capitalism, there has been the strong
conservative tendency to label outcast groups as unworthy, undeserving,
antisocial, indigent out of inertia rather than because of public apathy or
private exploitation. These outcasts then came to symbolize, and in turn
stigmatize, the larger groups who resembled them in their poverty, ethnic
identity, or other demographic characteristics.

Conservatism, of course, predates industrialism. The Roman playwright
Plautus, for example, gives these words to one of his characters: "He deserves
ill of a beggar who gives him to eat or to drink, For he both loses that which he
gives and prolongs for the other a life of misery." Alas, Plautus lived out his
later life in poverty.

The historical dialectic of love and hate, compassion and contempt for the
outcast has also played itself out in our own time, first in "the war on
poverty," in which the poor themselves played an active and sometimes even
violent political role, and on into the darkening period of reaction to welfare,
street crime, "big government," and high taxes. Accordingly, those who
traded on rising welfare costs and street crime delivered this message at the
polls: the poor are not only undeserving and expensive to support, they are
made even more miserable and antisocial by public assistance. Plautus
revisited.

In New York City and elsewhere, a new group has appeared to join the poor
and outcast, relieving to some degree the stigmatizing pressures on older
outcast groups. The public response is far more charitable than its response to
the old outcast groups, perhaps because its composition is quite different; that
is, it contains many women, whites, elderly, and large numbers of those who
are indisputably and conspicuously disabled.

This new impoverished group has come to be known as "the homeless." It
included some older inhabitants of the central city and skid row: males
without families, jobs, homes, often disabled by alcoholism or other infirmi-

ties. The ranks of these "old-timers" have been joined by at least two other groups. The first resemble the "hobos" of the 1930s in that they are mainly able-bodied young males who have been displaced by hard times from their jobs, families, shelters.

The second group, which is of special concern here, is almost unique in our times, made up as it is of people who were, in other days, locked up in mental hospitals but now are "deinstitutionalized" or denied voluntary admission to these hospitals. In the two decades following 1960, more than half a million people throughout the country were deinstitutionalized, and an unknown, but perhaps similar, number have been refused voluntary hospitalization.

Estimates derived chiefly from the Department of Health of the State of New York indicate that more than 36,000 people in New York City are homeless. The city challenges the figure but the fact that every public shelter newly opened by the city is soon filled suggests that demand far exceeds supply.

While growing numbers of these homeless are apparently young jobless males who are relatively sound of mind and body, there is evidence that one-third or more of the city's homeless (estimates range up to two-thirds) suffer from some disabling pyschological disorder, including chronic alcoholism.

The designation for these new and old street people—"the homeless"— reflects the response of a new group of their advocates and the causes and "cures" they perceive from homelessness. The term is neutral rather than pejorative, unlike such designations as underclass, lower class, lower depths—or such popular words as bums, tramps, or drunks. The term "homeless" does not attach blame or a degraded "lower" status to people. It merely says that they are "without homes" and that their primary need is for shelter.

An impressive group (or movement) has been formed, first in New York City and now nationally, the Coalition for the Homeless. The group's leanings are toward advocacy and the law as means, and toward establishing small-scale residential communities for the homeless. The group does not seem to count much on extensive research, conferences, or actions by the homeless as means—or on the remedial efficacy of psychiatric or other professional services for them.

The successes of the Coalition for the Homeless, at least in New York City, have been notable. City shelters and soup kitchens have been opened, the conversion of single-room occupancy hotels to more profitable purposes and the consequent eviction of their residents has been impeded, and new money for the homeless and for small residences has been obtained. The Coalition's major limitation has been (as some observers see it) that, while its goals involve political advocacy, it does not have either the political skill or the drive to mobilize available public support. The Coalition may indeed be the only potentially large-scale movement concerned with the poor to survive the current war against poverty programs.

Homelessness, then, is symbolic not only as a designation but as a new direction in the public response to the poor. Many citizens, of course, are repelled or terrified by the sight of so many disturbed and homeless people on their doorsteps, but an astonishing number of them respond to the homeless, especially to the "deinstitutionalized," with perplexed compassion and charity. In that sense, it may be a tragic but somewhat fortunate political circumstance that the institutionalized were so abruptly released from their confinement, even though they have not yet found the care and welcoming communities that were supposed to follow their release, along with an extension of their basic civil rights.

Appalling as their condition is, it may serve some social purpose. The deinstitutionalized are far more visible than most of the poor and, more important, they are obviously "deserving" poor. Many are especially sympathetic figures because, for the first time in memory, they are women, "shopping-bag ladies," who have known better times and are now far down on their luck, just as our own kin could some day be.

The stigma attached to the outcast, as previously noted, tends to spill over onto adjacent groups with similar characteristics, but the deinstitutionalized have no related groups. They are isolates, and their visible presence tends to distract people from other stigmatized groups—the "undeserving and dangerous poor."[1]

In New York City, the most effective advocacy has been carried out in the courts, and by one lone ranger, a young lawyer, Robert Hayes, who successfully sued the city on behalf of homeless men—using the language of the state constitution concerning public responsibility for shelter. Hayes now has left his Wall Street law firm to work full-time for the Coalition. More recently, he has filed suits against the city on behalf of homeless women, and against the state for its failure to provide suitable voluntary hospital care for those suffering from chronic mental illness.

As for the response of religious groups, Catholics have been notably more active than others (though working far from full capacity), and to some extent the medieval poetry of the poor, the sense of the hapless and deranged being closer to God, has reappeared with the Catholic Worker group providing an active, enduring model for others. Of course, the Salvation Army is there but is not much involved in the new advocacy movement. Other religious groups, such as the Moravian Church (which predated the Lutheran Church), have also been active. And the major religious groups of the city—Protestants, Catholics, and Jews—collectively decided to work on behalf of the homeless. The Community Service Society, a civic group, has taken some major organizational initiatives, and the city of New York has also been there, with a human service record at least equal to that of other American cities.

The importance of the city's relative receptivity, plus the religious connection, can be seen in a Coalition news report on an "extermination program" underway in Phoenix, Arizona. In July 1981, a Phoenix ordinance made it a misdemeanor to lie down or sleep on public property, and that November a new zoning ordinance excluded soup kitchens and missions from the renewed downtown area. On January 1, 1982, the Lighthouse Rescue Mission was condemned by the city after 28 years of operation, along with the Helping Hand Mission, which had functioned 34 years. A major park was closed to discourage sleeping, and all existing public shelters and a Salvation Army program are being shut down, along with existing soup kitchens. In May the editor of the *Arizona Republic* hailed such actions: "We didn't tolerate prostitutes—why tolerate bums?" The sole remaining refuge will be the St. Vincent de Paul Society, which, the Coalition reports, "has decided to fight."

Based on the wholly unsupported view that big is beautiful, or cost-effective (or better for managers), even the best public officials are likely to favor huge public institutions (schools, asylums, medical complexes, shelters) over more intimate and self-managing ones. Private tax-paying citizens, on the other hand, may be persuaded to prefer, for their communities, the more modestly proportioned establishments, all else but size being equal.

The Coalition claims that smaller residences, run by nonprofit groups, can do a better job for less money than big public institutions; but it also urges New York City to adopt a large, planned crash program to meet urgent need. The program should include:

- the identification of thousands of emergency beds to be used on an as-needed basis for the winter;
- employment of shelter clients on the staff of all new shelters;
- initiation of a pilot public-works program of jobs and stipends for willing shelter residents;
- reimbursement of nonprofit groups and the substantial assistance of religious groups that set up shelters; [and]
- the conversion into longer-term residences of city-owned properties in all five boroughs.

In New York, the charitable mettle of residents is being tested as perhaps never before. It's not the usual test; no collection plates are being passed, and there is no demand for impersonal credit-card giving. The test is one-to-one, hands-on giving, and it involves more than money or mere symbolic currency.

A case in point is a student who told me of a young man who lives in front of one of the city's super-luxury hotels by day and in steam tunnels near the hotel by night. The hotel's doormen provide showers for him and others on the hotel staff, as well as passersby, regularly give him food. My student spent many hours of many days trying to befriend this desperately troubled man and in the end broke through his silence, and told him of other food and shelter options available to him. She learned that he had been in mental institutions but much preferred his present quarters to hospitalization. She also learned that he knew his condition was deteriorating and that he would probably accept an offer of decent public shelter, were it forthcoming.

Obviously, the hands-on charity of passersby is no substitute for proper housing and public welfare. But as a supplement to the latter, this hands-on exercise can benefit the giver as well as the recipient; and its absence can allow citizens a certain detachment and moral distance from the harsh, punitive decisions now being made about public welfare.

The medieval system of hands-on charity was an imperfect model. It led to the institutionalization of begging, and it failed to provide the poor with the welfare entitlements that we now cherish. But, these entitlements are slipping away fast and leaving no charitable tradition of *moral* rights and obligations in their place.

The organizational division of labor that established poor laws, workhouses, and public welfare allowed individuals, in a sense, to turn over their charitable impulses and obligations to those specialists who were supposed to "care for" the poor—and who often "cared very little" for them. Thus the private citizen was let off the hook while the welfare system was institutionalized, bureaucratized, and, in the worst of times, corrupted by those who dispensed welfare in an exceedingly uncharitable way.

To keep that system open, honest, vigorous—and charitable—there may be no substitute for the application of hands-on charity, to all varieties of outcast and impoverished people, by as many citizens as can be reached.

The deinstitutionalized homeless are only the most conspicuous and most compelling group of outcasts. Their presence has helped to open the doors of public shelters to other homeless people, so it may also help extend more adequate public welfare and hands-on charity to others.

Quite obviously, the mini-movement for the homeless, generated by concerned citizens, as well as by those who simply want the poor off the streets, cannot by itself turn around the nation's voters or the welfare system; but it may be one part of the overall political strategy of those who favor decent welfare policies.

The young leaders of the Coalition for the Homeless are perhaps right to be suspicious of academic studies and statistics, so often offered as substitutes for action. We already know a great deal about who the homeless are and what they need, but we know much less about how to win the votes and resources needed to deal with their problems. This is basically a political issue and one of crucial importance to the homeless and to other impoverished people.

NOTE

[1] Oddly enough, during the great depression of the 1930s, the mentally ill apparently played a very different role. Appearing to the public as a "dangerous class" that resembled the unemployed in their homelessness, age, race, etc., they tended to stigmatize the sturdy unemployed and the legions of hobos with whom they were associated in the public mind.

7

The Homeless of New York

Thomas J. Main

IN MOST NEIGHBORHOODS of New York City it is possible to see a large number of people in the streets who are variously described as "vagrants," as "bag people," or, most often, as "the homeless." It is not at all unusual today to see several homeless people stretched out in a subway station; tourists in Greenwich Village seem surrounded by these aimless wanderers; and everyone who uses Pennsylvania Station or the Port Authority Bus Terminal must have seen those who have made these public places their homes. Such a situation could not fail to attract attention, and in fact New York's news media frequently run reports on the homeless, community service organizations devote much effort to advocacy and research work on the subject, and the city spends considerable resources on the problem. In fact, it is no exaggeration to say that, in terms of public attention and growth of government involvement, this is one of the city's most pressing problems.

New York's many homeless people have a very strong impact on the other people who use the streets. Obviously, the sight of tattered or disoriented people sleeping on the street, sifting through garbage cans, or otherwise behaving bizarrely, is very disturbing, and when the number of people doing such things begins to increase in a neighborhood, the reaction can be quite strong. Recently, when the opening of a shelter for homeless people in a nearby church brought more of their numbers to one neighborhood, the secretary of the community board wrote to Mayor Edward I. Koch as follows:

> Since the program opened, this has been a disaster area. Our brownstone steps, doorways and vestibules have been invaded by derelicts and bag people—and

Reprinted with permission of the author from: *The Public Interest*, No. 72, Summer 1983, pp. 3-28. © 1983 by National Affairs, Inc.

their urine and feces. Some of us have been physically attacked by the more violent of the church's clients.

A bag person couple were seen fornicating on the church steps one afternoon. Some of their male clients lie on our sidewalks exposing their genitalia. All of this, and there is more, is not only disgusting and dangerous to our adult population, but we have young people living here as well.[1]

With such passionate feelings aroused, the press began to pay a great deal of attention to the problem. *The New York Times*, local TV stations, and other New York media have run many stories on the homeless, and *New York* magazine went so far as to have John R. Coleman (a former president of Haverford College who once used his sabbatical to investigate the conditions of the disadvantaged by working as a garbage collector) write a long article describing the ten days he chose to spend living on the city's streets. As Mayor Koch has said, "Whenever I pick up a newspaper, or listen to the news, I find stories about one of our most pressing problems—that of the homeless."[2]

Not only are the media paying attention to the homeless, but so are the city's many community service and "advocacy" organizations. Moreover, as other cities find that they too must find a way to deal with this population, still more advocacy groups are becoming involved. For example, in Washington, D.C., the Community for Creative Non-Violence established, as a way of protesting the plight of homeless people, two tent cities for them on the Mall and in Lafayette Park.

Before many other advocacy groups resort to such desperate tactics, perhaps a closer look at the situation in New York, and at the policies the city has adopted, is in order. Sobriety has been in short supply in discussions of the terrible plight of the homeless, yet without it we cannot determine whether current thinking and policy are well tailored to the problem at hand.[3]

Legal Advocacy Work Begins

One of the New York groups that is most active in the cause of the homeless is Coalition for the Homeless (CFTH), whose director is Robert Hayes, a New York lawyer. CFTH coordinates the activities of the various advocacy groups involved with the homeless, but is primarily involved with public interest litigation on their behalf.

Robert Hayes began investigating the condition of the homeless in 1978. Then, as now, the city ran a shelter system—a system of lodging houses and auxiliary services for those who have nowhere else to go. Hayes investigated the various kinds of lodging to which the city directed homeless people: the Men's Shelter at 8 East Third Street, which is the principal intake point for the rest of the men's shelter system; the Bowery hotels—or flophouses—to which the Men's Shelter issues vouchers; and later the Keener building (an abandoned mental institution on Wards Island opened in 1979 to accommodate the growing demand for shelter). At the time Hayes began his work, the city sent men applying for shelter to the Bowery hotels, or to Camp La Guardia, a shelter 60 miles from the city designed to accommodate older clients. If both these places were filled men slept in the "big room," the largest room of the Men's Shelter. After the "big room" was filled, other applicants were simply turned back on the streets.[4]

Hayes interviewed many homeless men and learned, according to CFTH literature, that they "found the streets and subways less dangerous and degrading" than the shelter system. "Streets were [the] preferred option . . . because conditions at the city shelter were so abominable." He therefore felt that "the demand for shelter beds was far lower than the true need since conditions at the municipal shelter effectively deterred many of the homeless from even seeking shelter."[5] Hayes had come to the conclusion that the shelters discouraged clients from using them, and were thus forcing people back on to the streets.

At this point Hayes decided to do something—and what he did seems to have been determined by his belief that what was needed was "recognition with the force of law of a right to shelter." The reasoning, apparently, was that if shelter was recognized as a right, rather than as a matter of social service, then no one could legitimately be deterred from claiming it. The conceptualization of the problem—as one of rights—also determined the avenue through which it would be settled: the courts. CFTH was aware of this implication, and of the problems it might raise. A CFTH report, "Litigation in Advocacy for the Homeless," states that, "It is rare that a 'right to shelter' will be forthrightly espoused in any jurisdiction. Instead, the more probable course would be one which would require creative interpretation of a more general statutory and constitutional language to arrive at an enforceable entitlement." In other words, open-ended rights are rarely granted to anything, so if one is searching for such a right one must tease it out of some apparently non-germane constitutional provision or statute.

Such creative work is what Hayes then began. He found entitlements to shelter implied in the New York State Constitution, the New York State Social Service Law, the New York Municipal Law, and even the equal protection provision of the U.S. Constitution. Thus, according to Hayes, the following lines from the New York State Constitution imply an enforceable right to shelter: "The aid, care and support of the needy are public concerns and shall be provided by the state . . . as the legislature may from time to time determine."[6] Whether the legislature has ever determined to establish a right to shelter is something the CFTH report does not discuss. But Hayes was convinced that advocacy through the courts was crucial to solving the problems of the homeless, and with such arguments in mind, he gathered together several homeless men, including one, Robert Callahan, to serve as co-litigants against the city and state.

The Courts Steps In

The case of *Callahan v. Carey* went to the New York State Supreme Court in October 1979. In December the court granted the plaintiffs a preliminary injunction that required the city to provide shelter to any man who requested it. On Christmas Eve the court entered a temporary order requiring the city to "provide shelter (including bedding, wholesome food and adequate security and supervision) to any person who applies for shelter at the Men's Shelter." To fulfill the court's requirement, the city quickly opened the Keener building as a shelter. Demand for shelter promptly shot up; Keener was filled to overflowing with more than 625 men by early 1980. Partly in response to this situation, the city eventually had a new building constructed on Wards Island—the Schwartz building—which has housed 400 men almost since it opened in 1982.

By the summer of 1981 the case of *Callahan v. Carey* had come to trial. At this point a compromise was reached: Hayes and the plaintiffs had been demanding not merely recognition of a right to shelter, but that this shelter be "community based," i.e., that shelters be scattered throughout the city and empowered to admit clients directly, to avoid the "deterrent effect" of having clients processed primarily in the Bowery. When the city pointed out that community opposition would make this plan nearly impossible, the requirement was dropped, with the city agreeing to supply all applicants with shelter of a quality to be mandated by the courts. This compromise was the basis for a consent decree, which was signed in August 1981 and which amounted to "recognition with the force of law of a right to shelter."

Since then CFTH has forced the city to live up to its obligation and to increase steadily the capacity of the system in order to eliminate the "deterrent" factor of limited beds. Usually after such an increase, demand for shelter has shot up until the new capacity is filled and the city is obliged to find more beds. Thus, six weeks after the consent decree was signed, the city ran out of beds.[7] CFTH then brought the city back into court, where the city was ordered to open another 400 beds within 24 hours. The city complied by housing men at an abandoned Brooklyn school building. Within a month, the school's capacity was filled. Again the city was brought back into court, and again a new shelter was opened, this one in an abandoned armory. But this action did not entirely satisfy the court, and in response to the court's demand that the city meet the growing demand for shelter, the city opened yet another armory to homeless men. Since the December injunction the city has been making a steady effort to provide for the homeless, and so no longer turns any applicants away.

One must be careful in asserting that the outcome of *Callahan v. Carey* was recognition of a right to shelter. The suit ended with the signing of a consent decree, and left all points of law—including the determination of a right to shelter—legally unsettled. However, it is true that since the December 1979 injunction the city has been obliged to follow a de facto policy which assumes such a right. Moreover, since the 1981 consent decree, the city has been obliged to meet certain quality standards which the consent decree lays out in detail and which remove the most obvious causes for any "deterrent" effect. Bedding and clothes issues must be clean, heat maintained, a minimum amount of space per person provided, a recreation program developed, etc.

Research and Advocacy Work

The homeless have also attracted the attention of advocacy groups whose primary interest is research. Most important among these is Community Service Society of New York (CSS). CSS has produced two extensive studies of homelessness, "Private Lives/ Public Spaces: Homeless Adults on the Streets of New York City" (February 1981) and "One Year Later: The Homeless Poor in New York City, 1982" (June 1982). The CSS reports dealt with the life of the homeless on the streets, and also with the quality of the shelter system. CSS advanced two claims that became especially influential.

First, CSS made an estimate of the number of homeless people in New York City. CSS held that there were 36,000, this figure being based on estimates made by the New York State Office of Mental Health (OMH).[8] In an internal memo dated October 12, 1979, OMH in turn based its figure of 30,000 on estimates made by the Men's Shelter that the approximately 9,000 different men they serviced represented 30 percent of the homeless men in the city. CSS then added to this the Manhattan Bowery Corporation's estimate of 6,000-6,500 "periodically homeless" women to arrive at the 36,000 figure.

CSS made this estimate public in February 1981. According to the New York City Human Resources Administration (HRA), for FY 1980-81 the overall daily average attendance in the shelters was 2,428.[9] Again, since December 1979 the city has been required to provide shelter to any man who requests it. (The city also voluntarily agreed to provide shelter to all women who request it.) How did CSS explain the fact that, while their estimate of the number of homeless people was 36,000, not even a tenth of that number had requested shelter from the city? The answer lies in the second main contention of CSS, which concerned the nature of the shelter system. CSS held, as did CFTH, that the conditions at these facilities were so bad that the homeless refused to use them and preferred to stay on the streets. According to CSS:

> What public resources do exist, moreover, have their own deterrent power. The deplorable conditions of the flophouses and Keener Building, high incidence of violence, routine contempt meted out to applicants for shelter, and the historical association of the Bowery as the abode of "bums," all make the Men's Shelter the place of last resort for many homeless men. For different reasons—namely exclusionary policies, limited beds, and the militaristic regime—the Women's Shelter can effectively service only a small proportion of homeless women. . . .Given the state of the public shelters—or perhaps more accurately given the nature of the personal costs extracted when one submits to their regimes and conditions—the decision made by many homeless people to fend for themselves on the streets gains at least a measure of intelligibility.[10]

In short, CSS came to very much the same conclusions about the plight of New York's homeless and about the condition of the shelter system that Hayes did: The problem was enormous and the shelter system was inadequate to help.

A New and Improved Shelter System

Callahan v. Carey and the publicity brought on by the advocates' work have had a large impact on the shelter system, especially in regard to increasing the supply of beds, improving conditions, and generally removing deterrent factors. Therefore, it is important to understand what the shelter system is like *now*, for it has changed quite a bit since Hayes first began his investigations back in 1978. (The emphasis here will be on the facilities for men, since they were the focus of the *Callahan v. Carey* suit, and since the overwhelming majority of the shelter clients are male.)

The Men's Shelter is located in the Lower East Side off the Bowery. Most of the men who use the shelters enter here, where they are given food, showers, and medical services (including psychiatric services). Within ten days of their coming to the shelter, all men receive a social service interview by the "5 x 8 staff," so called because the client's records are entered by the interviewer on 5" x 8" index cards. Interviewers may refer clients to one of several special social service units, such as the psychiatric unit, or the under-21 unit.

Very few men actually sleep at the Men's Shelter, however; it contains only a few beds in its infirmary. Rather, clients are generally sent to one of several principal types of lodging. The majority are given housing vouchers, which entitle them to spend the night in one of the Bowery hotels: These are the Union, the Kenton, the Palace, the Sunshine, the Delevan, and the Stevenson. These are among the least comfortable lodgings in the shelter system. Some of the men sleep in small cubby-like rooms covered on the top with chicken wire; other accommodations are dormitory style. About 1,150 men sleep in the hotels.

After processing at the Men's Shelter, men may also be sent to a city-run shelter for lodging. The exact assignment will depend on the vacancy rate at the various shelters. The principal city-run shelters are the Charles H. Gay Shelter Center on Wards Island, the East New York Shelter in Brooklyn, and the Harlem Shelter. Men who are assigned to these shelters receive free transportation there and back to the Men's Shelter in the morning.

Of these shelters, the Gay center is by far the largest, lodging 816 men in its two buildings (East New York houses 350 and the Harlem Shelter holds 200).[11] The Gay center consists of the Keener building and the Schwartz building, which is newly built and which opened in the spring of 1982. The entire center is run by the private charitable organization, the Volunteers of America, under contract to the city.

While CSS reports that conditions at the Keener building are "deplorable" the fact is that conditions there are now quite good. Men in the Keener building are assigned to fair-sized "semi-private" rooms which sleep two or three people. Accommodations in the Schwartz building are dormitory style, but still fairly spacious. The Schwartz building, since it is brand new, has a clean and modern look to it. Both buildings have a TV room. The Schwartz building also has kitchen and dining facilities. The center has a medical clinic and mental health services on site.

When the shelters and Bowery hotels are filled, the city will send people to one of the armories it has opened for the homeless with the cooperation of the state. The Flushing Armory and the Lexington Avenue Armory are for women; the Kingsbridge Armory in the Bronx, the Fort Washington Armory in Manhattan, and the Park Avenue Armory are for men. The Fort Washington Armory, which holds 600 people, is the largest of these sites. All the armories are open on a 24-hour basis, which means that clients can be admitted there directly, without having to go first through the East Third Street site.

The city also runs a facility some 60 miles outside the city, Camp LaGuardia, which sleeps approximately 950 men. This shelter is primarily intended for use by older clients. It is currently undergoing extensive renovation. New dormitories are being built which will eventually house 600 men by the fall of 1984.

There are also three main shelters for women. The Women's Shelter, which is also the principal intake center for women, is in the Lower East Side. It provides meals, showers and social services for the women in the shelter system, and has 51 beds. Other sites are the Women's Shelter Annex, which holds 150 women, and the Bushwick Center.

As can be seen, the city has developed an extensive system to comply with the first requirement of the *Callahan v. Carey* consent decree—that all applicants be given shelter. But the city is also making efforts to comply with the other aspect of the consent decree—the quality standards. According to CFTH, "the shelters remain dangerous and forbidding, continuing to deter many homeless men from coming off the streets."[12] But the city disagrees. It holds that it is in substantial compliance with all aspects of the quality requirements. According to Mayor Koch:

> I don't agree with the way the court is trying to implement the consent agreement. I think it is enough to provide shelter for the evening, three hot meals a day, showers, medical care, clothing and counseling. The court says we have to provide all these services in shelters that are open 24 hours a day so that the homeless will not have to be bused from where they shower and eat to where they sleep. We bused only a small percentage of the homeless anyway, but this requirement has made it difficult to find appropriate facilities as the number of homeless has grown, and it also has made the program more expensive than it needs to be.[13]

It seems then, that there is no substantial dispute over whether the city is in compliance with the requirement to provide shelter, food, and auxiliary care of essentially decent quality. Such dispute as there is arises over such less than central matters as shelter hours and transportation.

Where Are the Homeless Now?

Clearly, the city has developed a large system and made great efforts to recognize the de facto right to shelter, and to eliminate any deterrent factors from the shelter system. The advocacy groups have therefore largely gotten their way, but at a high price. In early 1978, when Robert Hayes began his work, the city's operating budget for the homeless was $6.8 million; for the current fiscal year it is projected to be $38 million.[14] What, then, has been the effect of instituting the advocacy group's policies on a large scale?

It is now turning out that some CSS research work, which was never intended to be very rigorous, is indeed rather shaky. The estimate of 36,000 homeless people especially seems very soft. The fact of the matter is that no one knows how many homeless people there are *on the street*. The city had plans to conduct a census of people actually on the street or in the shelters, but they were dropped after CSS severely criticized the project and funds were unavailable. We do know, however, how many people are in the shelters, and it is nowhere near 36,000. For FY 1982-83 to date (i.e., July 1982-April 1983) the overall daily average attendance in the shelters was 4,235.[15] When cold weather set in, attendance began to rise. On Friday, February 11, 1983, a large blizzard hit New York with more than 20 inches of snow. Attendance at the shelters that night was 4,771.[16] The next night, the twelfth, attendance was 4,873, and on the thirteenth it began to drop again to 4,825. (Interestingly, the figure of 4,771 for the eleventh represents a *decrease* from the night before the blizzard hit, the tenth, when attendance was 4,909.) What, one wonders, happened to the additional 31,000 homeless people who were presumably out in the street or subways during the blizzard, assuming the CSS estimate is accurate? No one knows, but for whatever reason, they did not show up in the shelters. This does not prove that there are not thousands of homeless people who are so deterred from using the shelters that not even blizzards will drive them in. On the other hand, it does not offer any support for the CSS figures either.

This brings us to another issue that CSS and other advocacy groups have raised: deterrence. These groups still think that conditions at the shelters deter a large number of homeless people from using the shelters. There are, by this account, many thousands still out on the streets or otherwise in some sense homeless, but deterred from using the shelters. And this is indeed the point that CSS makes. According to *The New York Times*:

> Ellen Baxter, a research associate at the Community Service Society, pointed out that the largest city shelter opened for women, on East Third Street, filled up within two weeks. "Where were those 80 women before that?" she asked. "Every time a decent shelter opens, it fills immediately."[17]

The implication here is that the shelter population pool is simply a group of people without homes, who live either on the street or in otherwise intolerable conditions until the shelters become decent. But how true is this picture? Who, indeed, are the homeless?

Types of Homelessness

Trying to categorize the shelter clients is very difficult. Indeed, the salient point to be made about them is that they are a very heterogeneous group. They have come to the shelters because of a variety of misfortunes and pathologies, and their housing situations before they come to the shelter are very diverse—many do not simply move from the streets into the shelter, although, of course, many do. In fact, the more one looks at the shelter clients, the less obvious it becomes that they share a common state which may be straightforwardly defined as "homelessness."

In 1982, the Bureau of Management Systems, Planning, Research and Evaluation of the City Human Resources Administration, under the direction of Stephen Crystal, released two extensive reports on the client population of the city's men's shelter system. They were, "Chronic and Situational Dependency: Long-Term Residents in a Shelter for Men" (hereafter the Keener report) and "New Arrivals: First Time Shelter Clients."[18] The Keener report was a study of 173 men who had been living in the Keener building for two months or more. "New Arrivals" presented the results of 687 interviews conducted with first-time clients either at the Men's Shelter or the East New York Shelter. Both reports asked a variety of questions regarding the men's background and their reasons for coming to the shelter. "New Arrivals" was principally concerned with determining where the clients were immediately before they came to the shelter. The Keener study's purpose was to determine in detail who long-time users of the shelter were and why they came to need the shelters' emergency services.

The Keener study is particularly important for understanding the heterogeneous nature of the shelter population, for it attempted to devise a typology of its subjects derived "from the overall interviewer assessments of primary problems" and found that the subgroups so classified "are very different from one another." The Keener report thus generated "relatively clear-cut categories for about two thirds of the men" (see Exhibit 7-1).

The largest category was "psychiatric only," which accounted for 34 percent of these men. These overlapped to a large extent with the "major subgroup [that] consisted of *those with major psychiatric* disabilities or histories. One third of the long-term men acknowledged past psychiatric hospitalization" (italics in original). The mean age of these men was 33. Thus the popular perception of the homeless as consisting of a large number of former mental patients seems to have some basis in fact.

The third largest category of the Keener study was "alcoholic only," which consisted of 6 percent of its subjects. The study also classified 2 percent of its subjects as "drug only." The study also found that of the men it directly interviewed, "Thirty-five percent were regular past or present alcohol abusers" and that "Almost a quarter . . . acknowledged that they were past regular users of hard drugs; an additional 3 percent state that they were current users." Thus, although the percentage of current "alcohol only" and "drug only" clients is relatively low, much higher percentages have had past experiences with alcohol or drugs that may have contributed to their becoming homeless. Thus the traditional vision of shelter-users as consisting largely of alcoholics has only some validity, although the study notes that "hard drugs abuse is beginning to catch up with the traditional alcohol abuse as the major substance abuse problem."

Exhibit 7-1
Categories of Long-Term Shelter Clients (Based on
Overall Interviewer Assessments of Primary Problems)[1]

Group	Number of Men	Percentage of Total	Mean Age
Psychiatric Only	59	34%	33
Alcoholic Only	10	6	41
Economic Only	33	19	32
Drug Only	4	2	30
Physical Disability Only	6	3	49
Total	112	64%	

[1]Source: Stephen Crystal, et al., "Chronic and Situational Dependency: Long-Term Residents in a Shelter for Men" (New York: Human Resources Administration, May, 1982), p. iv.

The Problematic Category: "Economic Only"

This brings us to the second largest category identified in the Keener study, and also in some respects the most interesting: those men classified as "economic only," who make up 19 percent of the subjects, and whose mean age was 32. Of them the report stated:

A group of particular concern is the group of 33 men considered "economic only." This relatively young group of men may fall into the category of "discouraged workers" whose numbers, particularly among younger minority men, have been increasing rapidly, and to disturbing dimensions, during the last year, according to Bureau of Labor Statistic reports.

The report also said of such "discouraged workers" that they "had in the past been able to function at quite high levels, both occupationally and socially."

In the introduction, the report discussed the problem that such "higher functioning young men" present to the shelters:

As a result of a meeting on June 23, 1981, which included City Council President Carol Bellamy and HRA Administrator James Krauskopf, it was agreed that a study be undertaken of "higher functioning young men" at the Keener Shelter on Wards Island. The need for such a study was prompted by a concern that, unlike the typical shelter men serviced at the 3rd Street site, some men at Keener appeared to be capable of more independent living. Many men appear to the eye to be without the usual self-evident disabilities associated with homeless men. There was concern that a group of such men might be settling into Keener on a long term basis. Such a situation, if true, not only would have negative consequences for the men who should be encouraged towards greater independence, but could also result in increased total demand for shelter space as new men continue to enter the system.

Ultimately, the Keener study was expanded to include not merely higher functioning young men, but all long term clients. But there was support for the suspicion that such people were settling into the shelter and driving up the total demand for shelter, primarily in the "New Arrivals" study, which found that:

Like the Keener study, the findings show that there are substantial numbers of men seeking services at the shelters who have significant job skills and histories, and that many have previously been able to support themselves through employment. This further supports the need to develop employment referrals, supported work, and other means of fostering economic self-sufficiency. The findings also suggest that the shelters are drawing from a potentially very large population pool, most of whom are not "homeless" in the sense of being undomiciled at the time of coming to the shelter. Thus future demand may be very large. It will be important to carefully assess client need and resources, to impose appropriate structure and make appropriate demands on clients' own efforts.

The report included considerable evidence that the shelters were drawing on a large pool of higher functioning men who were not homeless before they came to the shelter. The subjects had been asked where they spent the night before they came to the shelter (see Exhibit 7-2). The report found that:

The majority of men had not spent the previous night in the street or subways, although this was the largest single category. Thirty eight percent of the men had done so, while friends (15 percent), family (14 percent), and own apartment (12 percent) accounted together for slightly more. The fact that *one of seven new men had spent the previous night with family* is particularly striking. It is also significant that *12 percent had spent the previous night in their own apartment*. Institutions of various sorts, including jail, account for almost all the rest, while hotels accounted for a smaller proportion than expected, only 4 percent. Just over sixty percent of the men had not been in the streets or subways in any of their last three sleeping arrangements [italics in the original].

Exhibit 7-2
Place of Previous Night's Stay of Shelter Clients[1]

Type of Place	Number of Men	Percentage of Total
Street or Subway	256	37.6%
Friends	105	15.4
Family	96	14.1
Own Apartment	80	11.7
Other Institution	57	8.4
Hospital	38	5.6
SRO	29	4.3
Jail	13	1.9
CLH (Bowery Hotel)	7	1.0
Totals	681	100.0%

[1]Source: Stephen Crystal, et al., "New Arrivals: First-Time Shelter Clients" (New York: Human Resources Administration, November 1982, Revised May, 1983), p. 13, Table 6.

In fact, the "New Arrivals" study found that together the categories of "friends," "family," "own apartment," and "SRO" accounted for the previous night's stay for 46 percent of the men. Of course, the fact that these men had spent the previous night somewhere other than the streets does not imply that they could easily return there immediately. The "New Arrivals" report also found that most of the men who spent the previous night with family or friends were—for whatever reasons—no longer welcome, and that most who have stayed in their own apartments had been evicted (although the report did not give exact figures in its final version). However, other findings in the report suggest that most of the men were not usually homeless. Only 4.7

percent of the men gave the street or subways as their usual place of residence; for 43 percent such usual residence was found either in their own apartment or with family or friends.[19] (The "New Arrivals" report defined usual prior residence as "the most recent place if that accounted for six months, the previous if that was longer or accounted for six months, or the last stable place within the last year.") Thus although most of these men may not have had any other option when they came to the shelter, most of them have had other housing available to them in the recent past, and conceivably might again in the near future if the proper help is available. This would be especially true of those who stayed with family and friends, which ties might still be alive. According to the report, "family contacts are recent and informal support systems may still be viable."

The points to be emphasized are that the shelter clients are an extremely heterogeneous group, and that the various subgroups of the homeless are homeless in very different senses. The clients in the Keener study classified as "psychiatric only" are homeless, but this is because they are severely mentally ill. The "alcoholic only" and "drug only" cases are another issue; these people are homeless, but again, their dominant problem is not homelessness but alcoholism or drug addiction. Finally we have the "economic only" cases. It turns out that in many instances, these people are not simply homeless before they come to the shelters at all. Many do, in fact, have other housing options available to them. These are the people who represent a really new and challenging development. The important question is: Why are they in the shelters at all?

The Background of "Economic Only" Clients

Many of these "economic only" clients enter the shelter system, not because they have nowhere else to go, but rather because their circumstances are such that the shelters become—if it may be so put—the most "attractive" choice among other options.

Of course, one must be careful not to exaggerate the "attractiveness" of the shelters, which is purely relative. They are, to be sure, rather rough and ready places, which no one with even moderate resources and established social connections would want to use. But the sad fact is that a large number of youths are not so fortunate. For a variety of reasons, the shelters can have a certain appeal to marginally situated youths.

Consider, for example, the effect of high unemployment among minority youths. Of course, unemployment by itself does not make one a candidate for homelessness. Indeed, it used to be received wisdom among shelter workers that demand for shelter was inelastic with regard to unemployment, because the unemployed had of course once been employed and therefore had the personal skills and resources necessary to find shelter. But high minority-youth unemployment affects many people who are marginally situated to begin with. For these young people, family ties are fairly tenuous; further, these families are often housed in relatively poor conditions. So, although an unemployed minority youth may have family members who would ordinarily be expected to put him up, these people may in fact be less than overjoyed to have him.

Of course, welfare benefits are available to someone so situated. New York State Home Relief grants a housing allowance of $152 a month to single adults, but this is not a flat grant.[20] It is applicable only to rent, and if one's rent is less, the difference is returned to the welfare office. Neither can clients rent an apartment with rent over $152 and then split the cost with others. Thus the housing allowance will buy housing of only the poorest quality, given the cost of New York apartments. Housing allowances are another factor to consider in determining the relative attractiveness of the shelters, for the allowance often simply cannot buy housing any better than the shelters.

This brings us to an especially important factor in determining the relative attractiveness of the shelters to marginal youths—the shelters themselves. The fact is that the shelters—although of varying quality—are by and large not such bad places to stay. The Gay shelter—particularly the Schwartz building—is in especially good shape. Other shelter lodgings are not so comfortable. However, even these lodgings have important advantages over other sorts of shelter that their clients might find available.

First of all, since the shelters and hotels are either run or regulated by the city, they are subject to regular inspection—both by the city and advocacy groups—which guarantees that basic services will be regularly provided. Thus heat, plumbing, and cleanliness are all maintained at a high level, and with no efforts by the clients. Moreover, shelters provide such auxiliary services as food, clothing, and medical attention to those who need it, services which are generally not included in the rent for private lodgings. Finally, unlike many landlords, and unlike the welfare system, the shelters are by design very easy to deal with. Their extensive staffs are paid to make things easy on the clients, and to help them where they can so that "low functioning" people will not be discouraged from using them. Moreover, in all these respects, the shelters are getting better: Provision of basic and auxiliary services continues to improve, and shelter personnel are being admonished—mostly by the advocacy groups—to become still more accommodating.

For a large number of marginally situated, but not necessarily destitute, inner-city youths, the shelters may represent the best of various housing options. Such people may have somewhat tenuous relations with family or friends who might put them up if all else failed. But there is nothing tenuous about the shelters—it is certain they will accept whoever applies. Again, unemployed single adults have access to Home Relief housing allowances. But the shelters very likely provide better lodging than they can find for themselves on Home Relief. Potential shelter clients may have at least the minimal employment skills necessary to maintain the menial sort of jobs that one in desperate circumstances might ordinarily take to avoid sheer destitution. But shelters obviate the necessity of taking such work merely to obtain basic resources and provide employment counseling to boot. For such people, there is simply no reason not to move into the shelters. So that is what they do.

The New York Times recently reported the case history of one such marginally situated youth who ended up in the shelter. The article tells of Gregory Jonassaint, who in some respects is representative of the shelter's higher-functioning young clients:

> A few months ago, Mr. Jonassaint was living in the spit-and-polish world of the Marine Corps. Now, at 19, he is homeless and moving through the city's seamy underside. . . . "After I got out of the Marines and before I came here, I was living at my mother's house in Brooklyn, but my stepfather threw me out . . . ." He is the product of what he describes as a "very strict" Haitian-American family and grew up in Brooklyn in an atmosphere of family disputes that he says often pitted his stepfather against his mother and siblings. . . . "I looked for cashier's jobs, mailroom jobs, general maintenance and clerk jobs but I couldn't find anything. . . . I tried to get welfare so I could find a place since I couldn't find a job. But welfare wanted my parents to support me. And my father kept saying that I had to get out. So I ended up here."[21]

Though he was lucky enough to have a background of military service (he was honorably discharged from the Marines after an accident), Mr. Jonassaint displays all the characteristics of an "economic only" client. He was unemployed, a situation that weakened his already shaky family life, and welfare was unable to help him because it was more restrictive than the shelter system. On the other hand, he did have a recent employment history and was not "chronically" homeless. In the end he was able to use his various resources to get out of the shelter: His mother eventually offered to take him back in, and he reapplied for welfare and seems likely to get it this time. He is an excellent example of a shelter client with many opportunities available to him who nonetheless feels it necessary to use the shelters.

Our Three "Homeless" Problems

The problem of homelessness thus turns out to be at least three very different problems in New York City. The first is a problem with former mental patients and others suffering from mental illness; this represents an organic, quasi-medical problem. The second is the problem of alcohol and drug abusers: Both of these groups are homeless largely as a result of their substance abuse problem and are in need of specialized treatment. The third is the difficult case—the "economic only" cases. These are people who are suffering from no disability. They are simply locked in a network of circumstances that makes the shelters "attractive" to them. Obviously this is a very different problem from the psychiatric and alcohol and drug abuse cases. We must not allow ourselves to mix these groups together simply because they all use the shelters.

Of the three groups described above, the most problematic is the higher-functioning young men. The presence of the other two groups in the shelters is widely recognized by the advocacy groups and everyone else. CSS first began its research over concern with the conditions of the mentally ill on the streets and in the shelters, and no one has ever doubted that there are many alcoholics and drug abusers among the shelter clients. But that the shelters are also housing people who are not chronically homeless, and are not undomiciled at the time of coming to the shelters, is a reality that has been harder for the advocacy group to face. They simply refuse to admit that the presence of such people should make any substantial difference for shelter policy. The following is typical of the CSS attitude on this subject:

> The city . . . argues that people who were living with family or friends before coming to the shelter are not homeless. Why they left is of no concern.
>
> This view animates the city's interest in distinguishing—as the April 23 draft proposal [of a census to count homeless people] puts it with disarming candor—the "truly homeless" from other marginally needy groups. The assumption, of course, is that large numbers of people are abandoning acceptable residences to take refuge in the public shelters. In support of this claim no data . . . has been advanced. Nor to our knowledge, are any data available to justify the recent claim by an HRA official that "certainly a hundred, maybe more" currently sheltered people are not "truly homeless.". . . No bolder invocation of the invidious distinction between the "deserving" and "undeserving" poor can be found.[22]

As we have seen, in fact there is ample data to suggest that a large portion of the shelter population is not "truly homeless" in the sense of being chronically without lodgings before coming to the shelter. Again, the "New Arrivals" report found that some 30 percent of its subjects had spent the night before with family and friends. And despite the CSS objections, there seems every reason to distinguish such people from other sub-groups of the homeless.

Surely someone who recently had family ties presents a very different problem for social service intervention than a chronically homeless former mental patient or alcoholic.

The *real* reason CSS will not acknowledge the problem of "economic only" clients is that to do so smacks of drawing the "invidious" distinction between the deserving and undeserving clients. In other words, the reluctance of CSS to come to grips with the problem that higher functioning clients present to the shelter system is a matter not of facts but of ideology. CSS is in principle against attempts to isolate such clients and to treat them differently from other clients. Everyone should be given shelter and that is the end of the matter.

The Ideology of the Advocates

What is the ideology of the advocacy groups? As we have seen, they reject the conventional distinction between the deserving and the undeserving poor—and not only for homeless people, but also for other welfare groups. CSS asks:

> How valid now is the conventional distinction between the deserving and undeserving poor, that relegates the homeless to the latter class and treats them accordingly? Can a policy of grudging relief be defended, in which what appears as the lineaments of aid mask what is in fact merely a means of containing and penalizing its recipients?[23]

And the authors also suggest that our experience with the homeless, which supposedly has refuted the "policy of grudging relief," should be applied to other welfare issues as well:

> For the homeless poor effectively to plead their case for relief, it will be increasingly critical for them to make common cause with other neglected victimized populations, to force the issue away from idiosyncratic pathology or eccentricity and into the realm of common suffering; to secure, in short, the recognition that what once could be dismissed as an alien sore on the body politic has now the character of an endemic disorder. Only in this way will an effective constituency of demand—the necessary inital step in the redress of grievance—be mobilized.[24]

The point seems to be that since welfare groups are "victims" of an "endemic disorder" they have a claim to "redress of grievance" and are thus all "deserving." This "declaratory" model of welfare, in which clients need only declare themselves in need to be eligible for relief, has always dovetailed with a radical critique of American society. And CSS does indeed suggest that its work on the homeless fits into such a critique. Leo Srole, Professor of Social Sciences at Columbia University, writes in the introduction to "Private Lives/Public Spaces":

> All [of the homeless] are the "fall out" rejects of a highly competitive, cornucopian socioeconomic system that cannot mobilize the fiscal wherewithal and organizational talents for quasi-family care of its casualties.

In short, according to the ideology of the advocacy groups, homelessness and welfare issues in general are matters of systematic failure, rather than of individual responsibility. This is why they have such trouble figuring out what to do with the higher functioning clients who may have other options available to them. To confront the presence of such people as an important sub-group in the shelters, suggests, as "New Arrivals" puts it, the need to "assess client needs and resources, to impose appropriate structure and make appropriate demand on clients' own efforts." But to do so would mean some element of individual responsibility should be incorporated into the shelter's social service programs, and this is anathema to the advocacy groups' ideology. And so they simply refuse to come to grips with the special case of "economic only" clients.

Guidelines for Shelter Policy

How, then, *should* we cope with the problem of the "economic only" clients and with the problem of the homeless in general? First, it must be recognized that homelessness is better understood as a matter of social service policy than as a matter of human rights. If we recognize shelter as "a basic human right," as the advocacy groups would have us do, then the logical arena for settling the problem is the courts. But the courts are not well suited to make shelter policy. As we have seen, the shelter population is very heterogeneous and the different sub-populations require specific policies devised for their needs. It is unlikely that courts will enter into such administrative detail. As CFTH admits, "courts may well be disposed to order a defendant to provide shelter, but unwilling to specify further the terms and requirements of shelter."[25] But such details are all-important in developing a shelter that will address the various sub-populations' needs and responsibilities. We need a new way of thinking about shelter policy, one that does not impose the language of human rights on an inappropriate subject.

The most important thing to realize in trying to develop realistic guides to shelter policy is that the shelters are not simply a straightforward response to a clearly defined problem called homelessness: Rather, they are residual institutions that deal with a variety of essentially independent problems that other welfare institutions avoid. The shelters take care of the mentally ill who are not in institutions, the alcoholics and drug users who are not in other treatment programs, and the marginally poor who are not on, or not getting enough help from, welfare. Institutions already exist for dealing with all these problems, but the people in the shelters have not been helped yet. *Thus the purpose of the shelters should be to act as a safety net for such people until they can be reintegrated into a standard social service program.*

From this principle, two general guides emerge for shelter policy. First, shelters should quickly size up the basic problems of each client and then refer him to one aid program or another. No one should stay in the shelter simply to put a roof over his head. The second implication for shelter policy is that every effort should be made to keep the client's stay there brief. A client should be allowed to stay in the shelters only until he can take care of himself again, or until he can be transferred to a more permanent institution, or program.

This approach is quite different from that advocated by CSS, which quite openly admits that its "basic thrust is to shift the focus from rehabilitation, the attempt to return the disabled to normalcy, to welfare." CSS takes as its model for shelter policy a men's shelter in Boston, the Pine Street Inn, whose basic philosophy it describes as follows:

> The object is emphatically not to "rehabilitate" the men, only to provide the essentials of life in a homelike atmosphere. The brochure distributed to volunteers put it this way: "the goal of the Inn . . . is to help the men optimally adapt to the lifestyle they sustain by choice or fortune, neither encouraging that lifestyle nor censoring it."

In this way, mental illness, drug abuse, alcoholism, and dependency become morally neutral "lifestyles" to which the shelters are to help their clients "adapt." Quite apart from the moral considerations such a position raises, the problem is that, since these pathologies are to a large extent the *cause* of the client's homelessness, simply allowing the clients to "adapt" to their problem will eventually increase demand for shelter to unacceptable levels as more and more people "adapt" to life there. Again, to prevent such an outcome, shelters must be seen as safety nets from which clients are to be referred to more permanent rehabilitation programs as soon as possible.

Separate Policies for Separate Sub-Populations

How could these general guidelines translate into specific policies for each of the three main shelter sub-populations: the mentally ill, the alcoholics and drug abusers, and the "economic only" youths?

As far as the mentally ill are concerned, the important point to make is that the shelters are not good places for them. The atmosphere in the shelters is not conducive to mental health. Nonetheless, the shelters do their best to treat mentally ill clients on the premises. After their routine social service interview, clients may be referred to the psychiatric unit, whose staff can treat them with psychotropic drugs and psychiatric social work. Mentally ill clients may also be referred for more intensive therapy to psychiatric units funded by Community Support Systems, or to the OMH-run Shelter Outreach Project.

Some psychotherapy is therefore available in the shelters; the problem is with referring the mentally ill out of the shelters. Admissions criteria to state mental hospitals are probably more restrictive now than they were before the advent of the deinstitutionalization movement. It is therefore not possible to reduce the number of the mentally ill in the shelters by institutionalizing more of them. It is usually argued that this is for the best since most mentally ill people do not need to be institutionalized and are capable of living quasi-independently in community-based, "halfway" psychiatric residences. Unfortunately, few such residences were developed. In New York State, the total capacity of such residences is 3,000 while the estimated state need is 13,000.[26] While deinstitutionalization proceeded apace during the 1960s and 1970s, no legislation provided for a transfer of mental health funding to the localities that were now supposed to care for the mentally ill. As a result, few community residences were developed. If mentally ill clients are to be referred out of the shelters, we need some combination of less restrictive state institutionalization requirements and development of local residences for the mentally ill.

Alcoholism and drug abuse are separate problems. As things now stand, the men's shelter has no specific program for dealing with drug abusers, since traditionally they have not been a major problem. But the Keener study found drug abuse to be on the rise among its clients. So the first thing the shelters ought to do for these clients is consider developing a special drug abuse unit.

A special program does exist for alcoholics. This is the Supported Work Program (SWP) in which about 60 clients are enrolled. SWP involves a kind of Alcoholics Anonymous group therapy which works its members up through four levels of functioning, of which the highest involves work for the shelter as clerks, janitors, and even bookkeepers. For at least some of its members SWP is enormously successful. (A few have even worked their way through it and into graduate school for social work certification.)

There is, however, an inevitable limitation to this and any other treatment program for alcoholics: It must be voluntary. Thus the alcoholic clients who do not enroll in SWP simply receive no treatment, and there is not much that can be done about them. Such incorrigible alcoholics may represent a "natural" shelter population, which it will be almost impossible to relocate no matter what policies are adopted. However, we should not conclude from this fact that such efforts are unnecessary for the shelter population in general.

Preventing Dependency

This brings us to the most difficult problem for shelter policy: what to do with the higher-functioning young men. As we have seen, such people move into the shelters because it makes sense for them to do so. What we must do is change the circumstances that make the shelters attractive to them without allowing conditions there to deteriorate significantly.

The shelters have improved tremendously in quality since the signing of the *Callahan v. Carey* consent decree. This has had the inevitable effect of making the shelters more attractive to the poor who are at the margin of moving into the shelter. But obviously the solution to this problem is not to reduce the quality of the shelters, nor is it to turn away some of the would-be clients. Another, more humane, way must be found for "deterring" higher functioning clients from using the shelters as anything but a last resort.

The most sensible way of achieving this would be to institute a work requirement for all who are capable of working. SWP clients already are put to work on a wide variety of chores, some of which involve a high degree of responsibility. While these clients are among the more capable in the shelters, experience with them indicates that clients can do a good deal of useful work around the shelters. A work requirement—to be restricted, of course, to those without disabilities that prevent them from working—would help eliminate dependency among higher-functioning clients in two ways.

First, a work requirement would change the incentive structure of the shelters. The alternatives to the shelters—menial work and the welfare system—both require one to accept considerable responsibility, and even welfare—which now requires that clients present themselves for periodic face-to-face interviews and which may impose work requirements of its own—in its own way imposes certain responsibilities. The shelters, on the other hand, give out something for nothing: Clients get plenty of services and have to give nothing in return. A work requirement would mean that clients have to give something back. Clients would no longer be able to get a better deal by switching out of the marginal economy or the welfare system and into the shelters. A work requirement would eliminate one incentive for using the shelter without lowering the quality of shelter services.

But more important than the incentive, a work requirement would change the atmosphere in the shelters—the way shelter personnel think about clients and the way clients think about themselves. If a work requirement were imposed, shelter clients would realize that the shelter system deliberately presents them with essentially the same responsibilities they would face outside the system. "Economic only" clients would realize that they were officially considered capable of ultimately functioning without the aid of the shelters. The expectation would be created that the functioning clients will eventually be able to find their way out of the shelters. And this is exactly the sort of expectation we should want to create, both in the minds of the shelter workers and in those of the clients.

It turns out that, contrary to the claims of CSS, it is not true that "the problems of the homeless run deeper than the services which mental health and social service professionals can supply." The only reason for giving way to such despair is to discredit the welfare system altogether, and to set the stage for its replacement with a new system that will no longer embody such "invidious" concepts as individual responsiblity. On the contrary, since the shelters should operate as bases from which the homeless are reintegrated into the appropriate social service programs, these very services turn out to be the answer to the problem of the homeless—in so far as one can speak of an answer. For the fact of the matter is that the homeless, like the poor, we will always have with us. The only question is how to help them without encouraging them in their pathologies and dependency. This is the central question of all welfare systems, but it is never raised by the advocacy groups except to dismiss its importance. It is time to insist on its relevance once again.

NOTES

[1]   Deirdre Carmody, "New York is Facing 'Crisis' on Vagrants," *The New York Times* (June 28, 1981): 1.

[2]   Edward I. Koch, "Homeless: One Place to Turn," *The New York Times* (February 26, 1983).

[3]   This article will deal primarily with New York's shelter system and the lodging of homeless people. In a second article I will consider the street life of the homeless.

[4]   Ellen Baxter and Kim Hopper, "Private Lives/ Public Spaces: Homeless Adults on the Streets of New York City" (New York: Community Service Society, February 1981), p. 57.

[5]   Kim Hopper and L. Stuart Cox, "Litigation in Advocacy for the Homeless: The Case of New York City" (New York: Coalition for the Homeless, May 1982), p. 8.

[6]   Quoted in Hopper and Cox, "Litigation in Advocacy for the Homeless," pp. 9-11.

[7]   Hopper and Cox, "Litigation in Advocacy for the Homeless," p. 16.

[8]   Baxter and Hopper, "Private Lives/ Public Spaces," p. vi.

⁹ Human Resources Administration of the City of New York, "Monthly Shelter Report" (November 17, 1982), Table A1.

¹⁰ Baxter and Hopper, "Private Lives/Public Spaces," p. 103.

¹¹ Human Resources Administration of the City of New York, "Providing Services for the Homeless: The New York City Program" (December 1982), pp. 9-13.

¹² Hopper and Cox, "Litigation in Advocacy for the Homeless," p. 17.

¹³ Koch, "Homeless: One Place to Turn."

¹⁴ Sarah L. Kellerman, "Is Deinstitutionalization Working for the Mentally Ill?" (New York: Department of Mental Health, Mental Retardation and Alcoholism Services, 1982), p. 9.

¹⁵ Human Resources Administration of the City of New York, "Monthly Shelter Report" (April 1983).

¹⁶ Interview, Kathryn Ruby, spokesman for the Human Resources Administration.

¹⁷ Robin Herman, "City to Make a Count of Homeless People," *The New York Times* (December 30, 1981): B1.

¹⁸ For the Keener study, Crystal and his staff developed a questionnaire that asked, "in addition to basic descriptive data (employment, education, medical and mental history, etc.) numerous questions relating to attitudes, values, and self image . . . to facilitate the differentiation of respondents into categories that realistically reflect their potentials for more independent, stable lives." Interviews were conducted with 128 men who had been at Keener two months or longer. In addition, 45 men were independently interviewed by OMH and their responses were collected from OMH interview forms and inscribed on the questionnaire.

For the "New Arrivals" study, a form of five basic questions regarding the client's recent accommodations was developed. For one month beginning January 22, 1982, clients at the Men's Shelter and East New York site who had never been serviced before were asked these questions during the regular 5 x 8 interview. A total of 687 completed interviews were analyzed, although since specific items were not necessarily completed for all respondents, there are variations in the total numbers on which the tables are based.

¹⁹ Stephen Crystal, et al., "New Arrivals: First-Time Shelter Clients" (New York: Human Resources Administration, November 1982, Revised May 1983), p. 14, Table 7.

²⁰ Vera Institute of Justice, "Apartment Hotel Project" (New York, August 1982), p. 7.

²¹ Sheila Rule, "More Men Under 21 Housed in City Shelters for Homeless," *The New York Times* (March 7, 1983): B3.

²² Kim Hopper et al., "One Year Later: The Homeless Poor in New York City 1982" (New York: Community Service Society, June 1982), pp. 45-46.

²³ Ibid., p. 51.

²⁴ Hopper et al., "One Year Later," p. 55.

²⁵ Hopper and Cox, "Litigation in Advocacy for the Homeless," p. 18.

²⁶ Human Resources Administration of the City of New York, Bureau of Management Systems, Planning, Research and Evaluation, "Deinstitutionalization and the Mentally Ill" (1982), p. 4.

8

The Politics of Displacement

Sinking into Homelessness

Marjorie Hope and James Young

HUNGER AND HOMELESSNESS are haunting the president these days. The public doesn't seem to buy the findings of his hunger task force, namely that it was unable to "substantiate allegations of rampant hunger." And on January 31 he referred to the "people who are sleeping on the grates" as "the homeless who are homeless, you might say, by choice." Yet two months later, he personally intervened to postpone the closing of a large shelter in a federally owned building in Washington—a shelter that hundreds of people seem to have chosen as preferable to the grates. It is possible, of course, that the president was uncomfortable with *his* choice, since the Community for Creative Nonviolence, which operated the emergency refuge, had planned a protest march that would have brought the issue up to the White House gates.

Homelessness has become an election-year issue. Clearly, the fact that some two million Americans are roofless represents only the tip of the iceberg; it is less a problem in itself than a symptom of deeper, ongoing problems. Although Mr. Reagan would hardly agree, it is a symptom of the bankruptcy of our militarized economic system.

Homelessness baffles the public. If official unemployment (i.e., all civilian workers) is down to 8,772,000, a "mere" 7.8 percent (a figure which excludes the involuntarily underemployed and those who have given up looking for

From *Commonweal*, June 15, 1984, pp.368-371. Reprinted by permission of *Commonweal* and Marjorie Hope and James Young.

work), why does this phenomenon persist? Why are there so many more undomiciled people in 1984 than in 1975, when the recession of the 1970s hit its worst point?

Let's compare the two years in terms of the four major causes of homelessness: unemployment, displacement from housing, deinstitutionalization of the mentally ill, and inadequacy of social benefits.

In 1975 official unemployment was higher: 8.5 percent. On the other hand, according to the Center on Budget and Policy Priorities, in that year 78 percent of the jobless enjoyed unemployment compensation; in March 1984 only 37 percent of the unemployed received it. (During the 1975 recession, unemployed workers were eligible for up to 65 weeks in benefits.) Today some 5,544,630 "officially" jobless and some 1,457,000 "discouraged" jobless, or a total of 7,001,630 Americans, are without work *and* without unemployment compensation. Never since the inception of the program have so many unemployed been left without benefits.

Back in 1975 black unemployment was 13.9 percent. Today it's 16.6. Black teenagers (whose unemployment rate is currently 46.7 percent) and blacks in their twenties are disproportionately represented among the chronically homeless. In nine years the economy has moved steadily in the direction of high technology, leaving behind those who are limited in education, work training, and job experience. The majority of the chronically homeless— however able-bodied they may be—are simply unemployable in today's economy.

Displacement from low-income housing is one of the most widespread factors in homelessness. According to the Legal Services Anti-Displacement Project, displacement afflicts some 2.5 million Americans each year; moreover, some half million lower-rent units are lost each year through conversion, abandonment, inflation, arson, and demolition.

Let us focus on one example. Condo conversion has been accelerating since 1975. Research shows that 86,000 units were converted between 1970 and 1975, and 280,000 more in the following four years. Most existing tenants cannot afford the converted units because monthly costs often double; HUD has estimated that about two-thirds of the occupants move out. Many such condos were single-room occupancy hotels (SROs), traditional havens for single persons on welfare. In New York City alone, SROs have declined from about 50,000 units in 1975 to less than 14,000 in 1982. On the Upper West Side of New York, where many of these SROs have succumbed to conversion, rents for one-bedroom apartments now bring $700 or more. Moreover, this process has been aided by tax abatements of up to 100 percent. This pattern is being repeated in all large metropolitan cities.

As homelessness was growing in the past decade, so, too, was the proportion of income that the poor pay for shelter. The 1977 *Annual Housing*

Survey reveals that in 1976 more than 5.8 million households paid over half of their incomes for shelter, including utilities. In 1980 (the latest year for which figures are available) more than 7 million households were paying over fifty percent of their incomes for shelter.

Space limitations preclude exploring the complexities of housing problems. The point is that displacement is a symptom of the overall shortage of low-income housing. The basic reason for the shortage is that housing for people with low and moderate incomes is no longer "profitable" on its own, without government subsidy. In the past decade, but especially during the first three years of the Reagan administration, the role of the federal government in the housing field has been shrinking. Even Congress's recent approval of 100,000 newly subsidized units (a victory for housing advocates over President Reagan's initial opposition) represents only a third of what it provided annually in the 1970s.

In virtually every city across the country, Americans have become alternatively repelled, mystified, and intrigued by the spectacle of men and women living in cardboard boxes, or washing their laundry in public restrooms, or getting on their knees in buses and screaming.

The mentally ill constitute about a third of the homeless population. Most have been discharged from institutions to community-based "systems." Yet according to Dr. John Talbott, president-elect of the American Psychiatric Association, fewer than 25 percent of the patients discharged from the state mental hospitals remain in any mental health program. Many are not even referred to such a program. Others are merely given a bus token and directions to a welfare office.

Despite mounting public criticism, the release movement, which began in the mid-1950s, has continued. In 1975 there were 193,721 persons in state mental hospitals; by 1982 they numbered only 125,200.

Community-based treatment and special housing facilities have not grown commensurately. In 1963 mental health professionals set 2,000 community-based centers as a national goal; only 717 have been created. In the years 1977-82 New York State spent $3.1 billion on mental hospitals and only $540 million on services in the community. The picture is similar in other states. Furthermore, growing numbers of the mentally disabled on the streets are young "chronics" who have *never* been in an institution.

For the mentally ill, sheer survival is even more important than treatment. Ten years ago thousands of them lived in SROs; now these hotels are disappearing. Three years ago many more were receiving social security disability or Supplemental Security Income (assistance for the indigent aged, blind, or disabled). During the first two years of the Reagan administration, more than 350,000 recipients—nearly a third of them psychiatrically impaired—were dropped from disability rolls. They included hallucinating ex-patients who had not worked for years, paranoid persons who had been fired from their jobs, and at least one incontinent man who wore seven pairs of pants at one time.

Under the Reagan administration, many recipients of assistance have been dropped from the rolls. Hundreds of thousands of "working poor" families receiving supplemental Aid to Families with Dependent Children (AFDC), have had their supplement (an incentive to work) cut down or cut out—despite the administration's avowed espousal of the work ethic. Supplemental Security Income has disqualified thousands of recipients. Daycare (which made it possible for poor mothers to work), Medicaid, and school feeding programs have been cut. True, overall outlays for food programs have increased, but only because of the increase in food prices and in the number applying. Over one million people have lost their eligibility for food stamps since 1981, and average food stamp benefits have been cut by 14 percent. Today the average stipend amounts to 47 cents per person per meal.

State governments were supposed to sew up any holes in the safety net. Instead, pressed by recession and cuts in federal aid, they *lowered* case welfare benefits by 17 percent betwen 1979 and 1983. In the largest state-federal public assistance program, AFDC, the average monthly stipend per person was $72.40 in 1975 (adjusted to 1967 figures, $44.89). In 1982 it was $102.80 (in 1967 values $35.67). Industry average weekly gross earnings, by comparison, rose from $190.79 in 1975 to $330.65 in 1982—nearly keeping up with inflation. Clearly, the poor have been the real victims. The National Low Income Housing Coalition points out that if we adjust for inflation, since 1980, for each dollar cut from low-income programs (housing and other programs) $4.15 has been added to the military budget and $2.26 to interest on the public debt.

Statistics are telling, but they don't tell the whole story. Bureaucrats in their office towers tend to assume that human needs are neatly segregated. Hence, if we have a food stamp program and some people are able to get along on that, then anyone who is hungry must be a poor manager, or a glutton, or a cheat. Or, in presidential confidant Edwin Meese's view, a lazylegs who finds standing in a line for food "easier than paying for it."

Real life isn't like that. Unemployment, lack of low-income housing, eroding welfare benefits, and lack of resources for the mentally disabled often converge to produce homelessness. And in real life, hunger and homelessness are two dimensions of the same problem. Let's look at a real case—in Washington, the president's own backyard.

Bill (a few details of Bill's life have been altered to conceal his identity; the figures and circumstances are nevertheless real) is twenty-five, unemployed, black, and mentally ill although he has never been hospitalized. He has an engaging smile and a playful manner; he likes to play hopscotch with imaginary companions.

For nearly a year Bill received General Public Assistance, $189 a month. To qualify for this he had to be judged temporarily disabled by District of Columbia doctors. (Doctors for the Supplemental Security Income program, which would have paid him up to $304 a month, turned him down as not sufficiently disabled.) For a run-down hotel room Bill paid $50 a week, leaving him with less than nothing to pay for all other expenses except those covered by food stamps and a medical card—i.e., clothing, transportation, non-prescription medications, tobacco, repairs, telephone calls, laundry, soap, toilet paper, and the like. How was he to survive? Bill had little choice. Sometimes he hustled; other men on the street persuaded him to be a runner in the numbers game. Sometimes he sold his food stamps—at about half their net worth. Since this left him quite hungry, he spent the last half of each month standing in line—often for one or two hours, sometimes in rain or snow—for a bowl of soup or spaghetti, dry bread, coffee, or Kool-Aid, and perhaps an apple. Some weeks he could not afford to pay the rent; then he was homeless and hungry.

Recently the D.C. doctors determined that because Bill had failed to fill out recertification papers that had come to him in the mail—papers that mystified and frightened him—he was no longer qualified as disabled. In D.C. an unemployed but "able-bodied" person is eligible for food stamps and some medical aid, but no cash assistance whatsoever. Today Bill lives on zero income—hustling when he can, eating where he can, alternating between sleeping on park benches and bedding down in barn-like public shelters. He has not taken his psychotropic medications in months, for no one is supervising them. He has lost weight, and developed a chronic cough and ulcerated legs.

As hunger and homelessness take on stronger dimensions in the election year, there is growing talk of solutions—short-term ones. The food stamp program can be expanded. City and state governments, as well as the Federal Emergency Management Administration and the Department of Housing and Urban Development, can provide more assistance for emergency shelters. Churches can make more pleas for funds, material, and volunteers.

Some advocates and workers in the field, notably those who belong to the National Coalition for the Homeless, are pushing for a three-tiered approach: basic emergency shelter; transitional accommodations where clients would receive intensive help in obtaining social and health services; and permanent housing (which can include, for the chronically mentally disabled, supportive residences where services are built into structures of everyday life).

In all three tiers of housing, religious groups have had the most humane—

and most economical—approach. As one worker put it: "The church brings a compassionate, caring dimension that you don't find in big bureaucratic city-run shelters." The churches have also pioneered with new efforts. For example Saint Francis Residence in New York offers its mentally disabled residents a variety of social services, comparative privacy, and opportunities to work out long-range individualized plans. Yet even Saint Francis cannot exist without considerable government support.

Almost no politicians are talking about preventive measures. Yet the homeless promise to be a long-term problem.

While those of the "new poor" whose jobs have not disappeared forever may be reabsorbed into the economy, the chronically homeless form a new class, or underclass. They are here to stay, unless Americans change their basic social philosophy from making it up by their bootstraps to one based on fair shares.

We should hardly be surprised by the number who have been sinking into homelessness during the last decade. It was predictable. In the past five years growing numbers of critics have pointed out that decarcerating mental patients into an uncoordinated, ill-funded community-based "system" was not working. For years we have talked anxiously about technological unemployment, yet never has government provided meaningful training or jobs programs, as many European nations have done. As for housing, clearly only the federal government can finance low-income housing on the scale needed. Yet the National Low Income Housing Coalition points out that only 19 percent of the renter households with incomes below $3,000 lived in subsidized units in 1980. Less than one American household in sixteen is living in such units. This is the lowest proportion among the so-called civilized countries.

Although most European countries have been struggling with high inflation and high unemployment, they do provide social supports. For example, in 1982 unemployment reached nearly 14 percent in Britain, yet few families were known to have been turned out of their homes or to have had to sell their possessions. (The government owns 60 percent of the rental housing stock, which makes eviction more unlikely, and also assures a more manageable waiting list.) In the same year, jobless Americans who did receive compensation got only an average of 63 percent of previous earnings; in West European countries the average was 85 percent. Family allowances have never been adopted here. The United States has the distinction of being the only industrialized country in the world without such allowances; sixty-one others, including many that are poor, find this an effective way to help keep families together and off welfare rolls. Because all European countries have some form of national health care, unemployed persons have not had to choose between food, shelter, and medical treatment, as thousands have had to do here. Moreover, deinstitutionalization has been carried at a slower, more controlled pace. It is no coincidence that in European countries, where real safety nets persist even in hard times, homelessness is a comparatively rare phenomenon.

Emergency shelters and breadlines are not the answer to homelessness in the richest and most powerful country in the world. We do have three major choices. We can decide that the homeless are redundant, non-productive casualities of today's society, and simply write them off or hope against hope that somehow the overburdened churches will fill the gap. We can, if we consider them to be nonproductive, provide supportive services and some sort of guaranteed annual income. Or, if we still believe in liberty and justice for all, government, churches, and individuals can make concerted efforts to *prevent* homelessness.

9

The Emergence of the
Homeless as a Public Problem

Mark J. Stern

URING THE PAST CENTURY the primary goal of social welfare has been to provide for the needs of individuals within our society. The provision of the most basic needs, such as food, shelter, and warmth, has been seen as the minimum goal of the welfare state. We are shocked when we realize our failure to provide these needs. Indeed, a popular slogan of the early 1980s, concerned with the forced choice between "heating and eating," gained notoriety precisely because it exemplified the failure to provide two things that we believe all persons should have.

Although our failures to provide warmth and food have been much in the news in the past few years, a third basic need—shelter—has received the most public attention. During the early 1980s, homelessness emerged as a significant public problem. It attracted a great amount of news coverage and became the target of public and private efforts at the national, state, and local levels. Yet, much confusion exists about the nature of the problem, who the homeless are, and what can be done about them.

In this article, I wish to address these questions from an unusual perspective. Rather than getting to the "facts" about the homeless, I want to ask how the homeless have been conceptualized in the public's mind and what this tells us, not about the homeless, but about ourselves, our officials, and our society. Thus, rather than holding the homeless under the microscope of public and professional enquiry, I want to use the homeless as a means of looking at ourselves.

First, I will examine the past two years to see how the homeless have

From *Social Services Review*, Vol. 58, June 1984, pp. 291-301. Reprinted by permission of the University of Chicago Press and Mark J. Stern.

become a public problem at the national level, and as a local issue in the city of Philadelphia. Second, I will place the homeless in a historical perspective and speculate about the historical significance of the emergence of this issue. Here I will make the case that the homeless as a public problem reflect the conservative drift in public policy symbolized most graphically by the Reagan administration's attack on the poor.

The Anatomy of a Public Problem

The starting point for my examination of the homeless is Herbert Blumer's seminal essay, "Social Problems as Collective Behavior."[1] Blumer's essential point is that "social problems are fundamentally products of a process of collective definition instead of existing independently as a set of objective social arrangements with an intrinsic makeup."[2] Thus, rather than using the common geological metaphor of social problems—their "discovery" or "uncovering"—it is more appropriate to use a construction metaphor: How do we build social problems? As much as any other element of reality, public problems are socially constructed.[3]

This insight has a number of important implications. First, it suggests that public problems are selective; not all phenomena become public problems. (For example, although by objective measures poverty was more extensive in the 1940s and 1950s, it was not until the 1960s that we "discovered" poverty.)[4] Second, once we agree that a social problem exists, there is competition over what the nature of the problem is. For example, Joseph Gusfield notes in the *Culture of Public Problems* that for most of the postwar period the issue of automobile casualities was seen as a problem of individual competence.[5] Then, in the late 1960s, thanks to the efforts of Ralph Nader and his supporters, a competing definition emerged that stressed problems of automobile design and manufacture as the source of the problem.[6]

Blumer specifies five steps that comprise the career of a social problem: its emergence (through agitation, violence, interest groups, or political attention); its legitimization (when the explanation of the problem is agreed upon); the mobilization of forces to attack the problem; the development of an official "solution"; and the implementation of the plan. Of these steps, perhaps the most interesting is the legitimization stage, for it is there that the issue of who "owns" a problem is decided. Only when a paradigm of the cause of the problem emerges can we be sure who has a right to "know" about the problem. Again using the automobile example during the 1950s, psychologists and doctors were the experts who explained the origins of the "drunk driver." In the post-Nader era, however, the ownership of the problem passed to reporters and other investigators of the unsafe automobile.

A final point: at any time in its career a social problem can be sidetracked from its course. When this happens, it recedes from public notice and becomes part of the accepted order of things. Here again, the example of the War on Poverty comes to mind.

The Homeless as a Public Problem

Emergence

The homeless slowly emerged as a public problem between 1980 and 1982. A combination of activism, publicity, self-interest and timing account for the power with which homelessness burst upon the public consciousness.

The initial factor in the emergence of the homeless as a public problem appears to have been the legal action undertaken by attorney Robert Hayes on behalf of vagrants in the Bowery section of New York City. As early as 1979, the city had agreed to provide more beds for the homeless on Ward's Island.[7] However, it was only the consent decree in the Callahan case signed by the city and the state in August 1981 that brought the issue forcefully to the public consciousness.[8] The decree committed the city to provide clean and safe shelter for every homeless man and woman who sought it and set standards against overcrowding in the shelters.

At the national level, this legal action was supported by direct political action. During the Democratic Convention in 1980, a coalition formed by the Community Services Society of New York, Catholic Workers, and other groups held a vigil at St. Francis of Assisi Church near Madison Square Garden in New York City. This demonstration was followed the next year by a veritable publicity blitz as first Ann Marie Rousseau's *Shopping Bag Ladies* and then Ellen Baxter's and Kim Hopper's *Private Lives, Public Spaces* were released.[9] The Baxter and Hopper study, a combination of ethnographic observation and advocacy research, was widely publicized and served to focus public attention on the issue.

In Philadelphia, local businessmen aided in pushing the homeless forward as a public problem. In November 1981, the *Inquirer* reported that businessmen in the area of the city most frequented by homeless men were complaining that the men on the street were hurting business. They demanded that the city take action to relieve the problem.[10] At the same time, other cities, including Washington, D.C., began to pay attention to the problem.

The culminating event in the emergence of the homeless as a public problem, however, was the severe winter of 1981-82. As the newspaper filled with grim stories of the homeless freezing to death, they gained a kind of "newsworthiness" that made them accessible to the television audience.[11]

Legitimization and Mobilization

The legitimization of the homeless is an example of the contestable character of public problems. As I have noted, the goal of legitimization is to forge a paradigm to explain the nature of a problem and to suggest its solution. The resolution of this issue determines who "owns" it. Thus, when there are competing groups interested in "owning" an issue, as has been the case with the homeless, there are competing paradigms to explain and legitimize it as a public problem.

The most successful attempts to legitimize the homeless as an issue point to the deinstitutionalization of mental patients during the 1970s.[12] According to this theory, most of the homeless are severely disturbed individuals who in earlier decades would have been safely warehoused in state facilities. However, because of deinstitutionalization they have been dumped on the street, where they maintain a marginal existence.

As with the emergence of the homeless as a problem, this proposed paradigm had its roots in self-interest, resulting from the overlapping responsibilities of various levels of government. As early as 1980, for example, New York City Mayor Edward Koch was resisting state pressure to open more shelters, while in turn the governor of New York reacted angrily to city officials' attempts to link the homeless to the state's release of psychiatric patients.[13]

The source of this controversy was not simply disinterested social research, but the division of responsibility between the state and city. If the homelesss were considered a welfare problem, the city had ultimate responsibility. If they were considered a mental health problem, the state needed to act. The deinstitutionalization theory was again voiced repeatedly by the Koch administration, leading to the mayor's call for legislation to allow the city to involuntarily commit the homeless.[14] The Callahan case rendered the issue moot by holding both the city and state responsible for providing shelter.

In Philadelphia, a similar use of the deinstitutionalization issue took place. During the winter of 1982, the city's Department of Public Welfare attempted to draw a distinction between the "homeless" and "street people." Department officials claimed that street people were deinstitutionalized mental patients and should be the responsibility of the health department, while the homeless were their responsibility.[15]

Interestingly, the recession in the winter of 1982-83 changed the paradigm of legislation. More and more news reports and "experts" linked the homeless explicitly to unemployment and foreclosures.[16] Thus, as the economic situation of the "normal" population declined, the homeless were portrayed as more normal.

The official plans ultimately agreed upon to fight the problem exemplified the conservatism that characterized the homeless as a public problem. Rather than entering into a complex analysis of the multiple causes of homelessness—housing shortages, gentrification, unemployment, mental problems, and other social and individual problems—almost all agreed on the most simple answer to the problem: providing food and shelter. New York City, under its commitments in the Callahan decision, led the way, and other localities followed.

The official plan had a number of important features. First, there was a central reliance on traditional voluntary agencies like the Salvation Army and church groups. The new shelter that opened in New York City in 1980 was under the authority of the Volunteers of America, and Mayor Koch was constantly calling on or berating the city's religious institutions to do their share. In addition, the efforts of the city were restricted to the provision of food and shelter. In the emergency of 1982, for example, the city of Philadelphia paid Giffre Hospital $22 per day to shelter those homeless who could not be housed in existing voluntary shelters. By that summer, the city council had passed a bill to provide annually for shelters.[17]

Although in 1983 the activist groups that had originally drawn attention to the homeless were still calling for more sweeping actions to get at the root of the problem, the evidence seemed to suggest that from a social perspective, the problem had been solved. Although the number of homeless had not diminished, they had become part of the accepted order of things. Much like the poor of the eighteenth and nineteenth centuries, the homeless (outcasts, psychotics, and physically impaired) would be with us for the foreseeable future. The only solution was palliative: keep them from freezing or starving and keep them out of fashionable areas where they might provide discomfort for those who were better off. As former Haverford College President John Coleman noted while he was "underground," "Watching people come and go at the Volvo tennis tournament at Madison Square Garden, I sensed how uncomfortable they were at the presence of the homeless. Easy to love in the abstract, not so easy to [love] face to face."[18]

A Public Problem for the Age of Reagan

The emergence of the homeless as a public problem is relatively easy to document. A far more difficult question is why the homeless struck such a responsive chord in our culture in the early 1980s. Although there was some evidence that the problem was getting worse, the increase in attention was totally out of proportion with the increase in the phenomenon. I propose that the emergence of the homeless was an element of the conservative reaction that brought Ronald Reagan to the presidency and, in Pennsylvania, led to

Governor Thornburgh's proposals for the cutoff of welfare to "able-bodied" recipients.

The conservative nature of welfare policy in the 1980s has been widely commented on elsewhere.[19] In its first two years, the Reagan administration took steps to reduce the federal government's role in most of the major welfare programs, including Aid to Families with Dependent Children, Food Stamps, federal housing and education programs, and legal services. At the state level, in Pennsylvania, these reductions were echoed in the governor's proposals to eliminate adult men from the state's general assistance program.

These developments had a complex impact on our society. On the one hand, they represent a return to a "traditional" American approach to poverty. Yet, at the same time, they go against fifty years of government action flowing out of the New Deal. Thus, they present those in control with a delicate issue of legitimization. The response to the homeless emerged as an issue that suited the situation by allowing the better off in society to affirm their continued belief in the New Deal tradition, while reimposing an older vision of the relationship of the poor to the nonpoor.

What is the basis for such a proposal? It rests on a historical perspective of the relationship between the well-off and the poor in America, and the changes that that relationship underwent in the postwar period. Traditionally, the relationship of charity was meant to underline the social position of both parties. The giver was able to conform his benevolence and the legitimacy of his position, while the poor were expected to understand their inferiority, the stigma attached to their position, and the docility and appreciation they should feel toward the giver. As Gareth Stedman Jones has noted in his under-read *Outcast London*, "In all known traditional societies, the gift has played a central status-maintaining function."[20]

Stedman Jones, following Marcel Mauss, associated the gift relationship with three conditions.[21] The gift implies the idea of sacrifice; it is a symbol of prestige; and it serves as a method of social control. In Jones's words, "To give, from whatever motives, generally imposes an obligation upon the receiver. In order to receive one must behave in an acceptable manner, if only by expressing gratitude and humiliation."[22]

Jones goes on to note that these three conditions imply that the gift entails a personal relationship. "If it is depersonalized, the gift loses its defining features: the elements of voluntary sacrifice, prestige, subordination, and obligation."[23] He claims that much of the motivation of the British Charity Organization Society in the 1860s and 1870s was to reestablish this set of relationships that urbanization had "deformed."

The United States, too, has traditionally used charity as a means of reinforcing the virtue of the rich and the immorality of the poor. As Michael Katz has recently noted, part of the "identifiable style" of welfare policy and practice in America is the "individual and degraded image of the poor."[24] Indeed, the often-used distinction between the worthy and unworthy poor has had much to do with issues of deference to authority. The worthy poor— widows, children, the insane, and disabled—were expected to be grateful for the beneficence of the welfare ladies, while the unworthy—the shiftless vagrants and other able-bodied recipients—were sly, ungrateful, and mendacious.

These images of the poor and the rich held up through the Great Depression. Indeed, the reports on the psychological impact of unemployment by Kamarovsky and Bakke suggest that self-blame, not anger, was a typical response to the great social crisis of the 1930s.[25] Yet, the dynamics of the Great Depression did set off forces that led to change.

The spread of welfare in the 1940s and 1950s and the spark of "community action" of the War on Poverty set off a new posture toward welfare that was symbolized by the welfare rights movement. Rather than seeing welfare as a gift, the National Welfare Rights Organization and like-minded groups attempted to cast it as right or entitlement, the product of structural, not individual, breakdown.

More important than the NWRO itself during the 1970s was a perceptible change in the stance of welfare recipients. The use of food stamps was no longer a stigma. A new, assertive attitude began to characterize the actions of welfare recipients. As James Patterson noted, "Despite the hostility of the middle classes to increases in welfare, poor Americans refused at last to be cowed from applying for aid. Despite the continuing stigma attached to living on welfare, they stood firm in their determination to stay on the rolls as long as they were in need. . . . Compared to the past, when poor people—harassed and stigmatized by public authorities—were slow to claim their rights, this was a fundamental change."[26]

This change in the attitudes of the poor had an immense impact on the beliefs of nonrecipients. Among conservatives, there was little need for change, since they had been preaching the moral inferiority of welfare bums for decades. Among liberals, however, a great discomfort set in.

Although liberals, like members of the welfare rights movement, had been preaching the structural origins of welfare, when the poor actually came to believe them, they were not happy with the results. First, the failure of the programs of the 1960s and 1970s to reduce poverty made it more difficult than ever to expose its "roots." The web of causality seemed too dense to penetrate. Furthermore, overlaid with issues of race, the new attitude of welfare recipients did not include gratitude or deference to their liberal "friends." In short, by the end of the welfare revolution of the 1970s, liberals no longer felt appreciated, the poor were no longer deferential, and the gift relationship, with its affirmation of the virtue of the rich, had broken down.

The way in which the issue of the homeless came to public consciousness in the early 1980s broke with this pattern in three decisive ways. First, it reestablished a direct relationship between the giver and receiver. Second, it was based on exacting "proper" behavior from the recipient. And finally, it simplified the web of causal attribution and strategy formulation that had so frustrated liberals during the 1970s.

The outstanding feature of the official plan to fight homelessness was its reestablishment of the bond between giver and recipient. Although the activists, like the Coalition for the Homeless, promoted the "entitlement" of the homeless to shelter and worked for government action to achieve this, the vast majority of action was directed at voluntarism and individual responsibility. Always in the forefront of the movement to evade governmental responsibility, Mayor Koch called for New York City's 3,500 houses of worship to take in ten homeless people each, and then berated synagogues for not doing their part.[27] Indeed, one notable feature of the homeless problem was the extent to which churches, lay organizations, and individuals did respond to the need by carrying out food drives, setting up shelters, and providing aid.

One of the reasons for this response was the comportment of the recipient. Although much attention was paid to their negative physical characteristics (bad smell, ulcerated sores), this was contrasted with their almost saintlike spirits. Docility and gratitude, not anger and suspicion, were the general images of the homeless. Thus, even for those who did not consciously advocate it, the reestablishment of a "proper" gift relationship was one element of the popularity of the homeless.

Finally, the homeless cut through the tangled web of causality that was typical of poverty policy in the 1970s. Although advocates attempted to draw continuities between the homeless and the explanations of poverty in the 1970s, the massive response of the public simplified the situation. For example, in my experience, a discussion of whether a shelter was a degrading form of aid for the homeless could be cut off with the claim, "People are hungry and cold. That's all there is to it." Although true enough, the homeless may have actually functioned to reduce the willingness of Americans to explore the complexities of need in the 1980s.

After two decades of guilt and worry, the framing of the homeless issue served to reestablish the gift relationship of a bygone era. Indeed, a particular irony emerged as the old "worthy" and "unworthy" distinction took on a new meaning. As I have noted, in the nineteenth century, the symbol of the worthy poor was the single mother (assumed to be widowed), and that of the unworthy poor was the vagrant and tramp. By the 1970s, the images had been reversed. It was the single mother (assumed not to be married), like those who came to Washington to denounce President Nixon's Family Assistance Plan

("You can't force me to work. . . . You better give me something better than I'm getting on welfare"), who came to symbolize the unworthy,[28] while the docile and appreciative homeless, like Bernice Martin, who asked Mayor Koch, "Can I go to the one [shelter] on Lafayette Street?" became the image of the worthy poor.[29]

The implications of this reversal are important. The distinction between worthiness and unworthiness is often seen as locked in demographic characteristics, while others have argued that it has fluctuated with the needs of the labor market. The experience of the homeless, however, suggests that a key element is comportment. Those poor who are willing to be polite and quiet, grateful and guilty, have a much better chance to be seen favorably than those who are assertive and loud, nondeferential and unbowed. The gift relationship, with all of its complexity, still haunts our welfare system. The American style of welfare remains.[30]

The development of the homeless as a public problem poses a severe dilemma for advocacy groups, such as the Coalition for the Homeless, that have been instrumental in drawing attention to the issue. Although the public prominence the problem has been given will undoubtedly provide more alternatives for those who wish to avail themselves of the services, the way the issue has been cast will frustrate the longer-term goal of activists: to use the homeless as an example of the general inequities of the American social welfare system.

In a sense they share an old radical dilemma. As long as radical activists clearly enunciated their position, they remained isolated from the mainstream of American politics. Only in those times when their concerns converged with those of a wider political sphere—the Socialist party's antiwar stand in 1917, the Unemployment Council in the early 1930s—have radicals broken out of this isolation. In the end, they have either had to face repression or surrender their issues to those who had different goals in mind.[31] One hopes that advocates for the homeless will not face this choice; however, events of the past two years do not provide much ground for optimism.

NOTES

This paper was an outgrowth of a student project that I directed at the University of Pennsylvania School of Social Work. I would like to thank my coadvisor on the project, Dr. June Axinn, and the students involved, Cynthia Armstrong, Ruth Bronzan, Catherine Clark, Anne Gibbons, Richard Koch, Sally Stephens, and Sister Joanne Williams. I would also like to thank the Lazarus-Goldman Center for the Study of Social Work Practice and its director, Dr. Joseph Soffen, for providing research assistance. Michael Katz and Susan Davis provided comments on an earlier draft.

[1]   Herbert Blumer, "Social Problems as Collective Behavior," *Social Problems* 18, no. 3 (Winter 1971): 298-306.

[2]   Ibid., p. 298.

[3]   Peter L. Berger and Thomas Luckman, *The Social Construction of Reality: A Treatise in the Sociology of Knowledge* (Garden City, N.Y.: Doubleday & Co., 1967).

[4]   On poverty in the immediate postwar period, see James T. Patterson, *America's Struggle Against Poverty 1900-1980* (Cambridge, Mass.: Harvard University Press, 1981), pp. 78-81.

[5]   Joseph R. Gusfield, *The Culture of Public Problems: Drinking, Driving, and the Symbolic Order* (Chicago and London: University of Chicago Press, 1981).

[6]   This leads to an important aside: the limited role of social science in the process of problem definition. For example, in spite of its prevalence during the 1950s, poverty was practically ignored by social researchers during that decade. Only after popular writers such as Michael Harrington and Dwight McDonald focused public attention on it did professional social researchers begin to "discover" poverty (Patterson, p. 99).

[7]   *The New York Times* (January 4, 1980).

[8]   *The New York Times* (August 27, 1981); Kim Hopper et al., *One Year Later: The Homeless Poor in New York City, 1982* (New York: Community Service Society, 1982), pp. 20-23.

[9]   *The New York Times* (February 15, 1981), (March 21, 1981); A.M. Rousseau, *Shopping Bag Ladies: Homeless Women Speak About Their Lives* (New York: Pilgrim Press, 1981); Ellen Baxter and Kim Hopper, *Private Lives/Public Spaces: Homeless Adults on the Streets of New York City* (New York: Community Service Society, 1981).

[10]   *Philadelphia Inquirer* (November 11, 1981).

[11]   *The New York Times* (January 27, 1982).

[12]   *The New York Times* (November 24, 1983).

[13]   *The New York Times* (December 30, 1980).

[14]   *The New York Times* (March 28, 1981), (March 25, 1983).

[15]   Cynthia Armstrong et al., "Homeless Adults: A Participant Observation Study" (M.S.W. project, University of Pennsylvania, 1982), pp. 65-66.

[16]   *The New York Times* (December 15, 1982).

[17]   Armstrong et al., p. 65.

[18]   John R. Coleman, "Diary of a Homeless Man," *New York* (February 21, 1983), p. 30.

[19]   See, e.g., Alan Gartner, Colin Greer, and Frank Riessman, eds., *What Reagan Is Doing to Us* (New York: Harper & Row, 1982).

[20]   Gareth Stedman Jones, *Outcast London* (London: Oxford University Press, 1971), p. 251.

[21]   Marcel Mauss, *The Gift: Forms and Functions of Exchange in Archaic Societies* (New York: W.W. Norton & Co., 1967).

[22]   Ibid., p. 253.

[23]   Ibid.

[24]   Michael B. Katz, *Poverty and Policy in American History* (New York: Academic Press, 1983), pp. 239-40.

[25]   Frances Fox Piven and Richard Cloward, *Poor People's Movements: Why They Succeed and How They Fail* (New York: Pantheon Books, 1977).

[26]   Patterson, p. 179.

[27] *The New York Times* (December 11, 1981), (January 20, 1983).

[28] Patterson, p. 195.

[29] *The New York Times* (March 25, 1983).

[30] See Katz, chap. 1, for a discussion of the charity organization movement's view of comportment.

[31] Hopper et al., pp. 51-55; Aileen S. Kraditor ("American Radical Historians on Their Heritage," *Past and Present*, no. 56 [August 1972], pp. 136-53) presents a provocative theory of the role of radicals in the American political system.

III

The Importance of
Numbers

10

The Extent of Homelessness in America

A Report to the Secretary on the Homeless and Emergency Shelters

U.S. Department of Housing and Urban Development

HOW PREVALENT is homelessness in America? To date, answers to this question have been based on a number of local studies and reports and on some not-so-very-well-documented guesses about the number of persons who are homeless nationally. The extent of homelessness throughout the nation has not, however, been studied systematically, nor has the question of whether homeless people are concentrated in certain parts of the nation or in certain types of cities. Clearly, such information is basic to an understanding of the scope and nature of the homeless problem in the United States.

Defining "Homelessness"

In order to assess the extent of homelessness, it is necessary to clarify how the term is defined in this report. "Homelessness" refers to people in the "streets" who, in seeking shelter, have no alternative but to obtain it from a private or public agency.

Homeless people are distinguished from those who have permanent shelter even though that shelter may be physically inadequate. They are also distin-

From *A Report to the Secretary on the Homeless and Emergency Shelters*, U.S. Department of Housing and Urban Development, Office of Policy Development and Research, Washington, D.C., 1984.

guished from those living in overcrowded conditions, often described as "doubled-up" (referring to people who have lost their homes or apartments and are forced to live with friends or relatives). While overcrowding is generally unsatisfactory, people in this situation are not homeless. On the other hand, because of the tensions arising from such living arrangements, some of them may be "evicted" into the street or their cars. Unless or until this happens, these people do have a roof over their heads and are not homeless.

For pupposes of this study, then, a person is counted as homeless if his/her nighttime residence is:

(a) in public or private emergency shelters which take a variety of forms— armories, schools, church basements, government buildings, former fire-houses and, where temporary vouchers are provided by private or public agencies, even hotels, apartments, or boarding homes; or

(b) in the streets, parks, subways, bus terminals, railroad stations, airports, under bridges or aqueducts, abandoned buildings without utilities, cars, trucks, or any other public or private space that is not designed for shelter.

Residents of halfway houses, congregate living facilities, and long-term detoxification centers are not classified as homeless because of the longer-term nature of such facilities. Furthermore, upon discharge, many residents of such facilities will probably not end up on the streets. However, persons who are temporarily in jails or hospitals, but whose usual nighttime residence is (a) or (b) above, are considered homeless.

While some people are chronically homeless by the above definition, others are homeless on a temporary or episodic basis for a variety of reasons. For example, an elderly person living in a single-room occupancy (SRO) hotel whose sole income is SSI payments may deplete his/her resources by the third week of the month and live in a shelter until the next check comes, at which time he/she can return to the hotel. Or, as noted earlier, a 20-year-old single male living at home, or with friends, may move to the streets or shelters occasionally as conditions within the home worsen. Or, an unemployed family may live temporarily in their car until employment is found.

A count of the homeless on a single night, therefore, will be less than the number of people who are homeless for any period of time throughout, say, one year. While this may seem an obvious point, some confusion has arisen over the meaning of certain published figures on the size of the homeless population, with "annual totals" used to represent the number of homeless on a particular night. Also, shelter operators generally maintain statistics on the total number of persons served during a year, and such figures have been used to estimate the total number of homeless persons. The figures do indicate (to the extent that those using the shelters constitute all the homeless) how many people were homeless at one time or another throughout a year, but they do not indicate the total number homeless at any one point in time throughout that year. While both figures are of interest, the latter is more crucial in understanding the size of the problem and the shelter needs of the homeless.[1]

How Many Homeless Persons Are There?

No one has done a thorough census of the homeless population in the United States. In the absence of one, some observers have claimed that the national total is as high as two or three million persons, and this estimate has achieved fairly wide circulation. Lower estimates, such as 250,000 to 500,000, have also been given, but the two million figure has been cited more frequently by the media, by witnesses at Congressional hearings, and by various organizations.[2] This estimate originated in testimony prepared by the Washington D.C.-based Community for Creative Non-Violence (CCNV) for the House Committee on the District of Columbia on July 31, 1980. In a subsequent published version of their 1980 testimony, the authors indicated that

(at) that time [1980], we concluded that approximately 1 percent of the population, or 2.2 million people, lacked shelter. We arrived at that conclusion on the basis of information received from more than 100 agencies and organizations in 25 cities and states. We have learned nothing that would cause us to lower our original estimate. In fact, we would increase it, since we are convinced that the number of homeless people in the United States could reach 3 million or more during 1983.[3]

However, while the testimony by CCNV contains information on the homeless situation in several localities, nowhere does the CCNV report to Congress on homelessness actually give a figure of one percent or 2.2 million. What is actually said is "How many people in the District of Columbia are homeless? Thousands. How many nationally? Millions. Of that we are certain. Precisely how many? Who knows?"[4]

There is a clear need for more systematic evidence to help in assessing existing estimates. In order to evaluate their validity, four approaches which rely on a variety of information sources and procedures are presented. The use of more than one approach to arrive at a national estimate helps to ensure the reliability of the results, given the difficulty of assessing the size of a population as fluid and often hidden as the homeless. While each approach, in and of itself, has strengths and weaknesses, when combined they tap many different information sources and extrapolation procedures. The approaches include: (1) published local estimates; (2) interviews with local observers in a national sample of 60 metropolitan areas; (3) interviews with a national sample of shelter managers; and (4) a combination of shelter and street counts.

The first procedure uses the highest local estimates available but makes no assessment of their reliability, in order to see whether extrapolating them to the Nation would produce a figure close to the highest existing national estimate. A second approach involves systematically collecting estimates, and assessing their quality, from a range of informants in a national random sample of metropolitan areas. A third approach is a variant of the second; estimates are gathered from one "front-line" group, the managers of shelters for the homeless. A fourth method differs from the first three in that it is based on actual counts of those in shelters or on the streets. The shelter population is based on a nationally representative probability sample of shelters; the street count was done by the U.S. Bureau of the Census, as part of the 1980 decennial census, in a non-random sample of cities.

1.   Published Homeless Estimates in Various Localities

One way of estimating the number of homeless nationwide is to take the highest published available local estimates, however derived, at face value and to extrapolate from them (see Exhibit 10-1). Since many of the localities for which estimates are presented are places where the problem of homelessness is likely to be more severe, a straight extrapolation from them is likely to be on the high side. This procedure assumes a constant rate of homelessness in all areas of the country, whether it be New York City or a rural county in Wyoming. Evidence will be presented later, however, to show that homelessness in small towns and rural areas is not as high as in metropolitan areas. Furthermore, this procedure is premised on the highest estimate being correct for each place shown.

The estimates presented in Exhibit 10-1 reflect the situation prior to the current winter. The earliest estimate used was published in November 1981, but most were published in 1982 and in 1983. The largest single source of this information is the *Report to the National Governors' Association Task Force on the Homeless*, but others include newspaper articles, studies, Congressional hearings and task force reports. Estimates which include only one category of the homeless, such as those in certain types of shelters or those served by particular city agencies, are excluded since these figures underestimate the total number of homeless persons in a metropolitan area. Also excluded are cumulative yearly totals of those who might have used shelters at any point in time throughout a year since these figures over-estimate the number of homeless on a given night. The number presented refer to the total number of homeless persons at a particular point in time. When more than one estimate exists for a locality, the highest and lowest figures are given in the table.

In calculating the rate of homelessness, the *highest* local homeless figures are taken from 37 localities in which they are available and summed over the total metropolitan population in those areas.[5] The metropolitan population is used since there is consensus among observers that there are few homeless persons in suburban areas. Homeless persons tend to be drawn to central city areas.[6] Most shelters and other facilities, such as soup kitchens and welfare agencies, are concentrated in the central city rather than the suburbs, and suburban ecology provides few sleeping places for those outside the shelters.[7] Most abandoned buildings, heating grates, bus and train terminals, etc., are located downtown.

If one uses the highest local estimates unquestioningly, the overall homeless rate is .25 percent, or 25 persons per 10,000 population. A straight extrapolation of this rate to the entire Nation produces a figure of 586,000 homeless. Because of the way this figure was arrived at, it is likely to be an outside estimate.

2. Interviews with Local Experts in a National Sample of Metropolitan Communities

A second approach to estimating the number of homeless people nationwide uses estimates by local observers, but attempts to resolve some of the problems inherent in the first approach. First, a valid national sample of 60 metropolitan areas was selected so that the estimated national total is not based only on those places where the homeless problem is severe or where published information exists. Second, over 500 telephone interviews were conducted in these areas. Third, instead of simply accepting the highest local figure provided during these interviews, the reliability of each of several local estimates was examined. Fourth, a more standardized information collection procedure was employed, using the same definition of homelessness from city to city and the same time period—the winter of 1984 (December 1983 or January 1984) as its basis.

The number of different estimates obtained for each area was as follows: three to five for smaller metropolitan areas; four to seven for medium-sized metropolitan areas; and eight to twelve for large metropolitan areas.[8] For large metropolitan areas estimates were obtained separately for both the central city and surrounding jurisdictions (usually counties).

Exhibit 10-1

Published Estimates of the Number of Homeless Persons
in 37 Localities

Place	Number of Homeless	Sources
Atlanta	1,500- 3,500	a, b, c
Baltimore	8,000-15,000	*Baltimore Sun* 9/24/82, *Atlantic* 10/83
Birmingham	291	*Birmingham News* 11/24/83
Boston	2,000- 8,000	a, b
Brockton	250	e
Buffalo	500	d
Chicago	12,000-25,000	a, c, *The New York Times* 6/3/83
Cleveland	400- 1,000	a, c
Denver	1,500- 5,000	b, c, *Denver Post* 3/6/83, *USNWR* 1/17/83
Detroit	2,000- 8,000	a, b, *New York Times* 6/3/83
Elizabeth	300	*Star Ledger* 4/22/83
Fresno	600	f
Jacksonville	150- 300	a
Los Angeles	22,000-30,000	b, *Los Angeles Times* 12/26/82, *USNWR* 1/17/83
Miami	4,000	*Miami News* 2/12/83
Minneapolis	900	*Minneapolis Tribune* 11/29/81
New York	36,000-50,000	b, *Atlantic* 10/83
New Orleans	700	a
Norfolk	100- 300	f
Orlando	400	f
Philadelphia	8,000	*Philadelphia Inquirer* 12/12/81
Phoenix	500- 6,200	a, b, c, *Newsweek* 1/2/84
Pittsburgh	1,500	*Pittsburgh Post Gazette* 1/2/82
Pittsfield	50	e
Portland	1,000- 2,000	a
Richmond	2,000- 4,000	a
Rochester	400- 500	*Rochester Times-Union* 3/11/82
Salt Lake City	600- 1,000	a, c
San Francisco	4,000-10,000	a, b, c
San Jose	1,000	a
Seattle	500- 5,000	a, b, f, *USA Today* 2/18/83
Springfield	570- 780	c, e
Syracuse	450	d
Tucson	3,000	*Los Angeles Times* 12/26/82
Tulsa	1,300	a
Washington D.C.	5,000-10,000	*Washington Post* 9/11/83
Worcester	2,500	e

Exhibit 10-1 (continued)

Notes:

a. Cuomo, Mario, *1933-1983, Never Again, A Report to the National Governor's Association Task Force on the Homeless* (July 1983).
b. *Editorial Research Report* (October 24, 1982).
c. *Homelessness in America,* Hearing before the Subcommittee on Housing and Community Development of the Committee on Banking, Finance and Urban Affairs, House of Representatives, 97th Congress, December 15, 1982 (Washington, D.C.: U.S. Government Printing Office, 1983).
d. Governor's Task Force on the Homeless, Albany, New York.
e. "Profile of the Homeless in Massachusetts," Governor's Office (April 28, 1983).
f. Jacksonville Community Council, *Downtown Derelicts Study* (May 1982).

A single metropolitan estimate was computed by assessing the information underlying each estimate and calculating an average which took into account the reliability of each estimate received. Estimates derived from "street counts" and "shelter bed statistics" received more weight than estimates dependent on "impressions of the street population." The overall expertise of the interviewee was also evaluated in terms of his/her involvement with the issue and level of knowledge about the homeless. Where estimates were considered totally unreliable, or "pure guesses," they were excluded from the analysis.

Exhibit 10-2 shows both the lowest and highest estimates, and the most reliable range of estimates for each of the 60 metropolitan areas in the sample. These data are the basis for calculating a national estimate of the homeless in all metropolitan areas, a figure of 210,000. To estimate the number of homeless persons in non-metropolitan areas, it was assumed that the rate of homelessness in smaller towns and rural areas was equal to that for the small metropolitan areas. Multiplying the population outside the metropolitan areas by this rate produces an estimate of 44,000 homeless.[9] Combining this figure with the 210,000 in metropolitan areas produces an estimate of 254,000 nationwide.

3. National Figure Based on Extrapolation of Estimates Provided by Shelter Operators

Since shelter providers have the most immediate and direct contact with homeless individuals, they were asked as part of a larger survey to estimate the

Exhibit 10-2

Local Estimates of Homeless Persons in 60 Metropolitan Areas

	Lowest Estimate	Highest Estimate	Most Reliable Range
Large Metropolitan Areas			
Baltimore	450	750	630- 750
Boston	2,300	5,000	3,100- 3,300
Chicago	17,000	26,000	19,400-20,300
Cincinnati	350	1,350	800- 950
Cleveland	200	2,000	400- 420
Detroit	3,000	9,000	7,200- 7,800
Hartford	250	1,800	600- 1,800
Houston	450	12,500	5,200- 7,500
Kansas City, MO	150	1,500	340- 400
Los Angeles	19,500	39,000	31,300-33,800
Miami	1,000	10,000	5,100- 6,800
Minneapolis/St. Paul	700	1,150	870- 1,150
New York	12,000	50,000	28,000-30,000
Philadelphia	450	8,050	2,200- 5,000
Phoenix	300	1,500	750- 1,400
Pittsburgh	50	1,500	600- 1,175
Portland	600	2,700	1,400- 1,700
San Francisco	7,500	11,500	7,700- 8,800
Seattle	1,300	5,000	3,100- 3,250
Washington, D.C.	3,000	10,500	3,000- 6,400
Medium-Sized Metropolitan Areas			
Baton Rouge, LA	100	200	150- 200
Birmingham, AL	300	1,000	550- 600
Charleston, SC	50	250	75- 90
Charlotte, NC	70	400	235- 315
Colorado Springs, CO	45	200	95- 100
Davenport, IA	75	500	330- 390
Dayton, OH	75	1,000	250- 340
Fort Wayne, IN	150	1,000	700- 750
Grand Rapids, MI	56	550	270- 430
Little Rock, AR	100	3,000	250- 770
Las Vegas, NV	400	2,000	950- 1,250
Louisville, KY	300	2,000	500- 650
Raleigh, NC	50	225	200- 225
Richmond, VA	325	2,250	1,100- 1,250
Rochester, NY	91	300	120- 150
Salt Lake City, UT	200	650	425- 650

Exhibit 10-2 (continued)

	Lowest Estimate	Highest Estimate	Most Reliable Range	
Medium-Sized Metropolitan Areas				
Scranton, PA	50	100	65-	75
Syracuse, NY	250	450	370-	380
Tampa, FL	250	1,500	550-	700
Worcester, MA	700	3,250	1,500-	1,900
Small Metropolitan Areas				
Annapolis, MD	10	125	70-	80
Athens, GA	10	75	25-	60
Binghamton, NY	44	75	40-	65
Bowling Green, KY	0	9	8-	9
Columbia, MO	15	85	55-	75
Danville, VA	0	150	30-	100
Durham, NC	10	50	40-	50
Fall River, MA	5	150	25-	40
Hazelton, PA	0	100	5-	20
Jackson, MI	25	88	40-	55
Lincoln, NE	50	150	115-	150
Lewiston, ME	22	30	25-	30
Lompoc, CA	2	55	20-	50
Merced, CA	20	50	35-	50
Monroe, LA	25	120	25-	105
Monroe, MI	15	37	20-	25
Pueblo, CO	35	55	45-	50
Reno, NV	100	400	285-	340
Sioux City, IA	50	73	50-	60
Tyler, TX	18	350	35-	50

total number of homeless in their metropolitan areas. Given the fact that the survey was based on a national random sample, their estimates can be generalized to the nation. However, unlike the previous method which involved assessing the reliability or basis of each local estimate, the figures given by the shelter operators were simply accepted as given.[10]

Extrapolating from the shelter operators' estimates, the number of homeless persons nationally for all metropolitan areas is 309,000. Adding the estimate of homeless persons in non-metropolitan areas (44,000) to this figure produces a total national estimate of 353,000. As in the second approach, this figure represents the average number of homeless persons on any given night in December 1983 or January 1984.

4.   Street and Shelter Counts

On any given night, the homeless are found either in emergency shelters or "on the streets." A fourth way of arriving at the homeless population is to estimate those in each place, and then sum the figures. The national shelter survey makes it possible to estimate the size of the former group with a high degree of confidence. According to the records of shelter operators, there were an average of 69,000 people in all shelters on any given day in January, 1984.[11]

The second group is, for several reasons, very hard to count because some homeless persons are able to maintain a reasonably good personal appearance and behave "normally" enough that they are often overlooked by casual observation. Furthermore, some homeless persons have an interest in concealing the places where they sleep, because they fear being harassed or victimized.[12]

Such factors have been used to explain why some attempts to contact or count the number of homeless have yielded very low numbers. Thus in early 1982, the Baltimore City Planning Department conducted a citywide street census using police officers as enumerators, and during a 24-hour count located only 29 homeless individuals. In Richmond, Virginia, two reporters searched the downtown area and discovered only 16 people. Yet the Greater Baltimore Shelter Network estimates that there are about 600 homeless at any one time in the city and in Richmond, the downtown homeless population was variously estimated at 50 to 125 by local experts.

In estimating the number of homeless "on the streets," two kinds of count data are used: the first from the 1980 Census "casual count," and the second from locally done street counts in three cities—Boston, Pittsburgh, and Phoenix.

1980 Census Count

The 1980 Census attempted to account for highly transient individuals, not counted using other procedures, by means of a "casual count" of homeless persons at places such as employment offices, bus and train stations, welfare offices, food stamp centers, pool halls, and street corners.[13] The number of persons enumerated during the "casual count" cannot be considered a national census of the homeless, however, since the count took place only in some census districts. The figure of 23,237 homeless discovered by this procedure, therefore, must be adjusted.

The census districts where the "casual count" was conducted contained 12 percent of the U.S. population; if it is assumed that they contain also the same share of the homeless population this amounts to a total of 166,000 homeless people on the streets in 1980. Since most local interviewees in the sample of 60 metropolitan areas estimated that the numbers of homeless have increased an average of about 10 percent a year, this figure is adjusted upward to account for changes since the census was taken. The adjusted figure is 233,000. However, since the street count was conducted only in larger cities, where the homeless rate is higher, this figure should be reduced by 35,000 to compensate for large city bias.[14] The resulting estimate of the national number of people "on the street," then, is 198,000.

Local Count Extrapolations

Street counts of the homeless were carried out in Phoenix (March 1983), Pittsburgh (June 1983) and Boston (October 1983). All three studies were conducted in a systematic fashion during periods of relatively mild weather when more people are likely to be on the street, by groups with considerable experience in studying the homeless. These counts are the only ones known to exist at the present time.

In all three cities, more people were found to be on the streets than in the shelters, as Exhibit 10-3 shows. Expressed as a ratio, for every 100 persons in shelters, there were 129 persons on the street in Boston, 273 in Phoenix, and 130 in Pittsburgh. The average street-to-shelter ratio for the three is 178:100. Given the estimate of 69,000 in shelters nationally, and assuming the ratio to be valid nationally, there would be 123,000 persons on the streets. While this method of arriving at the street population is based on only three cities, the result (123,000) is not all that different from the Census count (198,000).

Depending on which method is used to calculate the number of homeless people outside of shelters, the homeless total varies between 192,000 and 267,000 (see Exhibit 10-4). The latter figure, in particular, is very close to that derived from the interviews with local observers (254,000).

Exhibit 10-3
Local Street and Shelter Counts

	Street Count Total	Shelter Total
Phoenix	1,813	664
Pittsburgh	485	372
Boston	1,190	925
Total	3,488	1,961

Exhibit 10-4
Summary: Shelter and Street Counts

Shelter Population in Metro Areas	57,000
Shelter Population in Non-Metro Areas	12,000
Total	69,000
Street Count (Local Area Data) in Metro and Non-Metro Areas	123,000
Street Count (1980 Census) in Metro and Non-Metro Areas	233,000
(Adjustment for Over-Sampling in Large Urban Areas)	-35,000
	198,000
Total Homeless	
Shelter Population plus Local Area Street Count	192,000
Shelter Population plus 1980 Census Street Count	267,000

Conclusion

The preceding analysis has presented four approaches to estimating the national number of homeless persons. The range of estimates is 192,000 to 586,000 (see Exhibit 10-5).

As best as can be determined from all available data, the most reliable range is 250,000 to 350,000 homeless persons. This represents the total number of people, nationally, who were homeless on an average night in December 1983 or January 1984, and includes anyone who meets the criteria for homelessness adopted in this study. It is important to note that this group consists of people who have been chronically homeless and those who are temporarily without shelter.

Exhibit 10-5
Summary of Four Approaches to
Estimating Number of Homeless Persons Nationwide

Approach 1:	Extrapolation from Highest Published Estimates	586,000
Approach 2:	Extrapolation from Estimates in 60 Metropolitan Areas Obtained in 500+ Local Interviews	254,000
Approach 3:	Extrapolation of Estimates from National Sample of 125 Shelter Operators	353,000
Approach 4:	Shelter Population and Local Area Street Count	192,000
	Shelter Population and 1980 Census Street Count	267,000
	Most Reliable Range: 250,000 - 350,000	

It should also be noted that there is considerable turnover in this group, i.e., not all of these people have always been or will continue to be homeless; a substantial number are either occasionally or temporarily homeless. It may well be that in another year the number of homeless would be the same, but that the group could consist of substantially different people because of high turnover.

Regional and City Size Differences

The severity of the homeless problem varies noticeably by region and city size. Contrary to the popular view that homelessness is most concentrated in the North East, the West has the highest share of the Nation's homeless. Almost one-third of all homeless people in metropolitan areas are in the West, even though only 19 percent of the country's population lives there. The other three regions have roughly similar shares—between 22 and 24 percent (see Exhibit 10-6).

Exhibit 10-6
Numbers of Homeless by Census Region
for Metropolitan Areas of 50,000+
January 1984

Region	Number	Percent of Total Homeless	Percent of 1980 Population
South	50,000	24	33
North Central	45,400	22	26
North East	49,500	24	22
West	65,500	31	19
Total	210,400	101	100

This pattern may become even more accentuated in the summer, since the homeless population in the West and Southwest grows during this time of the year. The greater concentration of homeless in the West probably reflects both the attractiveness of its climate and perceived employment opportunities which attract itinerant job-seekers as well as those who may have been displaced from jobs in the Midwest. Local officials also noted the relative lack of old, low-cost housing, such as boarding homes or SRO-type hotels, as a reason for homelessness. A unique situation in the Southwest is the migration of Indians from reservations with very high unemployment rates to neighboring metropolitan areas in search of employment.

The Southwest is also experiencing an increase in the number of Mexican immigrants who enter the United States in search of employment. However, most of these people do not become homeless because, according to local

Exhibit 10-7
Estimates of Homeless Persons by Size
of Metropolitan Area

Estimate of homeless in large metropolitan areas (1,000,000+)	150,000
Estimate of homeless in medium metropolitan areas (250,000 to 1,000,000)	41,000
Estimates of homeless in small metropolitan areas (50,000 to 250,000)	19,000
Total	210,000
Extrapolated estimate for non-metropolitan areas	44,000
Total	254,000

Number of Homeless Per 10,000 Population

Large Metropolitan Areas	13.0
Medium Metropolitan Areas	12.0
Small Metropolitan Areas	6.5

officials in Los Angeles, they are cared for by their families and friends, "doubling-up" so that few actually end up on the streets.

The great majority of the homeless are found in large metropolitan areas. As Exhibit 10-7 shows, the ratio of homeless to total population is 13 persons for every 10,000 population in large and medium-sized metropolitan areas; it drops by about one-half in small metropolitan areas (to 6.5 persons per 10,000). Therefore, the homeless share of the population is greater in metropolitan areas over 250,000 than in less populous areas. Larger metropolitan areas do not, however, have proportionately more homeless persons than medium-sized areas.

The reasons why there is a higher rate of homelessness in large cities than in small cities parallel those given for why homelessness is more prevalent in central cities than in suburbs: there are more shelters and more social services in large cities. In addition, unemployed homeless people may be attracted to large cities because of the perception of more job opportunities. Finally, large cities have always contained relatively more poor households who have a greater chance of being homeless at one time or another than do higher-income households. . . .

NOTES

[1]   The number homeless at any point in time constitutes the population of potential shelter users on any given day—not the number of people who have been homeless for one or more days over a year's time period.

[2]   They include for example: *Newsweek* (December 27, 1982), *Congressional Quarterly* (February 12, 1983), *The Atlantic* (October 1983), *Newsweek* (January 2, 1984), *U.S. News and World Report* (January 17, 1983), and *Christian Science Monitor* (January 27, 1983). The two million figure was also used by the U.S. Conference of Mayors and the National Coalition for the Homeless. The most recent estimate by the Coalition for the Homeless is that there are three million homeless throughout the United States (*Los Angeles Times*, December 11, 1983).

[3]   Mary Ellen Hombs and Mitch Snyder, *Homelessness in America, A Forced March to Nowhere* (Washington, D.C., 1982), p. vi.

[4]   *Homelessness: A National Priority*, Report of the Community for Creative Non-Violence. Prepared for U.S. Congress, House District Committee (September 1, 1980), p. 79.

[5]   The total metropolitan figure is based on the population residing within the boundaries of the Ranally Metropolitan Areas for these 37 places in Exhibit 10-1: The RMAs are defined on a township and locality basis in contrast to the official SMSAs which are generally defined in terms of whole counties. In 1980, the 300 RMAs that approximate the 286 SMSAs comprise 92 percent of the SMSA population but only 28 percent of the SMSA area.

[6]   Or, sometimes, they are sent there. One city official in Chester, Pennsylvania said, "Frankly, we refer a lot of people to Philadelphia. At least there are shelters there and places where people can get off the street. There is nothing here in Delaware County." *Philadelphia Inquirer*, March 6, 1983.

[7]   In the Washington D.C. metropolitan area, for example, 76 percent of the total shelter capacity is in the District of Columbia; in the Baltimore metropolitan area, even more, 96 percent, is in the City of Baltimore.

[8]   Usually the number of interviews in any metropolitan area exceeded the actual estimates obtained since some people felt they could not give reliable figures.

[9]   For the rate of homelessness in different-sized metropolitan areas see Exhibit 10-7. The non-metropolitan areas contain 29 percent of the Nation's population.

[10]   In some of the metropolitan areas, either because there were no shelters or because shelter operators were not willing or able to respond, no estimates were obtained. In those places where more than one shelter was sampled, all the estimates were simply averaged.

[11]   Again, since the sample represents only metropolitan area shelters, it was necessary to estimate separately the shelter population in non-metropolitan areas. To estimate the non-metropolitan shelter population, the shelter population rate in small metropolitan areas, for which estimates were available from the shelter survey, was used. This rate was then multiplied by the population in the non-metropolitan areas. The metropolitan shelter population was 57,000 in January 1984; the estimate for those in non-metropolitan shelters is 12,000.

[12] Hombs and Snyder, *op. cit.*, p. 9; Baxter and Hopper, *Private Lives/ Public Spaces* (New York: Community Service Society, 1981), p. 14; Caro, F., "Estimating the Numbers of Homeless Persons," unpublished manuscript (New York: Community Service Society, 1981).

[13] U.S. Bureau of the Census, *1980 Census Special Place Operations Manual*, D-565.

[14] The 35,000 reduction is arrived at in the following manner. The homeless rate, using the 254,000 estimate (obtained via the second approach) is .0011, or 11 persons for every 10,000 population. The homeless rate for larger metropolitan areas where the census count occurred is 13 persons per 10,000 population (see Exhibit 10-7). To adjust for the large-city bias of the census count, the 233,000 figure, therefore, is multiplied by 11/13 and the product is subtracted from 233,000. The difference is 35,000. This represents one estimate of the overcount of street people nationally when simply extrapolating from the census count in the larger urban areas.

11

A Strategy for Helping America's Homeless

S. Anna Kondratas

Introduction

TO JUDGE from recent media reports, America faces a growing crisis of homelessness. The staggering figure of two to three million homeless Americans has been repeated so often that it has now acquired the status of conventional wisdom. Yet this figure vastly exaggerates and distorts the number of homeless: even the author of the study first containing the figure describes it as "meaningless." In fact, America's homeless probably number no more than 350,000.

The vast majority of today's homeless, moreover, are not otherwise typical Americans who have suffered massive economic catastrophe; rather, they are either dependent on drugs or alcohol, or they are mentally ill and on the streets because of the movement more than a decade ago to empty a large share of the nation's mental institutions. A smaller group among the homeless are the very poor, often welfare families, unable to find affordable housing due to change in the nation's rental housing market over two decades.

The homeless are not neglected and ignored. In fact, efforts to feed and house them have been growing in recent years. Ironically, the greater visibility of the homeless stems in part from these attempts to help. The federal government has several programs to aid the homeless. But emergency food and shelter only treats the problem, it does not cure it. An attack must be made on the underlying causes of homelessness and this requires that the states accept the obligations they have sought to avoid. New federal programs

Excerpted from S. Anna Kondratas, "A Strategy for Helping America's Homeless," *The Heritage Foundation Backgrounder*. No. 431. May 6, 1985. pp. 3-6. Reprinted by permission.

will simply produce another coalition of bureaucrats and activists with a vested interest in prolonging the homeless "crisis."

There are several steps to alleviate some of the causes of homelessness that the federal government could take immediately. Federal law should be amended to require states to provide adequate community mental health care before releasing patients from state institutions and to admit them if community care is inadequate. The federal government should also ensure that federal redevelopment grants are not used to lessen the low-income urban housing stock. Federal housing policy should continue to redirect subsidies from costly construction to rehabilitation and direct aid to the poor to make most efficient use of available funds.

How Many Homeless Are There?

The CCNV Estimate

During congressional hearings in 1980, Mitch Snyder of the Community for Creative Non-Violence (CCNV), a homeless advocacy group, charged that official data on the homeless were woefully inadequate. To "correct" this, CCNV undertook a survey of its own. It was a completely nonscientific study which presented only the sketchiest data from a very limited number of locales but nonetheless has been treated as hard fact.[1]

There is no indication in the 1980 CCNV report that the sampling of 14 "key cities" (which included one of just 55,000 residents) was random, or that any demographic factors were taken into account in selection. No systematic explanation of the study's methodology has ever been produced by CCNV, despite congressional requests. It appears that an unspecified number of unstructured telephone interviews were conducted with private and public service providers and agencies to elicit their opinions. CCNV chairman Snyder claims that information was received from "more than 100 agencies and organizations in 25 cities and states," averaging four calls per locale, although the report provides homeless estimates only for 14 cities.[2]

There is little reason to believe respondents for this survey were chosen by other than arbitrary and subjective criteria. The CCNV data yielded widely differing estimates of homelessness for each locale, and no attempt was made to explain, reconcile, or verify these estimates. The 1980 report includes, for example, one informant's bizarre estimate of 250,000 homeless in Chicago. Some estimates appear to be for metropolitan areas, others for cities only; some appear to be point-in-time counts, others annual counts. In one case, numbers of families, rather than family members, are enumerated.

In short, the CCNV data are useless as a means of estimating the number of America's homeless. Indeed, Snyder never claimed that this study was scientific, nor did his initial 1980 report include a U.S. homeless total. Nevertheless, according to a 1982 version of the report: "At that time [1980] we concluded that approximately 1 percent of the population, or 2.2 million people, lacked shelter . . . we are convinced the number of homeless people in the United States could reach 3 million or more during 1983."[3] The 1980 study reported some sketchy data and no homeless total; the 1982 version omitted some of the original data, expanded the narrative, and claimed to have produced a total of 2.2 million in 1980.

Even the upper range of the estimates Snyder presented in 1980 would yield homeless rates ranging from only several hundredths of a percentage point to half a percentage point in half the cities he enumerates. Only three individual estimates—one each in Louisville, Chicago, and Washington, D.C.—lead to a homeless rate over 1 percent, even using the city, rather than metropolitan area, population in all cases.

So where did the widely publicized statistic come from that two to three million Americans, one percent of the population, are homeless? Why does it still appear in CCNV documents? With disarming honesty, Snyder told a congressional panel last year:

> . . . These numbers are in fact meaningless. We have tried to satisfy your gnawing curiosity for a number because we are Americans with western little minds that have to quantify everything in sight, whether we can or not.[4]

Counting the Homeless—The HUD Report

The Department of Housing and Urban Development in 1983 decided to compile official data on homelessness. Last May, the results of HUD's six-month study were released.[5] The report's conclusions were based on a review of nearly 100 local and national studies, over 500 interviews with local observers in a nationally representative sampling of 60 metropolitan areas, site visits in ten localities, a national survey of shelter operators, a 50-state survey of state activity, and discussions with representatives of national homeless advocacy groups.

Based on four different approaches, each with a different rationale and methodology meticulously explained in the report, HUD concluded that on an average night in December 1983 to January 1984, the homeless numbered from 192,000 to 586,000. HUD considered the "most reliable range" to be from 250,000 to 350,000. The HUD figure was a "point-in-time" estimate.

Since many of the homeless are only temporarily without a residence, the number of people who experience homelessness during any year, of course, would be far greater than this range. But the point-in-time estimate is a far more meaningful indication of the extent of the problem. It is the method, for instance, by which unemployment is measured. HUD clearly states what its figure signifies. In contrast, the CCNV study does not explain whether its numbers are annual or point-in-time.

One of HUD's methods made use of the highest published local estimates in 37 localities. Ten of the localities were among the fourteen surveyed by the CCNV report. Since CCNV later accused HUD of making conscious efforts to minimize the problem, the CCNV and HUD estimates should be compared for these ten cities:

	HUD (1981-83)	CCNV (1980)
Atlanta	3,500	1,000
Baltimore	15,000	8,000
Boston	8,000	5,000
Chicago	25,000	250,000
Detroit	8,000	500
Los Angeles	30,000	8,500
New York	50,000	75,000
Pittsburgh	1,500	135
Seattle	5,000	(Not clear)
Washington	10,000	15,000

If Chicago, clearly an anomaly in the CCNV data, is discounted, the total HUD estimates are actually 30 percent higher than those of CCNV. So why are HUD's national totals so different from CCNV's? HUD's method for extrapolating a national homeless rate from their data is clear and methodical—CCNV's method is unexplained and inexplicable.

Reaction to the HUD Report

The HUD study used routine and rarely questioned survey and statistical techniques, yet it immediately encountered intense criticism—presumably because it did not find that two million homeless were camping on America's sidewalks and sleeping on grates. The press emphasized that the HUD results were disputed by homeless advocacy groups, and HUD was accused of "playing games."[6] Critics claimed that the HUD study was not objective (although it was conducted by professional civil servants whose tenure at HUD predated the Reagan administration), and that the "low" numbers were simply cooked to justify "callous" Reagan administration budget cuts. It was not noted that HUD's numbers were "low" only by comparison to CCNV's unsubstantiated figures. Instead, the HUD report itself was compared to Nazi propaganda by the chairman of the congressional hearings on the HUD study.[7]

The criticism of HUD's methodology simply does not bear scrutiny. Many of the allegations by critics are misinformed or false. The complaint that people living on temporary vouchers in hotels and motels were not counted by HUD is simply erroneous, as is the accusation that HUD had used a ridiculously low estimate of 12,000 for New York City's homeless to establish their reliable range. Nor did HUD obtain "artificially" lower rates by counting only inner-city homeless while dividing by the metropolitan area population to obtain the rate. HUD obtained its homeless rates by employing credible and consistent techniques. In the several hundred pages of testimony presented at hearings on the study, there was not a single valid methodological criticism that the HUD report itself did not raise or that HUD spokesmen did not subsequently answer.[8] Curiously, despite the careful attention critics paid to HUD's methodology, they almost universally overlooked the totally unscientific basis of the CCNV estimate that there are two to three million American homeless.

The attack on HUD left the Reagan administration reeling. Take the Federal Emergency Management Agency [FEMA], which is charged with administering a substantial portion of federal funds for the homeless. FEMA recently released a study that ignores the HUD figures. When asked why HUD's figures were not used, Dennis Kwiatkowski of FEMA replied that HUD's numbers have been seriously discredited.[9] The fact is that HUD's figures have not been discredited; they only have been attacked—unconvincingly.

Many commentators have suggested that an argument over numbers is somehow irrelevent and that discussion should focus only on solutions. Yet the numbers are of critical political significance at the federal level. If the U.S. is swamped with millions of homeless Americans, then a better case can be made for treating the matter as a federal problem. But if the homelessness is on the scale that the HUD figures suggest, there is little justification for asking Washington to intervene—in yet another area. Instead, current federal efforts could be redirected rather than expanded. The main burden of responsibility for the homeless—and society does have a moral responsibility for them—is with state and local governments and private organizations. . . .

NOTES

¹   Community for Creative Non-Violence, *A Forced March to Nowhere*, Washington, D.C., September 1, 1980.

²   Written testimony by Mitch Snyder, in *Joint Hearing on HUD Report on Homelessness*, House Banking and Government Operations Committees, May 24, 1984, pp. 33-34. For a new edition of the study, the information was supplemented by calling "another couple of hundred people" in unspecified locales.

³   Mary Ellen Hombs and Mitch Snyder, *Homelessness in America, A Forced March to Nowhere*, Community for Creative Non-Violence, Washington, D.C., 1982, p. xvi.

⁴   *Joint Hearing, op. cit.*, May 1984, p. 32.

⁵   HUD Office for Policy Development and Research, *A Report to the Secretary on the Homeless and Emergency Shelters*, May 1, 1984.

⁶   Colman McCarthy, "Just What the Homeless Needed," *Washington Post*, May 12, 1984.

⁷   *Joint Hearing, op cit.*, May 1984, p. 9.

⁸   Ibid., pp. 281-287 and 297.

⁹   Telephone interview with Dennis Kwiatkowski, Chief of the Division of Individual Assistance, March 11, 1985. The FEMA study was released as *The National Board Emergency Food and Shelter Program Study of Homelessness*, March 1, 1985. It talks of percent increases without mentioning specific numbers. Since a percent is a ratio between two numbers, the lack of a reference point makes the percentage useless. So FEMA intends to base its policies only on whether the homeless problem is getting better or worse, without reference to its scale.

12

Testimony on *A Report to the Secretary*
on *The Homeless and Emergency Shelters*

Chester Hartman

M Y COMMENTS on HUD's just-issued study, *A Report to the Secretary on the Homeless and Emergency Shelters*, will focus in part on thoughts as to how such a study might have been undertaken, and still ought to be.

. . . Since the problem of homelessness has grown so rapidly, both in reality and in our consciousness, it is not surprising that the numbers that exist are not terribly reliable; they are drawn largely from impressions rather than scientific attempts at counting and estimating. A certain number gets into currency and then is repeated by others; and while this sometimes becomes accepted as the real number, it is not necessarily the more reliable simply because lots of people who know about and are involved in the homeless issue repeat it. People working day to day with the homeless and their problems cannot be expected to know and be the source of reliable overall numbers of how many homeless there are altogether. They are too busy providing needed help to become statistical experts. All they know reliably is that the number of people who need help is far more than the number they can . . . help.

What is troublesome about the HUD report in terms of overall numbers is that the agency assembles these commonly used and believed local numbers, which no one regards as wholly reliable, aggregates them, throws in some assumptions and extrapolation techniques, and derives what then is regarded

Reprinted from Chester Hartman's testimony prepared for a Joint Hearing before the Subcommittee on Housing and Community Development of the Committee on Banking, Finance and Urban Affairs, and the Subcommittee on Manpower and Housing of the Committee on Government Operations. United States Congress. House of Representatives. May 24, 1984.

as a "hard" number. It is useful to have [their] compendium of what estimates and commonly used numbers exist in various localities, useful to have [their] review of the literature. But the mere act of compiling these figures and studies should not lead anyone to believe—as HUD has done and as the public will be led to believe by virtue of HUD's imprimatur—that the totals HUD had produced are any more reliable and firm than the unreliable, unfirm numbers from which that total was derived. Systematically aggregating lots of guess-work does not produce a reliable number, no matter how scientific the procedure with which all these guesses have been collated. And HUD's statement that "the use of more than one approach to arrive at a national estimate helps to ensure the reliability of the results" (p. 9) is sheer nonsense: if none of these approaches is based on any scientific, reliable methods, no amount of piling approach on approach will ensure reliability. And using accredited sampling techniques to arrive at a sample of locales for inclusion in the study gives a further misleading impression of accuracy and reliability: scientific sampling of localities doesn't mask poor numbers. If solid numbers are not available for the sampled locales, the figures derived from this sample will be equally unsolid. The aphorism about silk purses and sows' ears holds for statistics and government reports as well.

At one point (p. 6) HUD says, regarding the option it rejected of doing an actual person count and in-person national survey, "It is not clear that the results would be that much more reliable than those presented here." But it is not clear either that the results would not be more reliable. Such efforts as national counts are indeed time-consuming and costly. But if the government [requires] really big numbers in order to begin to deal effectively with an important social problem, perhaps Congress or HUD ought to authorize and undertake such a national count.

I also have trouble with the report's lack of any estimates of the growth and change in the homeless population in the coming years. Most, if not all, experts would agree that homelessness is on the rise. Based on what we know of its growth in the past few years, surely HUD might have used some of its statistical techniques to come up with a high and low figure for homelessness, say two or five years from now. [Does their failure] to do this [reflect] a desire to minimize the problem?

Likewise, the number of homeless the report puts forth is the number on any given night. The report acknowledges (p. 9) that another important figure is "how many people were homeless at any one time or another throughout the year." It regards this figure only as "of interest," but [asserts] that the single-night figure "is more crucial in understanding the size of the problem and the shelter needs of the homeless." I do not agree with this argument. The number [who are] homeless at one time or another is terribly important in determining the shelter needs of the homeless; since it is not a constant group, but a group of shifting composition and location, we *must* know about the group's composition over time if we are to plan for their needs. And, if in a given year the reality of homelessness affects several times the number . . . homeless on a given night, that is a social, human, and political fact that needs to be known. Again, why did not HUD offer an estimate of this figure? Is it because the news stories would then have put forth a number far higher than the 250,000-350,000 figure of this report? The problem, of course, in terms of public and political consciousness, is that a report like this leads to a popular perception that only a relatively small number of people are homeless, when, even with the limited data available, a very different picture might have been given of the number homeless over the course of a year.

Another misleading impression is given in how the report treats households that are "doubled up." While it is technically accurate not to count as homeless such households, the HUD report recognizes that the potential for "eviction" into the streets or their cars is high. Since this change of status may happen overnight, an honest assessment of the homelessness problem would attempt a count or estimate of these involuntarily doubled-up households, so that public consciousness and public policy would include this immediate potential for homelessness as part of the issue and needed solutions.

Let me turn now from narrower issues of methodology to how the Department has handled the entire research question. . . . I am troubled by the approach HUD took to [this volatile] task. In very general terms, HUD . . . [had a] choice of two modes of research: doing the job totally in-house, or doing it with some input from outside experts. In the latter mode, a contract can either be let to a private or nonprofit research group, or there can be substantial input from outside experts in the form of review panels, consulting committees, and other bodies.

In this instance, HUD chose to do the work entirely in-house, through its Office of Policy Studies (save the the survey of shelter providers, done by an outside survey research firm), and did its work apparently in a great rush. . . .

One can—and should—ask, why the big rush in doing such a study, and why the need to keep the research totally in-house? It seems to me that on a question of such great social importance, nationally and in specific locales—how large is the problem of homelessness, what are its characteristics and causes, what's being done about it?—HUD ought to have taken a more broadly based, participatory approach to its work. Public and private providers of services to the homeless, advocates of their needs, academic experts, representatives [from] the homeless themselves—all these groups should have been represented on a research panel assembled at the outset, and that body, with HUD staff, should have designed the research task, decided who would carry it out, supervised its implementation, analyzed the data, and collectively issued a report. That kind of approach would have produced a document far more credible, far less divisive and controversial than what we have before us today.

And it is easy to find [precedents] for [HUD having taken] this alternative approach. . . . When [the Department] wanted to learn the impact of the Community Development Block Grant allocations, it set up a user panel of experts and funded it through the Urban Consortium, with much of the research carried out under University of Pennsylvania auspices. When HUD wanted to learn about the modernization needs of public housing projects it established and funded a broadly based advisory committee of experts from the National Association of Housing and Redevelopment Officials, Congressional staff, and other sources. Is homelessness less important an issue,. . . an issue of lesser concern to a range of groups and people all over the U.S.? It is important that Congress ask HUD why in this case it did not adopt that mode of research and investigation, which is bound to lead to better, more widely accepted results.

If the answer HUD gives you to this question is "speed"—that procedures of the type I've described take longer—then we have to ask what the rush was, in view of the total absence of proposed solutions in the HUD document under review. Research on the extent and nature of a social problem and what is currently being done to alleviate it [are] valuable endeavor[s]. But when such research is carried out by a public agency with major responsibility in this area, and especially when that research is done in so rushed a manner, one should legitimately expect that agency to come up with a proposed plan to remedy the problem it has found. Even if the true number of homeless in the U.S. is "only" 250,000-350,000, that's a vast problem calling for immediate remedies. Yet nothing in the HUD study, not in any accompanying documents or statements, suggests HUD has a real sense of urgency in doing something about the problem of homelessness, except minimizing its importance.

In some sense, I agree with those who take the position that whether the actual number is a quarter of a million, a half million, a million, or two million is not so important; we likely never will have a firm number everyone will agree to, and the real issue is that in a society with the wealth of the United States, there should not be a single involuntarily homeless person. If the "real" number is 250,000-350,000 rather than 2,000,000, as the HUD report claims, one could even say, all the easier for HUD and other government agencies to solve the problem. Simply stated, I would feel far less uncomfortable with and hostile to this HUD report if it were accompanied by a real commitment, a sense of urgency, an allocation of resources, to *solve* the nation's homelessness problem, whatever the number of homeless is.

HUD's somewhat cavalier stance to this problem is all the more disturbing, given the agency's direct and indirect role in creating and adding to the very problem it now is belittling. Program cuts this Administration and agency have instituted since 1981—in public housing, Section 8, rehabilitation loans, and other areas—have reduced low-income housing subsidies at the very time the need for these subsidies has been dramatically rising. Malign neglect of existing public housing projects has reduced the stock of housing potentially available to the homeless. Increasing the proportion of income demanded from public housing and Section 8 [tenants] from 25 percent to 30 percent has placed an intolerable additional burden on low-income families and likely forced many onto the streets.

That homelessness now is afflicting a full range of Americans—all ages, races, household types—suggests that it is not a problem to be looked at apart from the nation's general housing problems, in particular the problem of affordability. With 8 million renter households paying more than 50 percent of their income for rent, as of the 1981 Annual Housing Survey, and mortgage foreclosures and delinquencies at an all-time high; with 2.5 million people being displaced each year from all causes; with overcrowding on the rise—at a minimum, 10 percent of all New York City public housing households are doubled up—the line between the housed and unhoused is a thin one. Those without a regular place to live can only increase in numbers over the coming years, unless there is a serious attempt to deal with the broader problem of housing affordability in America. Neither HUD nor the Administration of which it is a part wants to touch that problem. It comes as no surprise to me that a report is issued downplaying the problem of homelessness, just as the national housing crisis more generally is downplayed by this Administration. We must deal honestly with the problem of homelessness—how many, who, and what to do about it—just as we must deal honestly with the housing crisis being faced by tens of millions of Americans lucky enough to have a roof over their heads. It seems to me the best place to begin that honest evaluation and fashioning of real solutions is with this report and the ultimate housing problem it speaks to.

In ending, I would recommend to the Congresss, and to HUD:

1. That a new study of the issues contained in this report be undertaken, but under the direction of a broadly based panel of government and private-sector experts, as outlined above [; a]nd that perhaps a scientific national count of the homeless be undertaken as part of this project. The problem is important enough right now, will become larger in coming years, and is so symptomatic of ills in the housing system as a whole, that we should take longer to analyze it and do it in the way that gives the public the most confidence in the reliability and independence of the study.

2. That pending completion of this new study, HUD voluntarily withdraw the current report and issue a statement clarifying what is and is not possible to state firmly based on the data gathering done for that document.

3. ... [f]inally, that pending completion of this new study, the Administration make serious efforts to end the unconscionable situation of involuntary homelessness in America for the 250,000, 350,000, or whatever number of persons the Administration acknowledges to be without homes.

13

Testimony on *A Report to the Secretary on The Homeless and Emergency Shelters*

Richard P. Appelbaum

THE HUD *Report to the Secretary on the Homeless and Emergency Shelters* (HUD Report)[1] suffers from methodological deficiencies which cast serious doubt on the validity of its conclusions. In the following [testimony] I will focus on the estimates of homelessness provided in chapter 2 of the Report. At issue are questions of overall methodology and internal consistency, rather than the adequacy of data collection procedures. I recognize that in this latter area as well, the study is often inaccurate and occasionally biased.

While the HUD study appears rigorous in employing four seemingly different approaches to arrive at its final estimates, I believe this promise is not fully realized in its actual execution. What I propose to do is briefly run through the various approaches, raising questions concerning each which I believe should be adequately addressed before the study becomes the basis for far-reaching policy reformulation. I might add that I have been hampered in this task because the Report itself does not provide the information necessary to evaluate either its sampling methodologies, or its extrapolations from sample to national totals.

Reprinted from Richard P. Appelbaum's testimony prepared for a Joint Hearing before the Subcommittee on Housing and Community Development of the Committee on Banking, Finance and Urban Affairs, and the Subcommittee on Manpower and Housing of the Committee on Government Operations. United States Congress. House of Representatives. May 24, 1984.

Approaches to the Estimation of Homelessness

1. Published Estimates

The first approach is intended to provide a "worst case" estimate of homelessness, by accepting at face value the highest published figures that satisfy certain minimal standards. These figures, primarily for 1982 and 1983, are presented for 37 localities in table 1 [Exhibit 10-1 of this reader]. The "high" estimates sum to 211,321. Since these 37 places represent an underlying population of approximately 84.5-million people, a rate of 0.0025 is derived (25 per 10,000) by simple division. When applied to an estimated national population total of approximately 234 million, a "high" total of 586,000 results—high because it is based on unverified reports from only those places whose problems are severe enough to merit study. It is all the more surprising, then, that this estimate is only one-quarter of the most widely cited figure.

The most significant problem with this estimate is one that troubles all of the projections in the study, to which I will several times return: the choice of denominator for the ratio employed in the projection. I believe the denominator is far too large, giving a ratio that is correspondingly too small. The 84.5 million people assumed to produce a homeless population of 211,000 are the total residents of the underlying "Ranally Metropolitan Areas" (RMA's), a geographic unit developed by Rand McNally for their *Commercial Atlas and Marketing Guide*. RMA's are similar to census "urban areas" in that they are based partly on density; unlike the census units, however, they include outlying commuter suburbs and can cut across county boundaries.[2] In the larger RMA's numerous cities may be involved. The New York City RMA, for example, includes Westchester, Rockland, Putnam, and parts of Orange counties in lower New York state, Fairfield County in Connecticut, and most of northern New Jersey and Long Island; it had a 1980 population of 16.6 million in almost 80 different cities. The Los Angeles RMA, with a population of 9.8 million, covers most of Los Angeles and Orange Counties, as well as parts of Ventura and San Bernardino; it also encompasses some 80 cities. As previously noted, the 1980 census reported a combined population for the 37 RMA's in table 1 [Exhibit 10-1 of this reader] of about 84.5 million people. This is 2.7 times the population of the central cities for those same places.

The HUD Report justifies RMA's—as opposed to central cities or other smaller units—on the grounds that most of the homeless reside in the central city rather than the suburbs. But the RMA's are not simply central city plus surrounding suburbs; the larger RMA's often include numerous different central cities, each one of which potentially has a homeless problem. The study nonetheless often appears to treat the RMA's as if they were cities; the two terms in fact are used interchangeably throughout the Report.[3] The decision to use studies of specific cities as if those studies in fact covered homelessness throughout their corresponding RMA's is unfortunate, because it results in homeless ratios which potentially underestimate the extent of the problem by a substantial margin. If, for example table 1 were based on central city population rather than RMA population, its projected result would be 2.7 times as large, or 1.6 million.[4]

2.   Interviews with Experts in National Sample

The second estimate is based on a stratified sample of RMA's, in which 20 RMA's are drawn from among all RMA's in each of three size categories (50,000-250,000; 250,000-1,000,000; over 1,000,000). The probability of an area being chosen is proportional to the square root of its population, meaning that larger RMA's have a somewhat higher chance of being represented than smaller ones. All RMA's over 4 million people—there are 6—are included in the sample. 500 telephone interviews were then conducted in the 50 sampled RMA's, with responses weighted according to reliability. The results are then combined into high and low estimates, as well as a single average which is used to generate the national figures presented in table 6 [Exhibit 10-7 of this reader]. The methodology by which the ranges and averages are derived is not revealed, except for a brief discussion of the reliability weights. . . . Once a homeless ratio is generated for the sample RMA's in each of the three strata,[5] it is then multiplied by the combined population of all RMA's in the strata (sampled and unsampled) to produce a national figure. The resulting estimate is 254,000 homeless people.

This method suffers from the same deficiency as the previous one; we do not know whether the numerator in the ratio (the number of homeless identified through the interviews in a particular locale) corresponds to the denominator (the population of the RMA). Did their Los Angeles interviews adequately cover the approximately 80 cities that comprise the Los Angeles RMA, with its 1980 population of 9.8 million? Did their Washington interviews cover the dozen or so cities in Virginia and Maryland that help comprise the 3.2 million people in the Washington RMA? The problem is especially acute for the large- and medium-size RMA's where most homelessness is concentrated, as the following table indicates:

Underlying Population Estimates:
Urban Areas and Central Cities

Size Category	Metropolitan Population	City Population	Ratio: M/C
large areas	77,583,000	27,329,000	2.8:1
medium areas	10,280,000	4,070,000	2.5:1
small areas	2,255,000	1,329,000	1.7:1

Source: Rand McNally, *Commercial Atlas and Marketing Guide for 1983*, and HUD Report, table 14.

If central cities were used as the basis of the projection, rather than RMA's, the final estimate would increase by 250% to 637,000.[6]

Since we are not provided with any information that would enable us [to] assess the match between homeless estimates and the population which presumably underlies them, it is impossible to determine the accuracy of the ratios which are then used to project to a national total.

Two additional comments are in order, concerning both the representativeness of the sample and the adequacy of the weighting system for combining differing RMA estimates into a single total.

It is impossible to independently judge the sample's representativeness, since the Report does not provide any information which would permit us to detect (and/or adjust for) sampling bias. It is customary when sampling to provide socioeconomic or demographic profiles of the sample and underlying population so the two can be compared. (Appropriate indices in the present instance might include region, median income, percent of population below poverty line, and total population for each strata.) However reasonable the method may appear on the surface, there are always errors introduced when moving from sample to population, and without additional information the representativeness of the Report's sample cannot be ascertained.

It is similarly difficult to evaluate the adequacy of the weighting system (summarized in appendix table A-4 [of the HUD Report]) without more detailed information, but my impression is that the system weighs "hard figures" (street counts, shelter records, official figures) relative to "softer" ones. While this appears reasonable, it inevitably favors the "official" homeless over the more numerous street homeless, who are harder to detect.[7] As the Report's discussion makes clear, there are numerous homeless people on the streets for every person in a shelter on a particular night [the Report estimates a ratio of 178:100]. Since there are only three "hard" street counts "known to exist at the present time" (Phoenix, Pittsburgh, and Boston), it is likely that the weighting system again underestimates the actual numbers by overvaluing data concerning the "official" homeless.

3. Extrapolation from Shelter Operator Estimates

In this third approach, operators surveyed in a sample of shelters were asked to estimate the extent of homelessness in their cities. These estimates were taken at face value, and used to extrapolate to a national figure by the same method employed in the preceding two approaches. The extrapolation for metropolitan areas yields an estimate of 309,000; when a nonmetropolitan estimate (44,000) is added, the final figure is 353,000 homeless.

The same concerns can be raised here that were raised previously: the choice of underlying population to which these projections refer, and the adequacy of the sampling methods. Concerning the first difficulty, I shall only repeat the point that has previously been made: to the extent that the shelter operators' estimates refer to smaller units than the RMA's, the projections will underestimate the actual extent of homelessness nationally. In the absence of additional information, the magnitude of this problem cannot be estimated.

Concerning the second difficulty, the previously discussed sampling problems associated with the selection of RMA's are now compounded by any additional problems associated with the further sampling of shelters from among the sampled RMA's. The 679 shelters in the 60 cities were used to generate a sample of 200, out of which 184 shelter managers responded to the questionnaire.... The sampling procedure is only briefly discussed,.. and no effort made to independently gauge the representativeness of the sample with regard to the underlying national "population" of shelters. It is impossible, therefore, to determine whether or not the homeless estimates derived from the sample of shelter managers adequately represents the actual figures.

4. Street and Shelter Counts

The fourth method of estimating homelessness combines data concerning two different groups of homeless people—those who are housed (on any given night) in shelters, and those who sleep in "any public or private space not designed for shelter."[x] ... The former estimate is obtained from the survey of shelter operators, and is subject to any statistical deficiencies that result from the two-stage sampling procedure employed (sampling of cities and shelters).

Again, the objection is not so much with the method, as with the lack of information in the Report by which the representativeness of the resulting sample can be evaluated. The Report estimates that there are 57,000 homeless in metropolitan shelters, and 12,000 in non-metropolitan shelters, for a total of 69,000.

Two separate estimates of the non-sheltered homeless are obtained: one by extrapolation from the census "casual count," and one a projection of street counts conducted in Phoenix, Pittsburgh, and Boston at various times in 1983. The census yields a national projection of 198,000, when certain adjustments are made. The three-city street count produces a national projection of 123,000. When combined with the population in shelters, two different estimates result: a census-based figure of 267,000, and a street-count based figure of 192,000.

As the Report seems to recognize, these are extremely weak estimates, with a large number of attendant problems.

1. The estimates of homeless people in shelters are subject to the deficiencies previously discussed, namely unknown sampling bias and the choice of underlying population used for projecting local figures to a national total.

2. The census "casual count" undoubtedly severely underestimates homelessness in those districts where it was conducted. As the Report correctly emphasizes, . . . homeless people are very hard to count; many look "normal" in appearance, and many have a strong interest in remaining invisible, especially to public agencies.[9] Furthermore, the census count was conducted in districts with only 12 percent of the U.S. population; this figure is then extrapolated to a national figure on the assumption that these districts experience the same degree of homelessness as the national population. Again, we are given no figures on which to judge the adequacy of this assumption, figures which could be readily provided given the source of the data.[10]

3. The local street count is used to generate a ratio of "street homelessness" to "shelter homelessness" in the three cities for which data are available. This ratio (178/100) is then applied to the national estimate of "shelter homelessness" derived from the survey, to yield a national estimate of "street homelessness." The projections are, of course, subject to any (unknown) bias associated with the two-stage survey of shelter managers. Additionally, it seems to me highly questionable to make a national projection on the basis of studies in three cities, however accurate those studies might be. For example, there is a wide range in the street/shelter ratio across the three places, with Pittsburgh

and Boston having ratios around 130/100, and Phoenix having a ratio twice as high (273/100). Such a large variance renders any effort to project to a national total extremely suspect.

Finally, a comparison of tables 2 and 3 [Exhibits 10-2 and 10-3 of this reader] reveals some potential difficulties with the data. For example, in table 2 the "most reliable range" for Phoenix is 750-1400 homeless; yet table 3 yields a "hard" total of 2,473 (1,813 + 664). In Boston the error appears to be in the other direction: table 2 provides a "most reliable range" of 3,100-3,300, while table 3 finds only 2,115 homeless. Only the Pittsburgh total from table 3 (857) lies within the "most reliable range" (600-1175). These discrepencies suggest a great deal of slack across the various methodologies employed.

Summary

The preceding points can be summarized as follows:

- The use of Ranally Metropolitan Areas (RMA's) as the basis of projections from sampled estimates of homelessness to national totals may result in significant under-estimation of the extent of the problem. This is because the RMA's are extremely populous areas which may encompass numerous cities and counties, while the homeless estimates derived from them refer to only one or two central cities. The Report fails to provide the information necessary to estimate this source of bias.
- The sampling procedures are complex and a potential source of unknown bias. Unfortunately, no population parameters are provided to permit a comparison of the sampled cities and shelters with the national "population" of cities and shelters they are intended to represent. It is standard operating procedure in any study that relies on a sample to have a discussion of possible sampling bias, and a study of this importance should be no exception.
- While the various approaches appear to be different from one another, they in fact all rely on similar RMA-based projection techniques; furthermore, all but the first are based in whole or in part on the sample survey. Any bias resulting from the use of RMA's in sampling or in making projections, or from the sampling methods generally, is likely to be reflected in all of the projections. The seeming convergence of the projections on similar estimates may therefore be an artifact of their common underlying methods.

- The methods for weighting "experts' responses" (approach 2) are likely to favor "official homelessness," discounting those homeless who are most removed from public or private agencies. This again introduced a bias towards underestimation in the results.
- The attempt to infer a national figure from ratios of "street homelessness" to "shelter homelessness" in three cities is highly questionable, as is the extrapolation from census estimates. This failed effort does point out, however, the fact that a large (and unknown) number of homeless people studiously avoid contact with census takers, surveyers, and agencies generally, and are therefore unlikely to be counted in any study.
- Finally, the operational definition of homelessness excludes people who are doubling-up out of necessity. While it would be very difficult to measure this group, it seems to me that they are clearly a part of the problem of homelessness also.

I have limited this discussion to possible methodological problems which, in my view, all converge to bias the Report's estimates in a downward direction. All studies are subject to flaws and biases. What concerns me is the absence of any serious discussion in the Report of potential difficulties, along with the failure to provide information which might permit an independent evaluation of its findings. These shortcomings are especially troubling given the thought and effort which apparently went into the study.

NOTES

[1]   *A Report to the Secretary on the Homeless and Emergency Shelters*, hereafter referred to as the Report.

[2]   Rand McNally defines RMA's as including "(1) a central city or cities; (2) any adjacent continuously built-up areas; and (3) other communities not connected to the city by continuous built-up territory if the bulk of their population [8% of population or 20% of labor force] is supported by commuters to the central city and its adjacent built-up areas, and provided their population density is fairly high." Rand McNally has identified 394 RMA's in the United States.

[3]   In the discussion of sampling and weighting in appendix A of the HUD Report, the Report acknowledges that the RMA's are "also referred to as cities." See page A-1.

[4]   Page 12 of the HUD Report states that using these estimates, "the overall homeless rate is .025%, or 25 persons per 1000 population." Both of these figures are incorrect; they should in fact be 0.25%, and 25 per 10,000.

[5] For large RMA's the ratio is .0013; for medium ones it is .0012; and for small ones it is .0065. This latter ratio is also applied to nonmetropolitan areas.

[6] This figure is derived by applying the M/C ratios in the above table to the HUD Report estimates in table 6 [Exhibit 10-7 of this reader].

[7] I use the term "official homeless" to refer to those who come into contact with public or private agencies, and are known by those agencies to be homeless.

[8] This is the definition of homelessness employed throughout the study; people forced to double-up are thereby excluded from the study by definition. I believe that a plausible argument could be made for including such people among the homeless, particularly if they are forced to frequently move from house to house [Report, p.7; first page of Chapter 10 of this reader].

[9] As noted in the Report, many homeless fear harrassment and victimization. Additionally, many locales require an address for receipt of food stamps or other forms of public asssistance; an undetermined number of homeless receiving such assistance provide the address of a friend or acquaintance if required to do so, thereby giving the appearance of having a home. Undocumented aliens who are homeless are a large and growing group who also have an obvious interest in remaining undetected.

[10] The 23,237 homeless revealed in the census "casual count" of districts containing 12% of the U.S. population should arithmetically produce a national estimate of 193,642 (23,237 divided by .12); the figure derived in the Report . . . is 166,000. The actual method either differs from that described in the Report, or the arithmetic is incorrect.

IV

Who Are the Homeless and Why?

14

Skid Row as an Urban Neighborhood, 1880-1960

John C. Schneider

RECENT JOURNALISTIC exposes of the "new poor" and homeless, of "street people" and overcrowded city missions, have served to remind us of that perennial urban phenomenon in the United States: skid row. It is more common these days to speak of "skid row types" than to think of skid row as a point in city space. Many cities have deliberately done away with their oldest and most objectionable "wino" areas. Nevertheless, skid row has a long history as a recognizable section of the inner city, dating from at least the last quarter of the nineteenth century.

Except for a few cameo appearances in studies of class and mobility, sub-areas of transient and unattached men have not figured in the work of urban historians. Sociologists have shown a good deal more interest in skid row's past, but mostly to provide historical background to their investigations of present-day skid row populations and social structures. The results have tended to be superficial glances, especially as far as skid row's spatial development is concerned. Sociologists might be excused for this, but curiously geographers have also been inattentive to the spatial evolution of skid row. The most ambitious historical study of skid row as an urban neighborhood is *Liquor and Poverty: Skid Row as a Human Condition* (1978) by a sociologist, Leonard Blumberg, and two associates. A student of Philadelphia's skid row for twenty years, Blumberg brought to *Liquor and Poverty* a strong interest in skid row's historical development. A major segment of the book is devoted to

Reprinted from *Urbanism Past and Present*, vol. 9, Winter/Spring 1984, pp. 10-19. An *in gratis* reprint of John C. Schneider's article has been granted by *Urbanism Past and Present* of the University of Wisconsin-Milwaukee, Board of Regents of the University of Wisconsin System, 1985.

a comparative examination of homeless men's areas in nineteenth-century Philadelphia, San Francisco, and Detroit. It is clearly the best work to date on the spatial history of skid row in American cities.[1]

Informative and suggestive, *Liquor and Poverty's* historical sections are nonetheless deficient on two counts. First, there is a tendency to assume that transient men's areas in the past were always decaying neighborhoods housing mainly "skid row-like" persons recognizable to us today. Second, the authors fail to integrate fully the sociological and geographical approaches to skid row. Contemporary investigations of skid row typically have discussed the social community apart from the physical neighborhood. Skid row becomes just an area in which the social problem—homelessness, disaffiliation, alcholism—happens to be concentrated. In fact, sociologists often scold each other for focusing exclusively on skid row populations when the social condition they are most interested in is found in many parts of the city. That very point is one of the principal themes running throughout *Liquor and Poverty.*

For studies such as Blumberg's that seek to provide guidelines for welfare and governmental agencies, a concern for the social problem rather than the neighborhood is to be expected, and it is hardly surprising, therefore, that many of their prescriptions for reform make little effort to preserve skid row's distinctive physical plant.[2] Yet there is every reason to believe that the homeless, disaffiliated, or alcoholic people who live on skid row share a quite different social experience than similar persons who live elsewhere. Skid row is a neighborhood in the simplest meaning of that term. Its buildings and spaces contribute to the skid row subculture, however one chooses to describe it. Interestingly, while sociologists such as Claude Fischer have been trying to free the concept of neighborhood from the constraints of place by exploring the complex social networks of modern urbanites, geographers such as David Ley have been rebelling against the economic and quantitative determinists in their own discipline by emphasizing the subjective and the role of imagery in urban geography, and in the process revealing that cities are not only broken into functional and descriptive units, but into perceptual ones as well. Ley's approach reminds us that neighborhoods and other well-defined urban spaces are important reference points that help to determine the different social experiences of urbanites.[3] This is as true for skid rowers as for other urban groups. Ben Reitman, the celebrated "tramp doctor" of early twentieth-century Chicago, certainly thought so. "Whatever the area of the homeless men is in any city," he once wrote, "it represents the world in which they live. Considering these men as behaving and thinking individuals, we must recognize their surroundings as the sources from which they draw so much that makes them what they are."[4]

The sketch that follows is an attempt to put skid row into clearer historical perspective, emphasizing its quality as a functioning neighborhood and as meaningful social space. The focus, consequently, is on several interrelated themes: the size and character of the population, the nature of institutional and associational life, and the extent of spatial cohesiveness. Three stages in the evolution of the modern skid row emerge from the investigation. The first coincided with the great hobo era around the turn of the twentieth century. A second followed in the late 1920s and 1930s when skid row became much less identified with migrant workers and more with the unemployed. And finally, by the post-World War II years skid row had become the familiar world of dropouts and derelicts. In the process of this long transition skid row changed dramatically from a vital and secure neighborhood to a fragmented and vulnerable one.

Skid Row in its Heyday: The "Main Stem," 1880-1920

The earliest skid rows formed in the context of an active labor marketplace during the second half of the nineteenth century. A male-dominated immigration, the rapid development and exploitation of the trans-Mississippi West, and the general absence of working-class job security were only the most significant of the factors that made the period between the Civil War and World War I an age of transient and seasonal workers.[5] Men on the tramp routinely passed through cities because transportation termini, employment agencies, and a good deal of casual work were located there. Transient workers were drawn to the downtown near the docks or railyards, where they established a highly visible subcommunity at a time when differentiated land use characterized American cities.[6]

The term skid row derives from Seattle's "skid road" (a lumberjack district of the late nineteenth century) but was not a term commonly used until the 1930s. Between the 1890s and 1920s it was more typical to hear tramping workers speak of the "main stem." Here a variety of places served the needs of transient and unattached men. In cheap lodging houses a man could spend as little as 7¢ for a night on a wooden bunk, a dirty hammock, or the bare floor.[7] Nearby were cheap restaurants, second-hand clothing stores, employment offices, and most importantly saloons, where tramping workers could eat and drink, socialize, perhaps talk to prospective employers who came there looking for men, and even spend the night.[8] At the turn of the century a well-defined homeless men's area was an established part of every city. New York's was famous. "From Canal Street to Bayard Street on the west side of the Bowery," wrote one investigator in 1909, every building is a cheap lodging house, and from Chatham Square to Cooper Square about every other

Exhibit 14-1
Center of the Transient Men's Area in Omaha, 1887

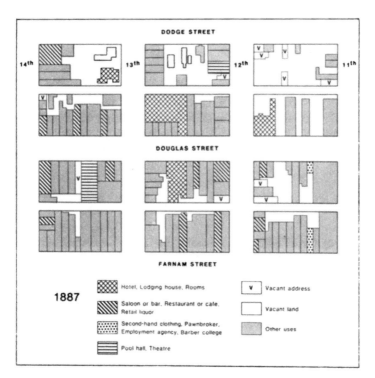

building on each side of the street is a lodging-house, and there are more saloons than lodging houses."[9] No less important in their own right were Chicago's West Madison Street (the largest homeless men's area). Seattle's Yesler Way, San Francisco's South of Market district, or the Gateway in Minneapolis, a twenty-five-block area that in 1900 had 109 saloons and 113 hotels and lodging houses.[10]

The city of Omaha was also an important regional center for tramping workers, and the development of its main stem serves as a useful case study. Omaha was situated on major rail lines and was near seasonal farm work and railroad construction jobs. It was first settled in the 1850s, progressed steadily over the next two decades, and then enjoyed spectacular growth in the 1880s as a railroad, commercial, and meatpacking center. A bustling city of around 100,000 people in the late 1880s, Omaha harbored large numbers of transient workers on their way to and from jobs throughout the American West. A scanning of the manuscript schedules of the 1885 Nebraska state census shows that the principal concentration of lodgers and roomers lay between 9th and

15th streets for several blocks above and below Douglas, one of the main east-west streets. Many of the city's cheapest lodging houses were located in the vicinity. The core of this area was the six blocks along Douglas between 11th and 14th streets. Here clearly was the embryo of a skid row.[11] Exhibit 14-1 reveals, however, that as of 1887 the area had not attracted a significant concentration of homeless men's services.[12] In fact, there were not even that many lodging houses and cheap hotels (although it is clear from press reports and the census schedules that many second and third floors above shops and stores were used for lodgings but were not so described in the city directories or Sanborn insurance maps.[13] So, while the Douglas Street area housed transient men in these years, it had still not acquired the look and feel of a "main stem."

This began to change in the 1890s. The nucleus of the central business district was inexorably moving west along Douglas, Farnum, and Harney streets, from 10th street in the early days, to 13th and then 15th by the 1870s, to 16th after the 1880s. As it did so, homeless men and their services rushed into the backwash created in the less attractive older business area. The westward drift of Omaha's business district probably speeded up the development of the city's main stem. It was a process not without some friction, for as main stem businesses crowded on to Douglas and the cross streets they created what one Omahan called a "line of respectability" around 14th and 15th streets. Businessmen to the west were determined to hold this line. In 1898 they prodded the police into raiding a gambling den that was operating in the back room of a store just west of 15th, threatening to draw other disreputable businesses to the block.[14]

Exhibit 14-2 exhibits the considerable change that had taken place in the Douglas Street transient quarter by 1912. Hotels and lodging houses had proliferated and were now joined by a host of supporting businesses: saloons, cafes, secondhand stores, pawnbrokers, employment agencies, even vaudeville theatres. Where only 16% of the addresses in the six blocks supported businesses serving tramping workers in 1887, by 1912 the figure had jumped to 45%. There were other areas around the downtown that catered to these men, but a check of the city directory and real estate surveys shows no area, even a relatively small one, with anything like the concentration of men's services that Douglas Street had. Douglas was now indeed Omaha's main stem.

Tramping workers came to this and other stems mostly out of economic necessity, but the areas were also social centers, instrumental in the making and reinforcing of the tramping subculture. They were, in fact, just another manifestation of the male ethic that prevailed in American culture during the latter part of the nineteenth century and early years of the twentieth. Male fraternizing in settings as diverse as the workplace, clubs, lodges, saloons, and

Exhibit 14-2
The "Main Stem" in Omaha, 1912

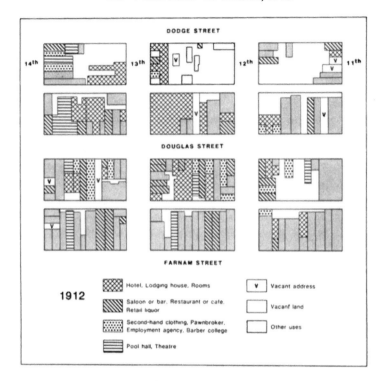

sporting events was an acceptable supplement to home life for bachelors as well as for married men.[15] This male ethic lent a distinct character to downtown city streets. Gunther Barth has written of the impact of the large department store in bringing women into a downtown world, once the domain of men, but I believe he overstates the democratization of the late-nineteenth century central business district. Despite the increased presence of women downtown much that went on there was still for men only. Hotels, taverns, restaurants, clothing stores, barber shops, tailors, cigar stores, newsstands, and even Turkish baths catered to the needs of business and professional men, male office workers, and shopkeepers. If main stem business failed to enjoy the status of some of their more respectable neighbors, they nonetheless gained a measure of legitimacy as lower-class versions of the same thing.[16]

Street life on the main stem therefore had a more positive quality than the often destitute and desperate condition of tramping workers would suggest. The crowded and busy sidewalks—"swarming with migratory workers" as one hobo recalled—offered the men an exhilarating experience. The sociologist Nels Anderson traveled the west as a hobo worker when he was a young man. In 1907 he arrived in Omaha on a freight out of Billings, Montana, and was impressed with the size of the city's main stem and the variety of its services. He and a companion seemed genuinely excited walking along what was undoubtedly Douglas Street and taking in the view. Anderson's friend stood on one corner and estimated that from there he could see at least a thousand men on the streets and sidewalks.[17] On main stems such as Omaha's, knots of men were likely to gather outside the employment agencies that displayed large placards announcing farm jobs or railroad section work. The agencies tended to cluster in Omaha (as they did in most cities), mainly on 10th, 11th, and 12th streets just south of Farnum. Men fresh from the freight yards added to the bustle of main stem sidewalks as they moved along in search of a lodging-house, second-hand store, cafe, or saloon. In saloons they took advantage of the free lunch given for the price of a schooner of beer. Jim Tully wrote in his tramp memoir about a large saloon on South Clark Street in Chicago where the "free lunch was always plentiful, and whether a hobo had a five-cent piece or not, he always ate there." The tramping professor, Walter Wyckoff, found the choices in Chicago overwhelming. He strolled past one saloon after another advertising such treats as "the best free lunch in the city" and "hot sausages with every drink."[18]

The main stem, to be sure, was not altogether upbeat. Observers often described scenes that revealed a dark side—the pathetic beggars, the men with black stares and drooping heads. "They huddle together perforce on the narrow benches," wrote one journalist about the tramps he saw in a New York park, "but they seldom speak to each other, and then in low and spiritless tones. . . . Sodden and hopeless they doze under the trees that bar the rays of the electric lights, living shadows of silent despair."[19] Still, the descriptions of homeless men's areas by Anderson, Wyckoff and others belie these unhappy views. There seems little doubt that at least in the midwestern and western cities where there were large contingents of robust seasonal workers the main stem was a lively place, a genuine workingmen's quarter in which much of the wretchedness was obscured by the comings and goings of harvest workers, construction gangs, lumber men, and even tramping artisans.

A Neighborhood in Decline, 1920-1940

The main stem began to change in the 1920s, principally as a result of new labor market conditions. Mechanization on the farm, in factories, and in the lumber industry, along with the decline in railroad construction, reduced the seasonal demand for unskilled and semi-skilled migrant labor. The migrant workers who remained, furthermore, more typically traveled by automobile or truck—the U.S. Department of Labor estimated in 1926 that 65% of the harvest workers in Kansas came to the wheat fields by car.[20] These and other factors, including the generally favorable employment conditions of the 1920s, had a marked effect on the main stem. The decline in seasonal migrant work opportunities meant fewer men stopping at job agencies and lodging houses, while the widespread use of motor vehicles deprived the main stem of the men who used to catch freights and pass in and out of the homeless men's districts that had always been an adjunct to downtown rail yards. As the main stem lost the visits from tramping workers, it became more closely identified with the "home guard," to use the tramping vernacular. These were the men who stayed on a particular main stem the year round and traveled primarily to settle on another stem. Augmenting this group were inveterate casuals who would have done more traveling had migrant work opportunities been greater. Anderson has written that while he did not realize it at the time, the "hobohemia" he studied in Chicago in the early 1920s was already changing significantly as the old-time hobo began to disappear and the home guard became more conspicuous. Milwaukee officials reported in 1925 that most of the men on that city's main stem were "steady casuals" who stayed in the Milwaukee area doing odd jobs three or four days a week.[21]

The changes in population had an impact on the main stem's services. Still filling their cots and rooms (especially during the 1921-22 depression) were municipal lodging houses for the destitute and the philanthropic "working-men's hotels" for steady laborers, but cities reported a decline in the numbers of cheap lodging houses that had always attracted tramping workers. In Minneapolis, for instance, total lodging-house accommodations were already 30% fewer in 1920 than they had been in 1915.[22] Saloons were also affected, and even more so as a result of prohibition. Drinking places on the main stem had to be underground at the same time that they were losing some of their best customers. Saloons were fewer and different in style. They no longer doubled as dance halls, flophouses, and employment agencies. The free lunch counter disappeared. "The saloon still lives in Hobohemia," Anderson wrote in 1923, "though with waning prestige'. . . one can still get a 'kick' out of the stuff that is sold across the bar, but the crowds do not gather as before Prohibition."[23]

With its changing and shrinking population and withered institutional life, the main stem lost much of its liveliness during the 1920s. A journalist's impression of the Bowery in 1929 was that the color and "picturesque wicked-ness" it had around the turn of the century had disappeared, and all that remained was a depressed scene personified in the lethargic men who resided in cheap lodging houses and attracted the momentary attention of fleeting passersby on the Third Avenue elevated:

> The noisy "L" rushes by its dingy windows,
> "The Lodging House for Men."
> And careless eyes may look upon its inmates
> (They seldom look again).
> Only a bunch of "has-beens," frayed and seedy,
> Wanting a bath and shave.
> Wastrels, who whistle down the wind of fortune
> The gifts that nature gave.[24]

The Bowery and other main stems changed as the heterogeneous transient population of the great hobo era gave way to a smaller, more stationary population of odd-jobbers and the handicapped and misfits for whom the main stem had always been a haven. The phlegmatic and dispirited atmosphere evident on the Bowery signalled the transition from the animated "main stem" to "skid row" as we know it today.

The Great Depression enlarged skid row's population and created a new public awareness of its problems. Social workers had concerned themselves with homeless men since at least the 1890s, when "model" lodging houses first appeared under both municipal and charitable auspices. By the 1920s the professionalization of social work was well underway and the individualized casework approach had become the ideal. Social workers hoped at the time to extend this approach to homeless men, but with the inundation of skid row in the 1930s by thousands of the unemployed there was little else to do but provide most homeless men with "congregate care" of the type they had received since the late nineteenth century. State and city governments helped unattached homeless men first by increasing support to established municipal lodging houses, then by making arrangements with private agencies such as The Salvation Army, and finally by establishing "shelters" in and around skid row in abandoned school buildings and factories. In 1933 Congress passed the Federal Emergency Relief Act creating the Federal Transient Program, and the New Deal came to skid row in the form of additional federal shelters.[25]

The various skid row shelters of the depression years were designed with the best intentions and paid lip service to casework professionalism but in practice they were just big impersonal lodging houses. This was especially true of the state and local shelters. Investigators reported on an affliction called "shelterization," a gradual debilitation among shelter residents brought on by the daily experience of living with a thousand other discouraged men in a cold institutional setting. The experience was seen as especially debilitating for the many depression homeless who came to skid row unwillingly. Edwin Sutherland and Harvey Locke made the classic statement of this thesis. The "shelterized man, they wrote, "shows a tendency to lose all sense of personal responsibility for getting out of the shelter, to become insensible to the element of time; to lose ambition, pride, self-respect, and confidence; to avoid former friends; and to identify himself with the shelter group."[26] How true this really was for the mass of men who spent time in the shelters is difficult to say, but there seems little doubt that the routine and regimentation of the shelters took their toll on a group of mostly unemployed men who spent much of their time just waiting in line. "The line is a long shuffle," wrote one investigator, "with the linesman expressionless, quiet and with the long, bored look as he waits for his food, his fumigation, his bath, his toilet. . . ."[27]

The Works Progress Administration superseded the federal shelter program in 1935, and when cities and states began to dismantle their own shelters that same year welfare officials were actually relieved. "Most dairy barns," one said "were better suited to their purpose than some of those buildings we set up for the care of human beings."[28] However, the new WPA programs more readily accepted family men or unattached men with no history of transiency, and in any case large numbers of unemployed men remained on skid row. Shelter care therefore continued in the old municipal lodging houses, as well as in city missions, The Salvation Army, and other private agencies.[29]

The ambitious shelter programs of the depression years inherited the role played by municipal and charitable lodging houses in earlier periods of unemployment, especially 1913-14 and 1921-22, but they left their own legacy on skid row. Although they were not a truly dominant institution—after all, most men on skid row at any given time were probably not living in shelters—they were nonetheless important in introducing men to skid row, perhaps now rivalling the depleted commerical lodging houses and job agencies.[30] More importantly, in the publicity they received and the controversy that swirled about them the shelters were symbols of skid row, not only to the outside world but also to the men themselves. Skid row, in short, was becoming identified with welfare. Shelter men were by and large products of the depression; between sixty and seventy percent of the men in Chicago's shelters were "non-hobohemians."[31] Such men were not independent agents in the labor marketplace as much as clients of the welfare state. They were on skid row but did not want to be; and the skid row regulars they joined were mostly, as we have seen, men of the home guard who had nowhere else to go. Skid row streets were not to any great extent anymore a way station in a progressive work life, but rather a siding, or even a dead end.

The streets themselves were changing as well, as a return look at Douglas Street in Omaha clearly reveals. The area between 11th and 14th streets—now

Exhibit 14-3
Skid Row in Omaha, 1934

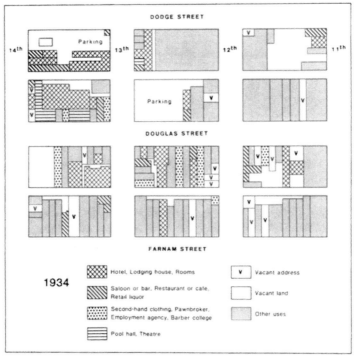

sometimes referred to as "pawnshop row"—remained the heart of the homeless men's district in Omaha, but it was not the area it had been before the First World War. Exhibit 14-3 shows that by 1943 the proportion of addresses serving homeless men had fallen sharply, from 45% to 34%. All the categories of services had declined in numbers. The Salvation Army had now taken over an old bank building on 13th south of Douglas and turned it into a sizable hotel that also served as a shelter under the Homeless Men's Bureau. At the same time, however, two large hotels on Douglas Street were gone and another was reduced in size. The legacy of Prohibition remained: there were no saloons or taverns anywhere, at least not listed as such, since liquor by the drink had yet to return to Omaha. Along Farnam Street on the fringes of the area mainstream businesses had made a noticeable comeback (the same thing had happened on the Bowery in the 1920s).[32] Moreover, in these depressed years vacant addresses were common and more broadly distributed than in 1912, and a large empty lot now met the eye at 14th and Douglas. Not dissimilar in their visual and communal effect were the intrusions of the auto age: two parking lots—one where a hotel had been—and also a filling station at Dodge and 14th. All in all, the old main stem had eroded. Its heyday was apparently over, its future uncertain.

A Neighborhood of Vulnerability: "Skid Row," 1940-1960

The 1940s were perhaps the most important short span of years in all the history of skid row. The wartime industrial buildup helped to end the depression and eradicate the unemployment problem that had brought so many men to skid row. While postwar economic adjustments probably led to some temporary increases in skid row populations, the overall trend continued to be downward. Detroit's skid row population, for example, fell by 17% between 1940 and 1950 and New York's by 50% between 1949 and 1964.[33] Soldiers returning home from this war were less likely than those in previous ones to end up on skid row now that there were veteran's benefits easing the transition to civilian life. In the meantime, automation in agriculture, industry, transportation, and warehousing continued to reduce the need for seasonal, migrant, and unskilled labor. As early as 1940 Nels Anderson could write that the old-time hobo had become little more than a curiosity.[34]

The men who remained on skid-row—mostly the home guard, handicapped, and pensioners—were an older and less mobile group. The average age of the men in Chicago's municipal shelters increased from 40 to 57 in just the short period from 1938 to 1942, and the men stayed much longer, about three months on the average in 1942 compared to only three weeks in 1938.[35] The long-term trend was clear. A census of Bowery lodging houses in 1930 had revealed that almost three-fourths of the men living there were under 50 years of age; by 1966 about three-fourths were over 45.[36] Half of skid rowers in Minneapolis in 1958 were past fifty, while in 1940 only a third had been.[37] And a substantial majority of the men in Los Angeles and Buffalo shelters in the early 1930s were under 45, while just as substantial a majority of skid row men in Sacramento, Philadelphia, and Chicago in the late 1950s were over 45.[38] As the population got older it became less mobile. Over half of the men on Chicago's skid row in 1958 had lived there continuously for at least a year, two-thirds of the men on the Gateway in Minneapolis did not leave the Twin Cities area during a twelve-month period in 1957-58, and almost 90% of the men on Philadelphia's skid row in 1960 had lived there off and on for at least a year—almost 50% for at least five years.[39]

Skid row seemed an anomaly in the postwar era. The nation was geared to a return to prosperity and consumer spending after a decade and a half of depression and war. Returning military personnel entered the ranks of young marrieds looking for housing to raise their growing families. It was a time of optimism built increasingly around the single-family house in new automobile-oriented suburbs. Not surprisingly the public became more interested in street and flophouse life on the old downtown skid rows. Newspapers in Boston, Chicago and Detroit did stunning exposes of their skid rows in 1949—the Chicago *Daily News* gained 20,000 readers during its twelve-part series. A number of cities formed special mayor's committees to study the problem, with a view to rehabilitate the men and to renovate skid row itself through urban renewal under the new Federal Housing Act of 1949. In fact much of the interest in skid row developed directly out of a desire to arrest the decline of central business districts at a time when cities were exploding outward.[40]

The public's new preoccupation with skid row focused on the problem of alcoholism among the homeless men living there. "Skid Row, U.S.A., to anyone who does not really know it from inside," reported one investigator in 1956, "is that place where alcoholics on their last legs have come to drink in peace."[41] The old main stem had been associated with drinking as well, but even its most pious critics saw the classic hoboes and tramps mostly as rough working men or social misfits who simply overindulged in low-life saloons and then went on the road again. Their sins were wanderlust and laziness, not alcoholic addiction. The typical skid row man of the 1950s, however, was supposedly a hopeless alcoholic, enslaved by his addiction to the point where he was totally unproductive. He was a pathetic creature lying in littered alleys, consumed by the daily quest for alcoholic oblivion. More sophisticated studies by sociologists and psychologists in these years pointed out that many skid row men were not alcoholics and that some did not drink at all. At the same time, however, these investigators left little doubt that drinking was indeed the most important activity that took place on skid row.[42]

Older and more socially inadequate as a group than their predecessors, the men on skid row in the postwar era were enveloped by the welfare state. A variety of agencies and institutions provided services. Washington D.C. and Detroit were pioneers with publicly run alcoholic clinics on their skid rows in 1950s, and by the 1960s the welfare system stretched from hospital care to half-way houses. Private social agencies with updated approaches and methods often worked closely with public agencies and were part of the larger professional welfare establishment on skid row. The Salvation Army, for example, moved away from simple lodging and work tests in the 1950s and began to offer much more counseling, medical assistance, and alcoholic treatment. Social security and other retirement programs added to the skid rower's status as a dependent client. Two-thirds of the men on the Gateway in Minneapolis received some sort of welfare payments or pension in 1958, as life (and crime) on skid row became "regularized by the monthly check."[43]

The rapid deterioration of skid row's image invited the municipal "clean-up" efforts first proposed in the late 1940s. The old main stem may have been an urban blight in the eyes of many people, but it was also a crowded and lively part of the city whose function as a men's quarter lent it legitimacy. By the 1950s skid row was not only less crowded and lively, it had lost its tie to the cultural mainstream with the decline since early in the century of the male ethic and the widespread bachelor-style fraternizing that went with it. Moreover, skid row usually occupied some of the least attractive areas of an urban downtown that was losing its soul to the suburbs. Little wonder skid rows were prime targets for new urban renewal schemes and interstate high-way routes. By the late 1950s Kansas City, Los Angeles, Sacramento, Denver, Minneapolis, New York, Philadelphia and Detroit had all pulled down large segments of their skid rows or were contemplating doing so.[44]

Omaha's Douglas Street skid row would also face the wrecking ball, but not before the 1970s. Until then it stood as a classic example of the decline of skid rows in postwar America. Its population had plummeted. One study estimated that there were at most only two thousand homeless men in downtown Omaha in 1950. There were probably four times that number around the turn of the century.[45] Exhibit 14-4 shows that by 1953 only 30% of the addresses in the Douglas Street area served homeless men, down even further from the 1930s. The concentration of job agencies just off the map south of Farnam had gone, along with the migrant seasonal work the agencies had specialized in; and the few that remained probably served more and more outsiders, as Keith Lovald found was the case on the Gateway in Minneapolis during the 1950s.[46] There were now as many retail liquor stores as bars, an indication not only of the drinking problems on skid row but also of the social environment in which much of it took place. Men were buying cheap bottles and drinking on the street, in alleys, and in hotel rooms.

As homeless men's services decreased in the Douglas Street area over the years they did not become more concentrated. Skid row in Omaha did not shrink that much, it just thinned out. Consequently, a much smaller skid row population in the 1950s used services that were distributed over roughly the same area as fifty years earlier in the heyday of the main stem. Moreover, the thinning out of Omaha's skid row did not mean the remaining services were mixed in with empty lots and abandoned buildings. There was actually a lower vacancy rate in 1953 than there had been in 1934. Skid row businesses operated alongside gas stations, wholesale suppliers, appliance repair shops, and other establishments with a markedly different function and clientele than places serving homeless men. The nucleus of Omaha's central business district had continued to move west, but its eastern edge still rested at 16th Street. Skid row, only two blocks away, therefore still had enough site value to attract "legitimate" businesses, although not enough to attract the glamor-

Exhibit 14-4
Skid Row in Omaha, 1953

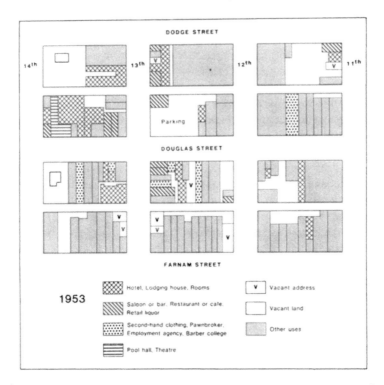

ous sectors of the downtown economy: new hotels, offices, banks, and chic retail stores. Lower Douglas Street remained largely the "zone of discard" in downtown Omaha.[47] Only in the 1970s would it become the focus of major urban renewal, mostly for a park designated to establish a visual link between the downtown and the riverfront in an effort to restore vitality to the heart of the city.

The implications of postwar development for street life on skid row are difficult to judge. One should never underestimate the adaptable social tendencies of homeless men. Investigators in Chicago and San Francisco during the 1950s and 1960s found a vigorous street life in which large crowds of men "promenaded" along the sidewalks, much in the fashion of students strolling on a college campus.[48] However, these were historically cities with unusually large and populous skid rows (Donald Bogue reported that they were still the nation's two most populous in 1950).[49] The fact remains that the spatial context of much of the socializing that took place on skid row had unquestionably changed, and with it the social experience itself. The Omaha evidence suggests that the typical skid row in the 1950s had fewer areas where the men, themselves fewer in number, would be likely to gather informally, such as along blocks where most if not all of the frontages opened to skid row services. Even in the heart of skid row, homeless men rubbed shoulders with outsiders. As a result, the men were more exposed, more vulnerable, with a less sure claim to the sidewalks they had dominated when Nels Anderson walked along Douglas Street in 1907. Their exposure was highlighted by the fact that their outdoor loitering was a throwback to a time when public spaces had many uses. This had given way during the twentieth century to the idea that streets and sidewalks, especially downtown, were exclusively thorough-fares for pedestrian and vehicular traffic moving quickly to a destination. The socializing that skid rowers enjoyed on the street was something other urban-ites did indoors, including in their automobiles.

As the skid row population got smaller and suffered further in its public image, and as skid row's physical plant changed, the police assumed a far greater role. By the 1960s patrolmen on skid row acted not so much in the interest of homeless men but rather in response to the sensibilities of the larger public and in particular those persons who worked in and around skid row in businesses unconnected with the skid row economy. The police on skid row were managers as much as order-keepers, seeing to it that the street made a presentable appearance. Patrolmen were encouraged in this approach by the fact that the street scenes they usually encountered now involved relatively small groups of men—isolated and intimate situations, easily comprehended, easily dealt with. Since skid rowers had become so immobile, they could become quite well-known individually to police officers, who sometimes developed a paternalistic relationship with them. However, this did not interfere with the absolute authority of the patrolman on skid row and his undisputed prerogative to make an arrest at any time. The police were clearly more tolerant of certain behavior on skid row than they were elsewhere—for example, men staggering about or lying down on the sidewalk—but skid rowers had to be prepared at almost any time to be picked up by police patrols. The charge was usually drunkenness, whether the men were actually drunk or not. It was often just a surrogate for a vagrancy charge, which posed questions of constitutionality and was under attack in the 1950s and early 1960s.[50]

The day-to-day interaction between skid rowers and the criminal justice system developed into a ritualistic one, and even served as induction cere-mony for men new to skid row. "The jail is perhaps the most important scene in the life of tramps," wrote James Spradley in his interesting work on skid row men in Seattle during the 1960s. "It is here they find the remaining shreds of respectable identity stripped away as they become participants in an elaborate ritual—that of making the bucket. Identity change takes place for these men as they are labelled 'bums,' cut off from former roles and identities, treated as objects to be manipulated."[51] Confronting the police had preoccupied tramping workers in the days of the main stem as well, but the men were much more numerous and mobile then. They stood a lesser chance of getting frequently arrested and jailed, and they could more easily elude the police, even carrying on what amounted to a heroic test of wit and skill with the "yard bulls" employed by the railroads. They were not helpless objects of police manipulation passing regularly through a humiliating criminal justice process.

The police problem inhibited street life on skid row. Homeless men had to be incessantly watchful, hoping not to draw attention to themselves by their actions. It became safer to socialize in alleys, under viaducts, or simply on the move, aping unconvincingly respectable society's sidewalk behavior, and all the while trying to stay within the skid row area. Once outside, the men became like a "fifth wheel," as one skid rower put it. In fact, between the decline of street life and the threat of the police, homeless men often beat a hasty retreat indoors, to the few bars and theatres that were open to them (and even these were often invaded by outsiders at night), as well as to the lodging house, which in the past had not been a place to linger. Hotel proprietors now commonly allowed the men to sit in the lobby and watch television. Half of Chicago's skid rowers in 1958 watched television on a daily basis. Even the tiny hotel rooms and cubicles became places to socialize or to sit alone and drink. For an increasing number of men, they became places to die.[52]

Conclusion

The evolution of skid row can be traced through the institution located there which served at different times as the most visible agent of outside interests. Before the 1920s that institution was the employment agency (and the saloons and lodging houses that often doubled as employment agencies or were connected to them). The men were "goods" in the labor market, used and abused no doubt, but still seasonal and itinerant laborers participating at least marginally in the economic mainstream. In the 1920s the "home guard" and others may have continued to use the job agencies still to be found on skid row, but migrant work in distant places was on the decline, and with the depression of the 1930s the public shelter emerged as the major representative of an outside world concerned about the crisis in unemployment and transiency. By the 1950s and 1960s the police were the most visible agents of the larger society, which now had little use or sympathy for homeless men. While welfare agencies abounded and pursued a strategy of rehabilitation, they were inextricably tied to the order-minded criminal justice system that sent them most of their skid row clients.

The transformation of skid row from labor marketplace to ward of policemen and the welfare state can be depicted in a superficial way by three imaginary street scenes, dated approximately 1900, 1930, and 1960. In the first we see great bunches of workingmen ambling along a city block crowded with men's services. The second reveals a more orderly yet disturbing scene. Hundreds of men, looking strangely alike in their overcoats, hats, and dazed expressions, stand in a long line stretching down the block and around the corner from a soup kitchen. The last view is striking for its less crowded appearance. Here we see a few lone pedestrians walking past a man sprawled out on the sidewalk. Several others crouch along a storefront and watch, and a foursome lurks in the shadows of an alley passing around a bottle of wine.

These images of skid row at various stages in its history are not drawn here for their accuracy. They are misleading in that much on skid row remained the same over the first half of the century. Beggars, handicapped men, social misfits, and other "skid row types" were always there. So too was excessive drinking. And the streets themselves have ever defined a special men's world, even as the great hobo armies of the past became what Howard Bahr has called the small "tribes" of homeless men in recent times.[53] Still, the images clearly belong to three distinct epochs in skid row's history and tell us a great deal about real changes that have taken place on skid row.

Critical to an understanding of these changes is an appreciation of skid row's physical plant. Since so little work has been done on the spatial history of skid row, this paper has examined Omaha's Douglas Street as a case study. Throughout the first half of this century Douglas Street remained Omaha's principal skid row area. The same fixedness was true of the larger area in which homeless men and their services could be found (including what amounted to a small secondary skid row a few blocks away on North 16th Street). There is a remarkable fit between the area Omaha officials described for Donald Bogue's survey of skid rows in 1958 and the distribution of lodgers and roomers in the 1885 state census. Spatial inertia has characterized homeless men's areas in most cities. The boundaries of skid row in urban America have always been clear to homeless men and outsiders alike.[54]

The fact that Douglas Street served as the traditional center of a larger homeless men's area extending loosely over part of the downtown only added to the importance of the strong concentration of men's services there in the heyday of the main stem early in the century. Small though it was, this four-to-six block concentration was critical in legitimizing, protecting, and reinforcing the subculture of the main stem. Their little patch of urban turf stood as a grand achievement to tramping workers—a sort of "home territory" over which they exercised a sense of control.[55] The decay of the main stem in later years, while by no means complete, blurred the spatial definition of the Douglas Street skid row, undermined the coherence of the area, and altered the social environment for its habitués, who had become fewer and undoubtedly older, less mobile, and dispirited. The evidence suggests a cruel paradox: as skid row men became more detached from the socio-economic mainstream and retreated more or less permanently to a particular skid row, they were less able to enjoy the sense of security afforded by a neighborhood they could truly call their own.

NOTES

[1] Leonard U. Blumberg, Thomas E. Shipley, Jr., Stephen F. Barsky, *Liquor and Poverty: Skid Row as a Human Condition* (New Brunswick: Rutgers Center of Alcohol Studies, 1978). Another excellent study is Alvin Averbach, "San Francisco's South of Market District, 1850-1950: The Emergence of a Skid Row," *California Historical Quarterly*, 52 (Fall 1973), 197-223. See also Keith Lovald, "From Hobohemia to Skid Row: The Changing Community of the Homeless Man" (Doctoral dissertation, University of Minnesota, 1960); James F. Rooney, "Societal Forces and the Unattached Male: An Historical Review," in Howard M. Bahr, ed., *Disaffiliated Man: Essays and Bibliography on Skid Row, Vagrancy and Outsiders* (Toronto: University of Toronto Press, 1970), pp. 13-38. Geographers who have touched briefly on the spatial history of skid row are Jim Ward, "Skid Row as a Geographic Entity," *Professional Geographer*, 27 (August 1975), 286-96; Gwyn Rowley, " 'Plus ca change...': A Canadian Skid Row," *Canadian Geographer*, 22 (Fall 1978), 211-24.

[2] For example, Leonard Blumberg, Thomas E. Shipley, Jr., Irving R. Shandler, *Skid Row and its Alternatives: Research and Recommendations from Philadelphia* (Philadelphia: Temple University Press, 1973), p. 204.

[3] Claude S. Fischer et al., *Networks and Places: Social Relations in the Urban Setting* (New York: Free Press, 1977); David Ley, *A Social Geography of the City* (New York: Harper & Row, 1983). For reviews of recent theoretical trends in urban sociology and geography, see Kenneth A. Scherzer, "The Unbounded Community: Neighborhood Life and Social Structure in New York City, 1830-1875" (Doctoral dissertation, Harvard University, 1982), Introduction and *passim*; David T. Herbert and Ronald J. Johnston, "Geography and the Urban Environment," in Herbert and Johnston, eds., *Geography and the Urban Environment: Progress in Research and Applications*, 4 vols. (Chichester, England: John Wiley, 1978-81), I: 1-33.

[4] Ben L. Reitman, "Following the Monkey," p. 8 (reverse side), Folder 11, Reitman Papers, Manuscripts Collection, University of Illinois-Chicago Circle Library. (On Reitman, see Roger A. Bruns, *Knights of the Road: A Hobo History* [New York: Methuen, 1980], pp. 170-76. A brief study that sensitively explores the role of the skid row neighborhood in the social experience of the men who live there is Ronald Vanderkooi, "The Main Stem: Skid Row Revisited," *Society*, 10 (September-October 1973), 64-71. I have made a more extended argument for a spatial view of urban social history in *Detroit and the Problem of Order, 1830-1880: A Geography of Crime, Riot, and Policing* (Lincoln: University of Nebraska Press, 1980). See also Theodore Hershberg, ed., *Philadelphia: Work, Space, Family, and Group Experience in the Nineteenth Century* (New York: Oxford University Press, 1981), pp. 121-23.

[5] Eric M. Monkkonen, ed., *Walking to Work: Tramps in America, 1790-1920* (Forthcoming, University of Nebraska Press).

[6] David Ward, *Cities and Immigrants: A Geography of Change in Nineteenth-Century America* (New York: Oxford University Press, 1970).

[7] Jacob Riis, *How the Other Half Lives* (Repr. ed. New York: Hill & Wang, 1957), pp. 59-67; Alice W. Solenberger, *One Thousand Homeless Men* (New York: Russell Sage Foundation, 1911), pp. 314-29.

[8] Jon M. Kingsdale, "The 'Poor Man's Club': Social Functions of the Urban Working-Class Saloon," *American Quarterly*, 25 (October 1973), 472-89.

[9] Frank M. White, "Eliminate the Tramp," *Harper's Weekly, 53* (February 6, 1909), 16.

[10] Lovald, "From Hobohemia to Skid Row," pp. 121-22.

[11] Reels 15-17, Nebraska State Census, 1885, Nebraska State Historical Society: "A Bed for a Dime," *Omaha Republican*, February 23, 1890, p. 4.

[12] Sources for the maps in this paper are the Sanborn Fire Insurance maps of Omaha (1887, 1934, 1953), *Baist's Real Estate Atlas of Surveys of Omaha* (Philadelphia: G. William Baist, 1910), and the Omaha city directories for 1887, 1912, 1934, and 1953. All are in the Nebraska State Historical Society except for the 1953 Sanborn maps, which are located at the Omaha Public Library. Obviously not all of the places I identify as serving homeless men necessarily did so most of the time. This is especially true of hotels and restaurants. However, I chose not to include other places that probably did serve homeless men at least part of the time, namely barber shops, men's clothing stores (not second-hand), and cigar shops.

[13] Later editions of the city directory identify second and third floor lodgings more fully, but it still ought to be said that lodgings are underrepresented in all the maps prepared for this paper. Where there were lodgings or rooms above a first floor with different uses, the addresses are displayed on the maps as divided into front and rear spaces.

[14] "Movement of the Business Center," *Omaha Daily Bee*, March 29, 1903, p. 21; "Omaha Realty," ibid., January 26, 1901, p. 4. "Grief to Gamblers," ibid., March 17, 1898, p. 1.

[15] Ned Polsky, *Hustlers, Beats, and Others* (Chicago: Aldine, 1967), pp. 32-34; Joe L. Dubbert, *A Man's Place: Masculinity in Transition* (Englewood Cliffs, Prentice-Hall, 1979), p. 99; Benjamin G. Rader, *American Sports: From the Age of Folk Games to the Age of Spectators* (Englewood Cliffs: Prentice-Hall, 1983); Kingsdale, " 'Poor Man's Club,' " pp. 472-89. For some contemporary views, G.S. Crawford, "Club Life vs. Home Life," *Arena*, 16 (August 1896), 418-31; John J. a'Beckett, "Man at his Club," *Harper's Bazaar*, 35 (June 1901), 149-54; "Men's Clubs and the Churches," *Independent*, 55 (January 1, 1903), 16-21. I have dealt more fully with the tramping subculture in "Tramping Workers, 1890-1920: A Subcultural Perspective," in Monkkonen, ed., *Walking to Work*.

[16] Gunther Barth, *City People: The Rise of Modern City Culture in Nineteenth-Century America* (New York: Oxford University Press, 1980), pp. 146-47; Philip Thomason, "The Men's Quarter of Downtown Nashville," *Tennessee Historical Quarterly*, 41 (Spring 1982), 48-66.

[17] Bruns, *Knights of the Road*, p. 163; Nels Anderson, *The American Hobo: An Autobiography* (Leiden: E. J. Brill, 1975), p. 85.

[18] Jim Tully, *Beggars of Life: A Hobo Autobiography* (Garden City: Garden City Publishing Co., 1924), pp. 176-77; Walter A. Wyckoff, *The Workers: The West* (New York: Scribners, 1898), p. 54. See also William Edge, *The Main Stem* (New York:

Vanguard, 1927), pp. 202-3. On employment agencies, see Frances Kellor, *Out of Work: A Study of Employment Agencies* (New York: G.P. Putnam's Sons, 1905); Don D. Lescohier, *The Labor Market* (New York: Macmillan, 1919), pp. 141-63.

[19] Mariner J. Kent, "The Making of a Tramp," *Independent*, 55 (March 1903), 667. See also Josiah Flynt [Willard], *Tramping with Tramps: Studies and Sketches of Vagabond Life* (New York: Century, 1899).

[20] John J. Hader, "Honk Honk Hobo," *Survey*, 60 (August 1, 1928), 453. On mechanization and the decline of the unattached migrant worker, see Wilson Compton, "Recent Developments in the Lumber Industry," *Journal of Forestry*, 30 (April 1932), 440-50; Paul S. Taylor, "Migratory Farm Labor in the United States," *Monthly Labor Review*, 44 (March 1937), 538-39; Nels Anderson, *Men on the Move* (Chicago: Univerity of Chicago Press, 1940), pp. 169-76; Thomas D. Isern, "Adoption of the Combine on the Northern Plains," *South Dakota History*, 10 (Spring 1980), 101-18; Rooney, "Societal Forces and the Unattached Male," pp. 18-20.

[21] Anderson, *American Hobo*, pp. 167-68; Edward Berman, "Odd Jobbers: The Placement of Casual Labor," *Survey*, 53 (January 15, 1925), 466-68. I have argued elsewhere that this large change in population character on the main stem may have begun as early as the turn of the century in the greater Midwest. See my "Omaha Vagrants and the Character of Western Hobo Labor, 1887-1913," *Nebraska History*, 63 (Summer 1982), 255-72.

[22] Philip Klein, *The Burden of Unemployment: A Study of Unemployment Relief Measures in Fifteen American Cities, 1921-1922* (New York: Russell Sage Foundation, 1923), pp. 158-60; Leah H. Feder, *Unemployment Relief in Periods of Depression: A Study of Measures Adopted in Certain American Cities, 1857 through 1922* (New York: Russell Sage Foundation, 1936), pp. 315-18. On municipal lodging houses and workingmen's hotels, see Alice C. Willard, "Reinstatement of Vagrants Through Municipal Lodging Houses," *Proceedings of the National Conference of Charities and Correction (1903)*, pp. 404-11; John L. Thomas, "Workingmen's Hotels," *Municipal Affairs*, 3 (March 1899), 73-94; "Decent Lodgings for Poor Men," *Independent*, 75 (September 11, 1913), 638.

[23] Nels Anderson, *The Hobo: The Sociology of the Homeless Man* (Chicago: University of Chicago Press, 1923), pp. 38-39.

[24] William N. Hubbell, "Adventures in the Bowery District," *Missionary Review of the World*, 52 (July 1929), 528-29. See also Anderson, *Men on the Move*, pp. 16-20.

[25] Roy Lubove, *The Professional Altruist: The Emergence of Social Work as a Career, 1880-1930* (Cambridge: Harvard University Press, 1965); Manfred Lilliefors, Jr., "Social Case Work and the Homeless Man," *Family*, 9 (January 1929), 291-94; Alvin Roseman, *Shelter Care and the Local Homeless Man*, Publication No. 46, Chicago Public Administration Service (Chicago: Public Administration Service, 1935); Russell H. Kurtz, ed., *Social Work Year Book, 1939* (New York: Russell Sage Foundation, 1939), pp. 441-44.

[26] Edwin H. Sutherland and Harvey J. Locke, *Twenty Thousand Homeless Men: A Study of Unemployed Men in the Chicago Shelters* (Chicago: J.R. Lippincott, 1936), p. 146.

[27] Jesse Walter Dees, Jr., *Flophouse: An Authentic Undercover Study of "Flophouses," "Cage Hotels," including Missions, Shelters, and Institutions Serving Unattached (Homeless) Men* (Francestown, N.H.: Marshall Jones, 1948), p. 131. See also Roseman, *Shelter Care*, pp. 7-8. The term "shelterization" might have been new, but the idea was an old one. Social reformers had long argued that many men were turned into tramps and hoboes as a result of extended association with homeless men on the

road or in lodging houses and other skid row places. For example, see Solenberger, *One Thousand Homeless Men*, pp. 213-14.

[28] Robert S. Wilson, "Current Relief Problems in the Care of Resident Homeless and Unattached Persons," *Proceedings of the National Conference of Social Work (1937)*, pp. 619-20.

[29] M. Starr Northrup, Malcolm J. Brown, and Katherine Gordon, *Survey of Transient and Homeless Population in 12 Cities*, Research Bulletin, Works Progress Administration (Washington D.C.: Government Printing Office, 1937); Russell H. Kurtz, ed., *Social Work Year Book, 1941* (New York: Russell Sage Foundation, 1941), pp. 256-57; "Temporary Shelter for Homeless or Transient Persons, 1936-1938, in 29 Urban Areas," *The Child: Monthly News Survey*, 4 (March 1940), supplement, pp. 6-11.

[30] Lovald, "From Hobohemia to Skid Row," pp. 189-90, 218-19.

[31] Sutherland and Locke, *Twenty Thousand Homeless Men*; pp. 50-69; Roseman, *Shelter Care*, pp. 10-11.

[32] Hubbell, "Adventures in the Bowery District," p. 528.

[33] H. Warren Dunham, *Homeless Men and their Habitats: A Research Planning Report* (Detroit: Wayne State University Press, 1953), pp. 11, 37-38; Howard M. Bahr and Theodore Caplow, *Old Men Drunk and Sober* (New York: New York University Press, 1973), p. 16. See also Donald Bogue, *Skid Row in American Cities* (Chicago: University of Chicago Press, 1963), pp. 8-12.

[34] Anderson, *Men on the Move*, p. 21. See also Samuel E. Wallace, *Skid Row as a Way of Life* (Totowa, N.J.: Bedminster Press, 1965), pp. 22-23; Bogue, *Skid Row in American Cities*, p. 476.

[35] Dees, *Flophouse*, pp. 143-44.

[36] "The Bowery Bum at Home," *Literary Digest*, 107 (November 29, 1930), 20-21, Bahr and Caplow, *Old Men*, p. 32.

[37] Lovald, "From Hobohemia to Skid Row," pp. 246-48.

[38] Pauline V. Young, "The New Poor," *Sociology and Social Research*, 17 (January-February 1933), 234-42; Herman J. Schubert, *Twenty Thousand Transients: A One Year's Sample of Those Who Apply for Aid in a Northern City* (Buffalo: Emergency Relief Bureau, 1935), pp. 10-12; Bahr and Caplow, *Old Men*, p. 32.

[39] Bogue, *Skid Row in American Cities*, pp. 111, 243-44; Lovald, "From Hobohemia to Skid Row," p. 303; Leonard Blumberg et al., *The Men on Skid Row: A Study of Philadelphia's Homeless Man Population*, lithograph, Department of Psychology, Temple University School of Medicine, December 1960, p. 24.

[40] Jerome Ellison, "The Shame of Skid Row," *Saturday Evening Post*, 225 (December 20, 1952), 13; "Land of the Living Dead," *Time*, 54 (August 29, 1949), 48: James O'Gara, "Chicago's Misery Mile," *Commonweal*, 50 (September 30, 1949), 598-600; *The Homeless Alcoholic: Report of the First International Institute on the Homeless Alcoholic* (Detroit: Mayor's Committee on Skid Row Problems and Michigan State Board of Alcoholism, 1955), p. 27; Harold W. Demone and Edward Blacker, *The Unattached and Socially Isolated Resident on Skid Row*, multilith, Boston Community Development Program, 1961, pp. 1-2.

[41] Sara Harris, *Skid Row, U.S.A.* (New York, Doubleday, 1956), p. 26.

[42] Robert Strauss, "Alcohol and the Homeless Man," *Quarterly Journal of Studies on Alcohol*, 7 (December 1946), 360-404; Robert Strauss and Raymond G. McCarthy, "Non-Addictive Pathological Drinking Patterns of Homeless Men," ibid., 12 (December 1951), 601-11; Joan K. Jackson and Ralph G. Connor, "The Skid Road

Alcoholic," ibid., 14 (September 1953), 468-86; W. Jack Peterson and Milton A. Maxwell, "The Skid Road 'Wino,' " *Social Problems*, 5 (Spring 1958), 308-16.

⁴³ *The Homeless Alcoholic*, pp. 15, 19-20, 33; Edward H. McKinley, *Marching to Glory: The History of the Salvation Army in the United States of America, 1880-1980* (San Francisco: Harper & Row, 1980), pp. 177-78; Lovald, "From Hobohemia to Skid Row," pp. 386-88.

⁴⁴ "Hallelujah Time for Bums," *Time*, 70 (October 14, 1957), 33, *The Homeless Man on Skid Row* (Chicago: Tenants' Relocation Bureau, 1961), p.i.

⁴⁵ Bogue, *Skid Row in American Cities*, pp. 6, 8. Chicago's skid row population had also fallen to a quarter of what it was in 1910, according to Wallace, *Skid Row as a Way of Life*, p. 24.

⁴⁶ Lovald, "From Hobohemia to Skid Row," pp. 352-62.

⁴⁷ On urban downtowns in the postwar era, see Raymond E. Murphy, J.E. Vance, Jr., and Bart J. Epstein, "Internal Structure of the CBD, *Economic Geography*, 31 (January 1955), 21-46.

⁴⁸ Jacqueline P. Wiseman, *Stations of the Lost: The Treatment of Skid Row Alcoholics* (Englewood Cliffs: Prentice-Hall, 1970), pp. 38-41; Bogue, *Skid Row in American Cities*, pp. 117-18.

⁴⁹ Bogue, *Skid Row in American Cities*, p. 6.

⁵⁰ Egon Bittner, "The Police on Skid Row: A Study in Peace-Keeping," *American Sociological Review*, 32 (October 1967), 706-14; Wiseman, *Stations of the Lost*, p. 67; Forrest W. Lacey, "Vagrancy and Other Crimes of Personal Condition, *Harvard Law Review*, 66 (May 1953), 1203-26; Arthur H. Sherry. "Vagrants, Rogues, and Vagabonds—Old Concepts in Need of Revision," *California Law Review*, 48 (October 1960), 557-67; Gary V. Dubin and Richard H. Robinson, "The Vagrancy Concept Reconsidered: Problems and Abuses of Status Criminality," *New York University Law Review*, 37 (January 1962), 121-36.

⁵¹ James P. Spradley, *You Owe Yourself a Drunk: An Ethnology of Urban Nomads* (Bowtown: Little Brown, 1970), p. 223.

⁵² Spradley, *You Owe Yourself a Drunk*, p. 124; Wiseman. *Stations of the Lost*, p. 23; Bogue, *Skid Row in American Cities*, p. 246; Lovald, "From Hobohemia to Skid Row," pp. 389-402; Wallace, *Skid Row as a Way of Life*, p. 121.

⁵³ Howard M. Bahr, *Skid Row: An Introduction to Disaffiliation* (New York: Oxford University Press, 1973), pp. 9-13.

⁵⁴ Bogue, *Skid Row in American Cities*, p. 34; Lovald, "From Hobohemia to Skid Row," p. 434. Interstate highway construction in the 1960s and urban renewal in the 1970s finally weakened the hold of Omaha's skid row on its traditional ground and led to the rise of at least one new skid row area downtown—about ten blocks to the west. See "24th , Farnum: 'A Dangerous Corner,' " *Omaha World Herald*, July 25, 1976, Sec. B, pp. 1, 6. The dispersion of skid row from its ancient turf was also true of other cities in the 1960s and 1970s, profoundly altering the social experience for many "skid row men." See Howard M. Bahr, "The Gradual Disappearance of Skid Row," *Social Problems*, 15 (Summer 1967), 43-45; Barrett A. Lee, "The Disappearance of Skid Row: Some Ecological Evidence," *Urban Affairs Quarterly*, 16 (September 1980), 104-5.

⁵⁵ Stanford M. Lyman and Marvin B. Scott, "Territoriality: A Neglected Sociological Dimension," *Social Problems*, 15 (Fall 1967), 236-49.

15

An Introduction to Chicago's Skid Rows—Survey Results

Donald J. Bogue

EVEN expert and long-time observers of Skid Rows in Chicago confess they cannot say reliably what kinds of men and how many of each kind live on Skid Row. The mission worker, the social worker, the tavern keeper, the policeman, the judge who sentences Skid Row men who have been arrested, or the labor contractor—each sees only a biased fragment. If one walks along a Skid Row street in the daytime, he notes only the dozens of idle men loafing in small clusters, drifting along the street, or leaning as solitary spectators against the buildings; he does not see those men who are at work. At night, a tour of the crowded taverns could give the impression that only heavy drinkers live here—unless it is counterbalanced by information concerning those who are sober and asleep in their cubicles, who are watching TV, visiting friends, playing cards in hotel lobbies, or attending mission services or meetings of Alcoholics Anonymous. The question, "How many of each kind?" is one that can be answered only by taking a sample census, that is, by interviewing a representative cross-section of the residents and getting from each one information which can help paint a composite picture when compiled.

Such a sample survey was made on Chicago's Skid Rows between December 22, 1957, and April 1, 1958. A total of 613 men were interviewed by carefully selected, trained, and tested interviewers. Men to be interviewed were selected on the basis of probability sampling in accordance with a predetermined sampling plan that was designed to give results that would represent an unbiased cross-section of each of Chicago's four major Skid Row areas. The questions asked in the interview covered the many aspects of the present situation and life history of the men that were hypothesized as having a bearing on their now being on Skid Row.

... It should be reported here that the degree of cooperation and apparent honesty in answering questions surpassed all expectations. The residents of these areas responded with amazing frankness, both with respect to themselves and with respect to conditions of their lives. Since each of the Skid Row areas has a very active "grapevine," news of the study traveled fast. The men correctly interpreted the purpose of the survey as one of objective fact-finding in an effort to understand how they got to this place and what might be done to help them. The resulting body of information is thought to be of a higher and more dependable quality, with less falsification and distortion, than has previously been assembled for this type of respondent. However,. . . this information is only the subjective self-reporting of a complete and emotion-laden set of experiences, and must be analyzed as such.

Physical Aspects of Chicago's Skid Rows

Chicago's Skid Rows: Definition and Location

It is impossible to establish a definition of Skid Row communities that will permit their clear-cut delineation. How, for example, does one differentiate between a slum and a Skid Row? Or between a rooming house area inhabited predominantly by workingmen and a Skid Row where many residents live in rooming houses? The definition used for the sample census of Skid Row residents was as follows: all cubicle-type hotels and all missions which serve homeless men or low-income chronic alcoholics are to be included, as well as all rooming houses and hotels with rooms where (a) the rent per night is less than $2.00 (or $12.00 per week), (b) more than three-fourths of the residents are men, and (c) the neighborhood has the general Skid Row characteristics— with employment offices for unskilled labor, many taverns, barber colleges, cheap clothing stores, missions, and second-hand stores.

At least five areas in Chicago qualify under this definition:

1. West Madison Street, from Canal to about 1200 West;
2. South State Street from the Loop to 1100 South, with a single cubicle hotel being located in the 3600 block on South State;
3. North Clark Street from the Loop to Chicago Avenue;
4. An "L" shaped area along South Clark Street from the Loop to 600 South and along Van Buren Street between State and Clark;

5. A small area near Wilson and Broadway, with a single cubicle hotel
    and a hotel with rooms catering exclusively to men.

Newer Skid Row type developments are emerging along Sixty-third Street,
along Halsted Street extending south from Madison, and along Madison
Street west of the 1200 block. They were not included in this survey because,
in every case, they are inextricably intermingled with a slum-family situation.

Number of Homeless Men in Skid Row Areas

A careful estimate was made of the homeless man population of the five
Skid Row Areas. This was done as the first step of the sampling procedure.
Each of the hotels and rooming houses, missions, and other places in which
these men live was canvassed, and a record was made of the number of
sleeping spaces (beds) available for these men. Data concerning the number of
beds occupied and vacant at the time of the canvass (winter, 1957-1958) were
also collected. The homeless man population was obtained by simply adding
the occupancy figures for each of the places. Because at any one time many of
these men are in the House of Correction or in Cook County Hospital, a
canvass was made of each of these institutions, similar to that for lodging
places. Finally, from discussions with persons familiar with the area, an
estimate was made of the number of men who sleep in boxcars, under bridges,
and in doorways, or who "carry the banner" (walk the streets all night or
lounge in restaurants and railway stations because they have no place to
sleep). The canvass yielded the following results:

	Number of Men	Percent of Total
Total homeless men of Skid Rows in Chicago	11,926	100.0
West Madison Street Area	7,525	63.1
South State Street Area	1,687	14.1
South Clark and Van Buren Street Area	1,223	10.3
North Clark Street Area	691	5.8
Wilson and Broadway, Other*	370	3.1
Jails, Hospitals, Sleeping out	430	3.6

* Includes missions that serve homeless men, but which are located outside the delineated Skid
Row areas.

As will be explained below, this count is an understatement of the number of men, because smaller rooming houses were not canvassed in the North Clark Street or "other" areas. The correct number of homeless men living in Chicago under Skid Row conditions in the winter of 1957-1958 was probably between 12,500 and 13,000.

Types of Residences in Which Homeless Men Live

More than two-thirds (67 percent) of the homeless men residents of Skid Row were found in cubicle-type hotels (see Exhibit 15-1). Hotels with single rooms housed 14 percent, while rooming houses provided accommodations for an additional 7 percent. Missions provided shelter for about one man in twelve, or 8 percent. About 3.5 percent were estimated to be in the Cook County Hospital, in the city jail, or sleeping out.

The cubicle-type hotels were divided into three classes:
Large—those with 300 cubicles or more
Medium—those with 200 to 300 cubicles
Small—those with fewer than 200 cubicles

Exhibit 15-1
Estimated Number and Percent Distribution of Residents on
Chicago's Skid Rows, by Type of Residence: Winter, 1958

Type of Residence	Number of Homeless Men	Percentage Distribution
Total, all Skid Row areas	11,926	100.0
Living in cubicle hotels	8,038	67.4
Large (300 or more)	4,624	38.8
Medium-Size (200-300)	1,779	14.9
Small (less than 200)	1,635	13.7
Living in hotels with rooms	1,677	14.1
Living in rooming houses	806	6.8
Living in missions	975	8.2
In Cook County Hospital	150	1.3
In House of Correction	170	1.4
Sleeping out	110	0.9

The larger cubicle-type hotels are by far the major place of residence. There are 13 such hotels in Chicago. Although they make up less than 20 percent of the 70 men's hotels canvassed, they house almost 40 percent of the men. The proportion of medium-sized cubicle hotels, small-sized cubicle hotels, and hotels with rooms, is about the same in each case—13-15 percent of the total number of residences. All three combined, however, hold only another 40 percent of the men.

It must be emphasized that this survey focused primarily upon hotel dwellers and made a systematic effort to canvass every rooming house only in the West Madison and South State Street areas. For this reason, an unknown number of lodgers in private homes was omitted. From the results obtained in the canvass of rooming houses on West Madison Street it could be inferred that perhaps as many as 1,000 homeless men live in rooming houses elsewhere in the city under Skid Row conditions.

The Sample and Field Work

A listing of all room numbers or bed numbers available for rent or free was obtained by calling on the management of each hotel, rooming house, mission or other place of Skid Row residence. This listing comprised the universe for sampling. A sample was drawn by taking every 15th bed (room) in the hotels and rooming houses and every 10th name in the missions. At the jail and Cook County Hospital, the complete roster of inmates was reviewed. Every 10th man committed from the Monroe Street Station and every 10th patient at the hospital with a Skid Row address were included in the sample. A quota of 10 men sleeping out was set to provide for those who were sleeping in doorways, under bridges, and so on, and most of them were interviewed as they came to the Reading Room to clean up. (Missions, the jail, and hospital were sampled at a greater rate in order to gain more precise data for the truly "down and out" population.)[1]

As each hotel was taken up as a field assignment, the names of the men registered for the sample rooms or beds on the day interviewing began there were taken as the list of persons to be interviewed. Also included in the sample were all transients or new customers who rented one of the vacant sample sleeping spaces during a 24-hour period following the taking of the names from the register. Intensive efforts were made to interview as promptly as possible the men whose names comprised the sample. Most transient men were interviewed either on the day the sampling began or on the following morning. The hotel management usually was very cooperative in helping the interviewers determine which rooms were occupied by "regular customers" who could be counted on to be around for several days, and which were occupied by the comparative newcomers or transients. The more permanent residents were interviewed within the week following the drawing of the sample. The procedure was relaxed from strict probability sampling rules to permit the substitution of a few new transients, drawn at random, for transients who could not be contacted during the 24-hour period and who were lost through no fault of the interviewers who had no opportunity to face them, explain the purpose of the survey, and ask for an interview. All refusals and break-offs were counted as irreplaceable losses.

It was quickly discovered that it was out of the question to interview men in their cubicles. Cubicle walls "have ears," and the interview disturbed other men who were trying to sleep in the daytime. Also, some interviewers acquired bedbugs or lice by sitting on the bed or chair in the cubicle, so other arrangements were made. Small portable interviewing booths, made of collapsible screens such as are used in homes were set up in a remote corner of the hotel lobby. Where it was impossible to use the screens, interviews were taken in strict privacy, out of the earshot of other men, to the greatest extent permitted by the circumstances. Often the manager made his office available.

The interviewers were carefully selected, trained, and field-tested before they were given an assignment. Special projective devices were used to detect and screen out applicants who would be unsympathetic, moralistic, or self-conscious in conversing with these men. Throughout, their work was carefully followed and supervised. On an average, an interview lasted about 2-1/2 hours. It was found that at the conclusion of the interview, a high percentage of the men asked for money. Since the study was indebted to them for a gift of so much time, it was difficult to refuse. In order to standardize the handling of this situation, each man was told in advance that he would receive $1.50 for the time he devoted to giving the interview. At that time, he was assured that he would receive the money even if he refused to answer some questions he thought too personal, and that in all cases we wanted him to tell exactly what he thought and not to give us a "dressed up" story about himself.

In general, the materials from these interviews are thought to be a very good representation of what the homeless men of Skid Row think and believe about themselves and their situation. This, of course, does not always correspond exactly to reality because of their biases, inability to view themselves objectively, and lack of information about several aspects of their situations. Quite possibly, the data for this group are somewhat less valid and less precise than similar data gathered for a more educated; happier, and better adjusted family type of population would be. However, the interviewers were impressed throughout at the almost pathetic eagerness with which many men sought to make themselves and their problems understood and the apparently deep sincerity with which most of them spoke as they tried to explain their lives. They seemed to accept readily the idea that at last "somebody is going to try to do something about Skid Row." They seemed to believe the interviewers when they said that knowing the men's stories would aid in developing plans to help homeless men.

After the interviewing was completed, samples of interviews were studied and used to establish codes for converting the information into categories for statistical analysis. These codes represent a compromise between the nice theoretical distinctions it had been hoped could be made and the often broad and vague answers received.

Extent of Problem Drinking and Alcoholic Dereliction on Skid Row

Obtaining a clear picture of the drinking behavior of homeless men and developing an understanding of the kinds of motives upon which their drinking is based are among the principal objectives of this study. Perhaps there is no more appropriate way to begin the analysis of the survey results than to classify the men according to their drinking behavior.

A Drinking Classification of the Homeless Men

At a point in the middle of the interview, after rapport had been firmly established, each man was asked, "How heavy a drinker are you? Do you consider yourself to be a heavy drinker, a moderate drinker, a light drinker, a periodic drinker, or don't you drink at all?" It would have been naive to rely solely upon the responses of the men to this question as the basis for classifying them according to their drinking behavior. What is "light drinking" to one man may be "heavy drinking" to another. In addition to this question, several others were asked about drinking which, taken together, provided enough data to permit each person to be given a classification which we believe rather accurately fits his drinking behavior [see Exhibit 15-2].[2]

Each respondent was placed in one of the following five classes:

Teetotaler—a person who says he never drinks and for whom there is no evidence to controvert his claim, including the observations of the interviewer.

Light drinker—a person who says he is a light drinker and who spends less than 15 percent of his income on drinking, and who drank less than 3 pints of whisky (or equivalent) during the week preceding the interview. Also included are persons who say they are moderate drinkers, but who drank less than 2 pints during the preceding week and spend not more than 10 percent of their income on drinking.

Exhibit 15-2

Age Composition of Chicago's Skid Row Residents,
by Drinking Classification: Winter, 1957-58

Age	All Skid Row Men	Drinking classification				
		Teetotal	Light	Moderate	Heavy	Derelict
Age, total	100.0	100.0	100.0	100.0	100.0	100.0
20-29 years	4.4	6.7	2.3	4.3	7.0	2.3
30-34 years	5.8	3.9	4.5	5.3	7.6	9.3
35-39 years	11.3	5.5	11.5	10.8	14.7	13.4
40-44 years	12.4	5.1	7.2	16.0	17.9	17.1
45-49 years	16.2	7.9	14.2	15.6	24.3	19.0
50-54 years	13.2	9.1	13.6	11.7	13.2	20.4
55-59 years	10.9	14.2	10.1	13.6	5.6	12.0
60-64 years	8.3	11.0	13.8	5.0	5.3	3.7
65-69 years	9.3	16.9	10.3	12.9	2.6	1.4
70 years and over	8.2	19.7	12.7	4.8	1.8	1.4

Moderate drinker—a person who says he is a moderate drinker and who spends between 15 and 35 percent of his income on drinking and who drank not more than 5 pints of whisky (or equivalent) during the week preceding the interview. Also included are men who call themselves "light drinkers" but who spend 20 to 40 percent of their income on drinking, men who call themselves "heavy drinkers" but who spend less than 20 percent of their income on drinking and drank less than 5 pints in the preceding week, or periodic drinkers whose spells of drinking are spaced 3 or more months apart and who spend less than 35 percent of their income on drinks.

Heavy drinker—a person who says he is a heavy drinker and who spends 25 percent or more of his income on drinking or who drank 6 or more pints of whisky (or equivalent) during the week preceding the interview; or who says he is a "light" or "moderate" drinker but spends 40 percent of his income on drinking and drank more than 5 pints of whisky (or equivalent) in the week preceding the interview.

Alcoholic derelict—a long-time heavy drinker who has sacrificed almost everything for drinking. These men qualify as heavy drinkers (as defined above) and, in addition, have been arrested at least 10 times for drunkenness (including once in the last 6 months), and who also are characterized by one of the following: (a) a health condition attributable to prolonged drinking, (b) D.T.'s one or more times, (c) 65 percent or more of their income spent on drinking, or (d) hospitalized one or more times as a result of drunkenness. If there was no record of jail or arrests, a heavy drinker was classified as an alcoholic derelict if he had 2 or more of the conditions listed above that did not refer to the same episode of drunkenness.

In those cases where the combinations of characteristics did not give a clear-cut and internally consistent classification, the man was allocated to the group that fit his behavior most nearly on the basis of all information in the interview, including the observations of the interviewer. In other words, the classification was based on all information that could be obtained from a rather thorough probing of drinking behavior. This classification will be used throughout the remainder of the report. The proportion of the sample that fell in each category, and the number of homeless men on Chicago's Skid Row implied by these proportions, are as follows:

Drinking classification	Percentage of men in the sample	Number of homeless men on Skid Row
Total	100.0	11,926
Teetotalers	14.8	1,765
Light drinkers	28.4	3,375
Moderate drinkers	24.4	2,910
Heavy drinkers	19.9	2,373
Alcoholic derelicts	12.6	1,503

It is difficult to translate this pragmatic definition of drinking behavior into the conventional terminology usually employed by students of alcoholism. The correspondence intended when the classification was made is as follows:

Teetotalers—Nondrinkers

Light drinkers—Controlled drinkers

Moderate drinkers—Incipient and borderline alcoholics

Heavy drinkers—Chronic alcoholics, initial stage

Alcoholic derelicts—Chronic alcoholics, terminal stage

The groups of moderate drinkers are "moderate" only by Skid Row standards; by the standards of the general public most of these men should be looked upon as a set of men who definitely have a drinking problem, by general standards, but who still maintain some curb cn their drinking.

In a similar way, the "light drinker" on Skid Row is not necessarily a light drinker to the general public. A man who drinks 2 or 3 pints of whisky per week or spends 10-15 percent of his income for drink is probably exceeding the average consumption of the general drinking population. Yet, such men must be regarded as light drinkers in the Skid Row situation, as they have control over their drinking activities.

This finding that about one homeless man in seven is a complete teetotaler and that 40-45 percent of the Skid Row residents are "controlled drinkers" is highly significant for the remainder of the analysis in this study. It supports strongly the views of those resource persons who maintained that a substantial number of persons live in Skid Row areas from economic necessity and for other reasons not related to drinking. It refutes those who have viewed Skid Row as solely a collection place for perennial drunks. Out of 12,000 men, only 1,500 are in the "alcoholic derelict" category.

Yet, it is abundantly clear that 30-35 percent of the men on Skid Row definitely fall in the "problem drinker" category. That 4,000 alcoholics, enough to populate a small city, are encamped on Skid Row and that 1,500 of them are so far "gone" in alcoholism as to be almost out of touch with reality and living with almost no objective other than that of procuring the next drink constitutes unmistakable evidence that this is a very serious problem.

A major theme throughout the book from which this chapter is taken will be that Skid Row is not one little world apart from society, but two worlds. Homeless men tend to fall in to one of two groups: those to whom drinking is at present the dominant activity in their lives, and those to whom drinking is only a pastime or a rejected form of behavior. (In between is a group which is sympathetic to both points of view, and whose members tend to call themselves "moderate" drinkers.) For this reason, the drinking classification will be used throughout this chapter . . . as a major dimension within which to examine other variables.

Disability Status

The substantial proportion of Skid Row men who are suffering from physical handicaps that are disabling to some degree constitutes another leading characteristic of this population. In order to explore this problem, several questions were asked on health, recent illness and symptoms of illness, and handicaps. A physician resident on the staff of the University of Chicago's Billings Hospital read the responses to these questions and, on the basis of all information available to him, assigned each man to one of six categories denoting degrees of physical disability. . . . The estimate of disability is oriented solely toward the man's capacity to do physical labor of the type expected of operatives, service workers, and unskilled laborers. Only as it produced symptoms of ill health was any account taken of the man's drinking problem. The physician's classification, when tabulated, produced the distribution of disability status of homeless men on Skid Row:

Disability status	Percent of homeless men
Total	100.0
Too old to work	8.8
Unable to work	1.5
Severely handicapped	9.4
Moderately handicapped	26.8
Slightly handicapped	25.1
Not handicapped	28.5

Physical handicaps are much more prevalent among the residents of Skid Row than among the general population. Seven out of each ten men on Skid Row are handicapped to such an extent that they have restricted capacity to hold a job requiring normal physical exertion as laborers or semi-skilled workers. One out of each ten men is either too old to work or is so severely ill or handicapped that he cannot work. From this it is quite clear that Skid Row is no longer (even if it once were) the labor pool of able-bodied manpower it has been reputed to be. Instead, it has the aspect of being a collecting place for unattached disabled laborers who make their services available to employers who will be content with a lower level of output or who will undertake to force a normal day's work out of bodies no longer normally capable of delivering it.

The extent of this disability should not be exaggerated, however. Only 10 percent of the men on Skid Row are incapable of doing at least some gainful work to help support themselves (those who are too old to work and those unable to work). Only an additional 10 percent are so severely handicapped that they need partial support, even when they are given highly "sheltered" employment at jobs they can perform. Assuming that the moderately handi-capped men could be placed in moderately sheltered employment that would allow them to earn at least their minimum necessities and that the slightly handicapped men could be fully self-supporting with only a little assistance in finding a job suited to their capacities, then not less than 80 percent of the men on Skid Row could be completely self-supporting, if physical health were the limiting factor rather than drinking or other problems. The notion that Skid Row is populated predominantly by helpless cripples and men too sickly to be rehabilitated is just as false as the notion that it is an economically valuable manpower pool.

Disability and Drinking

What is the relationship between disability and drinking? Are the heaviest

Exhibit 15-3
Disability Status and Drinking Classification of Homeless Men,
Chicago: Winter, 1957-58

Disability Status	All Skid Row Men	Drinking classification				
		Teetotal	Light	Moderate	Heavy	Derelict
Distribution by drinking classification, total	100.0	14.8	28.4	24.4	19.9	12.6
Unable to work	100.0	36.0	24.0	12.0	20.0	8.0
Severely handicapped	100.0	18.0	29.2	26.1	13.7	13.0
Moderately handicapped	100.0	12.6	25.4	22.0	22.4	17.6
Slightly handicapped	100.0	7.2	24.2	30.7	23.5	14.4
Not handicapped	100.0	14.9	30.9	23.9	21.3	9.0
Too old to work	100.0	35.8	41.1	15.2	4.0	4.0
Distribution by disability status, total	100.0	100.0	100.0	100.0	100.0	100.0
Unable to work	1.5	3.5	1.2	0.7	1.5	0.9
Severely handicapped	9.4	11.4	9.7	10.0	6.5	9.7
Moderately handicapped	26.8	22.8	24.0	24.2	30.2	37.5
Slightly handicapped	25.1	12.2	21.4	31.6	29.6	28.7
Not handicapped	28.5	28.7	31.0	28.0	30.5	20.4
Too old to work	8.8	21.3	12.7	5.5	1.8	2.8
Distribution by both variables, total	100.0	14.8	28.4	24.4	19.9	12.6
Unable to work	1.5	0.5	0.3	0.2	0.3	0.1
Severely handicapped	8.4	1.7	2.7	2.4	1.3	1.2
Moderately handicapped	26.8	3.4	6.8	5.9	6.0	4.7
Slightly handicapped	25.1	1.8	6.1	7.7	5.9	3.6
Not handicapped	28.5	4.3	8.8	6.8	6.1	2.6
Too old to work	8.8	3.1	3.6	1.3	0.3	0.3
Comparison of actual with theoretical distribution, total	—	—	—	—	—	—
Unable to work	—	0.3	-0.1	-0.2	—	-0.1
Severely handicapped	—	0.5	—	0.1	0.6	—
Moderately handicapped	—	-0.6	-0.8	-0.6	0.7	1.3
Slightly handicapped	—	-1.9	-1:0	1.6	0.9	0.4
Not handicapped	—	0.1	0.7	-0.2	0.4	-1.0
Too old to work	—	1.8	1.1	-0.8	-1.5	-0.8

drinkers the most disabled or the least disabled? These are very important questions, and worthy of careful analysis. Exhibit 15-3 furnishes information with which to study them. According to the exhibit, disability and drinking are almost, but not quite, unrelated to each other. The men who control their drinking tend to fall at the extremes: either they are severely disabled (too old, unable to work) or not disabled at all. The "moderately handicapped" and "slightly handicapped" groups contain the highest percentages of alcoholic derelicts and heavy drinkers. The large group of men with no disabilities has a disproportionately large share of teetotalers and light drinkers, but it also contains a substantial number of heavy drinkers.

The bottom panel of Exhibit 15-3 compares the actual cross-classification of disability and drinking with a theoretical distribution in which they would be randomly distributed with respect to each other. From this exhibit, one could conclude that for only about 4 percent of the homeless men could disability have led to above-average drinking; actually, above-average drinking may have created this amount of disability. While these differences are statistically significant and worthy of consideration, they should not be over-dramatized. On the one hand, they support in still another way the contention that there are many men on Skid Row who are there for economic reasons—primarily because of severe disability or old age. The disproportionately large share of teetotalers and light drinkers among the most severely disabled suggests that this is true. On the other hand, they lend some support to a theory that drinking is one way that partially disabled men sometimes take to escape the disappointments of being unable to really "make good."

If we were to simplify Exhibit 15-3 to its fundamentals, we could conclude that all Skid Row men could be grouped into four categories of drinking and disability:

Men whose drinking problem is:	Men whose disability problem is:	Percent of all homeless men
Total		100.0
Serious	Serious	3.5
Serious	Moderate	10.7
Serious	Light	18.2
Moderate	Serious	3.9
Moderate	Moderate	5.9
Moderate	Light	14.5
Light or zero	Serious	11.9
Light or zero	Moderate	10.2
Light or zero	Light	21.0

The largest single group of men is not that of the able-bodied drunkards; it is that of the teetotalers and light drinkers who are not disabled or who have only slight disability. In the course of the field work, time and again the men would express themselves in the following vein: "You know, West Madison (South State, North Clark) Street wouldn't be a bad place to live if they would just take the drunks off it. They are what gives the street a bad reputation, and there are more good men here than drunks."

The Drinking-Disability-Age Classification

If the men on Skid Row are to be rehabilitated, three factors would seem to stand out above all others in determining the extent to which they can be helped: their disability status, their drinking classification, and their age. By grouping all possible combinations of these three factors into the fewest possible meaningful categories, it was possible to construct a single 12-category drinking-disability-age classification that was then used throughout this study to analyze various other aspects of the men's behavior. The categories of this classification, and the percentage of homeless men falling in each category, are as follows:

Drinking-disability-age classification	Estimated percent of all men on Skid Row
A. Severely and moderately handicapped*	46.6
1. Elderly — 65 years of age or older	
Teetotaler and light drinkers	9.7
Moderate and heavy drinkers**	4.3
2. Young and middle-aged—20 to 64 years	
Teetotaler and light drinkers	12.6
Moderate drinkers	6.8
Heavy drinkers and derelicts	
20-44 years of age	4.3
45-64 years of age	8.9
B. Slightly and not handicapped	53.5
1. Elderly — 65 years of age or older	
Teetotaler and light drinkers	2.3
Moderate and heavy drinkers**	1.2
2. Young and middle-aged — 20 to 64 years	
Teetotaler and light drinkers	18.6
Moderate drinkers	13.3
Heavy drinkers and derelicts	
20-44 years of age	10.4
45-64 years of age	7.7

*Includes those unable to work
**Includes alcoholic derelicts

This classification leads to the following findings that might be highly significant for those seeking to understand what types of men live on Skid Row.

a. Of the elderly men 65 years of age or older who comprise 17.5 percent of Chicago's Skid Row populations, only about one-third may be said to have a drinking problem (moderate or heavy drinker). Of all elderly men, both those with and those without a drinking problem, about 80 percent are seriously handicapped.

b. About one-fifth of the men on Skid Row seem to be in no immediate need of physical rehabilitation or treatment for alcoholism in that they do not have a drinking problem, they are in the working ages, and have no serious handicap.

c. The group of heavy drinkers that would seem to be the "most promising" prospects for rehabilitation are the younger men (20-44 years of age) who are not handicapped. Ten percent of the men on Skid Row (roughly 1,200 men) fall into this group.

d. The group of heavy drinkers that are the "least promising" prospects for rehabilitation would seem to be the older men (45-64 years of age) who also have a serious physical disability. They comprise only about 9 percent of all men on Skid Row.

e. The "intermediate groups" with respect to potentiality for rehabilitation are those who are (a) older but not handicapped, or (b) younger and handicapped. About 12 percent of the men fall into one of these two groups.

A little speculation on the above categories suggests that the size of Skid Row could be substantially reduced if selective action were taken deemed appropriate to each of these groups. Suppose a program were devised that could:

a. Provide improved low-cost housing for all elderly men without a drinking problem;

b. Provide better housing (minimum standard) for all men with no drinking problem and no physical disability;

c. Help all handicapped men who have no drinking problem to live at a higher standard of living by rehabilitation training, aid in finding jobs or even employment under semi-sheltered conditions, and by making improved low-cost housing available;

d. Absorb into a rehabilitation program one-third of the "most promising" group, one-fifth of the "intermediate" group, and one-tenth of the "least promising" group of alcoholics listed above;

e. Commit to institutions or special homes or farms all hopelessly incurable alcoholic derelicts who have lost all ability to care for themselves.

Such a program would shrink the size of Skid Row by roughly 70 percent. In Chicago, it would take about 8,400 men off Skid Row. The remaining core of 3,600 alcoholics and other persons who would not respond to treatment or who would refuse to be helped could easily be housed in the 8 or 10 newest and most fireproof of the men's hotels already built. Perhaps these places could be remodeled somewhat to provide more adequate living arrangements, and operated in such a way that the offer of rehabilitation would always be present.

If such a program were also successful in working with newcomers to Skid Row, helping them before they become enmeshed, in only a very few years the process of aging and death would lead to further shrinking of the "hard core." It is entirely possible that a coordinated 5-year program of redevelopment, rehabilitation, and treatment for alcoholism could reduce the size of Skid Row to one-tenth or less of its present size, and leave that tenth living within one square block on a much more self-supporting, humane, and more nearly normal plane than previously has been thought possible.

Economic Status

Employment Status

The picture one gets of the employment situation on Skid Row in midwinter is that there are three major groups of men:

	Percent of homeless men
Men with jobs	40
Men looking for work	23
Men too old or too disabled to work	22

This is supplemented by a fourth group, roughly 15 percent of the total, of men who usually work but who did not care to work at the time of the interview because they were drawing temporary unemployment compensation, were on a spree drinking up wages earned previously, were temporarily ill, or did not care to work for other reasons.

Only about 40 percent of the men living on Skid Row were employed at the time of the survey (Exhibit 15-4). Of the remaining 60 percent, about one-third were not in the labor force at all because of retirement, disability, or disinclination, while two-thirds were in the labor force but unemployed at that particular time. Thus, the number of unemployed men was roughly equal to the number with jobs. Skid Row workers are among the first to be laid off or otherwise affected by a downturn in business conditions.

Exhibit 15-4
Employment Status of Chicago's Skid Row Residents,
by Drinking Classification: Winter, 1957-58

Employment Status	All Skid Row Men	Drinking Classification				
		Teetotal	Light	Moderate	Heavy	Derelict
Employment status, total	100.0	100.0	100.0	100.0	100.0	100.0
Employed	39.8	31.4	39.2	43.8	50.7	25.9
Steady job	21.9	15.7	24.4	27.5	20.8	13.9
Spot job	17.9	15.7	14.8	16.3	29.9	12.0
Unemployed	38.5	24.8	35.4	37.1	39.6	62.4
Applied for work	23.4	11.0	21.8	25.4	29.3	28.2
Did not care to work	9.0	8.3	7.4	4.5	4.4	29.6
Temporary illness	6.1	5.5	6.2	7.2	5.9	4.6
Not in labor force	21.7	43.7	25.5	19.1	9.7	11.6

Spot Job Workers

Many workingmen on Skid Row depend on a unique kind of employment—the "spot job," or temporary day work. Men are hired by employment agencies and labor contractors who are able to deliver any desired number of unskilled workers to a firm to meet an emergency or a peak work load. Unloading freight cars and trucks, washing dishes in restaurants on weekends or when conventions are in town, peddling popcorn and candy bars at major public events are examples of such work.

One of the most important economic functions of Skid Row is performed by these men who are willing to accept temporary work when it is available and to sit idle when it is not. With these men as a resource, the industrialist and the businessman can meet emergencies without having to retain men on the payroll when their services are not actually needed.

Work Status and Drinking Classification

As Exhibit 15-4 shows, it is neither the teetotalers nor the light drinkers who are most likely to be employed; they are often the old or disabled men who are retired or cannot work. Instead, it is the moderate drinkers and the heavy drinkers who have the highest percentage of men working. Even these drinking classes contain scarcely more than a majority of working men. A high percentage of alcoholic derelicts are incapable of working or else are not inclined to work except on a temporary basis. No more than one-half of the men in each drinking class had worked during the week preceding the interview. Hence, drinking is only one of several factors that make men on Skid Row unable or indisposed to work.

Nevertheless, if a man does work there are very definite relationships between his drinking classification, the amount of work he gets, and the types of jobs he holds. Unemployment rates are much higher among those who drink excessively than among those who do not. And an extraordinarily high percentage (30 percent) of alcoholic derelicts frankly stated that they had not cared to work during the preceding week. Working men who are light drinkers or moderate drinkers are much more inclined to hold steady jobs than those who are heavy drinkers or alcoholic derelicts. If these are employed at all, it is likely to be on a day-to-day basis as spot job workers.

Income

The income distribution of the Skid Row residents may be viewed from two perspectives: comparison with the national average and comparison with minimum levels of living. From the first point of view, these men earn a very small income in comparison with other citizens. From the second point of view, it is a small income that is to be expected, since they hold some of the lowest paying jobs in the economy. In fact, it may be surprising that as many of the men are able to be completely self-supporting as is the case.

In 1957, the median money income of the average U.S. male 14 or older was $3,684 (among those who received any income at all). The estimated median total income of men on Skid Row was $1,083. This comparison minimizes the difference between the Skid Row man and the average man because included as income of Skid Row residents is the value of food and lodging provided on disbursing orders to public assistance recipients. Exhibit 15-5 reports the income distribution of the Skid Row residents in more detail. A disproportionately large share of the men is concentrated in the $500 to $1,000 bracket, and also in the $1,000 to $1,500 bracket. Whereas 37 percent of U.S. men earn $4,500 or more, only about 3 percent of Skid Row men earn this much.

Exhibit 15-5
Income Distribution of Chicago's Skid Row Residents,
by Drinking Classification: Winter, 1957-58

| Income | All Skid Row Men | Drinking Classification | | | | |
		Teetotal	Light	Moderate	Heavy	Derelict
Income per year, total	100.0	100.0	100.0	100.0	100.0	100.0
Less than $750	22.3	17.7	24.0	26.3	18.8	21.3
$750-$999	19.7	25.6	26.3	13.2	14.1	19.4
$1000-1,499	15.5	10.2	15.2	15.6	18.5	17.6
$1,500-2,499	17.2	11.4	14.0	18.9	19.6	24.5
$2,500 and over	15.9	17.7	12.3	13.9	23.5	13.4
No information	9.4	17.3	8.2	12.2	5.6	3.7

The second point of view examines the standard of living of these men. A man on Skid Row usually has no family to support and may spend all he earns for his own maintenance. If $100 per month is accepted as the income with which a man can feed and clothe himself and provide the necessities of life at a minimum desired level of comfort and enjoyment, then almost one-half of the residents of Skid Row fall in this category. About one-third of the men have incomes of $1,500 or more, which permits them to live at a comparatively adequate level. If $75.00 per month is regarded as the minimum income on which a man can subsist, then about one-fourth of Skid Row residents, roughly 3,000 men, are in this plight, and about 1,600 men earn less than two-thirds of this minimum. Because most recipients of old age assistance get $65.00 or more per month, it appears that there is a sizeable group of self-supporting men who earn less than the average relief client gets.

Income and Drinking Classification

The men on Skid Row with the lowest incomes tend to be either teetotalers and light drinkers (the older and disabled men) or the alcoholic derelicts. The groups of moderate and heavy drinkers, which contain a higher percentage of earners, also have higher average incomes. Nevertheless, about one-third of the men in each drinking class receive less than $1,000 per year, and may definitely be regarded as poverty-stricken. Between 30 and 40 percent of the men in each drinking class received incomes during the preceding year which would permit them to live at minimum adequate comfort. Surprisingly, this included a substantial number of men who at the time of the study were classified as alcoholic derelicts. Thus, many of the men who are the very heaviest drinkers manage to hold jobs for at least a part of the year which yield a minimum adequate annual income. Many of these are gandies who work in summer and drink in winter.

Pension Status

Pensioners on Skid Row

When surveyed, 47 percent of the men were drawing some form of pensioner public assistance payments. The largest source of aid was public assistance relief. It is estimated that about one man in five on Skid Row is on the relief rolls of the Cook County Department of Welfare. It has been observed in several different cities that inflation has driven many low-income people without families to live on Skid Row, and Chicago appears to be no exception. Many of the older men who are reaching retirement age at the present time have managed to acquire only the minimum amount of Social Security coverage, which provides only $30.00 per month upon retirement. When the retirement allotment is insufficient to cover the minimum expenses of living even on Skid Row, public assistance funds are used to provide this minimum to those citizens of Illinois who meet residence requirements and have no other source of help. Many of the men have worked in industries that were not "covered" and hence have no Social Security insurance rights; they seek public assistance when old age or ill health arrives and no family is caring for them.

About 10 percent of the residents are drawing Social Security benefits. (Almost 60 percent of these have the combination of Social Security and public assistance described above.) Approximately one-ninth of the men were drawing unemployment compensation in some form. Much of this is the "rocking chair pay" (railroad unemployment compensation) that had been accumulated during the summer months by gandy dancers.

Number of Pensioners of Each Type

On the assumption that Chicago's Skid rows contain 12,000 men, the best estimate of the number of pensioners of each type is as follows:

Pension status	Estimated number of men on Chicago's Skid Rows, 1957-1958	Percent distribution
Total	12,000	100.0
Non-pensioners	6,372	53.1
Pensioners, total*	5,628	46.9
Public assistance	2,640	22.0
Old-age assistance	264	2.2
Social Security	1,236	10.3
Military pension	660	5.5
Railroad retirement	204	1.7
Unemployment compensation	1,428	11.9
Combination of pensions:		
Public assistance and Social Security	696	5.8
Public assistance and railroad retirement	60	.5
Railroad retirement and old-age assistance	60	.5

*Some of these men hold pensions from two sources. These combinations are indicated in the lower part of the table.

For purposes of analysis, the pensioners may be grouped into three major types as follows:

1. Earned-retirement pensioners—men with Social Security, military, or railroad retirement pensions;
2. Welfare pensioners—men on public assistance (relief), or old age assistance;
3. Temporary pensioners—men who are drawing unemployment compensation.

When grouped thus, with the combinations of pensions divided among the types, the number of pensioners in each major type is as follows:

Major type of pensioners	Estimated number of men on Chicago's Skid Rows, 1957-1958	Percent of all men on Skid Row	Percent of all pensioners on Skid Row
Total	5,628	46.9	100.0
Earned-retirement pensioners	1,694	14.1	30.1
Welfare pensioners	2,502	20.9	44.5
Temporary pensioners	1,432	11.9	25.4

Thus, of roughly 5,700 pensioners on Skid Row, 30 percent are living on pensions earned while they were younger, almost one-half are supported as public dependents, and one-fourth are temporary public dependents receiving unemployment compensation. This last figure includes the large number of men spending the winter on their "rocking chair pay" from railroad maintenance work during the summer.

Pension Status in Relation to Drinking Behavior

Very few men who are on earned-retirement pensions are problem drinkers. Exhibit 15-6 shows that only 18 percent of this group of pensioners are heavy drinkers or alcoholic derelicts, which is only about one-half of the proportion of heavy drinkers among the Skid Row population as a whole. This finding belies the assertion sometimes heard that when elderly men who have spent a lifetime as common laborers get their Social Security or railroad retirement pensions, they voluntarily retire to Skid Row and spend the rest of their days doing what they like to do best—drink. Instead, the facts seem to indicate that more than 80 percent of the earned retirement pensioners who live on Skid Row live there against their will, because inflation has destroyed the purchasing power of their monthly pension check and their ability to live elsewhere.

A very surprising aspect of Exhibit 15-6 is the finding that more than one-half (55 percent) of persons on public assistance are teetotalers or light drinkers. It has been believed by many that public welfare cases are relegated to Skid Row hotels and restaurants only when they are known to be confirmed alcoholics who cannot be trusted with cash for meals or lodging. Such men are given a "disbursing order" addressed to a particular cubicle hotel or Skid Row restaurant, usually one chosen by the recipient or recommended by the social worker. If it is sincere in wishing to conquer Skid Row, the public

Exhibit 15-6
Pension Status by Drinking Classification of Homeless Men, Chicago Skid
Row: Winter, 1957-58

Pension Status	All Skid Row Men	Drinking Classification				
		Teetotal	Light	Moderate	Heavy	Derelict
All Skid Row men, total	100.0	14.8	28.4	24.4	19.9	12.6
Not a pensioner	100.0	13.5	25.8	24.4	24.4	11.9
Welfare pensioner	100.0	18.4	37.0	20.9	13.9	9.8
Retirement pensioner	100.0	24.5	33.9	23.7	11.3	6.6
Temporary pensioner	100.0	3.8	17.5	30.6	20.2	27.9
Pension status unknown	—	—	—	—	—	—
Vertical percent distribution	100.0	100.0	100.0	100.0	100.0	100.0
Not a pensioner	51.9	47.2	47.2	51.9	63.6	49.1
Welfare pensioner	18.4	22.8	24.0	15.8	12.9	14.4
Retirement pensioner	15.0	24.8	17.9	14.6	8.5	7.9
Temporary pensioner	10.7	2.8	6.6	13.4	10.9	23.6
Pension status unknown	4.1	2.4	4.3	4.3	4.1	5.1

can reduce the number of Skid Row residents by at least one-eighth (and probably more, because moderate drinkers were not considered), simply by seeing that enough welfare funds are appropriated to make it unnecessary for homeless welfare cases to live on Skid Rows.

A fact that is not surprising is that the men living on temporary pensions (unemployment compensation) are highly concentrated in the heavy drinking and alcoholic derelict groups. Only 4 percent of these men are teetotalers and 18 percent are light drinkers. Almost 50 percent of unemployment compensation recipients are heavy drinkers, and 28 percent are alcoholic derelicts. A high percentage of these men are the gandy dancers who are here only in winter. It is reputed that they are joined by men who cannily hold steady jobs just long enough to qualify for unemployment compensation and then suddenly become "unemployed" until their accumulated compensation rights expire. Thus, on Skid Row two programs of social legislation to protect men from unemployment have been perverted by some to institutionalize alcoholic dereliction.

However, it should not be concluded that all heavy drinkers on Skid Row are gandy dancers or men living on unemployment compensation. Exhibit 15-6 shows that more than one-third of the men who are not pensioners are heavy drinkers. The bottom part of this exhibit shows the pensioner status of the various drinking groups. As the above discussion suggests, a high percentage of teetotalers and light drinkers are earned retirement or welfare pensioners, while the alcoholic derelicts and heavy drinkers tend to have no pension or to be on a temporary pension.

The findings shown here about unemployment compensation are not intended to damn the programs; the gandy dancers who do not want to spend the winter drinking apparently do not come to Skid Row, but stay in other towns or other parts of Chicago.

Race and Nativity

Racial Composition

Chicago's Skid Rows are predominantly white (about 86-89 percent).[3] However, on South State Street there are three cubicle-type hotels that cater exclusively to Negroes. As a result, 39 percent of the residents of this area are Negro. Among the white residents, anti-Negro feelings tend to be quite intense, and hotels tend to be either all-Negro or all-white. The only mixed Negro-white sleeping accommodations are in the missions, and even here the management tries to restrict the proportion of Negroes. There seem to be fewer restrictions against admitting American Indians to the hotels than against other minority groups.

A small minority of Skid Row residents are American Indians (estimated at about 2 percent). Large numbers of Indian families are found in the vicinity of North Clark Street, but individual members become disorganized and drift onto Skid Row.

A rather large and long-established colony of Mexicans is situated just South of West Madison Street, along Halsted Street. Puerto Ricans have been settling on both south State and North Clark, as well as near the Mexican colony. But these Spanish-speaking residents tend to live in family groups. Although they live under slum conditions in very poor circumstances, they are not "homeless" and hence are excluded from this study. Only occasionally are Mexican or Puerto Rican men found living in cubicle-type hotels. Very few of the hotels will admit them. Because they were suspicious of the survey (as they are of any official-seeming inquiry), the refusal rate among the few Spanish-speaking persons who fell in the sample was very high.

The central and western sections of the West Madison Street Skid Row are surrounded by slums which are now occupied by Negro families. This encirclement by Mexicans, Puerto Ricans, and Negroes is bringing a steadily greater frequency of contact among the races in all Skid Row areas. In restaurants, movies, and in public facilities such as the Reading Room, the missions, and the public welfare agencies, there is much more interracial contact now than in the past. Also, the white residents of Skid Row must compete for jobs with workers from these races and often work side by side with them.

To summarize: The Skid Rows tend to be Caucasian islands in a sea of Negroes, Puerto Ricans, and Mexicans who have settled in the oldest and most deteriorated slum areas around the central business district. Despite feelings of antagonism toward these groups held by white residents, Skid Row facilities now are operated on an interracial basis more than ever before.[4]

Nativity and Parentage

Some sociologists have tended to explain Skid Rows as groups of persons who are socially disorganized as a result of changing cultures. Migration from Europe to America and from farm to city have been cited as two of the more disorganizing types of experiences. Exhibit 15-7, which shows the race-nativity-parentage characteristics of the homeless men, casts indirect doubt

Exhibit 15-7
Race, Nativity, and Parentage of Chicago's Skid Row Residents,
by Drinking Classification: Winter, 1957-58

Race, Nativity, Parentage	All Skid Row Men	Drinking Classification				
		Teetotal	Light	Moderate	Heavy	Derelict
Race, nativity, parentage, total	100.0	100.0	100.0	100.0	100.0	100.0
White, total	85.7	—	—	—	—	—
Native born— both parents native born	42.8	24.4	37.6	41.6	56.9	56.0
Native born— father native born, mother foreign born	3.5	2.0	3.5	3.6	5.3	2.3
Native born—mother native born, father foreign born	4.7	6.7	4.7	2.2	6.5	4.2
Native born—both parents foreign born	20.7	27.6	20.3	20.6	16.7	20.4
Foreign Born	15.0	25.2	20.1	13.2	7.6	6.5
Nonwhite, total	11.5	—	—	—	—	—
Negro	9.2	11.4	10.5	13.2	3.2	5.6
Indian	2.3	1.2	2.7	0.7	2.9	5.1
Nativity unknown	1.8	1.6	0.6	5.0	0.9	—

upon this thesis concerning immigration. Disproportionately fewer men born abroad were found to be in the uncontrolled drinker category while by far the disproportionate majority of men in this category were native-born of native parentage. Native-born persons of foreign parentage tend to fall in the teetotaler category rather than in the heavy-drinker category where the sociological theory would tend to place them. It is quite obvious that the theory, if valid at all, would account for only a minor part of alcoholic dereliction.

Marital Status

The very fact that they are middle-aged and familyless dictates that the homeless men of Skid Row have a marital-status composition radically different from the general population. Exhibit 15-8 indicates that in comparison with men 20 and over in the general population, there is a considerable preponderance of men who have never married and of men who are widowed, separated, and divorced. Along Skid Row there is a saying that "95 percent of the men are here because of a woman." It certainly cannot be disputed that the residents are unique both in that an extraordinarily high proportion failed to marry and in that if they did marry, their marriages ended in separation or divorce.

Exhibit 15-8 does not show fully the extent of the discrepancy because the difference in age composition between the general population and the Skid Row population is not accounted for. A more exact comparison can be made by standardizing the marital-status distribution for Skid Row men. This

Exhibit 15-8
Marital Status of Chicago's Skid Row Residents,
by Drinking Classification: Winter, 1957-58

Marital Status	All Skid Row Men	Drinking Classification				
		Teetotal	Light	Moderate	Heavy	Derelict
Marital status, total	100.0	100.0	100.0	100.0	100.0	100.0
Single (never married)	43.1	48.4	51.5	34.4	40.5	38.9
Separated	15.9	13.8	12.5	15.6	20.5	19.4
Divorced	28.4	21.3	23.0	27.5	37.5	36.1
Widowed	10.4	16.5	12.3	14.8	1.5	4.2
No information	2.2	—	0.6	7.7	—	1.4

consists of estimating what proportion of Skid Row men would be single, married, widowed, separated, or divorced if they had the same age composition as the general male population of the nation. The results of such a comparison are shown as follows:

Marital status	Percent of males 20 years and over, U.S., 1950	Percent of Skid Row men, standardized, 1957-1958
Total	100	100
Never married	17	64
Married	74	2
Separated	2	8
Widowed	5	6
Divorced	2	20

Thus, the proportion of single men among the Skid Row population is about 4 times as great, and the proportion of divorced men is about 9 times as great, as among the general population when the factor of age is controlled. More than 40 percent of all men on Skid Row have had a marriage which ended in divorce or separation.

Marital Status and Drinking Classification

Widowed men on Skid Row tend to be teetotalers or light drinkers, whereas divorced or separated men tend to be heavy drinkers. A substantial proportion of single men fall in each of the drinking classifications.

Educational Attainment

Residents of Skid Row have considerably lower educational attainment than the general population (see Exhibit 15-9). However, this is to be expected of a group of older men who are retired or employed primarily as operatives, service workers, and unskilled laborers. A comparison between their educational attainment and that of men in the general population who have similar occupations is more revealing. A "composite" educational attainment was made by averaging the national statistics of educational attainment for low-income workingmen: male operatives, service workers, and nonfarm laborers. The differences between the educational attainment of the Skid Row men and this composite were quite small:

Educational attainment	U.S composite 1950	Skid Row men 1958
Total	100.0	100.0
No education	3.2	2.9
Grade school, 1-4 years	12.9	14.7
" " 5-7 years	22.4	21.5
" " 8 years	24.3	20.5
High school, 1-3 years	18.7	21.2
" " 4 years	14.5	13.3
College, 1-3 years	3.0	4.7
" 4 years or more	1.0	1.1

On the one hand, a slightly greater proportion of Skid Row men failed to graduate from eighth grade than is true for the composite. But a slightly larger percentage of Skid Row men said they had attended college. Since both sets of statistics are based upon small samples, the differences between them could easily be due to chance variations.

Exhibit 15-9
Educational Attainment of Chicago's Skid Row Residents,
by Drinking Classification: Winter, 1957-58

Educational Attainment	All Skid Row Men	Drinking Classification				
		Teetotal	Light	Moderate	Heavy	Derelict
Educational attainment, total	100.0	100.0	100.0	100.0	100.0	100.0
None or less than 5 years	17.0	31.5	25.1	9.6	6.2	13.0
Grammar school 5-7 years	20.8	20.9	24.6	16.5	16.4	27.3
Grammar school 8 years	19.8	16.1	17.7	23.2	22.3	18.5
High School 1-3 years	20.3	11.0	20.1	20.8	27.3	19.4
High School 4 years	13.1	15.0	7.0	13.6	19.6	13.0
College 1 or more years	5.7	4.3	4.3	5.0	7.3	8.8
No information	3.4	1.2	1.2	11.2	0.9	—

Two important implications may be drawn from this information. First, contrary to a popular conception, Skid Row is not populated by large numbers of highly educated men who land here because of excessive drinking. Such cases are known, but they are quite rare. Second, about one-fifth of the men report they have graduated from high school, which means they have educational preparation much more than adequate for the jobs they now hold. Thus, Skid Row is neither the "last stop" for alcoholic business and professional men, nor is it a collecting place for the semi-illiterates and uneducable men of the nation. Its educational composition is just about average for the occupational composition of its residents.

Educational Attainment and Drinking Classification

On Skid Row, the men with the most education are heavy drinkers in a higher percentage of cases, while the men with the least education are teetotalers or only light drinkers in a higher percentage of cases. Much of this relationship is due to the age distribution described above (younger people tend to have more years of formal schooling than older); but even when the effect of age is controlled, this tendency persists. This suggests that uneducated men have two reasons for being on Skid Row—personal disorganization and poverty—whereas most of the more educated men have only one reason for being there—personal disorganization.

Migration Status

Each man was asked, "How long have you lived on Skid Row since the last time you arrived from some other place outside of Chicago?" The results destroy rather effectively any notion that Skid Row is composed entirely of a group of highly transient persons. Less than 10 percent of the men had been on Skid Row for less than a month, and 55 percent had lived there longer than a year. One man in six (18 percent) had lived on Skid Row continuously for 10 years or more, and an additional 11 percent had lived there between 5 and 10 years [see Exhibit 15-10]. Moreover, these statistics count as short-term residents the gandy dancers and others who have a seasonal cycle that brings them into Chicago for a part of each year. The transients "just passing through" and the hoboes who follow the harvests are much fewer than they were 35 years ago when Nels Anderson wrote about Chicago's Skid Row and named it Hobohemia. Today, much of the migration of homeless men follows a pattern of changing from one Skid Row to another rather than following seasonal work as in the time of the hobo.

Exhibit 15-10
Length of Residence on Skid Row
Since Last Coming to Chicago: Winter, 1957-58

Length of Residence	All Skid Row Men	Drinking Classification				
		Teetotal	Light	Moderate	Heavy	Derelict
Length of residence, total	100.0	100.0	100.0	100.0	100.0	100.0
Less than 3 months	20.8	18.9	17.0	17.5	29.6	24.1
3 to 5 months	13.3	10.2	14.2	10.5	15.8	16.7
6 to 11 months	9.8	11.0	4.7	11.2	12.6	12.5
1 to 2 years	10.0	10.6	11.5	11.2	7.0	8.3
2 to 5 years	16.5	13.4	20.3	20.3	11.1	12.5
5 to 10 years	10.8	5.9	11.7	10.3	13.2	12.0
10 years or over	18.1	28.7	20.5	17.0	10.6	13.9
No information	0.6	1.2	—	1.9	—	—

Years of Skid Row-Type Living

The interview tried to determine the total number of years each respondent had spent in Skid Row-type living, combining all residence on Chicago's Skid Row with residence on Skid Rows of other cities (see Exhibit 15-11). The median duration and the percentage of men who have lived 10 years or more on Skid Rows, by drinking status, are as follows:

Drinking status	Median length of residence	Percent with more than 10 years
Skid Row, total	5 years	38.1
Teetotalers	8 years	52.2
Light drinkers	6 years	36.3
Moderate drinkers	4-5 years	37.3
Heavy drinkers	4 years	18.5
Alcoholic derelicts	6 years	34.4

It is surprising, perhaps, to discover (as the preceding section suggested) that heavy drinkers really·are short termers on Skid Row, and teetotalers are those with the longest average tenure. This is due in part to their old age (and hence longer opportunity to accumulate more years of Skid Row residence). Another factor may be that the alcoholic derelict runs much greater hazards

Exhibit 15-11
Years Spent in Skid Row-Type Living by Chicago's Skid Row Residents,
by Drinking Classification: Winter, 1957-58

Years in Skid Row Type of Living	All Skid Row Men	Drinking Classification				
		Teetotal	Light	Moderate	Heavy	Derelict
Years in Skid Row type of living, total	100.0	100.0	100.0	100.0	100.0	100.0
Less than 1 year	18.0	10.3	20.3	17.6	24.8	12.1
1 year but less than 2	6.4	6.9	2.4	9.5	8.7	5.7
2 years but less than 3	8.0	2.0	9.5	9.5	9.1	7.6
3 years but less than 4	5.9	6.4	5.5	6.9	4.3	7.0
4 years but less than 5	5.2	3.9	3.7	6.9	7.9	2.5
5 to 6 years but less than 7	7.7	5.4	6.1	3.9	12.6	14.0
7-8-9 years but less than 10	10.5	12.8	6.3	8.2	14.2	16.6
10 to 14 years but less than 15	13.7	19.2	14.7	14.4	8.7	10.8
15 to 19 years but less than 20	6.5	11.8	7.1	6.9	—	7.6
20 to 29 years but less than 30	7.6	9.9	8.9	5.9	3.5	11.5
30 years or more	6.5	5.9	11.6	6.9	2.0	1.3
More than 1 year but number unknown	3.8	5.4	3.2	3.6	4.3	3.2
No information	0.2	—	0.8	—	—	—

of death, imprisonment, or accident which tend to remove him from Skid Row. Also, by changing their ways, some alcoholics can make a "comeback," get off Skid Row, and rejoin the normal community. It may be even harder for a non-alcoholic unemployable to make a comeback from poverty than for an alcoholic to conquer his drinking, so that when a man once slides down to the level of Skid Row for economic reasons, he may be almost sentenced to die there—and hence the long residential terms for controlled drinkers.

Health Status

Each respondent was asked "How is your health? Would you say it is excellent, good, fair, or poor?" Although this is a somewhat subjective way of measuring the health of a population, it has been found to differentiate quite effectively among sick and well people. In general, the men of Skid Row tend to be less healthy than the general population, even when allowance is made for their older age composition. The following proportions bear this out:

Percent in each health category	Skid Row men standardized for age	U. S. general population*
Excellent health	18	32
Good health	46	38
Fair health	23	23
Poor health	12	7

*Source: Jacob J. Feldman and Paul B. Sheatsley, Chapter 5A in an unpublished manuscript entitled "Subjective Factors in Utilization of Medical Facilities."

The proportion of homeless men who report themselves to be in excellent health is only about one-half as great as among the general population, and the proportion which says that they are in poor health is 70 percent greater than among the general population. This substantiates the materials presented above concerning physical disability.

In addition to this general question about health, each man was asked in detail about illnesses during the past three months and during the past year, so that all disabilities and sicknesses were recorded. . . .

Conclusion

When a true cross-section of the Skid Row population is taken, the notion that Skid Row is solely a community of bad men reaping a just punishment is shaken. Instead, the contention of the resource persons . . . that it is a complex neighborhood where several different categories of men are living for a variety of reasons, is amply supported. In addition to alcoholism there are problems of physical disability, welfare budgets inadequate to care for needy familyless clients, poverty, chronic unemployment, abuse of unemployment compensation programs, and broken marriage. Blaming this situation on the disorganization of immigrants appears to be unwarranted. A most encouraging finding is that a fairly straightforward program of eliminating poverty, of semi-sheltered employment, and of improved low-cost housing, with a modest program of rehabilitation of potentially salvageable alcoholics and institutionalizing the comparatively small fraction of "hopeless cases" could cause Skid Row virtually to disappear in a short time, and certainly to take on a different character. Such a program would depend for its success, however, on the men themselves. . . .

NOTES

[1] One large Skid Row hotel located apart from regular Skid Row areas on the edge of the Loop was excluded from the sampling because it is very large and does not fit the Skid Row prototype very well. It charges higher rates, maintains unusually good lobby facilities, and seems to cater to single men working at low-wage jobs in the Loop. It has a more restrictive policy with respect to excessive drinking and seemed to be as much a very inexpensive rooming house as a Skid Row type of operation. To have included it would have used up a substantial part of the research funds on a group of men who seemed to be definitely outside of, or very marginal to, the core problems. Another isolated cubicle-type hotel, located at a considerable distance (several miles) from any of the other established Skid Row areas, was excluded because the manager refused admission. The hotel was undergoing major repairs at the request of the city, and the manager reported that his customers were already so irritable at the inconvenience that he feared having them labeled as Skid Rowers and subjected to an intensive interview about themselves would drive them away. It is believed that this hotel did contain a substantial number of men with drinking problems and other Skid Row characteristics while many of its clients were simply truck drivers stopping over for a few hours or days before going back on the road. The universe that was sampled was very nearly 100 percent of the sleeping facilities in the well-established and generally recognized Skid Row areas in Chicago.

[2] The classification was based on the following additional interview items: "About how much of the money you get do you spend on drinking?" "Do you have spells when you drink very heavily?" "How often do you have these spells?" "Why do you suppose you drink more at those times than at others?" "What do you usually drink?" "Do you usually buy at a bar or do you usually buy a bottle?" "About how many days last week did you have some wine or whiskey or beer to drink?" "About how much did you drink in one day?" "Do you ever feel like you have to take a drink in the morning just before or after breakfast?" "About how many of these times were you sentenced to jail?" "Have you ever been hospitalized for drunkenness or as a result of being drunk?" "How many times, if any, have you had the D.T.'s?"

[3] The definitions of "race" and "nativity" used here are those of the U.S. Census. Practical difficulties of collecting data make it almost impossible to employ more refined measurements.

[4] The considerable number of Negroes who walk the streets and use the Reading Room, missions, and other facilities created especially for the homeless men caused the research staff initially to suspect that all of Chicago's Skid Rows were doomed to extinction at their present sites (with possible removal to other spots) simply through the process of invasion which has been so commonplace in other types of areas where residential facilities are old and substandard. They suspected that job competition would eventually result in Negroes and Puerto Ricans taking over the jobs available to Skid Row residents with the result that the economic basis for Skid Rows as now constituted would disappear or pass to other racial groups. Long-term observers conceded that this may be the case on South State and North Clark Streets, but not on West Madison Street.

16

A Descriptive Portrait of the S.R.O. World

Harvey A. Siegal

THE QUALITY OF LIFE of those living in slums, welfare hotels and S.R.O. tenements differs radically from that of their more affluent neighbors. In part, their physical environment can be held responsible. Below, some of the physical aspects of S.R.O. living will be examined. Specifically, the nature of the accommodations, the facilities provided, and their ramifications on social interaction will be discussed.

Using the concept of "community" discussed in the previous chapters, this chapter will consider the S.R.O. community and the units or "stations" that are to be found within its boundaries. These stations will be differentiated and described. At the entrance of each station, however, a gatekeeper is located to control the flow of human traffic. As such, this gatekeeper occupies a pivotal place in the S.R.O. world. The functions, modes of operation, and social characteristics of these gatekeepers will be investigated.

Ecology

You know, I just can't seem to put my finger on it—but there's something just right about the S.R.O.'s being there.

This was the impression of a young, midwestern VISTA worker newly assigned to the urban renewal project on Manhattan's upper West Side. Whether or not other residents of the area would agree with him is very

Published by permission of Transaction, Inc. from *Outposts of the Forgotten* by Harvey Alan Siegal, copyright© 1978 by Transaction, Inc.

doubtful at best. It has been estimated that there are approximately one hundred thousand units of S.R.O. and S.R.O.-type housing in New York City and almost one-third of them are to be found between West 59th and West 110th Streets. The experience of other cities across the nation is similar. While the absolute size of the S.R.O. population is smaller, there is some tendency towards concentration in certain parts of the city. The way in which the housing turns into S.R.O. accommodations is similar; very few, if any, buildings are built to be S.R.O.'s, instead, through one or several renovations they are so transformed.

Returning to New York City, it is illustrative to note that one quarter of the city's S.R.O. buildings contain more than one hundred units, while one half have from ten to ninety-nine units. The average building on Manhattan's West Side is larger than the citywide pattern, and contains relatively more S.R.O. units per structure. Thus, the lone person, and the problems generally associated with him, is more concentrated on the West Side. A large number of S.R.O.'ers living in an area further increase the social isolation of the S.R.O. tenants through their being labeled as "neighborhood nuisances." Once this label has been affixed, the mobilization of higher status residents is likely and the larger community pressures for the elimination of the S.R.O. resident's bothersome presence.

Description

If one were to walk down a street on Manhattan's West Side, how would one be able to recognize an S.R.O. building or welfare hotel? From the outside, most buildings in this area look approximately the same. They are evenly covered with the same layer of soot and grime, which has quietly been depositing itself year after year from the industry on the east, and New Jersey's oil refineries on the west. Externally, little dilapidation is visible. Most of the buildings were constructed during a period when housing was expected to last forever giving the structures a massive, solid facade. Those buildings, originally constructed as hotels, still have signs affixed to them, with legends such as:

HOTEL MOUNT ROYALE
Transients and Permanents Accommodated
CLEAN AIRY ROOM-KITCHENETTE SUITES
ROOMS FROM $2 PER DAY & UP

S.R.O. hotels are unlike skid row flophouses in which one typically has to climb a flight of stairs to reach the lobby, which is located on the second floor.

(Street level in the skid row hotel is characteristically taken by businesses.) It is interesting to note, however, that both present a basically nondescript appearance. Often, the only external clue to their identification is the presence of several persons, some shabbily dressed or in various stages of intoxication, loitering around the entrance way. If, however, several buildings cluster on a single block, one of them will become the focus of the street sociability and business transactions. Many buildings are recognizable, at least during the warmer months, by the accumulated refuse, or "airmail" as area residents call it, of broken bottles and other trash that is simply thrown out of the windows. Ultimately, this accumulation of refuse becomes such an eyesore that after the landlord receives repeated police citations it is removed, then only to begin accumulating again.

As soon as one enters the lobby of an S.R.O. building, any resemblance to a conventional apartment building stops. The lobbies of conventional, higher class buildings in the areas are usually comfortably furnished with several pieces of old yet elegant furniture. The lighting in the lobby area is subdued, focusing social activity on a well-lit panel of mailboxes located in close proximity to the elevators.

Conversely, the lobby of a welfare hotel impresses one by its starkness: the absence of any furniture is striking. The management has removed it to discourage any loitering or sociability in the lobby area. In some buildings, one is struck by the decaying remnants of past grandeur—broken, soiled marble colonnades, cracked mirrored paneling and ornate but damaged tile mosaics decorating the floors present the flawed props for lobby dramas.

The most striking feature, however, presented by the S.R.O. or welfare hotel lobby is the caged enclosure through which business is transacted. In some hotels, the precautions are so elaborate as to include electronically operated doors, bullet proof glass with a narrow opening, set at right angles to the base panel, through which mail or communications can be passed, or thick plexiglass carousels to move material between tenant and management. Looking through glass or bars from the lobby into the enclosed areas, one sees the wooden pigeonholes into which mail is sorted—most residents, however, seldom inquire about mail since they receive it so infrequently. Prominently visible from the outsider's perspective is an armamentarium of baseball bats, taped pipes, nightsticks, heavy clubs and even firearms, hanging in mute anticipation of any sort of trouble. In some of the larger hotels, which in their halcyon days hosted affluent guests, the large safe with its interior divided into separate locked compartments to provide security for the guests' valuables, stands with its doors thrown open, benignly accumulating the dust and cobwebs of disuse.

When a building is converted into an S.R.O. the enclosed area is situated so that it commands a view of the street entrance. In theory this was done to make it possible to control traffic through the hotel. All the hotels prominently display signs over these areas proclaiming that no visitors are to be received after 10 p.m. (In some, no visitors are allowed at all.) The lobby is further secured by a system of mirrors that reveals the presence of anyone standing in any part of the lobby. These have been installed by managers fearful of robbery or other violence. Looking directly out through the bars or protective screen of the manager's cage one sees the door to the street, and then, by inspecting the mirrors, one observes the rest of the lobby and the entrance to the elevators. The lobby area is brightly lit with glaring high-watt bulbs that make it and everyone in it visible from the street.

S.R.O.'s, roominghouses, and some hotels each have different floorplans. Predictably, the plan of each floor is dependent upon what the original structure was like. . . .

There are, however, certain aspects of S.R.O. living that transcend any given unit or building. The walls of every S.R.O. building can be characterized by their dreary color: walls are unfailingly painted either a shade of dark green or brown. In addition, the omnipresent grime tends to quickly permeate even the newest coat of paint and soon it too has a dulled, dismal appearance. Hallways are generally poorly lit; burned out or broken lamps are not promptly replaced; or, the fluorescent lighting is so defective that the area is bathed in the eerie, flickering glow of the dying lamps. Windows in hallways are glazed with heavy, opaque glass, covered with so much grime and old paint that they allow little light through. Many others have had the original glass replaced by metal sheets after they were broken. Some floors still have the remains of the carpets that they had before the hotel began accepting welfare tenants. On these, water damage and ingrained grime has obscured all but the faintest remains of their original color and patterns, giving the floor a grubby, lackluster appearance. Fixtures, such as railings and staircase railings are likely to be dirty to the touch and have been painted and repainted so many times that the ornate designs of the iron work are almost imperceptible.

In most buildings, the limited, poorly paid staff of maids and porters finds itself unequal to the task of cleaning the constantly accumulating garbage. Common trash cans on each floor overflow with unsightly and noisome garbage through which vermin can be seen scurrying. Dirt is the omnipresent companion of the S.R.O. dweller. Garbage is often simply thrown into the halls, as well as from the windows. The level of hygienic abuse is primarily a function of how much the manager will tolerate. Some managers demand a higher level of cleanliness than others, and specify that if a tenant is not willing or able to meet it he will be evicted from the building.

Dogs kept for pets or protection by some tenants often present an additional source of uncleanness. While most pet owners observe the amenities involved in maintaining an animal in an apartment dwelling, others refuse to walk their animal outside of the building during spells of severe weather (or in some instances, during an alcoholic bender.) Instead, it is simply released in the hotel corridor for its daily exercise and attendant functions with the inevitable consequence of aggravating an already unpleasant situation.

Perhaps one of the most striking memories that I retain of the S.R.O.'s that I worked in was that of two infant black girls, one completely naked and the other in a torn pink shift, playing on the floor of a hotel corridor, littered with broken bottles, garbage and dog feces; cockroaches were crawling on the walls and the entire scene was bathed dimly by the flickering light of a dying fluorescent lamp.

Social Adaptations to the Physical Environment

As dreary and colorless as one finds the S.R.O. corridors and halls, it would be incorrect to describe the S.R.O. as bland and devoid of variability. A DOSS [Division of Social Services] caseworker who had spent more than two years working in the Hotel Enfer described an impression he had:

> Harvey, I know you're not aware of it yet, but when you get to know this place you'll find that each hallway has its own smell. Man, I'll be willing to bet that you could take me to a place [in the hotel] blindfolded and I'd still be able to tell you exactly where we were. Sometimes it's the smells that really get to me, man.

The S.R.O. building is considerably less neutral than its higher class counterpart since there is very seldom any effort made at standardizing or removing smells. Often the smell of an entire corridor is dominated by a single tenant. A certain corridor, for instance, was recognizable through the smells of a women who had had a colostomy; or, the corridor in which the notorious "cat-lady" (a woman who kept more than two dozen cats in a small room) lived was at times almost impassable.

Because many S.R.O. people have come to define the environment in which they operate as actively hostile, they have learned a set of skills which they believe can aid in their protection. People learn how to listen, or conversely, how to not hear, a lot more carefully than the middle-class person who has to confront a different type of isolation. At least partially responsible is the way in which the S.R.O. units are constructed. In many buildings the only separation between the individual units are partitions fabricated from a single layer of plasterboard. With conditions such as these one must be careful that his public recognition of others does not appear to be constructed upon information which may be construed as having been received in an illegitimate manner. In the S.R.O. world one's public or social face is accepted literally;

members do not look back into another's background or history to validate his claims or social presence. For example, if several persons are conversing together, and another, well known to each singularly, enters the room and directly attempts to penetrate the conversation, anyone already in the group, who might resent the intrusion, need only say, "Am I talking to you?" This will effectively insure that the newcomer's social presence is not acknowledged, thereby removing him from the conversational sphere. In terms of this interaction, then, he is expected to remove himself, and whatever he might have learned from having overheard the conversation is to be treated in the same manner as information that might have "come through the wall."

The S.R.O. world is a noisy one. There is a constant background of random sound: the phonographs, radios, clanking pipes, loud laughing or strident arguing, all blend into an omnipresent cacophony. Punctuating this, however, are episodic incidents that S.R.O. people readily respond to. For example, I was sitting with several people in a common room in the Enfer, when from somewhere above there was a loud noise, sounding as if a sizeable object had hit the floor. The room got very quiet and a moment later someone said: "That was too heavy to be a body." This struck me as very funny and I began to laugh. However, since no one else laughed, or even smiled, I quickly stopped. A little later the faux pas was carefully explained to me. The comment was offered in all seriousness, therefore my response was deemed to be entirely inappropriate. On many other occasions there were opportunities to observe the ability that S.R.O. people have to distinguish different sounds; some tenants, for example, could positively identify the several individuals in a group outside of his door by their footsteps alone.

S.R.O. Living Facilities

The living facilities provided by S.R.O.'s place significant constraints on the satisfaction of one's most basic needs. In a conventional apartment unit one finds a kitchen sink, electric refrigerator, four burner stove with oven, and storage cabinets, making the preparation of food possible. These facilities are wholly lacking in the S.R.O.'s. If private kitchen facilities (i.e., in the tenant's room) are provided, they consist, more often than not, of an older model electric or gas two burner range. Most rooms do not provide refrigerators. Because of the absence of refrigeration, an S.R.O. building can be distinguished during the winter months by the array of foodstuffs precariously perched on the exterior window sills. Room sinks are of the type found in older bathrooms: a shallow bowl with separate hot and cold spigots. Although the New York Housing Code clearly specifies what facilities must be present in a room to be rented as a unit with "cooking facilities," landlords have discovered that the only essential item is the hotplate. For most tenants the sleeping or rooming accommodations are the primary consideration; complaints are seldom voiced vociferously enough, if at all, to affect the addition of other facilities or the reduction of rents.

Since private storage and preparation of food is precluded for most S.R.O.'ers, they might be expected to use the common facilities located in the communal kitchen. Like other public areas in the S.R.O.'s, this communal kitchen has no one who is directly responsible for its up-keep. Because of this, most evidence a state of extreme uncleanliness, are vermin-infested, and are littered with discarded refuse and trash. Although a refrigerator and storage cabinets are provided, a cursory inspection finds them empty. Residents are very reluctant to store any food in these common areas because of the absolute certainty of having their food taken by someone else. As one resident reported:

Respondent:	She-it baby. I won't put nothing there. I rather buy my grub every day. If some nigger don' get it, them rats'n roaches will.
Interviewer:	But aren't you entitled to use these facilities—don't you even complain to the landlord?
Respondent:	Mr. Turkel—what he care? He just say that every time he put a new box in here with a new lock, someone up and come and break it off. He doesn't care. And man, I don't wanna catch nobody messin with my shit—I just don't want no hassels, ya dig?

Ideally, the communal kitchen should provide a focal point for group life (like the kitchen in Mrs. Grundy's folksy rooming house); instead it is avoided by most residents. Since it is a public area, access is freely available. One can never be sure of whom he might encounter in the kitchen and therefore, whether his person or property might be placed in jeopardy.

The bathrooms are equally noisome. Since only a poorly paid porter is directly responsible for their maintenance, most are in poor condition. All show evidence of extensive water damage, such as paint and plaster falling from the walls and ceilings. Floors are filthy and often partially inundated with water from leaking pipes and malfunctioning facilities. Amenities such as toilet tissue are seldom to be found. Because sanitary facilities so often malfunction, an entire floor is forced to rely on a single set of accommodations. In these cases residents complain of the landlord's seeming hesitancy in repairing broken equipment. In reply, landlords report that the tenants break the facilities faster than they are able to repair them.

For most residents, their complaints are subordinated to concern about physical security. Public areas such as bathrooms and kitchens are accessible to anyone. One can never be certain that someone is not lying in wait in the lavatory. Among older and female residents this is a frequently stated fear. Many S.R.O.'ers can recount incidents in which either they, or an acquaintance were so accosted. The trip and return from the bathroom, especially at night, is one that provokes much anxiety for these S.R.O. people. The moment when the person has his back to the corridor, as he inserts and turns his key in the lock to open his room, is when he is particularly vulnerable. One outspoken woman, at a tenants' meeting dealing with the problem of security at the hotel, stated:

Youse people, [referring to the social workers leading the meeting] youse don't know nothing. . . . Couple a week ago some muther trieda duff me [assault] when I came back from the john. I told the Man, and he say he'd take care of it—course, nothing happened. Now, I tell you, I just don't go out at night—no how! Got me a piss-pot 'neath my bed. . . . [At this point there was an appreciative chuckle from the audience. Encouraged by this she went on.] Yeah, that what this whole joint is—a piss-pot! [This was answered with several enthusiastic "right 'ons!" from the audience.]

Lavatories are used by persons who are not tenants of the building. Addicts who have "scored" in the hotel will often use a hotel lavatory to "shoot-up," since their dealer will refuse to allow his customers to congregate in his room and use it for a "shooting gallery." Occasionally, if the drugs are exceptionally good, addicts will drop into a stupor right in the lavatory and remain there until some of the effects of the drug have worn off. (Occasionally the drug proves to be so powerful that the user actually dies from an overdose.) During the winter, homeless people or those so inebriated that they are unable to return home, will wander in and use the hotel bathrooms, especially the bathtubs, to sleep in. Since most hotels lack any effective internal security, and few tenants are willing to do anything on their own, their use of the facility is not precluded.

In response, S.R.O. people have adjusted their life-rhythms to this situation. Some report having structured a daily round so that they can attend to all functions at times, and in ways that they assume to be the safest. For example, when I was confronted by the problem of making a before-bed toilet, and not wishing to travel to the next floor because the facilities on my floor were out of order (it was more than three weeks before they were fixed), I discovered that the sink right in the room served as well for urination as it did for washing.

Individual rooms found within an S.R.O. or welfare hotel vary from large and spacious to those with cubiclelike proportions; the room specifications are dependent upon how the building was renovated. In a hotel on Riverside Drive, for example, on a single line of rooms, the room overlooking the river was large (measuring about twelve by fifteen feet) and airy, dominated by three dormer windows. The room closest to the elevator, (the one I stayed in) on the other hand, had only a very small window and measured a scant six by eight feet. The room was so small that only a bed and a straight-backed chair could be accommodated.

Vermin are always present in an S.R.O. dwelling—cockroaches are so numerous and common that most tenants have learned to ignore them. The insects seem impervious to even the most determined pesticide spraying— merely returning the following day. Rodents are common and S.R.O. dwellers seldom leave food unattended; mice are accorded little, if any, notice. In some buildings, mothers slept with their infant children and forbade older children to bring any food into bed with them for fear of rats. Stories of small children molested by rats are not uncommon; many S.R.O. people will keep clubs and brooms within handy reach.

One tenant reported that when he complained to the manager about seeing a rat in his room, he was simply told to plug the rat's hole with steel wool. The tenant plugged the hole and a few days later he discovered a new hole within inches of the first. When he complained again, the manager suggested that the tenant speak to his caseworker about it. The caseworker was contacted and she promised to look into the matter. After several weeks, the tenant simply gave up. The experience of this resident is in every way typical.

If the caseworker had filed a formal complaint with the Health Department, the city would be obliged to intervene. This would entail dispatching an inspector to the building. The inspector will investigate and if evidence of rats is discovered (usually by the presence of fresh droppings), he will issue a warning. The landlord then has two weeks to correct the problem before the premises [are] reinspected. If the violation has not been eliminated in that time, a summons (which carries the possibility of a fine upon conviction) may be issued. If the summons is not answered, the landlord may be liable to arrest and the revocation of his permit to operate an S.R.O. Legal action appears to present little threat for S.R.O. landlords. Landlords often speak of how crowded the court calendars are, and how it can take up to two and a half years to get to court. If represented by counsel, and if the attorney requests additional time in order to prepare a defense, the process continues for at least another three months. With this much time, as one landlord philosophically said:

Who knows—God willing I should be alive in three years—by then, who

knows, I'll sell this joint, and then what? I should live and be well, and I'll worry
about it then.

The municipal housing code specifies that every owner or lessee of an
S.R.O. building must obtain a permit annually from the Department of
Buildings, authorizing the operation of the S.R.O. Issuance of a permit is
conditional on the absence of building violations. In theory, the need to
secure such an annual permit would compel all S.R.O. operators to maintain
their property at a minimum level and ameliorate any conditions which
violate the housing code. In fact, though, many S.R.O. buildings are currently
operating without a permit. The existence of manifold violations prevented
them from obtaining permits, but operating without a permit is simply
another violation. Since landlords pay little attention to control agencies,
partly due to the cumbersome and ineffective nature of enforcement machin-
ery, little is (or probably can be) done to improve the living condition in the
S.R.O.'s.

S.R.O. rooms tend to reflect the characteristics of their occupants less than
those of higher status persons. The S.R.O. *room* is less of a vehicle for the
presentation of self than the *person* of the S.R.O. dweller. Materially impoverished, the S.R.O. dweller has little furniture of his own. The furnishings of
an entire room, characteristically consisting of a bed, a chair, and a bureau,
have been provided by the management. The furniture and the overall conditions of the room are entirely congruent—both are dilapidated. Rooms are
poorly lit, the major source of lighting generally being an overhead fixture,
often fluorescent. The walls and ceiling are painted the same dark, character-
less green, grey or beige as the corridors, and are in need of repair. Due to
water damage, walls and ceilings generally show large cracks and areas of
peeling paint; and, during the winter, often feel clammy to the touch. Carpet-
ing is old and threadbare, showing ingrained stains and dirt. Wooden floors
are broken and linoleum is often worn and old.

Stations of the S.R.O. Community

In [Chapter 2 of *Outposts of the Forgotten*] we briefly discussed the quality
of "social navigation," that is, the ability to recognize symbolic markers
within a community and orienting one's geo-social action towards them. The
most important of these symbolic markers are the recognized "stations"
found in the S.R.O. world. These stations are actual S.R.O. buildings that can
be distinguished from each other. Indigenous S.R.O. people recognize the
different buildings for what they are, and fairly consistent value judgments

are held throughout the larger community. Below we shall examine the characteristics, qualities and organization of these S.R.O. stations.

All S.R.O. buildings, however, are not identical; some are considered by S.R.O. people as "better" places to live. Two major criteria are considered in this evaluation: (1) the appearance and facilities of the building; and (2) the matter of security. The latter far outweighs the former as a determinant of desirability and choice. In many ways, the condition that the building is in is a function of who has access to it. If we were to construct a continuum, the opposing poles of the S.R.O. world are signified by those buildings considered "*open*"—anyone may enter at any time; to, "*closed*"—one's person and packages are searched upon entry for the possession of alcohol, or whatever else the manager has declared as contraband. In this second group, rules regulating the entrance of nonresidents into the building are not only stated but rigidly enforced.

The "openness" of the building determines the quality of life for the residents ensconced there. Openness, however, is defined in two ways. In the first, an "open building" is simply one in which there is more than one entrance and there is little or no control placed upon who enters or leaves the building. Anyone, therefore, has unimpeded access to the building, its residents, and their possessions. Such buildings are often the scenes of violent street crime, in which the perpetrator will loiter outside of the hotel until a likely victim is spotted. The crime—typically a "grab and run" (purse snatching) or "yoking" (mugging)—occurs with the perpetrator(s) fleeing into the hotel. Generally, he does not remain there but will exit from the building via another entrance which fronts a different street. Understandably, the victim or civilian witnesses are extremely reluctant to pursue anyone into an S.R.O. building. In other instances, "people from the outside," as building residents describe them, "come into the building to bust into people's houses [burgle their rooms] when they are not there." In addition to free access to the hotel or buildings from the street, the open buildings do not enforce the municipal rule requiring that the original apartment door be locked and only people living in that wing have keys.

The second and even more significant factor determining an "open" building is the manager's willingness to give a room to almost anyone who can pay for it. The "closed" S.R.O. or hotel, conversely, demands that its prospective tenants meet certain standards of dress (such as clean, not overly shabby clothing,) deportment, employment or finances, before a room will be rented to them.

Stations within the S.R.O. world are defined through these characteristics. The most feared, the most notorious hotels or S.R.O. buildings, are those that are the most open. When talking with S.R.O. people in New York City, names such as Harvard, Whitehall, the Mount-Royale, the Marseilles and others, are mentioned time and again. A veteran of one of the most infamous describes his brief sojourn there:

> Got outta the joint [Manhattan State Hospital] and the Welfare sent me uptown [to the Harvard]. 'Vestigator said it was cool . . . she called up a couple of hotels and this one had room. Man, I didn't know nothing . . . soon as I walked up to the place I had a feelin, you know, like something just ain't right. The man cashes my check and I get a room. They got all these dudes just hanging' in the lobby, and this cat droppin' into a deep nod right there. Man, I knew it wasn't cool then. Man, just outta the joint and this place ain't gonna do me no good. One day I come back from the bathroom and this dude in my room, lookin' all around. He sees me and whips out this shank [a knife]. I say, it's cool, baby, it's cool—man, I sure that motherfucker was gonna cut me—I backed outta that room fast and hauled ass right downstairs. Got my shit together, man, and told Miss L. [the caseworker] I hadda get outta that joint . . . then I came here. Man, I be sleepin' in the subway trains 'fore I go back there.

Most S.R.O. dwellers, even if they haven't had firsthand experience with these hotels, have at least a very strong impression that they are to be avoided if at all possible.

These open buildings tend to be populated by those people who have had difficulty finding accommodations elsewhere. They are the ones most likely to continually manifest bizarre and unusual behavior and / or the most regressed alcoholics or addicts. These open buildings prove to be the most dilapidated and the dirtiest.

In contrast, the "closed" buildings are characterized by the rigid exclusion of those persons considered by the management to be a poor risk. Public access to these S.R.O. buildings is radically circumscribed. Only one entrance is provided and a key is needed to open the front door. The manager (or his agent) is on duty at all times and all strangers are excluded. Visitors must be collected at the desk, and often a sign-in-sign-out policy is in effect. Inside, each wing of rooms is kept locked and often a listing of that corridor's residents is posted. This population tends to be less mobile, quieter and less likely to be considered a neighborhood nuisance. These S.R.O.'s tend to have greater proportions of whites, orientals, and students. In New York City, certain landlords are especially interested in recruiting tenants of Haitian and/or Dominican nativity. They assume that many are in the country illegally and consequently make a much more pliant and docile tenant because of their understandable reluctance to seek any sort of official assistance in dealing with housing complaints. Members of these groups recruit newly arrived, fellow countrymen by word of mouth, stressing that the managers will not ask any questions when renting rooms. Many of these immigrants report that the presence of their countrymen living in close proximity is an advantage to the newcomer, especially if he wishes to call little attention to himself. A parallel phenomenon is in operation in the southwest where many Mexicans can be found.

The wholly "open" and wholly "closed" S.R.O.'s represent the polar extremes of the S.R.O. world. Between these two are the majority of buildings in which the management attempts some sort of restrictive admissions policy and ongoing control of behavior. Since the buildings can be located on a continuum, observers (cf. Shapiro, above) tend to attribute a "personality" to each building. While each building or hotel should not be seen as a distinct step on a scale, groups or clusters of similar buildings can be identified as differing steps by indigenous S.R.O. people. These clusters are not defined geographically. On one side street, for example, one of the most notorious buildings in the area could be found: the hotel was reputed to be a major point of distribution for heroin on Manhattan's Upper West Side. Almost directly across the street was an S.R.O. building of the "closed" variety which had been designated by the local police precinct as a "model S.R.O." While the "open" hotel always had people loitering in front of it, trash regularly thrown from windows, and many of the building's residents were well known to the police, the closed building presented a radically cleaner, quieter appearance and was never mentioned as a source of nuisance or anxiety by higher status residents of the area. Stations, in the S.R.O. world, are wholly socially defined.

Initial Contact With the S.R.O. World: The Gatekeepers

Since few questions are asked of one who is attempting to procure S.R.O. accommodations, and there is hardly ever any attempt at verifying a prospective tenant's claims, one's place of entry into the S.R.O. world is not necessarily a determinant of which station he might next progress to. Entrance and mobility depend, instead, upon the observable conditions of the person, the resources which he can mobilize, and the impressions and consequent judgment that the *gatekeeper* he first encounters makes about him.

It is these gatekeepers who occupy a pivotal place in the S.R.O. social structure. By a differential admissions policy, they ultimately decide what the character of the building will be. Although legal title to the building might change hands frequently, or the landlord may rent the property to different individuals or groups to manage, the building retains its character because the individual(s) who specifically handles the gatekeeping function generally remains with the building regardless of its change of higher management and/or ownership.

Many of these gatekeepers, whose official title is "room clerk" or "bookkeeper," have many years of tenure with the hotel. They demonstrate a notable similarity in their sociodemographic characteristics. In the eleven New York City hotels and buildings which I intensively studied, eight of the gatekeepers were Jewish women, between forty, fifty and sixty years of age, foreign-born, who had either been interned in the Nazi concentration camps (most still retain the tatooed number on their left forearm) or fled their native lands immediately before the occupation. They came to the United States right before or directly after the war, found employment in the hotel, and have remained since then. The other three gatekeepers were men, but in all other background characteristics they were identical to the women. None live in the hotel in which they work; however, one who was a sabbath observer had a room reserved as part of her contract.

In all of the hotels, the admissions function is relegated entirely to these women. If a person should inquire about a room when the usual gatekeeper is off duty, he will be told that either the establishment is full and he should try somewhere else, or that rooms are rented only between the hours of 8:00 a.m. and 6:30 p.m.; if he is still interested, he is advised to return the following day.

The gatekeeper has a realistic picture of the existing conditions within the hotel. She demonstrates a sophisticated outlook regarding the admission of an individual who differs significantly from most of those already ensconced in the hotel. Her primary loyalty is to the organization and she clearly recognizes that the presence of such an individual could mean trouble for the establishment. Trouble is defined as calling additional notice to an already tenuous situation by police or other control agencies. The gatekeeper, in the successful execution of her role, must be able to make a number of almost instantaneous judgments about the suitability of a prospective tenant. One described her role in this way:

> This place ... you know ... it's no Waldorf, we got all sorts here. Some of them are O.K. We also got some *ganuvim* [thieves] here. ... It's not as bad as some, let me tell you. You asked why I didn't give that man a room ... the little Puerto Rican fella? I didn't give him a room on account of he looked like too much of a *mensch* [gentleman] for here. That Clarence [referring to a particularly suspect tenant] would take one look at him and he would just eat him up alive. ... Let me tell you, the biggest favor I did that man today was to tell him that we were full up.

Judgments are made in the opposite direction as well. An individual will approach the gatekeeper and she might judge that his appearance indicated that he was an addict, or perhaps too "tough" for the hotel. The gatekeeper's is the last word, there is no appeal and once she judges someone as ineligible, there is almost no way he can get accommodations at the hotel.

One woman who had been working at a hotel for eighteen years recounts some of her experiences and some of the cues that she looks for when interviewing a prospective tenant.

Respondent:	*Boychick*, you just listen to me. When I first started here I was really a *greener* [newcomer]. . . . *Gottinu* what I didn't know . . . but that was years ago. When I first came here there was an entirely different element, but who's to say . . . times change and now Mr. Bloom and Mr. T., they have to make money too. . . . Ah, but I've seen it change. The *Schwarzes* [black people] . . . all the *Schwarzes* they all know they can't pull nothing over Bea. . . . I know from all their *stiplach* [tricks].
Interviewer:	But Bea, exactly what do you look for?
Respondent:	You remember that boy that was here yesterday . . . the colored boy who wanted a room?
Interviewer:	The one you thought was a narcotics addict?
Respondent:	He couldn't fool me . . . I know he was taking needles. [Here she paused, nodded her head with a knowledgeable expression on her face and mimed someone using a hypodermic syringe on his left elbow.]
Interviewer:	But how exactly did you know?
Respondent:	How do I know, how do I know anything. I use my *kepela* [head]. You look at him, he's so skinny you'd think he'd never eaten. . . . Also, you remember how warm it was yesterday? Who would wear such a heavy sweater on a day like that? I know, there's no fooling me—he was on needles.

It was problematic, of course, whether or not the prospective tenant was an addict. What was not at all problematic, however, was that he was defined as being an addict, and solely on the basis of this judgment was denied accommodations at the hotel.

Some gatekeepers are adept at structuring the interaction so that the prospective tenant is forced into making some revelation about himself. One woman, when confronted by young, black males who inquired about accommodations, would take out the stack of F.B.I. wanted posters that are routinely sent to large hotels, and begin leafing through them with the prospective tenant standing directly before her. On at least several occasions, she reported, the prospective guest suddenly remembered that he had already obligated himself for accommodations elsewhere. Another gatekeeper confronted the prospective tenant with the house rules, presenting them as stringently as possible. If his response was not satisfactory—usually measured in terms of docility—she would discover that the hotel was full.

Since the gatekeeper is often the most visible of the hotel's management to the tenants, it is she who is most likely to be the recipient of information about what might be happening in the building. She, of course, has direct access to the management and her judgments can be crucial in having a tenant evicted. Within the S.R.O. social system it is these persons who perhaps wield the most power. Since they persist even in the face of management/ownership changes, they assure that the nature of that building's population retains continuity over time, even though many of the individuals who had originally peopled it have left. It is in this way that the character of the several S.R.O. stations remains constant and the community retains its integration.

The S.R.O. Population: Brief Notes on its Sociodemographic Composition

At the outset of *Outposts of the Forgotten* we suggested that the typical population of the nation's S.R.O's are socially terminal. At this time, this should be qualified to some extent. The material in this chapter treated some of the differences between the "closed" and "open" S.R.O. buildings. The closed buildings contain a much more intact population, one that aspires to upward mobility. For this group the S.R.O.'s provide a relatively inexpensive and nonrestricting (in the sense of time commitment) residence. The notion of social terminality, however, figures considerably more importantly into our picture of the open S.R.O.'s. These are the buildings that contain a preponderance of social casualities: people with no place to go, people that we as a nation would rather forget. To complete this descriptive portrait of the S.R.O.'s, a look at some of the social and demographic characteristics of this population is appropriate.

Valid, reliable data about this population is hard to come by. The population is not one that is seen as deserving of in-depth research. What data we do have generally reinforces part or all of our assumptions having to do with the nature of this population. For instance, we see that nonwhites are strongly overrepresented in this population. A majority of the S.R.O. population in New York is black. Also, the population tends to be older; in a large way we are considering people who are well into the middle and even older age cohorts. Some researchers have observed that the white population tends to be even older than the nonwhite, especially the black, population. The hypothesis employed here suggests that the white person has a greater social distance to travel than the black before he finds himself living in S.R.O.'s. Questions such as these will hopefully provide direction for future S.R.O. research.[1]

In the economic sphere, the population is, of course, a poor one. S.R.O. people tend to be employed in low status, low paying occupations or not employed at all. Their family backgrounds tend to reflect this as well; only a minority of people come from higher status backgrounds.[2]

There is a certain amount of ambiguity considering the proportion of people who are receiving public assistance or welfare in the S.R.O. population. One New York City study suggested that more than three-quarters of the population in the surveyed hotels were welfare recipients. (This figure is probably biased because people who were gainfully employed, even in marginal occupations, probably were invisible to the social workers.)[3] Other research has estimated the proportion of people receiving some sort of welfare or public assistance at around 40 percent.[4] An additional proportion, probably as high as 15 or 20 percent, receive some sort of fixed-income such as social security, veteran's benefits, or other kinds of disbursements. This places some very severe economic restrictions on the population.

Some of the most telling statistics, however, have to do with health. Unfortunately, here too systematic research is unavailable. It is apparent through nonsystematic observations, interviews with health professionals (such as public health nurses and social workers in the community), as well as from the small amount of research data we do have that the population is not a healthy one. In addition to widespread reports of nonspecific poor health, aches and pains, frequent upper respiratory infections, and digestive disorders and the like, substantial proportions of the population report more serious difficulties: cardiac and vascular problems are quite common, people report that it is because of a "heart condition" that they are incapable of working. People with physical debilities are quite common in the S.R.O. world. It is not uncommon to encounter amputees, deaf, and wholly or partially blinded people.

The same can be observed for mental health. Here, too, we are lacking in any objective measure or assessment. In the population, reports of mental hospitalization(s) or extensive psychiatric treatment are so common that little question or stigma is attached to mental illness in the S.R.O. world. Other indicators of mental difficulties seem to abound as well: alcohol abuse is very common. The social workers attached to the St. Luke's project projected that some 90 percent of their case loads, that is, people in the hotels, had some sort of problem with alcohol.[5]

If data (again, for the most part unsystematic) from other cities is considered, essentially the same pattern emerges. Depending upon the area of the country, one substitutes, for instance, Spanish Americans for blacks, or one substitutes Native Americans (Indians) for other nonwhite groups. Regardless of the locale, it's clear that the core population of the S.R.O. world contains poor, unhealthy, predominately nonwhite and underclass people. This is a population that is excessively troubled, that holds little hope of being able to initiate any kind of significant change or self-improvement. It is a population to whom we are reluctant to provide anything but the barest supportive services, believing that there is little that they can benefit from what resources we would be willing to expend upon them.

NOTES

[1] Barbara Hoffberg and Joan Shapiro, "S.R.O. Service-Research Project," mimeographed (New York: Columbia University Urban Center and St. Luke's Hospital Center's Division of Community Psychiatry, 1969), pp. 26-27.

[2] Ibid.

[3] Ibid.

[4] Center for New York City Affairs, New School for Social Research. *A Program for Tenants in Single Room Occupancy and for their New York City Neighbors.* New York, 1969, pp. 7-8.

[5] Barbara Hoffberg and Joan Shapiro, "S.R.O. Service-Research Project."

17

Gentrification and Homelessness

The Single Room Occupant
And the Inner City Revival

Philip Kasinitz

Introduction: Gentrification As Value Shift

I N RECENT YEARS, the downtown sections of many American cities have undergone extensive renovation and revitalization. This "back to the city" or "gentrification" movement has been both hailed as an urban renaissance and condemned for disrupting urban neighborhoods and displacing inner city residents. The effects of this movement on working class neighborhoods (Levy, 1980; Clay, 1977) and specifically on the elderly (Henig, 1981) have all been widely discussed. In this paper, I will focus on the effect of the rapid increase in the desirability of city land on what is usually considered the nation's least desirable housing stock: single room occupancy hotels, rooming houses, and shelters. While these types of land use have long been seen as the very symbols of urban decay, they serve the vital needs of populations with few resources or alternatives. Gentrification has placed these powerless people in direct competition with relatively powerful and privileged actors for inner city space. The results may be at least a partial explanation for the growing ranks of the homeless on the streets of many cities.

From *Urban and Social Change Review*, Vol. 17, Winter 1984, pp. 9-14. Reprinted by permission of *Urban and Social Change Review*.

"Gentrification" (the term is British in origin and was coined by the movement's detractors, though in recent years it has been used by its proponents) is generally conceived of as private market, piecemeal renovation. It stands in contrast to large, publicly funded "urban renewal" projects, and is at times compared favorably to urban renewal as evidence of the success of private enterprise. A body of literature has grown up that virtually canonizes the urban pioneers, the small investors and individuals credited with saving the city in the face of bureaucratic resistance and indifference (Stratton, 1977; Anderson, 1977; Reed, 1979).

This view, while correctly granting recognition to the innovation and savvy of many small investors, presents an unrealistic distinction between private and public renovation efforts. The "private" revitalization of inner city America has been undertaken with the aid of municipal planning departments (Fitch, 1976), zoning changes (Zukin, 1982), landmarks designations (Tournier, 1980), federal tax breaks (Nesson, 1978) and municipal tax abatements (Mandelker, et al., 1980; Eibott and Kempney, 1978), as well as various governmental grants often funneled through quasi-public local development corporations (Zukin, 1982). Political initiatives are often vital tools used to save neighborhoods, and political clout is among the foremost resources brought into any conflict over inner city land use. The commodity being sold in the real estate market is more than a physical structure or piece of acreage. It is also the neighborhood: a political and cultural entity created at least in part by the beliefs and perceptions of residents, policy makers, and real estate speculators. As Sharon Zukin states: ". . .By this late point in capitalist economies probably no real estate market develops without state intervention" (Zukin, 1982). Therefore it is necessary to understand gentrification both as a shift in the values of urban residents and as governmental policy.

The suburban aesthetic of post-World War II America emphasized the spatial separation of public and private realms. If "downtown" was the world of public activity, then middle class people did not live "downtown," but in the private world of the suburb, where even shopping is segregated from living by the enclosed shopping mall. The suburban ideal of a home is a single-family home, sufficiently large and private to protect the family from scrutiny by the outside community. Downtown, by contrast, is made up of public spaces, where interactions are strictly limited, regulated and perhaps even ritualized. This is the public world captured so brilliantly in Erving Goffman's early work.

During the post-World War II period, urban planning and suburban growth sharpened this public/private distinction to the point where (to paraphrase Hopper and Baxter) a spilling of private lives into public spaces—street life—was perceived as symptomatic of poverty, degradation and social marginality. Hence, visual depictions of slum living generally show families on stoops or fire escapes, social workers endeavor to get ghetto youth "off the streets," the lowest form of destitution is to be a "bum on the streets," and the most degraded form of prostitution is to be a "streetwalker."

Gentrification, in contrast, promotes the positive value of the street and of street life, which is to say public life. "The real ingredient," Irving Allen writes, "that is missed in the suburbs is diversity." "The proximity of variety" is one of the basic "amenities" of the urban center. This positive view of density and human diversity has made its way from a slightly eccentric, fringe point of view first promoted by Jane Jacobs (1961) to a virtual tenet of urban planning orthodoxy with almost universally positive coverage in the press ("Cities are Fun" proclaims a recent *Time* magazine cover story.) At first ignored by governmental bureaucracies and shunned by wary financial institutions, downtown revival has today become the stock in trade of a network of private corporations, state agencies and local development corporations, encouraged by banks and insurance companies who had until recently written off the inner city.

The new image of the inner city celebrates the pedestrian street as a kind of permanent festival. Ghirardelli Square in San Francisco and the inner city "red brick shopping centers" of developer James Rouse in Boston, Baltimore and now New York combine a recycling of industrial and commercial space with an idealized image of the pre-automotive city. Indeed, a newly paved pedestrian mall is now a major tourist attraction in that most automotive of American cities, Los Angeles. Guidebooks for the would-be renovators, such as Richard Reed's *Return to the City* (1978) and Raquel Ramati's *How to Save Your Street* (1981) emphasize visual aspects and the need for "themes" for downtown streets. The variety of the inner city street (as contrasted with suburban sterility) is promoted as an almost voyeuristic experience for the generally young professionals who are depicted as courageously coming back to the city. These books also provide, along with a fashionable disdain for big government, useful information as to how private groups and individuals may tap government funds and resources to aid in private renovation.

Yet the diversity currently being celebrated is a limited and, as Wilson notes, a "safe" diversity (1975). It does not extend to people who, for whatever reasons, make middle class people feel uncomfortable. Ironically, that includes many of those who had traditionally, and during the 1970's increasingly, made downtown streets their home.

Single Room Housing: Its Residents and Functions

If the suburban aesthetic required abandoning the downtown streets at nightfall, there were many people who did not leave the central city. There are, of course, the working class neighborhoods of the older cities where family life goes on in close proximity to the central business district, under somewhat less private and more crowded conditions than in the suburbs (Gans, 1965). There are also the marginal people for whom downtown provided alternatives not available elsewhere. While neighborhoods, urban and suburban, are generally comprised of family units, commerical and industrial areas, as well as fringe areas in decaying working class districts, have tended to provide the single room housing stock vital to poor persons not living in conventional families. Single room occupancy hotels, rooming houses, and even skid row flophouses, have all provided low cost single accommodations for those who might not be able to come by them elsewhere.

Downtowns in many older cities have also traditionally contained the cities' skid rows and red light districts, which provided shelter and a degree of tolerance for deviant individuals and activities. Being close to transportation and requiring little initial outlay (often renting by the week), single room housing has traditionally been utilized by the elderly poor (National Council on the Aging, 1976), seasonally employed single workers, the addicted (Spradley, 1972; Wiseman, 1970) and the mentally handicapped (Segal and Baumohl, 1980).

In recent years, these populations have been supplemented by growing numbers of deinstitutionalized mental patients and unemployed young men (Baxter and Hopper, 1981). These trends, coming at a time when competition for inner city space has been intensified due to gentrification, have been sharply reflected in shelter populations and on the streets. Men under 21 years old constituted approximately 7% of New York City's shelter population in late 1982, whereas there had been virtually none in that age group as late as 1980 according to a city Human Resources Administration report (*The New York Times*, 3/7/83).

Exactly how many persons in each of these categories utilize single room housing is difficult to assess. Most studies are done of shelter populations. Shelters, temporary dormitory-type facilities run by state or charitable agencies, are generally seen as housing of last resort for homeless persons. Ethnographic data seem to indicate that many shelter users have already been displaced from private rooming houses or SRO hotels (Baxter and Hopper, 1981), and that there is some movement back and forth between shelters and more established SROs and rooming houses. In New York City, for example, a 1979 survey of 100 first time women's shelter users revealed that 50% had lived in SRO hotels immediately prior to coming into the shelter (Vera Institute of Justice, 1981). Therefore while we cannot generalize from shelter data to the entire single-room population, trends within the shelter population may indicate changes in the "single room" population.

It is therefore important to note recent studies indicating that, at least in

New York City, the shelter population is becoming younger and blacker, while a large minority seem to have had a history of psychiatric problems (New York State Office of Mental Health, 1981; *The New York Times*, 3/7/83; Vera Institute, 1980.) Contrary to the traditional image of the shelter population as predominantly aging, white and alcoholic, and almost entirely male, the Vera study shows a female population that is only 40% white and predominantly under 40. About 13% of these women had come to shelters directly from hospitals. A 1982 survey showed 33% (56) had histories of psychiatric hospitalization (Hopper, Baxter, et al., 1982).

The populations of the legal, privately owned single room occupancy residential hotels known as SROs have been less studied. Most indications are that the SRO population contains many of the same elements as the shelter population, though probably with more working persons. In New York City, the Mayor's Office of SRO Housing estimated the 1979 SRO population at 150,000, a figure which differs drastically from the estimate of 23,134 by the Human Resources Administration. (Apparently, the Mayor's Office includes a number of "illegal" rooming houses discussed below as well as higher-priced residential hotels in its definition of "SRO.") The Mayor's Office has also conducted a detailed survey of 2,110 residents of 13 SROs in which it provides special services, with the results indicated in Exhibit 17-1.

Exhibit 17-1
Demographic Breakdown of the SRO Residents
at Project Hotels, July 1978

Total Residents: 2,110 (Male, 70%; Female, 30%)

Population Type	Percentage Represented
Drug Abusers	5%
Ex-offenders	6%
Physically Handicapped	9%
Elderly	18%
Psychiatric Patients	32%
Alcoholics	25%
Others	5%

Source: "An Evaluation of Housing Alternatives in SRO Hotels," Mayor's Office of SRO Housing, June 1979

It must be noted, however, that the 13 hotels surveyed all were serviced by the SRO Housing Office and, as the report indicates, probably contained an unusually high proportion of deinstitutionalized mental patients and an unusually low proportion of working poor and ex-offenders (Coe and Whiteman, 1979.)

Finally, the single room housing category about which the least is known are the "illegal" rooming houses. "Illegal" because they are not licensed as hotels and are often in areas not zoned for cohabitation by large numbers of single adults, many of these houses have evaded census and social agencies, remaining statistically invisible. Where they have turned up, ironically, is in studies of gentrifying neighborhoods where new residents often report shock at just how many persons had previously lived in the houses they take over.[1]

Rooming houses have been the traditional homes of young working people and the elderly poor since at least the 19th century. During recent years, zoning restrictions on the number of unrelated persons per bathroom have served to drive such establishments underground. Today the quality of such establishments seems to vary widely. Nevertheless, they continue to provide essential shelter for many of those not able to utilize conventional housing stock.

Gentrification As Policy

The movement to revitalize the inner city of many U.S. communities may have started as the grassroots, almost anarchic, efforts of small preservation groups and individuals. However, downtown renovation is today a matter of policy in many U.S. cities. As the waves of new "gentry" move out from tiny, formerly working class enclaves to large-scale renovation projects in or near the central business districts, they have increasingly come into direct competition with the marginal single room population. The following are examples of what happens when the needs of the two groups collide.

In Phoenix, Arizona, the elimination of missions and SROs has been made a cornerstone of downtown renewal efforts. In November of 1981, a new zoning ordinance excluded shelters and soup kitchens from the newly renovated downtown. On January 1, 1982, two long-operating, religious-run missions were condemned by the city (Sexton, 1982.) The last refuges for the homeless in Phoenix won reprieve by large-scale publicity and the efforts of religious groups (Stark, 1982.)

In Newark, New Jersey, privately funded renovation efforts have been aided by political efforts to remove "bums" and "bag ladies" from the downtown area. Of the two legal SROs in the city, one was condemned in 1982 and the other was closed in the spring of 1983. While a coalition of religious and private groups did manage to open a trailer as a shelter for the winter of 1982-1983, it provided no sleeping facilities. The logic was that if services for the homeless were "too attractive," such people would migrate to Newark from nearby Jersey City or New York City (Prupis, 1982.) Similarly, Henig (1982A) notes that the first step in the much-publicized renovation of the historic Nicollet Island section of Minneapolis was the destruction of its skid row district. The inhabitants of the area, being socially isolated and chronically dependent, were unable to mobilize any effective resistance, and were easily and quickly displaced.

Between 1975 and 1979, San Francisco lost 5,723 (17.7%) of its 32,214 SRO units. Much of this decline was the direct result of the renovation of the city's famous "Tenderloin" district, where 10 SROs (1,192 units) have been converted into tourist hotels (Hartman, Keating and Legates, 1982.) Ironically, other units were lost to government-subsidized Section 8 renovation; while Section 8 seeks to provide housing for low-income tenants, its minimum, property standards mandate a separate bathroom and kitchen for each unit, thereby encouraging the conversion of SROs and rooming houses into standard apartments (Lincoln, 1980.)

Opposition to the displacement of SRO tenants in San Francisco brought about a moratorium on SRO conversions from November 1979 to December 1980. Yet, during this period, conversion continued, due to lax enforcement and numerous legal loopholes. An October 1980 study by the North Market Planning Commission found that 2,374 more SRO units had been lost during the moratorium period, many of them converted to tourist hotels and high income housing following illegal evictions and harassment of tenants. Only after this additional loss, were permanent and somewhat more effective, restrictions imposed to protect the city's declining SRO stock (Hartman, Keating and Legates, 1982).

Downtown renovation had a similar effect on the single room housing stock of Portland, Oregon and Seattle, Washington during the 1960s and 1970s. Seattle has lost approximately 15,000 units to code enforcement and to civic and commercial renovation; in Portland, 1,345 units have been eliminated, leaving fewer than 700. In both cities, joint local-H.U.D. efforts to preserve and upgrade a few of the remaining units have been undertaken in the last few years, but no attempt has been made to replace units lost (Lincoln, 1980).

In New York City, shelters in renovating areas have come under increasing attack. In Manhattan's Upper West Side and in the Murray Hill section, the newly arrived gentry have come face to face with shelter and SRO populations, while the "Brownstone revival" in Brooklyn has displaced countless illegal rooming houses. The mayor himself has repeatedly asserted that the presence of the special needs populations of shelters will disrupt neighborhoods and "impede economic development" (*The New York Times*, 12/30/80, 9/18/81, quoted in Baxter, Hopper, et al., 1982).

New York City's SROs have tended to be concentrated in inner city areas of Manhattan, particularly on the Upper West Side and in the Midtown areas. Thus, they have stood directly in the path of the renovation movement. The result has been that, despite some legal efforts to ensure SRO residents their rights as tenants (the right of SRO tenants to a written lease was won in 1981), SRO after SRO has been converted into luxury housing, in many cases with generous tax subsidies awarded to the landlords who have undertaken such conversions.

As Exhibit 17-2 shows, the number of legal hotels charging less than $50 per week dropped from 298 in 1975 to 131 in 1981. Of course, some of this is merely the result of rising prices due to inflation.[2] However, of the 167 hotels that dropped out of the lower priced category between 1975 and 1981, 89 (53%) are no longer hotels at all. They are closed, converted to apartments, co-ops or some other use—all of this at a time when demand for SRO rooms was rising, as the declining vacancy rates indicate.

It should also be recalled that this drop in the number of SROs followed the extension of the city's controversial J-51 tax abatement program to SRO hotels. J-51 is a program that provides property tax abatements as incentives for landlords to renovate buildings in New York City. Administered by the city finance department, the program was initiated in 1955, long before the current real estate boom and the displacement it produced. However, it was only in 1975 that the program was extended to cover the conversion of SROs and other large structures into apartments.

As Exhibit 17-2 indicates, this extension was followed by an almost immediate decline in the number of SRO rooms in the city, despite an increased demand for such rooms, as indicated by the sharp decline in the vacancy rates. Furthermore, in many SRO conversions, residents appear to have been driven out of buildings to make way for renovation by a variety of illegal and sometimes brutal methods including lock-outs, assaults, and even arson (*The New York Times*, 5/10/82). In 1982 this was brought to public attention when a member of the New York City Council disclosed that a landlord who was at that time in jail for harassing tenants in a five-story rooming house he was planning to convert into apartments, had since 1977 been granted 2.1 million dollars in city tax abatements for similar conversions in other buildings. Further, the councilwoman pointed out that once the landlord was released from jail he would be eligible to receive a J-51 abatement on the building in question in the harassment conviction (*The New York Times*, 2/24/82.)

The following summer, a New York City Arson Strike Force memorandum on housing assistance programs and arson was leaked to the press. The memo noted that the J-51 program produced "an atmosphere conducive to arson" and, in a study of 17 former SROs on the Upper West Side, it concluded that ". . . arson accompanies J-51 benefits, at least in the case of SRO conversions" (Auslander and Dougherty, ASF memo, p. 18.)

While defenders of J-51 and similar programs admit that there have been abuses, they are quick to point out that since the period covered in the Arson Strike Force study, J-51 has been modified. Since 1981, restrictions have been placed on exemptions for SRO conversions, and abatements in Manhattan south of 96th Street have been limited. However, by that time, much of the SRO housing in the city was gone and the destruction of the rest was proceeding unabated. Today, even the Bowery, New York's archetypical skid row, is feeling the pinch of renovation.

Exhibit 17-2
SRO and Low-Priced Hotels* in New York City

	January 1975	March 1978	July 1979	April 1981
Hotels	298	230	189	131
Rooms	50,454	35,708	28,332	18,853
% Vacant	26%	14%	9%	+
Residential Population	35,150	30,516	23,134	N.A.
% Receiving Public Assistance** or SSI	32%	40%	46%	N.A.

* Hotels charging less than $50 per week
+ Not available. On 2/22/81 *The New York Times* estimated the vacancy rate in SRO or low-priced hotels as approximately "0%."

** Public Assistance = Public Assistance housing funds administered by the N.Y.C. Human Resources Administration.

SSI = Supplemental Security Income, administered by the Social Security Administration.

Source: New York City Human Resources Administration

The Current Problem

Clearly, then, the traditional single room tenant is no longer welcome in the newly valorized central city. Certain types of housing stock, which is to say certain types of people, are apparently incompatible with policies of revitalization, particularly policies of partially subsidized "private" sector revitalization. The problem is, then, where should these people go? As former resources (rooming houses and SROs) have been priced beyond their reach or have simply ceased to exist, many single room tenants have had to turn to an increasingly reluctant public sector for help. This has served to politicize greatly the simple question of where single room tenants would be located.

If the central city is no longer appropriate, suburban communities and family neighborhoods remain largely closed to groups of single adults and openly hostile to the more marginal of the single room occupants.

> No community in New York City wants live-in shelters for bums and bag ladies. . . . Derelicts are the least desirable neighbors. Irresponsible, drunk, drugged, often crazy, they are a form of street pollution frightening to children and disgusting to adults. They are the embodiment of failure, despair and death. . . . (*New York Daily News*, 8/28/81)

The placement of new public shelters reflects both the recent positive reevaluation of downtown space and the negative evaluation of these traditional center city residents. We now insist that they suffer privately, and towards that end efforts are made to hide them. Hence New York City recently built its new men's shelter on isolated and unpopulated Ward's Island, one of the few places in the city that might be deemed (in the words of Baxter, Hopper, et al.) "an appropriate site in part because it had no potentially offendable constituency."

There is a danger in romanticizing the SRO, the rooming house, and the shelter. Many of these buildings provided—and provide—the most squalid conditions of the housing market. Landlords have at times abused tenants with few options, and private shelters have been known to exact penance, prayer, and conversion as the price for the meanest of accommodations. While at least one report emphasizes the element of choice exercised by SRO residents (Coe and Whiteman, 1979,) it must be said to be a "choice" made by those with very few options. Nevertheless, it is a housing stock that does provide shelter·for persons who might otherwise lack shelter. It is being destroyed. It is not being replaced.

Many renovation efforts have been made with sympathy towards the single room residents. However, starting with efforts to bring rooming houses "up to code" in the 1960s, these efforts were made without understanding. The only way for many rooming houses to come "up to code" given legal and economic constraints was for them to cease to exist.

The single room occupant may be incompatible with gentrification. The deinstitutionalized, the ex-offender, the addicted, the poor, sick and elderly, all bring to the central city a "diversity" that the new investors in cultural pluralism want no part of. Yet these people will not go away simply because their housing is eliminated. They remain on our streets and tax the strained resources of the remaining shelters. Therefore the return to the city implies a return to civic responsibility for these, our weaker brethren. Unlike the suburb, the newly gentrified inner city cannot close its gates to marginal members of society. It therefore becomes imperative that new alternatives be provided.

NOTES

[1] It should be remembered that while gentrification is generally conceived of as middle class *in-migration*, in most cases the number of persons leaving a gentrifying area far exceeds the number moving in (Anderson, 1977).

[2] Of course, it must be remembered that while inflation rose during these years, the SSI housing allowance did not. Therefore, for many SRO residents, a hotel becoming higher priced amounted to much the same thing as if it had ceased to exist.

REFERENCES

Allen, Irving. (1980) "The Ideology of Dense Neighborhood Redevelopment," *Urban Affairs Quarterly*, 15(4).
Allman, T.D. (1978) "The Urban Crisis Leaves Town," *Harper's Magazine*, December.
Anderson, Jervis. (1977) "The Making of Boerum Hill," *The New Yorker*, 17 November, p.81.
Auslander, Andrew and John Dougherty. (1982) Memorandum to Housing Assistance Grants Program Advisory Board—4/30/82. New York City Arson Strike Force.
Bahr, H. (1973) *Skid Row: An Introduction to Disaffiliation*. New York: Oxford.
Baxter E. and K. Hopper. (1981) *Private Lives, Public Spaces*. New York: Community Service Society.
Baxter, E., K. Hopper, et al. (1982) *One Year Later*. New York: Community Service Society.
Clay, P. (1979) *Neighborhood Renewal*. Lexington, MA: D.C. Heath.
Coe, S. and A. Whiteman. (1979) "An Evaluation of Housing Alternatives for Tenants in Single Room Occupancy Hotels and a Design for a Community Response." Report prepared for the Mayor's Office on SRO Housing. New School for Social Research, New York, June 1979.
Eilbott and Kempey. (1978) "New York City's Tax Abatement and Exemption Program for Encouraging Housing Rehabilitation," *Public Policy* 26.

Fitch. (1976) "Planning New York," in Alcaly and Mermelstein (eds.) *The Fiscal Crises of American Cities*. New York: Vintage.

Fried, M. (1964) "Grieving for a Lost Home" in Duhl (ed.). *The Urban Condition*.

Gans, H. (1965) "The Failure of Urban Renewal," *Commentary*, 39(4).

Goldfield, D.R. (1980) "Private Neighborhood Renovation and Displacement. *Urban Affairs Quarterly*, 15.

Hartman, Keating and Legates. (1982) *Displacement—How To Fight It*. Berkeley, Calif.: Legal Services Anti-Displacement Project.

Henig. (1981) "Gentrification and Displacement of the Elderly." *The Gerontologist* 21.

———(1982) "Neighborhood Response to Gentrification: The Conditions of Mobilization," *Urban Affairs Quarterly*, 17(3).

———(1982A) *Neighborhood Mobilization: Redevelopment and Response*. New Brunswick, N.J.: Rutgers University Press.

Jacobs, J. (1961) *The Death and Life of Great American Cities*. New York: Random House.

LeGates and Hartman. (1981) *Displacement*. Berkeley, Calif.: Legal Services Anti-Displacement Project.

Levy, P. (1980) "Neighborhoods in a Race with Time," in Liska and Spain (eds.). *Back to the City*. New York: Pergamon.

Lincoln, Sheryl. (1980) "Single Room Residential Hotels Must Be Preserved as Low Income Housing Alternative." *Journal of Housing*, July.

Lovell, A. and S. Makiesky-Barrow. (1981) "Psychiatric Disability and Homelessness: A Look at Manhattan's Upper West Side." Presented at the Conference on "The Community Support Population: Designing Alternatives in an Uncertain Environment." Syracuse, New York, November 19, 1981.

Mandelker, Feder, and Collins. (1980) *Reviving Cities with Tax Abatement*. New Brunswick: Center for Urban Policy Research.

National Council on Aging. (1976) *The Invisible Elderly: Older Persons Who Live in Inner City Hotels and Rooming Houses*. Washington, D.C. (May).

Nesson. (1978) "Treasure Houses," *Harper's Magazine*, December.

Prupis, S. (1982) "Homeless Individuals in Newark: A Case Study." Unpublished paper. New York: New York University.

Ramati. (1981) *How to Save Your Street*. Garden City, N.Y.: Doubleday.

Reed, R. (1979) *Return to the City*. Garden City, N.Y.: Doubleday.

Segal, S.P.; Baumol, J. and E. Johnson. (1977) "Falling Through the Cracks: Mental Disorder and Social Margin in a Young Vagrant Population." *Social Policy*, 21(3).

Sexton, P.C. (1982) "Homelessness, A Symbol and the Politics of Poverty." Unpublished paper. New York: New York University.

Stark. (1982) "Phoenix: War on the Homeless," *Village Voice*, 28 December, pp. 10-11.

Stratton, J. (1977) *Pioneering in the Urban Wilderness*. New York: Urizen.

Spradley, J.P. (1970) *You Owe Yourself A Drunk: An Ethnography of Urban Nomads*. Boston, Ma: Little Brown.

Tournier. (1980) "Historic Preservation as a Force in Urban Change," in Liska and Spain (eds.). *Back to the City*. New York: Pergamon.

Vera Institute of Justice. (1980) "First Time Users of Men's Shelter Services: A Preliminary Analysis." New York.

———. (1981) "First Time Users of Women's Shelter Services: A Preliminary Analysis." New York.

Wiseman, J.P. (1970) *Stations of the Lost: The Treatment of Skid Row Alcoholics*. Englewood Cliffs, N.J.: Prentice-Hall.

Wilson, W.J. (1975) *Thinking About Crime*. New York: Basic.

Zukin (1982) *Loft Living: Art and Culture in Urban Change*. Baltimore, Md: Johns Hopkins Press.

18

The Homelessness Problem

Ellen L. Bassuk

ORE AMERICANS were homeless last winter than at any time since the Great Depression. Estimates of the size of the vagrant population vary widely. The National Coalition for the Homeless puts the figure at 2.5 million for 1983, an increase of 500,000 over the preceding year. The Federal Department of Housing and Urban Development (HUD) estimates that only 250,000 to 350,000 are homeless nationwide. Whatever the number is, everyone agrees it is growing.

Particularly in the past five years government officials and private groups in cities around the country have responded by opening emergency shelters to try to meet the immediate needs of the homeless. Beds in these shelters fill as soon as they become available, and still only a fraction of those in need are provided for. Some of the rest seek temporary refuge elsewhere, for example in hospitals, but most probably fend for themselves on the streets, huddling in doorways or over subway ventilation grates. When the weather turns cold, some die.

At night in New York City 18 public shelters house some of the thousands of men and women who roam the streets during the day; 16 of these shelters did not exist before 1980. Private groups in New York have also stepped up their efforts. In 1982, 10 churches offered a total of 113 beds to homeless people; by the end of 1983, 172 churches and synagogues were providing a total of 650 beds in 60 shelters. In Boston two large shelters recently doubled their capacity. Nevertheless, on a snowy night in January, Boston's largest shelter, the Pine Street Inn, reported a record number of "guests": the 350 beds were filled, as always, and 267 people crowded onto the Inn's bare cement floors.

From "The Homelessness Problem" by Ellen L. Bassuk. *Scientific American*, Vol. 251, July 1984, pp.40-45. Copyright© 1984 by Scientific American, Inc. All Rights Reserved. Reprinted by permission of W.H. Freeman and Company (Publishers).

Who are these people? Unfortunately there are no reliable national data on the homeless, even though they have always been numerous in American cities. Anecdotal evidence suggests that in the decades before 1970 most of the homeless were unattached, middle-aged, alcoholic men—the denizens of Skid Row. Since about 1970 the population appears to have been getting progressively younger. Moreover, the sparse literature on the subject and my own experience as a psychiatrist working with homeless people in Boston leads me to believe a more important change has taken place: an increasing number—I would say a large majority—of the homeless suffer from mental illness, ranging from schizophrenia to severe personality disorders.

At a time when the accepted solution to the homelessness problem is to establish more shelters, this finding has disturbing implications. Shelters are invaluable: they save lives. The trouble is that many shelters do little more, and the mentally ill need more than just a meal and protection from the elements. Those whose disorders are treatable or at least manageable require appropriate psychiatric care, which they do not get at shelters. The chronically disabled people who will never be able to care for themselves deserve better than to spend their lives begging on the streets and sleeping on army cots in gymnasiums. Shelters have been saddled with the impossible task of replacing not only the almshouses of the past but also the large state mental institutions. At this task they must inevitably fail, and thus American society has failed in its moral responsibility to care for its weakest members.

The statement that a majority of the homeless are mentally ill does not in itself explain why their number is growing or why a particular individual joins their ranks. Without reliable data it is difficult to answer the first question, but several factors may have contributed to the recent swelling of the homeless population. The most obvious one is the recession. Unemployment reached a peak of 10.7 percent in November, 1982, its highest level since the 1930's. Some of those who lost their jobs and incomes undoubtedly lost their homes as well.

The effects of unemployment are intensified by another problem: the dearth of low-cost housing. According to an analysis of the Federal Government's Annual Housing Survey by the Low Income Housing Information Service, the number of renter households with incomes below $3,000 per year dropped by about 46 percent, from 5.8 to 2.7 million, between 1970 and 1980; at the same time however, the number of rental units available to these households at 30 percent of their income fell by 70 percent, from an estimated 5.1 to about 1.2 million (excluding dwellings for which no cash rent was paid). As the "housing gap" widened, the median rent paid by households in the lowest income bracket rose from $72 a month in 1970 to $179 a month in 1980. That works out to 72 percent of an annual income of $3,000 and leaves $71 a month to cover all other household needs. A family devoting such a large fraction of its income to rent is in a precarious position: it may easily be dislodged by a drop in its income or by a further rise in its expenses. Unemployment and the lack of low-cost housing help to account for the increasing number of homeless families (as opposed to individuals), which once were rare.

Recent cuts in government benefit payments may also have thrown some people onto the streets, although the evidence is inferential. One of the Federal Government's most controversial measures in this area has been its effort to reform the Social Security Disability Insurance program, which in 1983 provided monthly benefits to a total of 3.8 million disabled workers and their dependents. To receive payments a worker must be physically or mentally unable to perform any kind of "substantial gainful work" for which he is qualified, regardless of whether such work is available where he lives. Following a report by the General Accounting Office that as many as 20 percent of the beneficiaries might be ineligible under the law, the Reagan Administration launched a "crackdown on ineligibility" in March, 1981. Between 150,000 and 200,000 people lost their benefits before the Administration halted its review of the beneficiary rolls in April, 1984, amid charges that truly disabled people, including some who were too mentally disabled to respond to termination notices, had been stricken from the rolls. Again, a lack of data makes it impossible to draw definite conclusions, but it seems not unreasonable to infer that the loss of disability benefits reduced some people to not being able to pay for their housing.

Far more important, however, in its impact on the homeless population has been the long-term change in the national policy for dealing with the mentally ill. A little more than 20 years ago state and county mental institutions began releasing large numbers of patients, many of whom suffered from severe illnesses. The "deinstitutionalization" movement followed the widespread introduction in the 1950's of psychoactive drugs, which seemed to offer the possibility of rehabilitating psychotic people within a community setting, under better living conditions and with greater respect for their civil rights. It was also thought the "community mental health" approach would be cheaper than operating large state hospitals. The movement was launched in 1963 when Congress passed a law promising Federal funding for the construction of community mental health centers.

Deinstitutionalization was a well-intentioned and perhaps even enlightened reform, but it has not proceeded according to the original plan. The first step has been accomplished: the patient population at state and county mental hospitals is now less than one-fourth of its 1955 peak level of 559,000. By and large, however, the various levels of government have not taken the second step: they have not provided enough places, such as halfway houses or group homes, for discharged patients to go. Other factors contributing to the problems of the system include the fact that fewer than half of the community mental health centers needed to cover the entire U.S. population have been built; moreover, existing centers often do not coordinate their activities with those of the institutions that are discharging their patients.

The inadequacy of the care available to deinstitutionalized patients is suggested by the large increases since the early 1960's in the rate of admissions to state mental hospitals and by the fact that a growing majority of admitted patients have been hospitalized before. The drop in the resident population of the institutions is accounted for by shorter average stays. Younger ill people who might have been institutionalized 15 years ago now receive only brief and episodic care; one major reason is that the courts have decided only those among the mentally ill who are dangerous to themselves or to others may be committed involuntarily. In the absence of alternatives to the institutions, respect for the civil rights of the disturbed sometimes conflicts with the goal of providing them with humane treatment and asylum. Chronically disturbed people are sent out into the community, often to empty lives in single-room-occupancy hotels and Skid Row rooming houses. With the growing unavailability of even these housing options many of the people end up on the streets.

Thus it should not be surprising to find that a significant fraction of shelter residents are mentally ill. In fact, a clinical study I designed and implemented last year found at a shelter in Boston a 90 percent incidence of diagnosable mental illness: psychoses, chronic alcoholism and character disorders. The shelter selected for the study, which was under the direction of Alison Lauriat of the Massachusetts Association for Mental Health and Paul McGerigle of the United Community Planning Corporation, was considered demographically representative of Boston-area shelters.

The demographic data are themselves interesting. Men outnumbered women by four to one, although the number of women at Boston shelters seems to be increasing. The median age was 34 and apparently decreasing. One-third of the guests were either recent arrivals or only occasional users of the shelter, whereas the other two-thirds had been staying in shelters for more than six months. Some 20 percent had been on the streets and in shelters for more than two years.

My colleagues (eight psychiatrists, psychologists and social workers) and I interviewed 78 guests at the shelter over the course of five nights. We diagnosed 40 percent as suffering from some form of psychosis: a generic term for major mental illnesses whose victims have difficulty distinguishing external reality from their own thoughts and feelings. The psychoses include some manic and depressive states and some organic brain syndromes, but most of the psychotics at the shelter were schizophrenic. Often subject to delusions and hallucinations, they have trouble coping with the demands of daily life.

A 42-year-old man, at one time a talented artist, is an extreme example.

When he was 24, he killed his wife with a baseball bat because she had been unfaithful to him. At the time he believed he was Raskolnikoff, the protagonist in Dostoevski's *Crime and Punishment*. The court psychiatrist diagnosed him as schizophrenic, and he was hospitalized in an institution for the criminally insane for the next 16 years. Since being discharged more than two years ago, he has lived both in shelters and on the streets; not long before we saw him he had been arrested for trespassing in a cemetery, where he was living in a tomb he had hollowed out. He says he receives messages from spirits who speak to him through spiders.

The story of an 18-year-old shelter guest is less striking but no less tragic. Until he became psychotic he was enrolled in an Ivy League college. He was hospitalized briefly in a state institution, where he was given antipsychotic medication, but when we saw him, he was receiving no treatment. For a while after his discharge his mother cared for him; eventually, however, she became too depressed to continue. Frightened and too confused to care for himself, he now wanders the streets by day, muttering incoherently and responding to voices he alone hears. At night he goes to a shelter where the staff are too busy feeding and clothing people to devote themselves to individual problems.

Many of the people we interviewed—we estimated 29 percent—were chronic alcoholics. One 33-year-old man had lived on the streets of Boston for 20 years and like many homeless alcoholics had been in and out of hospitals, detoxification centers and various treatment programs. In the past year he had made several suicide attempts, and he had recently been treated for pulmonary tuberculosis. (About 45 percent of the study group reported serious physical problems, including heart disease and cancer, in addition to their psychological difficulties.) Finally, about 21 percent suffered from personality disorders that made it hard for them to form and maintain relationships or to hold a job.

Chronic mental illness, even when it is severe enough to impair the ability to function in society, does not by itself cause homelessness, any more than unemployment does. For the great majority of shelter guests lack of a home is symptomatic of total disconnection from supportive people and institutions. Consider for a moment what would happen if a crisis were to strike your life—if you were to lose your job, say, or contract a serious illness. Most likely you are surrounded by family and friends, by co-workers and even by professional caretakers at various social agencies whose help you could call on to prevent a downward slide. You are insured, both in the literal sense of having coverage against financial loss and in the figurative sense of having a reliable support network.

To talk with homeless people is to be struck by how alone most of them are. The isolation is most severe for the mentally ill. Family and friends grow exhausted or lack the ability to help; overburdened social workers may be less responsive; the homeless themselves may be unwilling or unable to communicate their needs and to make use of the support available. Some 74 percent of the shelter residents we interviewed said they had no family relationships, and 73 percent said they had no friends, even within the shelter community. Those who had been hospitalized before for psychiatric reasons (about one-third of the group) reported even less social contact: more than 90 percent of them had neither friends nor family. About 40 percent of all the guests said they had no relationship with anyone or with any social institution; although only 6 percent worked steadily, only 22 percent received any financial assistance.

There is usually no single, simple reason for an individual's becoming homeless; rather, homelessness is often the final state in a lifelong series of crises and missed opportunities, the culmination of a gradual disengagement from supportive relationships and institutions. A final example illustrates the point. A 45-year-old man whom I shall call Johnny M. has lived on the streets and in the shelters of Boston for four years. The youngest of four siblings in a lower-middle-class family, Johnny spent most of his adolescent years in an institution for the mentally retarded. He remembers washing dishes, going to classes and looking forward to the visits of his mother and older sister. When he turned 16, he moved back home and spent time watching television and puttering in the garden. Ten years later his older sister died suddenly and Johnny had a "nervous breakdown." He became terrified of dying, he cried constantly and his thoughts became confused. Because he was unable to care for himself, he was involuntarily committed to a state hospital, where he remained for the next eight years. He became very attached to a social worker whom he saw twice a week for therapy.

Although the hospital had become Johnny's home, he was discharged at the height of deinstitutionalization into a single-room-occupancy hotel. His father had died, his mother was in a nursing home and neither his remaining sister nor his brother could afford to support him. Within six months he had lost contact with the hospital. Johnny was forced out of the hotel when it was converted into condominiums; unable to find a room he could afford, he roamed the streets for several months until an elderly woman and her daughter took him into their rooming house.

When the daughter died unexpectedly of a stroke, Johnny became depressed, thought the other residents were trying to harm him and grew increasingly belligerent. His landlady evicted him. Without resources or supports and with an incipient psychosis, he ended up homeless. Resigned to street life, he now spends his days walking endlessly, foraging in dumpsters. Occasionally he collects bottles, sells his blood for transfusion or takes part in medical experiments to make pocket money. Itching from lice, wearing tattered clothes and suffering from cellulitis of one leg, he feels lucky that he can depend on an evening meal at the shelter and that on most nights he has access to a bed.

Shelters help to keep Johnny M. and his companions in misfortune alive. That is a shelter's function: to provide food, clothing and a bed. At a typical shelter guests line up outside until the doors open in the early evening. A security guard checks each person for alcohol, drugs and weapons. New guests are also checked for lice. At some shelters volunteers cook hot meals; at others dinner consists of soup, sandwiches and coffee. Some guests spend the evening socializing and playing cards, but most are too weary or too detached and go directly to sleep. The dormitory is typically a barren auditorium-size room with rows of cots or beds and one or two cribs. Sometimes groups of six or more beds are separated by partitions. Shelter guests usually have few opportunities to wash during the day, and so at night the bathrooms at the shelter are generally overcrowded. By 10:00 P.M. the lights are turned out, and the next morning the guests are awakened early, given coffee and a doughnut and sent out, even if the temperature is below zero.

The atmosphere in a shelter is sometimes volatile, and occasionally violent fights erupt that have to be broken up by the staff or the police. On the other hand, the anonymity and invisibility fostered by shelters is comforting to many of the guests, who spend their days as highly visible social outcasts. Shelter providers try to treat their guests with dignity and respect, asking no questions and attaching no strings to the help they offer.

Do they offer enough? In my view they do not. Shelters would be the appropriate solution if the homeless were simply the victims of unemployment, or of disasters such as floods or fires. Although these factors undoubtedly contribute to the problem, the overriding fact about the homeless is that most are mentally disabled and isolated from the support that might help to reintegrate them into society. Moreover, many are chronically, permanently ill and will never be able to live independently.

Although various innovative model programs exist, including one sponsored by St. Vincent's Hospital in New York City, shelters as a rule offer only minimal medical, psychological and social services. They are generally understaffed and have few personnel specifically trained to care for the severely disabled. Because they are open only at night, they cannot offer the continuing support and supervision that many chronically ill people need. People whose condition might improve with properly supervised treatment (for example the 18-year-old student I mentioned above) do not get it at the shelters. And it hardly needs saying that shelters are not a humane solution to the problem of providing a place to live for those who suffer from permanent mental disabilities.

The precise extent to which mental illnesses are prevalent among the homeless remains a matter of controversy. Recent clinical studies at shelters in Los Angeles, New York and Philadelphia support my contention that a majority of the homeless suffer from psychiatric disorders, but other estimates have put the incidence of mental illness among shelter populations as low as 20 percent. All these studies, including our own, have been largely descriptive and have been plagued by methodological problems. Differences in results can be attributed to the different theoretical biases of the various investigators, to the use of different standardized scales as the basis for psychiatric evaluation and most of all to the difficulty of obtaining a representative sample of a constantly shifting population. In addition, there is no reason to expect the characteristics of the homeless population to be constant throughout the country when mental health policies and economic conditions vary regionally.

The public debate on homelessness would undoubtedly be enlightened by more rigorous research into the causes of the problem. It can already be said, however, that at the very least a significant fraction of the people who frequent shelters have diagnosable mental disturbances. Public servants of all ideologies have failed to recognize the implications of this fact. Many political conservatives seem to believe the Government has little obligation to care for the homeless; this attitude is perhaps best exemplified by President Reagan's often quoted remark that "the homeless are homeless, you might say, by choice." For political liberals the plight of the homeless serves as ammunition in their attack on the Administration's economic policies, but the solution they tend to support is the expansion of emergency shelters: simply putting a temporary dressing on what has become a large, festering wound in the social body.

There is no mystery about the nature of a more appropriate solution. Essentially it would call for carrying out the aborted plans of the 1963 community mental health law by providing a spectrum of housing options and related health-care and social services for the mentally ill. These would entail living arrangements with varying degrees of supervision, from 24-hour care at therapeutic residences for patients with severe psychoses to more independent living at halfway houses for patients with less severe disorders. Some patients would receive counseling and therapy with the goal of rehabilitating them and even getting them jobs in the community. The one major change needed in the community mental health program, however, is a greater recognition of the limitations of psychiatry: given the current state of the art many chronically disturbed people simply cannot be rehabilitated, and the goal in these cases would be to provide the patient with comfortable and friendly asylum.

The community mental health movement failed primarily because the Federal and state governments never allocated the money needed to fulfill its promise. American society is currently trying to solve the problem cheaply, giving the mentally ill homeless at best emergency refuge and at worst no refuge at all. The question raised by the increasing number of homeless people is a very basic one: Are Americans willing to consign a broad class of disabled people to a life of degradation, or will they make the commitment to give such people the care they need? In a civilized society the answer should be clear.

19

Deinstitutionalization
and the Homeless Mentally Ill

H. Richard Lamb

Is DEINSTITUTIONALIZATION the cause of homelessness? Some would say yes and send the chronically mentally ill back to the hospitals. A main thesis of this chapter, however, is that problems such as homelessness are not the result of deinstitutionalization per se but rather of the way deinstitutionalization has been implemented. It is the purpose of this chapter to describe these problems of implementation and the related problem of the lack of clear understanding of the needs of the chronically mentally ill in the community. The discussion then turns to some additional unintended results of these problems, such as the criminalization of the mentally ill that usually accompanies homelessness. The chapter concludes with some ways of resolving these problems.

To see and experience the appalling conditions under which the homeless mentally ill exist has a profound impact upon us; our natural reaction is to want to rectify the horrors of what we see with a quick, bold stroke. But for the chronically mentally ill, homelessness is a complex problem with multiple causative factors; in our analysis of this problem we need to guard against settling for simplistic explanations and solutions.

For instance, homelessness is closely linked with deinstitutionalization in the sense that three decades ago most of the chronically mentally ill had a home—the state hospital. Without deinstitutionalization it is unlikely there would be large numbers of homeless mentally ill. Thus in countries such as

From: *The Homeless Mentally Ill*, a Task Force Report of the American Psychiatric Association on the Homeless Mentally Ill. Edited by H. Richard Lamb. Washington, D.C., American Psychiatric Association, 1984, pp.55-74. Used with Permission.

Israel, where deinstitutionalization has barely begun, homelessness of the chronically mentally ill is not a significant problem. But that does not mean we can simply explain homelessness as a result of deinstitutionalization; we have to look at what conditions these mentally ill persons must face in the community, what needed resources are lacking, and the nature of mental illness itself.

With the mass exodus into the community that deinstitutionalization brought, we are faced with the need to understand the reactions and tolerance of the chronically mentally ill to the stresses of the community. And we must determine what has become of them without the state hospitals, and why. There is no evidence that nationwide very substantial numbers of the severely mentally ill are homeless at any given time (Arce et al. 1983; Baxter and Hopper in press; Lipton et al. 1983). Some are homeless continuously and some intermittently. . . . We need to understand what characteristics of society and the mentally ill themselves have interacted to produce such an unforeseen and grave problem as homelessness. Without that understanding, we will not be able to conceptualize and then implement what needs to be done to resolve the problems of homelessness.

With the advantage of hindsight, we can see that the era of deinstitutionalization was ushered in with much naivete and many simplistic notions about what would become of the chronically and severely mentally ill. The importance of psychoactive medication and a stable source of financial support was perceived, but the importance of developing such fundamental resources as supportive living arrangements was often not clearly seen, or at least not implemented. "Community treatment" was much discussed, but there was no clear idea as to what it should consist of, and the resistance of community mental health centers to providing services to the chronically mentally ill was not anticipated. Nor was it foreseen how reluctant many states would be to allocate funds for community-based services.

It had been observed that persons who spend long periods in hospitals develop what has come to be known as institutionalism—a syndrome characterized by lack of initiative, apathy, withdrawal, submissiveness to authority, and excessive dependence on the institution (Wing and Brown 1970). It had also been observed, however, that this syndrome may not be entirely the outcome of living in dehumanizing institutions; at least in part, it may be characteristic of the schizophrenic process itself (Johnstone et al. 1981). Many patients who are liable to institutionalism and vulnerable to external stimulation may develop dependence on any other way of life outside hospitals that provides minimal social stimulation and allows them to be socially inactive (Brown et al. 1966). These aspects of institutionalism were often not recognized or were overlooked in the early enthusiasm about deinstitutionalization.

In the midst of very valid concerns about the shortcomings and antitherapeutic aspects of state hospitals, it was not appreciated that the state hospitals fulfilled some very crucial functions for the chronically and severely mentally ill. The term "asylum" was in many ways an appropriate one, for these imperfect institutions did provide asylum and sanctuary from the pressures of the world with which, in varying degrees, most of these patients were unable to cope (Lamb and Peele in press). Further, these institutions provided such services as medical care, patient monitoring, respite for the patient's family, and a social network for the patient as well as food and shelter and needed support and structure (Bachrach 1984).

Fernandez (1983), working in Dublin, recognizes these needs that used to be met, though not well, by state hospitals. He warns about the tendency to "equate the concept of homelessness exclusively with the lack of a permanent roof over one's head. This deflects attention from what is believed to be the essential deficit of homelessness, namely, the absence of a stable base of caring or supportive individuals whose concern and support help buffer the homeless against the vicissitudes of life. In this context, it is felt that the absence of such a base, or the inability to establish or to approximate such a base, is the essential deficit of patients with 'no-fixed-abode'." . . .

In the state hospitals what treatment and services that did exist were in one place and under one administration. In the community the situation is very different. Services and treatment are under various administrative jurisdictions and in various locations. Even the mentally healthy have difficulty dealing with a number of bureaucracies, both governmental and private, and getting their needs met. Further, patients can easily get lost in the community as compared to a hospital, where they may have been neglected but at least their whereabouts were known. It is these problems that have led to the recognition of the importance of case management. It is probable that many of the homeless mentally ill would not be on the streets if they were on the caseload of a professional or paraprofessional trained to deal with the problems of the chronically mentally ill, monitor them (with considerable persistence when necessary), and facilitate their receiving services.

In my experience (Lamb 1981) and that of others (Baxter and Hopper 1982), the survival of long-term patients, let alone their rehabilitation, begins with an appropriately supportive and structured living arrangement. Other treatment and rehabilitation are of little avail until patients feel secure and are stabilized in their living situation. Deinstitutionalization means granting asylum in the community to a large marginal population, many of whom can cope to only a limited extent with the ordinary demands of life, have strong dependency needs, and are unable to live independently.

Moreover, that some patients might need to reside in a long-term, locked, intensively supervised community facility was a foreign thought to most who advocated return to the community in the early years of emptying the state hospitals. "Patients who need a secure environment can remain in the state hospital" was the rationale. But in those early years most people seemed to think that such patients were few, and that community treatment and modern psychoactive medications would take care of most problems. More people are now recognizing that a number of severely disabled patients present major problems in management, and can survive and have their basic needs met outside of state hospitals only if they have a sufficiently structured community facility or other mechanism that provides support and controls (Lamb 1980b). Some of the homeless appear to be in this group. A function of the old state hospitals often given too little weight is that of providing structure. Without this structure, many of the chronically mentally ill feel lost and cast adrift in the community—however much they may deny it.

There is currently much emphasis on providing emergency shelter to the homeless, and certainly this must be done. But it is important to put the "shelter approach" into perspective; it is a necessary stopgap, symptomatic measure, but does not address the basic causes of homelessness. Too much emphasis on shelters can only delay our coming to grips with the underlying problems that result in homelessness. We must keep these problems in mind even as we sharpen our techniques for working with mentally ill persons who are already homeless.

Most mental health professionals are disinclined to treat "street people" or "transients" (Larew 1980.) Moreover, in the case of many of the homeless, we are working with persons whose lack of trust and desire for autonomy cause them to not give us their real names, to refuse our services, and to move along because of their fear of closeness, of losing their autonomy, or of acquiring a mentally ill identity. Providing food and shelter with no strings attached, especially in a facility that has a close involvement with mental health professionals, a clear conception of the needs of the mentally ill, and the ready availability of other services, can be an opening wedge that ultimately will give us the opportunity to treat a few of this population.

At the same time we have learned that we must beware of simple solutions and recognize that this shelter approach is not a definitive solution to the basic problems of the homeless mentally ill. It does not substitute for the array of measures that will be effective in both significantly reducing and preventing homelessness: a full range of residential placements, aggressive case management, changes in the legal system that will facilitate involuntary treatment, . . . a stable source of income for each patient, and access to acute hospitalization and other vitally needed community services.

Still another problem with the shelter approach is that many of the homeless mentally ill will accept shelter but nothing more, and they eventually return to a wretched and dangerous life on the streets. A case example will illustrate.

A 28-year-old man was brought to a California state hospital with a diagnosis of acute paranoid schizophrenia. He had been living under a freeway overpass for the past six weeks. There was no prior record of his hospitalization in the state. After a month in the hospital he had gone into partial remission and was transferred to a community residential program. There he was assigned to a skilled, low-key, sensitive clinician. Over a period of several weeks he gradually improved and returned to what was probably his normal state of being guarded and suspicious but not overtly psychotic.

Though he isolated himself much of the time, he appeared quite comfortable with the program and with the staff and indicated that he would, if allowed, stay indefinitely. He denied possessing a birth certificate, baptismal certificate, driver's license, or any other proof of identity. He steadfastly refused to give the whereabouts of his family or reveal his place of birth or anything else about his identity, even though he realized such information was necessary to qualify him for any type of financial or housing assistance. Clearly his autonomy was precious to him. And in an unguarded moment he said, "I couldn't bear to have my family know what a failure I have been." At the end of three months, the maximum length of stay allowed by the community program's contract, he had to be discharged to a mission.

What was not foreseen in the midst of the early optimism about returning the mentally ill to the community and restoring and rehabilitating them so they could take their places in the mainstream of society was what was actually to befall them. Certainly it was not anticipated that criminalization and homelessness would be the lot for many. But first let us briefly look at how deinstitutionalization came about.

A Brief History of Deinstitutionalization

For more than half of this century, the state hospitals fulfilled the function for society of keeping the mentally ill out of sight and thus out of mind. Moreover, the controls and structure provided by the state hospitals, as well as the granting of almost total asylum, may have been necessary for many of the long-term mentally ill before the advent of modern psychoactive medications. Unfortunately, the ways in which state hospitals achieved this structure and asylum led to everyday abuses that have left scars on the mental health professions as well as on the patients.

The stage was set for deinstitutionalization by the periodic public outcries about these deplorable conditions, documented by journalists such as Albert Deutsch (1948); mental health professionals and their organizational leaders also expressed growing concern. These concerns led ultimately to the formation of the Joint Commission on Mental Illness and Health in 1955 and its recommendations for community alternatives to state hospitals, published in 1961 as a widely read book, *Action for Mental Health*.

When the new psychoactive medications appeared (Brill and Patton 1957; Kris 1971), along with a new philosophy of social treatment (Greenblatt 1977), the great majority of the chronic psychotic population was left in a state hospital environment that was now clearly unnecessary and even inappropriate for them, though, as noted above, it met many needs. Still other factors came into play. First was a conviction that mental patients receive better and more humanitarian treatment in the community than in state hospitals far removed from home. This belief was a philosophical keystone in the origins of the community mental health movement. Another powerful motivating force was concern about the civil rights of psychiatric patients; the system then employed of commitment and institutionalization in many ways deprived them of their civil rights. Not the least of the motivating factors was financial. State governments wished to shift some of the fiscal burden for these patients to federal and local government—that is, to federal Supplemental Security Income (SSI) and Medicaid and local law enforcement agencies and emergency health and mental health services (Borus 1981; Goldman et al. 1983).

The process of deinstitutionalization was considerably accelerated by two significant federal developments in 1963. First, categorical Aid to the Disabled (ATD) became available to the mentally ill, which made them eligible for the first time for federal financial support in the community. Second, the community mental health centers legislation was passed.

With ATD, psychiatric patients and mental health professionals acting on their behalf now had access to federal grants-in-aid, in some states supplemented by state funds, which enabled patients to support themselves or be supported either at home or in such facilities as board-and care homes or old hotels at comparatively little cost to the state. Although the amount of money available to patients under ATD was not a princely sum, it was sufficient to maintain a low standard of living in the community. Thus the states, even those that provided generous ATD supplements, found it cost far less to maintain patients in the community than in the hospital. (ATD is now called Supplemental Security Income and is administered by the Social Security Administration.)

The second significant federal development of 1963 was the passage of the Mental Retardation Facilities and Community Mental Health Centers Construction Act, amended in 1965 to provide grants for the initial costs of staffing the newly constructed centers. This legislation was a strong incentive to the development of community programs with the potential to treat people whose main recourse previously had been the state hospital. It is important to note, however, that although rehabilitative services and precare and aftercare services were among the services eligible for funding, an agency did not have to offer them in order to qualify for funding as a comprehensive community mental health center.

Also contributing to deinstitutionalization were sweeping changes in the commitment laws of the various states. In California, for instance, the Lanterman-Petris-Short Act of 1968 provided further impetus for the movement of patients out of hospitals. Behind this legislation was a concern for the civil rights of the psychiatric patient, much of it from civil rights groups and individuals outside the mental health professions. The act made the involuntary commitment of psychiatric patients a much more complex process, and it became difficult to hold psychiatric patients indefinitely against their will in mental hospitals. Thus the initial stage of what had formerly been the career of the long-term hospitalized patient—namely, an involuntary, indefinite commitment—became a thing of the past (Lamb et al. 1981.)

Some clearly recognized that while many abuses needed to be corrected, this legislation went too far in the other direction and no longer safeguarded the welfare of the patients. (For instance, Richard Levy, M.D., of San Mateo, California, argued this point long and vigorously.) But these were voices in the wilderness. We have still not found a way to help some mental health lawyers and patients' rights advocates see that they have contributed heavily to the problem of homelessness—that patients' rights to freedom are not synonymous with releasing them to the streets where they cannot take care of themselves, are too disorganized or fearful to avail themselves of what help is available, and are easy prey for every predator.

The dimensions of the phenomenon of deinstitutionalization are revealed by the numbers. In 1955 there were 559,000 patients in state hospitals in the United States; today at any given time there are approximately 132,000 (Redick and Witkin 1983.)

What Happened To The Patients

What happened to the chronically and severely mentally ill as a result of deinstitutionalization? In the initial years approximately two-thirds of discharged mental patients returned to their families (Minkoff 1978.) The figure is probably closer to 50 percent in states such as California, which has a high number of persons without families (Lamb and Goertzel 1977.) This discussion is limited to those aged 18 to 65, for those over 65 are a very different population with a very different set of problems.

In more recent years, there has been a growing number of mentally disabled persons in the community who have never been or have only briefly been in hospitals. . . . Problems in identifying and locating them make it difficult to generalize about them. But we do know they of course tend to be younger and often manifest less institutional passivity than the previous generation, who had spent many years in state hospitals.

A large proportion of the chronically mentally ill—in some communities as many as a third or more of those aged 18 to 65—live in facilities such as board-and-care homes (Lamb and Goertzel 1977.) These products of the private sector are not the result of careful planning and well-conceived social policy. On the contrary, they sprang up to fill the vacuum created by the rapid and usually haphazard depopulation of our state hospitals. Suddenly many thousands of former state hospital patients needed a place to live, and private entrepreneurs, both large and small, rushed in to provide it.

"Board-and-care home" is used in California to describe a variety of facilities, many of which house large numbers of psychiatric patients. These patients include both the deinstitutionalized and the new generations of chronically mentally ill. The number of residents ranges from one to more than a hundred. Board-and-care homes are unlocked and provide a shared room, three meals a day, dispensing of medications, and minimal staff supervision; for a large proportion of long-term psychiatric patients, the board-and-care home has taken over the functions of the state hospitals of providing asylum, support, structure, and medications. And for many, the alternative to the board-and-care home would be homelessness.

There is a great deal of variability in facilities such as board-and care homes. Generally, they could and should provide a higher quality of life than they do, and services should be made more available to their residents. Services should include social and vocational rehabilitation, recreational activities, and mental health treatment. But considering the funding available, these facilities are for the most part not bad in the sense that there is no life-threatening physical neglect or other gross abuses (Dittmar and Smith 1983.)

What does stand out is the significantly higher funding for similar resources for the developmentally disabled, and the resulting increased quality in terms of location of the facility, condition of repair, general atmosphere, and staffing. For instance, as of 1984 the rate paid to operators of board-and-care facilities for the developmentally disabled in California varies from a min-

imum of $525 a month for easily manageable residents to $840 a month for
"intensive treatment." For the mentally ill there is only one rate of $476 per
month, regardless of the severity of the problem and the need for intensive
supervision and care; many of the better board-and-care home operators have
stopped serving the mentally ill in order to take advantage of the higher rates
for the developmentally disabled. Clearly this is a gross inequity.

But facilities such as board-and-care homes and single-room-occupancy
(SRO) hotels, even when adequate, often do not attract and keep the homeless (Arce et al. 1983.) If they do enter one of these facilities, their stay may be
brief—they drift in and out, to and from the streets. Further, these facilities
are not prepared to provide the structure needed by some of the chronically
mentally ill, as discussed below.

. This chapter is, of course, concerned with those chronically mentally ill
persons who live neither with family nor in board-and-care homes nor in SRO
hotels nor in nursing homes nor in their own homes or apartments. Some are
homeless continuously, and some intermittently. While estimates of the
extent of the problem are highly variable, and there are no reliable data, ... it
seems reasonable to conclude that nationwide the homeless mentally ill
number in the tens of thousands, and perhaps the many tens of thousands.
They live on the streets, the beaches, under bridges, in doorways. So many
frequent the shelters of our cities that there is concern that the shelters are
becoming mini-institutions for the chronically mentally ill, an ironic alternative to the state mental hospitals (Bassuk in press.)

The Tendency To Drift

Drifter is a word that strikes a chord in all those who have contact with the
chronically mentally ill—mental health professionals, families, and the
patients themselves. It is especially important to examine the phenomenon of
drifting in the homeless mentally ill. The tendency is probably more pronounced in the young (aged 18 to 35), though it is by no means uncommon in
the older age groups. Some drifters wander from community to community
seeking a geographic solution to their problems; hoping to leave their problems behind, they find they have simply brought them to a new location.
Others, who drift in the same community from one living situation to another,
can best be described as drifting through life: they lead lives without goals,
direction, or ties other than perhaps an intermittent hostile-dependent relationship with relatives or other caretakers (Lamb 1982.)

Why do the chronic mentally ill drift? Apart from their desire to outrun
their problems, their symptoms, and their failures, many have great difficulty
achieving closeness and intimacy. A fantasy of finding closeness elsewhere

encourages them to move on. Yet all too often, if they do stumble into an intimate relationship or find themselves in a residence where there is caring and closeness and sharing, the increased anxiety they experience creates a need to run.

They drift also in search of autonomy, as a way of denying their dependency, and out of a desire for an isolated life-style. Lack of money often makes them unwelcome, and they may be evicted by family and friends. And they drift because of a reluctance to become involved in a mental health treatment program or a supportive out-of-home environment, such as a halfway house or board-and-care home, that would give them a mental patient identity and make them part of the mental health system: they do not want to see themselves as ill.

Those who move out of board-and-care homes tend to be young; they may be trying to escape the pull of dependency and may not be ready to come to terms with living in a sheltered, segregated, low-pressure environment (Lamb 1980a.) If they still have goals, they may find life there extremely depressing. Or they may want more freedom to drink or to use street drugs. Those who move on are more apt to have been hospitalized during the preceding year. Some may regard leaving their comparatively static milieu as a necessary part of the process of realizing their goals—but a process that exacts its price in terms of homelessness, crises, decompensation, and hospitalizations. Once out on their own, they will more than likely stop taking their medications and after a while lose touch with Social Security and no longer be able to receive their SSI checks. They may now be too disorganized to extricate themselves from living on the streets—except by exhibiting blatantly bizarre or disruptive behavior that leads to their being taken to a hospital or to jail.

The Question of Liberty

Perhaps one of the brightest spots of the effects of deinstitutionalization is that the mentally ill have gained a greatly increased measure of liberty. There is often a tendency to underestimate the value and humanizing effects for former hospital patients of simply having their liberty to the extent that they can handle it (even aside from the fact that it is their right) and of being able to move freely in the community. It is important to clarify that, even if these patients are unable to provide for their basic needs through employment or to live independently, these are separate issues from that of having one's freedom. Even if they live in mini-institutions in the community, such as board-and-care homes, the facilities are not locked, and the patients generally have access to community resources.

However, the advocacy of liberty needs to be qualified. A small proportion of long-term, severely disabled psychiatric patients lack sufficient impulse control to handle living in an open setting such as a board-and-care home or with relatives (Lamb 1980b.) They need varying degrees of external structure and control to compensate for the inadequacy of their internal controls. They are usually reluctant to take psychotropic medications and often have problems with drugs and alcohol in addition to their mental illness. They tend not to remain in supportive living situations, and often join the ranks of the homeless. The total number of such patients may not be great when compared to the total population of severely disabled patients. However, if placed in community living arrangements without sufficient structure, this group may require a large proportion of the time of mental health professionals, not to mention others such as the police. More important, they may be impulsively self-destructive or sometimes present a physical danger to others.

Furthermore, many of this group refuse treatment services of any kind. For them, simple freedom can result in a life filled with intense anxiety, depression, and deprivation, and often a chaotic life on the streets. Thus they are frequently found among the homeless when not in hospitals and jails. These persons often need ongoing involuntary treatment, sometimes in 24-hour settings such as locked skilled-nursing facilities or, when more structure is needed, in hospitals. It should be emphasized that structure is more than just a locked door; other vital components are high staff-patient ratios and enough high-quality activities to structure most of the patient's day.

In my opinion, a large proportion of those in need of increased structure and control can be relocated from the streets to live in open community settings, such as with family or in board-and-care homes, if they receive assistance from legal mechanisms like conservatorship, as is provided in California. But even those who live in a legally structured status in the community, such as under conservatorship or guardianship, have varying degrees of freedom and an identity as a community member.

Some professionals now talk about sending the entire population of chronically and severely mentally ill patients back to the state hospitals, exaggerating and romanticizing the activities and care the patients are said to have received there. To some, reinstitutionalization seems like a simple solution to the problems of deinstitutionalization such as homelessness (Borus 1981; Feldman 1983.) But activity and treatment programs geared to the needs of long-term patients can easily be set up in the community, and living conditions, structured or unstructured, can be raised to any level we choose—if adequate funds are made available. The provision of such community resources, adequate in quantity and quality, would go a long way toward resolving the problems of homelessness. In the debate over which is the better treatment setting—the hospital or the community—we must not overlook the patients' feelings of mastery and heightened self-esteem when they are allowed their freedom.

Criminalization

Deinstitutionalization has led to the presence of large numbers of mentally ill persons in the community. At the same time, there are limited amounts of community psychiatric resources, including hospital beds. Society has a limited tolerance of mentally disordered behavior, and the result is pressure to institutionalize persons needing 24-hour care wherever there is room, including jail. Indeed, several studies describe a "criminalization" of mentally disordered behavior (Abramson 1972; Grunberg et al. 1977; Lamb and Grant 1982; Sosowsky 1978; Urmer 1971)—that is, a shunting of mentally ill persons in need of treatment into the criminal justice system instead of the mental health system. Rather than hospitalization and psychiatric treatment, the mentally ill often tend to be subject to inappropriate arrest and incarceration. Legal restrictions placed on involuntary hospitalization also probably result in a diversion of some patients to the criminal justice system.

Studies of 203 county jail inmates, 102 men and 101 women, referred for psychiatric evaluation (Lamb and Grant 1982, 1983) shed some light on the issues of both criminalization and homelessness. This population had extensive experience with both the criminal justice and the mental health systems, was characterized by severe and chronic mental illness, and generally functioned at a low level. Homelessness was common; 39 percent had been living, at the time of arrest, on the streets, on the beach, in missions, or in cheap, transient skid row hotels. Clearly the problems of homelessness and criminalization are interrelated.

Almost half of the men and women charged with misdemeanors had been living on the streets or the beach, in missions, or in cheap transient hotels, compared with a fourth of those charged with felonies ($p < .01$, by chi-square analysis.) One can speculate on some possible explanations. Persons living in such places obviously have a minimum of community supports; committing a misdemeanor may frequently be a way of asking for help. It is also possible that many are being arrested for minor criminal acts that are really manifestations of their illness, their lack of treatment, and the lack of structure in their lives. Certainly these were the clinical impressions of the investigators as they talked to these inmates and their families and read the police reports.

The studies also found that a significantly larger percentage of inmates aged 35 or older had a history of residence in a board-and-care home, compared with those under age 35 ($p < .02$, chi-square analysis.) Obviously the older one is, the more opportunity one has had to live in different situations, including board-and-care homes. However, in talking with these men and women, other factors emerged: the tendencies of the younger mentally ill person to hold out for autonomy rather than living in a protected, supervised setting, and to resist both entering the mental health system and being labeled as a psychiatric patient, even to the extent of living in a board-and-care home.

Board-and-care homes had been repeatedly recommended to a large number of the younger persons as part of their hospital discharge plans, but they had consistently refused to go. It appeared that eventually many gave up the struggle, at least temporarily, and accepted a board-and-care placement. However, most left the homes after relatively brief periods, many to return to the streets. In some cases this living situation did not appear to be structured enough for them. In other cases, they seemed to want to regain their autonomy, their isolated life-style, and their freedom to engage in antisocial activities. Despite the fact that a high proportion of the study population had serious psychiatric problems, only eight men (out of 102) and five women (out of 101) were living in board-and-care homes at the time of arrest.

Clearly the system of voluntary mental health outpatient treatment is inadequate for this population, who are extremely resistant to it. If they do agree to accept treatment, they tend not to keep their appointments and not to take their medications, and to be unwelcome at outpatient facilities (Whitmer 1980.) This is confirmed by our findings, which showed that only 10 percent of the inmates were receiving any form of outpatient treatment, such as medication, at the time of arrest, and that only 24 percent ever received outpatient treatment.

The need for mental health services in jails is apparent (Lamb et al. 1984.) Even so, many mentally ill inmates will not participate in release planning and will not accept referral for housing or treatment. As a result they are released to the streets to begin anew their chaotic existences characterized by homelessness, dysphoria, and deprivation. To work with this population of mentally ill in jail is to be impressed by their need for ongoing involuntary treatment.

Conclusions

The majority of chronically mentally ill persons live with their families or in sheltered living situations such as board-and-care homes. Some live in situations such as single-room-occupancy hotels or otherwise alone. Many are in and out of hospitals. Some are continuously homeless, and some intermittently so. While a minority of the total population of chronically mentally ill are homeless at any given time, very substantial numbers of persons are involved, and homelessness of the chronically mentally ill is a critical nationwide problem.

What have we learned from our experience with more than two decades of deinstitutionalization? First of all, it has become clear that what is needed is a vast expansion of community housing and other services and a whole revamping of the mental health system to meet the needs of the chronically mentally ill. Markedly increased funding is needed to increase the quality, quantity, and range of housing and other services, improve the quality of life for this population, and meet their needs for support and stability. The availability of suitable services should make it possible to attract many of the homeless to stable living arrangements and retain them there.

Many of the chronically mentally ill are not able to find or retain such community resources as housing, a stable source of income, and treatment and rehabilitation services. The need for monitoring and treating these patients by means of aggressive case management has become increasingly apparent. Aggressive case management for all of the chronically mentally ill, given the availability of adequate housing and other resources, would probably minimize homelessness.

It is one of the injustices of deinstitutionalization that, compared to the developmentally disabled, the chronically mentally ill in the community do not fare well in terms of funding, housing, and services. Surely the mentally ill should be given equal priority. The success of deinstitutionalization for the developmentally disabled, however, does demonstrate what can be accomplished when there is determined advocacy and adequate funding and community resources.

We have learned in this era of deinstitutionalization that many of the homeless mentally ill feel alienated from both society and the mental health system, that they are fearful and suspicious, and that they do not want to give up what they see as their autonomy, living on the streets where they have to answer to no one. They may be too acutely and chronically mentally ill and disorganized to respond to our offers of help. Their tolerance for closeness and intimacy is very low, and they fear they will be forced into relationships they cannot handle. They may not want a mentally ill identity, may not wish to or are not able to give up their isolated life-style and their anonymity, and may not wish to acknowledge their dependency. Thus we are dealing with an extremely difficult and challenging population.

As with most problems, we have learned that there are no simple and universal solutions to the problems of homelessness. Let us take the shelter approach as an example. Some of the chronically mentally ill will accept food and shelter, but nothing else, and sooner or later return to the streets, despite the efforts of our most sensitive clinicians. A few will not accept simple shelter, even with no conditions attached.

Certainly we must provide emergency shelter, but we also need to be aware that this is a symptomatic approach. Instead our primary focus should be on the underlying causes of homelessness, and we should work to provide a full range of residential placements, aggressive case management, changes in the legal system, a ready availability of crisis intervention including acute hospitalization, and other crucial community treatment and rehabilitation services.

We have also learned that some of the chronically mentally ill, because of their personality problems, their lack of internal controls, and their resort to drugs and alcohol, will not be manageable, or welcome, in open settings, such as with family or in board-and-care homes, or even in shelters. Some will need more structure and control; they may need involuntary treatment in a secure intermediate or long-term residential setting or in the community, facilitated by mechanisms such as conservatorship or mandatory aftercare. Such intervention should not be limited to those who can be proven to be "dangerous," but should be extended to gravely disabled individuals who do not respond to aggressive case management and are too mentally incompetent to make a rational judgment about their needs for care and treatment. In this way we can help those homeless mentally ill who are unwilling to accept our assistance and whose self-destructive tendencies, personality disorganization, and inability to care for themselves result in lives lived alternately in jails, in hospitals, and on the streets. In some cases such intervention is the only act of mercy left open to us.

We have learned that we must accept patients' dependency when dealing with the chronically mentally ill. And we must accept the total extent of patients' dependency needs, not simply the extent to which *we* wish to gratify these needs. We have learned, or should have learned, to abandon our unrealistic expectations and redefine our notions of what constitutes success with these patients. Sometimes it is returning them to the mainstream of life; sometimes it is raising their level of functioning just a little so they can work in a sheltered workshop. But oftentimes success is simply engaging patients, stabilizing their living situations, and helping them lead more satisfying, more dignified, and less oppressive lives.

The reluctance of mental health professionals and society to fully accept the dependency of this vulnerable group, inadequate case management systems, the preference of many mental health professionals to work with more "healthy" and "savory" patients, and an ideology that "coercive" measures should be used only in cases of "extreme danger" leave the homeless mentally ill in extreme jeopardy. If deinstitutionalization has taught us anything, it is that flexibility is all important. We must look objectively at the clinical and survival needs of the patients and meet those needs without being hindered by rigid ideology or a distaste for dependency.

REFERENCES

Abramson, MF: The criminalization of mentally disordered behavior. Hosp. Community Psychiatry 23:101-105, 1972.

Arce, AA, Tadlock M, Vergare MJ, et al: A psychiatric profile of street people admitted to an emergency shelter. Hosp. Community Psychiatry 34:812-817, 1983.

Bachrach LL: Asylum and chronically ill psychiatric patients. Am. J. Psychiatry 141:975-978, 1984.

Bassuk EL, Rubin L, Lauriat A: Back to bedlam: are shelters becoming alternative institutions? Am. J. Psychiatry (in press.)

Baxter E., Hopper K: The new mendicancy: homeless in New York City. Am. J. Orthopsychiatry 52:393-408, 1982.

Greenblatt M: The third revolution defined: it is sociopolitical. Psychiatric Annals 7:506-509, 1977.

Grunberg F., Klinger Bl, Grument BR: Homicide and the deinstitutionalization of the mentally ill. Am J. Psychiatry 134:685-687, 1977.

Johnstone EC, Owens DGC, Gold A, et al: Institutionalization and the defects of schizophrenia. Br J. Psychiatry 139:195-203, 1981.

Joint Commission on Mental Illness and Health: Action for Mental Health: Final Report of the Commission. New York, Basic Books, 1961.

Kris EB: The role of drugs in after-care, home-care, and maintenance, in Modern Problems of Pharmacopsychiatry: The Role of Drugs in Community Psychiatry, vol. 6. Edited by Shagass C. Basel, Karger, 1971.

Lamb HR: Board and care home wanderers. Arch Gen. Psychiatry 37:135-137, 1980a.

Lamb HR: Structure: the neglected ingredient of community treatment. Arch Gen. Psychiatry 37:1224-1228, 1980b.

Lamb HR: What did we really expect from deinstitutionalization? Hosp. Community Psychiatry 32:105-109, 1981.

Lamb HR: Young adult chronic patients: the new drifters. Hosp. Community Psychiatry 33:465-468, 1982.

Lamb HR, Goertzel V: The long-term patient in the era of community treatment. Arch. Gen. Psychiatry 34:679-682, 1977.

Lamb HR, Grant RW: The mentally ill in an urban county jail. Arch. Gen. Psychiatry 39:17-22, 1982.

Lamb HR, Grant RW: Mentally ill women in a county jail. Arch. Gen. Psychiatry 40:363-368, 1983.

Lamb HR, Peele R: The need for continuing asylum and sanctuary. Hosp. Community Psychiatry (in press.)

Lamb HR, Sorkin AP, Zusman J: Legislating social control of the mentally ill in California. Am. J. Psychiatry 138:334-339, 1981.

Lamb HR, Schock R, Chen PW, et al: Psychiatric needs in local jails: emergency issues. Am. J. Psychiatry 141:774-777, 1984.

Larew Bl: Strange strangers: serving transients. Social Casework 63:107-113, 1980.

Lipton FR, Sabatini A, Katz SE: Down and out in the city: the homeless mentally ill. Hosp. Community Psychiatry 34:817-821, 1983.

Minkoff K: A map of chronic mental patients, in The Chronic Mental Patient. Edited by Talbott JA. Washington, American Psychiatric Association, 1978.

Redick RW, Witkin MJ: State and County Mental Hospitals, United States, 1979-80 and 1980-81. Mental Health Statistical Note No. 165. Rockville, Md., National Institute of Mental Health, Aug. 1983.

Sosowsky L: Crime and violence among mental patients reconsidered in view of the new legal relationship between the state and the mentally ill. Am J. Psychiatry 135:33-42, 1978.

Urmer A: A study of California's new mental health law. Chatsworth, Calif., ENKI Research Institute, 1971.

Whitmer GE: From hospitals to jails: The fate of California's deinstitutionalized mentally ill. Am. J. Orthopsychiatry 50:65-75, 1980.

Wing JK, Brown GW: Institutionalism and Schizophrenia. New York, Cambridge University Press, 1970.

20

The Plight of Homeless Women

Madeleine R. Stoner

L
AST WINTER Rebecca Smith, age sixty-one, died in New York City. She froze to death in the home she had constructed for herself inside a cardboard box. She preferred it, she said, to any other home. Rebecca Smith had spent much of her life in a state psychiatric hospital under treatment for schizophrenia. Life in the box was preferable. In a sense, many people watched her die: her neighbors, the police, the Red Cross and finally a city-dispatched social worker and psychiatrist. In a larger sense, the nation watched too, because her death made the front page of the *Washington Post*.[1]

The senseless tragedy of Rebecca Smith's death immediately prompted nationwide concern for the plight of the homeless. Those who have worked with the homeless find this new acknowledgment of the thousands of homeless people in our midst rather strange. They also find somewhat remarkable the morbid curiosity demonstrated about them and the quickness with which they are branded a bunch of smelly sociopaths, chronic "crazies," to be dealt with someplace, but not here. Yet people and organizations are beginning to pay thoughtful attention to the problems of the homeless, and programs and services are emerging to meet the needs of this long neglected population. Concerned groups are organizing to provide an increasingly vocal advocacy network for coping with the needs of the homeless. Despite this activity, however, existing public and private welfare policies preclude adequate service delivery for the homeless population.

The intent of this article is to describe the homeless population and the special needs of women within it. In carrying out this intent, the article first reviews apparent causes of homelessness and the types of programs that currently exist for women. It then suggests a design for a comprehensive

From *Social Service Review*, Vol. 57, December 1983, pp. 565-581. Reprinted by permission of the University of Chicago Press and Madeleine R. Stoner.

service system for homeless women and concludes with a proposal for political and social action that will be essential if the systemic causes of homelessness are to be eliminated.

The rapidly increasing number of homeless people in America poses a new challenge to cities all over the nation. New York City has had to divert major resources to cope with an expanding street population because a court decree requires the city to provide public shelter for homeless men.[2] Throughout the country the capacity of agencies to make a place for everybody is being severely tested. Columbus, Ohio, a city badly hit by the declining economy, was forced to open the first public shelter accommodating 150 people a night.[3] The Traveler's Aid Society in affluent Houston has housed as many as 1,000 economically disabled people a month. This is nearly 40 percent more than the previous year.[4] In Denver, one church opened a shelter and within a week 400 people had applied.[5] In 1981 the Community Services Society of New York estimated that 36,000 people in that city were without homes.[6] More recently, Los Angeles County Department of Mental Health officials estimated that a minimum of 30,000 people are living on its streets.[7]

While these numbers are alarming, they also are misleading because there are so many methodological barriers to obtaining a sound census of the homeless. What is important is that public and private agencies, researchers, and the media are reporting readily visible evidence that the number of homeless people is rising and that radical changes in their circumstances and composition have taken place over the past fifteen years. These changes call into question the propriety of relief measures that traditionally have been applied to the contemporary homeless population.

Workers with the homeless report that more women, elderly, and young people—particularly black women and members of other minority groups— have slipped into a population once dominated by older alcoholic white men.[8] Any profile that attempts to develop an aggregate notion of the type of person in today's homeless population obscures the most distinctive features of this group: its variety and its heterogeneity. Surveys of these people are unreliable as they include only those who have been in public or private-shelters. Yet, these clearly serve only a small proportion of street people.

Clarification of the picture of who the homeless are is possible by considering why people find themselves homeless. Summary evidence from those who have studied the homeless population indicates that the antecedents of homelessness are: (1) lack of housing, (2) unemployment and poverty, (3) deinstitutionalization, and (4) domestic violence and abuse.[9]

Research conducted by the Vera Institute of Justice on user characteristics of homeless people in a women's shelter demonstrated that there is a direct link between such factors as evictions and lockouts and the consequence of homelessness.[10] As economic pressures for the reclamation of land for renovation and upgrading mount, evictions will continue to increase. The City of New York's Human Resources Administration has reported that a fourth of the recent applicants to its men's shelters are there due to job loss.[11]

Census data on poverty reveal that from 1980 to 1981 an additional 2.2 million people entered the official poverty index as unemployment figures increased.[12] According to the Census Bureau figures, the burden of this poverty falls disproportionately on families headed by women, on children, on young adults, and on ethnic minority groups.[13] The "feminization of poverty" has particular significance in the growing and shifting homeless population. Many women have no place to turn but to the streets. Significantly related to both income and homelessness is another fact, namely, that public assistance is denied to people who have no address.[14] People lose their benefits when they become homeless and, in turn, the means of finding another home.

There is considerable documentation to indicate the presence of large numbers of severely disturbed individuals in streets and shelters, many with histories of psychiatric hospitalization. Ill-planned deinstitutionalization, such as that leading to the death of Rebecca Smith, often is cited as the most prominent cause of homelessness. Whether or not this is so, recent studies have attested to the growing number of psychiatrically disabled among the homeless poor. An informal census conducted in the Los Angeles skid row district indicated that 90 percent of the women there were mentally ill and had histories of psychiatric hospitalization.[15]

Many homeless women and adolescent females report that they left their homes after repeated incidents of abuse by their spouses, rape, incest, and desertion. Despite the strengths of the Domestic Violence Prevention Act, cutbacks in expenditures for welfare programs include severe slashes in provisions for battered and abused women and displaced homemakers.[16]

Living and Coping Patterns of Homeless Women

Although there is a substantial body of literature concerning male vagrants and transients, until recently very little existed concerning unaffiliated women who are not alcoholic. Bahr and Garrett[17] conducted studies comparing dislocation factors among men and women in urban shelters and explained the differences by sex in the etiology of homelessness and the family backgrounds of this population. They also examined the drinking habits of men and women admitted to emergency shelters in New York City. Judith Strasser[18] provided a sensitive descriptive profile of the shopping bag lady population, exploring personal appearance, hygiene, daily routines, health conditions, and their use of services. Ambulatory schizophrenic women were described in a report by the New Orleans Traveler's Aid Society.[19] Most recently the media have exposed the box people—the Rebecca Smiths who have come to inhabit city streets or live underground in subway stations.

Because the little that has been written about homeless women has focused on the skid row environment and alcoholism, research is needed that does not treat women as derelicts but as homeless people with specific women's problems and needs. This is necessary because the apparent systematic avoidance of dealing with homeless women in research and literature suggests that women receive harsher judgment and less adequate services than men even at this marginal level of society. As women and their families continue to enter the ranks of the homeless—as victims of the economy, of landlords, of a depleted mental health system, and of spouses—society can no longer neglect them.

What may be a benchmark study of this problem was conducted by the Manhattan Bowery Corporation in 1979.[20] The strength of this report, which was not widely circulated, lies in the fact that it dispels many of the myths about shopping bag ladies. Several of its findings are particularly important.

1. Little is known about the homeless population, except that we are sure its numbers are growing.
2. The three municipal shelters for women in New York City are unable to to meet the growing demands of the homeless population. It is the only city in the United States providing public shelter for women.
3. Homeless women are singularly vulnerable to crime, the elements, and other hazards of the streets.
4. Some characteristics, viewed as bizzare (e.g., foul odors) are conscious defense mechanisms.
5. Mental disability per se is not a pervasive reason for women's alleged refusal to use available services.
6. The primary causes of their disaffiliation are to be found in the socioeconomic circumstances of poor, middle-aged, and elderly women—in particular, their isolation. Homeless women do not choose their circumstances. They are victims of forces over which they have lost control.

One of the first studies that looked beyond the alcoholic woman was conducted by Baumohl and Miller in Berkeley, California, in 1974.[21] They observed that there was a substantial presence of women among the homeless in that city, larger than had been found in comparable studies of the homeless. Their report pointed out several differences between men and women of the street. The women are younger, less educated, away from home for shorter periods of time, and they more frequently obtain income from legitimate sources. Despite the fact that more women than men receive either public assistance or money from home in order to survive, many are forced to panhandle, deal drugs, shoplift, or become prostitutes. This homeless style of life, hazardous for anyone, holds acute dangers for women, rape being high among them. The study reported that most women trade sexual favors for food, shelter, and other necessities, and it described frustrated desires for conventional monogomous relationships and intense conflicts following coercive sexual encounters.

A 1982 study of vagrant and transient women in Columbia, South Carolina, reported that the study sample was predominantly Caucasian, forty years of age or younger, natives of South Carolina, and none having more than a high school education. The majority were not employed, and most had incomes of less than $3,000 per year.[22] An important distinction between this study and previously cited ones is that it encompassed a broader environment than skid row and did not specifically focus on alcoholism. In relation to problems perceived by the study sample, the majority were dissatisfied with their present lives and identified as their most serious problems lack of money, nowhere to live, unemployment, separation from family, lack of friends, and illness. The majority who were sick sought professional care in health clinics. Most respondents hoped to be employed and have a place to live within one year.

This study also produced findings that significantly differed from previous descriptions of disaffiliation. One was that although the study sample complained of loneliness and isolation, there was a greater sense of affiliation than in earlier studies. Another finding pertained to the use of services: the majority of the sample received meals from a women's shelter and had sought help from social service agencies, but a sizable minority had not sought such help. Most services used by the study sample were general or lay community oriented rather than specifically designed to meet the needs of women and, in particular, homeless women.[23] This suggests that homeless women may turn to shelters only when other social services are unavailable.

In a survey of 100 first-time applicants in 1979,[24] the Vera Institute of Justice has produced the most detailed study of user characteristics of the New York City Women's Shelter. The demographic data closely parallel the men's shelter population and disclose that: (1) half of the women were under forty, with 16 percent sixty years and older: (2) 40 percent were white, and 44 percent were black: and (3) 61 percent had lived in the city for at least one year.

The most useful data from the Vera Institute Study for application to the design of services and preventive measures are those citing reasons for selecting shelter. Of those women who gave information on prior residence, 13 percent had come directly from hospitals. Nearly half had lived in single rooms in hotels immediately prior to coming to the shelter. Over a fourth of the first-time applicants cited as their reason for seeking shelter illegal lockouts or evictions, or ejection from a household (by family or friend).

The question of who the homeless women are cannot be completely answered without considering how they are portrayed. Earlier research, reinforced by popular notions, supported views of homeless women as derelict eccentrics who choose their life-style. The persistent denial of women's existence on skid row only served to consolidate long-held beliefs that homeless women are even more derelict and eccentric than homeless men, and thus the most socially undesirable of all marginal people. Equating the term derelict with homelessness has contributed to a belief that this is a "less needy" population. Because women have been less visibly homeless and less troublesome or feared than men, society and social agencies have regarded them as even "less needy" than homeless men. As a consequence, these unacknowledged women have tended to fall between the threads of the safety net, into the streets.

A personal testament to this notion has come from Jill Halverson, director of the Downtown Women's Center in Los Angeles, who reports that she always perceived skid row as being only for men. During her ten years first as a public welfare caseworker and then as a caseworker in alcoholic rehabilitation programs, she saw women sleeping in parking lots, in X-rated movie houses, and in roach-infested cheap hotel rooms. She discovered that women were on skid row, but that all of the agencies on Los Angeles' skid row were geared to serve men, not women.[25]

Images portrayed in the popular press appear to be changing. The tendency to blame the victim and the notions of dereliction and eccentricity are fading. At a conference in Orange County, California, in August 1982, conferees attested to the fact that homelessness is not confined to large cities. It is a national problem that reaches the smallest communities as well. Estimates that there are 4,000 homeless women in Orange County bear this out.[26] As Orange County and other communities across the nation are witnessing the increasing numbers of homeless single women and homeless women with children, there is an increasing awareness that these women are the by-products of the "feminization of poverty," often the result of family breakdowns through divorce, desertion, and abuse that have led to mortgage foreclosures or evictions for nonpayment of rent.

Implications for Social Work Practice

The growing population of homeless women holds immediate and far-reaching implications for social work practice and for the design of effective social services. With the exception of a loosely organized system of emergency shelters, little exists among traditional and alternative service agencies to meet the special needs of this population. The prospect of starting from the beginning to tackle this social problem is especially daunting in an atmosphere of declining resources, but to do so is imperative. We need a system that goes beyond emergency shelter to provide food, services, and a range of living facilities to meet the varied but basic needs of the wide spectrum of women who are now homeless. And to meet this urgent need it is necessary that preventive activities include political and economic elements. However, the formulation of any systematic and comprehensive plan must take into account the strengths and weaknesses of the programs for homeless women that currently exist and assess their potential as effective answers to this serious problem.

The current programs for homeless women appear to have four characteristics: (1) they are predominantly under private auspices, (2) they are proportionately fewer than those available for homeless men, (3) there are fewer professional social workers or other professionally trained people directly involved in staffing women's shelters, and (4) existing shelters for women tend to operate with lower standards of care than those for men.

Until very recently, there were 800 beds in Los Angeles' skid row for homeless men, but only two for women. Now there are thirty-five beds for women.[27] Similar patterns prevail throughout the nation, suggesting a woeful failure to serve the population of women in need of shelter. It is likely that life for many women outside the shelters is worse, but it may also be possible that the prevailing substandard conditions in many women's shelters makes life on the street more attractive. Rebecca Smith believed this.

New York City now has four public shelters for women. Four years ago, it had one.[28] New York City is notable for operating public shelters because of the court decree requiring the city to provide meals, clothing, and beds; social and medical services are limited. The admissions procedures are more stringent than those for men in public shelters. At intake a delousing shower is required, just as it is in shelters for men, along with an inventory of all belongings and evidence of psychiatric clearance from Bellevue Hospital. Gynecological exams are required by two of the shelters.

Whatever their bed capacity, shelters are overcrowded, and they accommodate more women than there are beds by filling hallways, chairs, and even using table tops. Facilities are adequate according to certification standards, but these standards are low. In one such shelter, Bushwick Annex, investigators found substantial fire code and food handling violations, inadequate toilet facilities, overcrowding, and inadequate staffing and security. These shelters tend to be located in fringe areas of the city, surrounded by dangerous and isolated neighborhoods where the women seeking the shelter are constantly harassed. Two of the shelters provide meals, but not on their premises. The women are transported by bus to another shelter for breakfast; they remain in the second shelter until they are bused back at night to sleep.[29]

New York City is an exception: most cities are not legally required to provide shelter. More typically, cities operate programs like Sundown in Los Angeles County. Sundown provides a list of hotels that will put people up for the night or a weekend. The program sometimes provides food, but essentially arranges one night's support for which transients do not qualify. Sundown staff report a growing demand. Approximately 1,300 people called the program asking for food and shelter in 1981. During the first few months of 1982, the calls averaged 1,400 a month and are expected to increase.[30]

Throughout the nation, the main source of refuge for homeless women consists of private nonprofit shelters. Public shelters that operate outside of New York, as in Washington, D.C., are restricted to men. On the whole, the private shelters are sponsored by organizations such as the Volunteers of America, churches and missions, and groups of concerned individuals. The Traveler's Aid Society, Salvation Army, and the Young Women's Christian Association also provide services, but these tend to be confined to the provision of food, drop-in centers, and travel arrangements home.[31]

There are two types of private shelters—the smaller, more casually run operation, and the longer-established institutions deeply rooted in mission work. Shelter provisions in the missions are characterized by intake and admissions procedures similar to those of public shelters. Waiting lists are common and rates are not cheap. Monies are taken out of Supplemental Security Income checks, and psychiatric care is often required of residents. Conditions vary among the missions but closely resemble those of the public shelters.

The more casual programs that prevail in the private sector attract full occupancy, primarily because they are smaller and offer a more humane and dignified quality of care according to most shelter residents. Operating costs are met by donations, voluntary labor, and contributions of clothes, furniture, and food. Social workers, psychologists,and psychiatrists are involved only peripherally on a consulting or emergency basis in most of these programs. Generally, these shelters are informal and stress the dignity and privacy of residents, many of whom are known only by first names. Many of the volunteer staff are residents of the shelters. A Catholic church in Boston's Pine Street has turned its basement over to a group of volunteers who operate a shelter there and have moved from their homes to live in the shelter. Some of these people have donated the proceeds from the sales of their homes to operate the shelter.[32] Social life is encouraged in these shelters, and it is known that strong bonds often develop among shelter residents, particularly in the less formal facilities. Because of their religious auspices, religious relics are seen everywhere. Religious services are held, but attendance is generally not required. Many of the shelters will accept no public funding, even when offered, because of their distaste for regulations and bureaucracy.[33]

Physical conditions in these private shelters vary. Some provide only mattresses on the floor, but the emphasis on human dignity and patience appears to compensate for less than adequate standards. An added advantage of many of these shelters is their connection to other services, such as religion-affiliated hospitals. They also operate as a network in some cities so that homeless women can be found by their families. There is reason to believe that women tend to prefer these smaller, casual shelters to the public shelters because of their nonjudgmental ambience as well as their less restrictive policies and practices.

The Christian Housing Facility in Orange County, California, provides a unique service for families. It offers temporary shelter, food, and counseling. Priority of services goes to families or victims of family violence. In 1981 this facility had 1,536 residents, a 300 percent increase from the previous year. The main facility is a remodeled house, but motels are used in emergency cases. This shelter views its function as that of helping people return to permanent housing. Residents are required to submit to counseling and search for jobs. Once they are hired, residents pay 10 percent of their salary to the house. According to its 1980 annual report, 504 persons, 103 of these children, left with a home, a job, and an income after an average twenty-day stay.[34]

Christian Housing is an example of a shelter designed to help people in transition. Its model of service differs from that of the mission and informal church settings in that it works with those people who are most capable of independent functioning rather than the "down and out."

Most night shelters provide little in the way of day services, and so, even with a meal and a bed, street life remains a reality for most of the homeless people who turn to such facilities. Drop-in shelters providing other services are beginning to emerge.

The Downtown Women's Center, opened by Jill Halverson in Los Angeles's skid row four years ago, is a prototype of drop-in centers. It is a former sheet metal shop that is now a bright and cheerful daytime drop-in center for as many as fifty homeless women a day. At the center the women can shower, eat a hot meal, and nap on one of four daybeds. A sense of community is fostered. A senior consulting psychiatrist from the community services division of Los Angeles County's Department of Mental Health who has studied and cares about the plight of homeless women visits the center regularly. He provides a range of services for the women, from individual therapy to group sessions and informal rap groups. The type of care given at the center departs from most traditional notions of what constitutes good psychiatric care, and there is a sense that no rules apply to therapy with homeless women except that they will respond positively when they have a sense that they are in a supportive environment where staff are patient, caring, and respectful. The director of the center possesses no professional training or qualifications and will not accept public funding. She does, however, accept offers of help from private individuals and groups.

In New York City, the Antonio G. Olivieri Center for Homeless Women opened in February 1981 as a daytime drop-in center for homeless men and women. However, male applicants so far outnumbered female applicants that the services were redirected to women only.[35] This center offers meals, showers, delousing, assistance with income entitlements, and access to medical and social services. Women are not required to give their names, nor are they obliged to take part in any activities. The center is open twenty-four hours daily, every day, and offers a form of shelter without beds. Women sleep on chairs, the floor, and desk tops. Tolerant and caring staff make this overcrowded, understaffed, and chaotic center a secure environment for women. Because of the high demand on the center, it has established a time limit of two weeks of continuous care, after which women are assured of seven days' lodging in the public shelter. They may then return to the Olivieri Center for another two weeks.

In addition to night shelters and drop-in centers, outreach services are expanding to deal with homeless people. The Manhattan Bowery Project sends out mobile vans with workers to locate homeless people and offer them food, shelter, and clothing.[36] Responses to such outreach programs vary. Center workers made every possible attempt to bring Rebecca Smith into care, but she refused.

As the number of homeless women continues to increase and the reasons for their plight extend beyond mental illness and alcoholism, women are turning to shelters that in the past they might have turned away from, or not sought at all. Some women who are homeless because of mental illness or alcoholism have tended to avoid shelters and escape from the rigors of mental hospitals and detoxification centers. This was Rebecca Smith's case history. The new homeless women who are increasingly in this plight for reasons related to unemployment, poverty, eviction, and abuse appear to be more accepting of social services and shelters.

What is clear from this survey of shelters and services for homeless women is the fact that public shelters operate under restrictive and demeaning policies and practices. Women prefer the private shelters and, among these, choose to be in a small and informal setting, no matter its conditions, rather than the more institutional missions with characteristics of public shelters. The overcrowding in all shelters dispels the myth that women choose life in the streets. Most women want shelter, but given the scarcity of private shelters and the harsh conditions of public and mission facilities, it is understandable why many homeless women continue to find themselves without any place to sleep at night.

A Comprehensive Service System for Homeless People

The evidence from drop-in centers, churches, missions, public shelters, and outreach efforts demonstrates the need for additional and better-quality shelter. Most programs presently operating are, at best, temporary and do not begin to approach the full dimensions of the problem.

Rational planning to meet the needs of homeless people in general, and homeless women in particular, must take into account the heterogeneity of the population and provide a range of housing and services. Some advocates for the homeless have proposed a three-tiered approach to the development of housing and services: (1) emergency shelter and crisis intervention, (2) transitional or community shelters, and (3) long-term residence.[37] Each would incorporate a cluster of elements, identified briefly below.

The *basic emergency shelter*, the first tier of shelter, should be made as accessible and undemanding as standards of hygiene and security allow. Clean bedding, wholesome food, adequate security and supervision, and social services should be available. Existing facilities such as school buildings, churches, armories, and converted houses could be adapted for such purposes. Each shelter should be community based as opposed to being in physically or geographically isolated locations.

Transitional housing would recognize that there are homeless people who, given the opportunity and supports, could eventually live independently. This type of shelter would make more demands on residents in terms of assuming self-responsibility and would provide longer-term social services and vocational rehabilitation. Staff would actively attempt to secure appropriate entitlements as well as necessary clinical care. Transitional housing settings could provide an address enabling residents to receive public assistance.

Long-term residence in effect would provide homes and offer services and aids necessary in the everyday lives of residents. The broad scope of such a program, incorporating aspects of low-income housing and a full complement of service personnel, does not make it a realistic prospect in today's political climate. Nonprofit sponsorship of such programming is more feasible than public funding and support.[38]

An outstanding example of such a three-tiered approach is the Skid Row Development Corporation in Los Angeles. Formed in 1978, the corporation is funded through private (the Los Angeles Central City Association) and public sources (the Los Angeles Community Redevelopment Agency,) but its goal is to be independent from city and county funding. Starting with a first-year operating budget of $95,000, after two years it generated an operating budget of $300,000, and the figure is growing.[39]

The primary service objective of the corporation is to provide an alternative housing resource to emergency shelter on skid row by recycling apartments in south central Los Angeles. The corporation has designed transitional housing for indigent women and men. Its Women's Transitional Housing Program calls for a separate building apart from its men's facility. Plans are under way for the completion of long term housing, and the corporation has planned a series of projects to relocate and rehabilitate apartment buildings slated for demolition in various parts of the city and county. Those who do well in transitional housing will be priority tenants, and the remaining units will be rented to individuals and families needing affordable housing.[40]

Ballington Plaza opened in July this year [1983] under the auspices of the Skid Row Development Corporation and is practical proof that long-term housing for the homeless population can be developed and filled where there is the interest and will to do so. This 270-unit housing complex located in Los Angeles's skid row is intended for low-income men and women who are elderly or handicapped and neither drug- nor alcohol-dependent. It offers the first real alternative to sleeping in the streets, transient hotels, or run-down missions. Rents range from $95 to $155 per month. It has full security, cooking facilities, and is an attractive three-story yellow stucco building with bay windows and a large central courtyard with grass, benches, and a parklike setting. This is a prime example of a suitable facility: it is the first in the nation to provide permanent housing for the homeless population. Most programs continue to be confined to the provision of temporary shelter, and many have time limits on the length of stay.

Recommendations for Policy Changes and Social Action

The underlying causes of homelessness show every sign of persisting, and the dimensions of the problem are increasing. Structural unemployment, inadequate and insufficient community-based psychiatric care, housing scarcity, domestic violence and abuse, and the recent cutbacks in income maintenance programs and social services are intensifying it. Given a confused and confusing political climate unsympathetic to the needs of the more vulnerable people in the country, it is difficult to gauge the prospects for a more enlightened public policy toward the homeless population in general and for bringing greater balance to providing for homeless men and women. There are hopeful signs, however, that the public is beginning to understand that the roots of mass homelessness lie in the pathology of society, not of individuals. There is increased public sympathy for the homeless and for their need for more adequate shelters. This is evidenced by the rapid rise of advocates for homeless people. Coalitions on behalf of the homeless are springing up throughout the nation: in Boston, Denver, Portland, Seattle, Los Angeles,

New York, and Philadelphia. A National Coalition for the Homeless has begun to provide an active lobby and information resource for homeless people and their advocates.[41] The leverage that these advocacy groups can muster at local and national levels in the courts, legislatures, and social agencies is critical in improving the lot of the homeless as well as reducing their numbers.

An important event, already mentioned, occurred in New York in 1981 when the Consent Decree settling the *Callahan v. Carey* case was signed and forced New York City to open more shelters for men and, indirectly, women. A subsequent court action was initiated when, on February 24, 1982, a class action suit, *Eldredge v. Koch*, was filed in New York State Supreme Court on behalf of homeless women in an effort to upgrade and expand shelters. The suit contends that the conditions in the public facilities effectively deter many homeless women from applying for shelter.[42] Resorting to the courts is a powerful tool that other cities and states have not utilized enough with respect to homeless women. Even though public shelters do not adequately deal with the needs of the homeless population, with the courts' help, these may nevertheless be a powerful beginning to securing entitlement shelter.

Many of the existing coalitions are actively attempting to educate the public about the homeless population and to dispel the many negative stereotypes, attitudes, and myths about them. This is an important strategy, and there have been discernible changes in public views of the homeless. In addition to securing improved shelter, changing attitudes, and legal action, advocates of the homeless must direct their energies toward changing policies in several areas mentioned below:

1. Every effort must be made to ensure a quantitatively and qualitatively adequate supply of emergency shelter and to apply equal standards to shelters for women and men. New York Governor Mario Cuomo's budget of $50 million to build or remodel 6,000 units of housing for the homeless is an example for other states.

2. Shelters should be accessible to the target population, and their admissions procedures should be simple. Shelters should be community based, in contrast to policies operating in some cities that support physically isolated shelters.[43]

3. Community efforts to develop transitional and permanent housing and vocational rehabilitation modeled on the Skid Row Development Corporation in Los Angeles should be undertaken and supported.

4. The diminishing rate of single-room occupancy hotels, despite their problems, should be reviewed. Cities and counties should drop tax incentives for conversion of these hotels. Despite their adverse conditions, single-room occupancy beds are at a premium, and many people consider themselves fortunate to obtain and keep them. Departments of

welfare should, however, implement programs that would guarantee that monthly checks go directly to beneficiaries, rather than the hotel owners.

5. Departments of mental health and mental retardation should expand their outreach programs so that their links with homeless people can precede—and possibly preclude—police intervention. Increasing the number of mobile vans, drop-in centers, and crisis-intervention provisions would be steps in this direction. Outreach efforts also need to provide clinical certifications necessary to obtain Supplemental Security Income and Disability benefits, for which some homeless men and women can only qualify once they obtain a residence. Staff of the Skid Row Project sponsored by the Los Angeles County Department of Mental Health have conducted training sessions for agencies that serve the homeless to inform their workers about the details and requirements for obtaining such benefits. Preliminary reports indicate that there was a 90 percent increase in the number of homeless people receiving such benefits in 1982 since these sessions took place.

6. Cities and states, along with private agencies, should be encouraged to build or convert facilities so that there are adequate supplies of transitional and permanent affordable housing.

7. Support for legislation to prevent further erosion of the single-room housing stock and illegal evictions or lockouts is needed. The Gottfried-Calandra anti-lockout and illegal eviction bill would allow city police in New York to intervene on the tenant's behalf when they are illegally locked out or dispossessed from their homes.[44] This bill can serve as a model for other cities.

8. Mental health agencies and health settings can redirect some of their programs to meet the needs of homeless women in spite of reduced operating budgets. This would include revised practices and increased support services related to deinstitutionalization. Recent policies that direct mental health services toward chronic mental illness provide the legal framework for developing these services.

9. The public assistance allowance should be raised to account for inflation. Unless this happens, homeless people who become ready to assume independent households will not be able to afford the necessary rents and the tide of building abandonment will continue.

There is evidence that public curiosity, sympathy, and genuine concern for the plight of homeless men and women are increasing. Examples of well-run supportive services for this population are also on the rise in communities throughout the country. But the comprehensive programming based on the three-tiered approach that offers a range of housing and linkages to services and a sense of community is seldom seen.

As the ranks of the homeless increase, and the numbers of women within those ranks rise, concerted and planned action must be taken to develop policies and programs that will prevent another Rebecca Smith from dying.in her cardboard home.

NOTES

1   *Washington Post* (February 4, 1982).
2   Callahan et al. v. Carey et al. Index No. 42582/79. Supreme Court of the State of New York.
3   These data were reported at a conference sponsored by the National Conference on Social Welfare (The Homeless: An Action Strategy, Boston, April 28-29, 1982.)
4   Ibid.
5   Ibid.
6   Ellen Baxter and Kim Hopper, "Private Lives/ Public Spaces: Homeless Adults on the Streets of New York City," mimeographed (New York: Community Service Society of New York, February 1981.)
7   Rodger Farr, "The Skid Row Project," mimeographed (Los Angeles: Los Angeles County Department of Mental Health, June 1982.)
8   *Los Angeles Times* (July 11, 1982.)
9   Baxter and Hopper, pp. 30-48.
10   Vera Institute of Justice, "First Time Users of Women's Shelter Services: A Preliminary Analysis," mimeographed (New York Vera Institute of Justice, 1981.)
11   Jennifer R. Wolch, "Spatial Consequences of Social Policy: The Role of Service Facility Location in Urban Development Patterns," in *Causes and Effects of Inequality in Urban Services*, ed. R. Rich (Lexington, Mass: Lexington Books, 1981.)
12   U.S. Bureau of the Census. "U.S. Poverty Rate, 1966-1981."
13   Ibid.
14   Los Angeles County, Department of Public Social Services General Relief Regulations, Regulations 40-131, Determination of Eligibility. Section 3.31 requires the following identifying information: proof of identity, social security number, proof of residence, statement of intent to continue living in Los Angeles, and proof of U.S. citizenship. Regulation 40-119.2 states that general relief applicants are to be referred to the district office where they first appeared to request aid. Interim relief can be given if the applicant possesses an affidavit from a salaried employee of a board-and care facility, alcoholism recovery home or detoxification center, or a recognized community agency within Los Angeles County. These regulations are prototypical of general relief regulations throughout the United States and serve as deterrents to homeless people who seek public assistance.
15   These data were first reported by Rodger Farr and Kevin Flynn, who directed the Skid Row Project of the Los Angeles County Department of Mental Health in June 1982.
16   Anne Minahan, "Social Workers and Oppressed People." *Social Work* 26 (May 1981): 183-84.
17   Gerald R. Garrett and Howard M. Bahr, "Women on Skid Row." *Quarterly Journal of the Studies of Alcohol* 34 (December 1973): 1228-43, and "The Family Backgrounds of Skid Row Women." *Signs* 2 (Winter 1976:) 369-81.

[18] Judith A. Strasser, "Urban Transient Women." *American Journal of Nursing* 78 (December 1978): 2076-79.

[19] New Orleans Traveler's Aid Society, *Flight Chronic Clients* (New Orleans, 1980).

[20] K. Schwam, "Shopping Bag Ladies: Homeless Women" (report to the Fund for the City of New York, Manhattan Bowery Corporation, April 1, 1979).

[21] Jim Baumohl and Henry Miller, "Down and Out in Berkeley" (report prepared for the City of Berkeley, University of California Community Affairs Committee. May 1974).

[22] John T. Gandy and Leonard Tartaglia, "Vagrant and Transient Women: A Social Welfare Issue," mimeographed (report prepared for the National Conference on Social Welfare, Columbia, South Carolina, May 1982). pp. 6-8.

[23] Ibid., pp. 13-16.

[24] Vera Institute of Justice (n. 10 above).

[25] This was reported in personal interviews with J. Halverson during the spring and summer of 1982.

[26] This estimate was reported at a conference on homeless women in Orange County, California, August 1982.

[27] Rodger Farr, "The Skid Row Project" (n. 7 above), and "Concerned Agencies of Metropolitan Los Angeles Directory of Services for the Homeless," mimeographed (Los Angeles, December 1982).

[28] Kim Hopper, Ellen Baxter, Stuart Cox, and Laurence Klein, "One Year Later: The Homeless Poor in New York City, 1982," mimeographed (New York: Community Service Society Institute for Social Service Research, 1982).

[29] Ibid.

[30] *Los Angeles Times* (July 11, 1982).

[31] This information is based on interviews with staff of the agencies, investigation of annual reports, and program descriptions on file with the United Way of America.

[32] These data were reported at the conference in Boston, April 28-29, 1982 (see n. 3 above).

[33] Reported at the Boston conference (see n. 3 above.) The Downtown Women's Center is another example of such refusal to accept public funds.

[34] Christian Temporary Housing Facility, *1980 Annual Report*: (Orange, Calif.: Christian Temporary Housing Facility, 1980).

[35] Hopper et al. (n. 28 above).

[36] Reported at the Boston conference (see n. 3 above) by Marsha Martin, director of the Manhattan Bowery Project.

[37] D. Sakano, "Homeless New Yorkers: The Forgotten Among Us" (testimony given at the New York State Assembly hearings, November 19, 1981).

[38] Hopper et al. (n. 28 above).

[39] Skid Row Development Corporation, *Annual Report, 1979-1980* (Los Angeles: Skid Row Development Corporation, 1981).

[40] Ibid.

[41] The National Coalition for the Homeless is based at the Community Service Society of New York.

[42] Eldredge et al. v. Koch et al., in pretrial discovery process at the time of this writing, Supreme Court of the State of New York.

[43] *The New York Times* (February 11, 1983).

[44] New York Senate, Illegal Eviction Law, 1982, Introduction 3538-B, Amendment to Multiple Dwelling Law of New York, Proposed Amendment Section 302-D.

21

Shelters for Battered Women

A Temporary Escape From Danger Or The First Step Toward Divorce?

Lorene Hemphill Stone

WITH THE GROWING RECOGNITION of the fact that wife battering is a recurring problem for many American women, the late 1970s ushered in the long overdue emergence of publicly and privately funded shelters and other crisis intervention services to aid the victims of domestic violence. These shelters have been established throughout the United States, and it is estimated that thousands of battered women each year make the decision to leave their assaultive husbands and escape to these shelters in search of safety. By definition, these emergency shelters for abused women are temporary havens from life-threatening situations. However, while women's shelters aid many women and their children, they, unfortunately, continue to be plagued with negative stereotypes and misconceptions about their specific role in helping battered women cope with their violent situations. In many instances, these shelters operate and survive in spite of a fairly hostile and insensitive community and without adequate or secure funding (Roberts, 1981.) This paper examines one major misconception that hinders the work of emergency shelters: their perceived role in family dissolution.

Present literature on domestic violence shelters is not clear on the role(s)

Reprinted by permission from *Victimology: An International Journal*, 9 (1984) 2:284-289.
© 1984 Victimology Inc. All Rights Reserved.

that these facilities play in the community. These facilities are called "shelters," implying a place to seek protection from danger and crises. It is recognized that battered women need a safe place to stay while they recover from violent beatings, because they cannot begin to think, relax, or make rational decisions about their futures unless they feel safe (Vaughan, 1979). However, Roberts (1981), in his national survey of 89 emergency shelter programs for abused women, reports that although the ultimate service a shelter provides is the option of leaving a crisis situation involving violence and finding a safe environment, the shelter facility also can be the logical extension of information and referral, crisis intervention, and advocacy services. Through its services, the shelter can help women who feel powerless to regain a sense of strength and control of their lives.

Battered women have two basic options for improving their situation: (1) they can stay in the marriage while trying to make basic changes, or (2) they can leave the marriage to build a new life for themselves and their children. When the battered woman enters the shelter, she has to come to grips with the realities of her situation and to face the difficult decisions that lie ahead. Inevitably, she has to determine what course of action she will follow: return home with the hope that it won't happen again or initiate some form of legal action (Roberts, 1981). Thus, the battered woman must assess her marital situation, including the anticipated outcomes and consequences of her actions, and make a decision about her future.

Because women's shelters offer victims an alternative to their problematic situation, they are viewed by some members of society as "homewreckers." These critics of women's shelters have difficulty with the philosophy of separation, divorce, and the possible breakup of the family unit, and they are under the impression that it is the shelter and its staff which persuade the battered woman to leave her husband permanently instead of encouraging her to return home and solve *her* problem with her husband. From this perspective, shelters are viewed as a threat to family life because they conflict with cultural beliefs about marriage and the family that have prevailed in American society for the past 200 years, including "marriage is a lifelong commitment," "a wife's place is at home," and "the husband is the ultimate decision maker." These critics point out that many of the refuges today are crucially different from those of the past in that today they unequivocally put the interests of the abused women who use them in the forefront instead of the family institution. These shelters, staffed largely by feminists, are seen as the place where abused wives go to seek support and encouragement in taking legal actions against their husbands, either in the form of assault charges or filing for divorce. As a result, the image of the women's shelter is one of being an initiator of family breakup.

This becomes a very important issue for women's shelters, because these "pro-family" critics recently have formed pressure groups and are working at the local and national levels to reinforce what they consider to be the proper form of family life. For example, the Family Protection Act was introduced in Congress to counter the perceived attacks on the traditional family. Among other things, the bill would deny federal funding to programs dealing with spouse abuse unless the state legislatures specially approve such funding. Thus, the Family Protection Act seeks to strengthen "traditional family life" by removing constraints against the physical abuse of wives. As pointed out by Kalmuss and Straus (1983), wife abuse is not viewed in all parts of the country as a social problem worthy of the same support as other "social problems." Therefore, many shelters would be forced to close because some state legislatures would not want to admit a need for them.

Roberts (1981) reports that obtaining operating funds is one of the most significant problems facing shelters, many of which survive on a shoestring budget. This funding becomes even more difficult when funding sources perceive shelters with this negative anti-family image. This is illustrated by a statement of an officer of a large Michigan bank: "The Foundations we manage have refused grants to women's shelters because of a fear by committee members that the shelters promote divorce" (Gardey, 1981). Hence, some shelters around the country have met financial resistance and rejection in their local communities; they are being victimized by this perception.

Therefore, the main objective of this present descriptive survey is to examine the role of shelters for abused women, specifically in relation to divorce. By answering the question—What proportion of battered wives who escape to an emergency shelter actually take legal action and file for divorce?—not only will we gain more information on the correlation between abuse and divorce, but we will also have a clearer idea about the primary function of shelters for domestic violence victims: a temporary escape from a life-threatening situation or an initiator for the severing of family ties.

Methodology

To examine this issue, information was collected from 133 abused women who came to a women's shelter in the state of Michigan for services from October 1, 1980 to March 1, 1981. Data were obtained through personal interviews conducted by one staff member who was not aware of the purpose of the survey. The initial interview was incorporated into the agency intake procedure conducted when the woman first entered the shelter. Questions were asked on the following general topics: husband's background characteristics, wife's background characteristics, history of abuse in the marital relationship, marital satisfaction, and views of violence. One-month and three-month follow-up interviews with these women provided data on subsequent abuse, their current marital status, and any divorce action.

The sample included women from a variety of demographic backgrounds. Following is a brief description of the abused women examined in this survey:

1. The women ranged in age from 17-56 years old, with the mean age being 27 years.
2. The sample was 90% white, 8% native American, and 2% black.
3. The income levels of these women varied greatly, with the mean income being $500 per month.
4. Educational information showed that 44% of the women did not complete high school, 36% had a high school degree, and 20% had college education.
5. The majority of abused women (63%) had minor children living with them; and
6. Only three women had not been assaulted previously by the same assailant, with the mean length of abuse being seven years.

This description is consistent with past research that clearly points out that there is no general profile of a battered woman, because abuse crosses all of the socio-economic strata (Martin, 1976; Straus et al., 1979).

Findings

As an examination of the relationship between being abused and filing for divorce, frequency distributions were compiled. As shown in Exhibit 21-1, an analysis of the data indicated that a small minority of abused women seek divorce from their assaultive husbands as a consequence of obtaining help from the women's shelter. Of the 124 women who were married to their assailants, approximately 58 percent of them chose the legal alternative of divorce as a solution to their problem. At first glance, this would appear to support the anti-family perspective, but closer examination of the percentages shows a marked distinction between those women who had made the decision to divorce their husbands and had taken the legal action *prior* to going to the shelter (34.7%) and those women who decided to sever their marital ties and filed for divorce *after* going to the shelter (7.3%). A sizable proportion of the sample chose to continue in the relationship and did not seek to divorce their mates (41.9%). It appeared that the shelter to which these particular battered women fled did not attempt to persuade them to leave their husbands permanently; many women had made that decision before they sought assistance at the shelter. The average length of stay at the shelter

Exhibit 21-1
Frequency Distribution of Battered Wives' Divorce Action

Divorce Action	N*	%
Woman made decision to file and filed for divorce prior to going to shelter	43	34.7
Woman decided to divorce before going to shelter but did not file until referral from shelter	20	16.1
Woman made decision to file and filed for divorce after going to shelter	9	7.3
Woman returned home and did not file for divorce	52	41.9
Total	124	100.0

*Nine cases are not applicable since the women were not married to their assailants.

for this sample of women was five days, implying that these women saw the shelter as a temporary escape from a violent home environment.

Conclusions

Impetus for developing shelters for victims of domestic violence has been generated by a growing awareness of the cultural oppression of women, more empirical research on the prevalence and causes of wife abuse, and the passage of domestic violence legislation by an increasing number of states. This legislation has resulted in state appropriations for shelter facilities. These refuges provide accommodation as well as protection, advice, and support.

It is the conclusion of this survey that shelters are not to blame for the dissolution of marriage and the family. While the findings of this survey cannot be generalized to all women's shelters in the United States, they do provide insight into the critical task of knowledge building for practice intervention with battered women. For instance, other factors may lead to high divorce rates among abusive spouses and thus, need to be considered. For example, the structures of the legal system and federal guidelines for financial assistance may be at fault. During their interviews, several women expressed frustration with the current legal and welfare services that were available to them. In many states, civil injunctions or restraining orders to protect a woman from an abusive assailant are available only if a petition for annulment, divorce, or separation or an existing divorce accompany the request. Thus, for some women, filing for divorce is the only way to guarantee some safety for themselves and their children. Also, the battered woman may be forced to begin divorce proceedings in order to obtain financial aid. The economically dependent married woman may try to obtain social services in her community. Because assistance is based on needs determined by federal guidelines, she may not qualify for the services. Even if she has no salary, her husband's income may be used to determine her eligibility. Thus, to obtain any financial assistance at all, the abused wife may have to file for divorce first so that her husband's income will not be used in assessing her own economic status. The victim is once again victimized. Because of the social service system's hesitancy to provide financial support unless the woman is in the process of divorce, the woman is forced to make difficult emotional choices regarding the future relationship with her spouse. These structural conditions appear to encourage family breakup.

The policy implications of the present survey become very relevant as federal legislation is being proposed that denies public funding to spousal abuse programs. This proposed legislation is based on the anti-family image of shelters for abused women. Public funding implies a public interest and a public commitment to the problems of domestic violence. Without public funds, these programs will lack public support, and the perception that violence within the family is a private problem, rather than a public issue, will continue in our society.

REFERENCES

Gardey, Kim. "Personal letter," 1981.
Kalmuss, Debra S. and Murray S. Straus. "Feminist, Political, and Economic Determinants of Wife Abuse Services." Pp. 363-376 in D. Finkelhor, R. Gelles, G. Hotaling and M. Straus (eds.). *The Dark Side of Families: Current Family Violence Research*. Beverly Hills, CA: Sage, 1983.
Martin, Del. *Battered Wives*. San Francisco: Glide, 1976.
Roberts, A.R. *Sheltering Battered Women: A National Study and Service Guide*. New York: Springer, 1981.
Straus, Murray A., Richard J. Gelles and Suzanne Steinmetz. *Behind Closed Doors: Violence in the American Family* (New York: Anchor, 1979).
Vaughan, S.R. "The Last Refuge: Shelters for Battered Women." *Victimology* 4:113-119, 1979.

V

Solutions to the Problem

22

Litigation in Advocacy for the Homeless

The Case of New York City

Kim Hopper and L. Stuart Cox

The State and the Needy

OR THE PAST one hundred and fifty years, the American state's attitude toward dependent populations has been a vexed mixture of self-interest, pity and resentment. The Gospel of Work appears to be firmly fixed in the American consciousness, and a pall of suspicion is cast on those who do not, or cannot, earn a livelihood. Such an attitude extends even to those people rendered "redundant" under the press of modern industrial processes—the aged, the incorrigible, the unemployable, or the merely mad. When confronted with the needs of such surplus populations, the state's policy has been guided by the English Poor Law principle of "less eligibility." Relief, especially "outdoor" (or non-institutionalized) relief, had to be made so onerous, so degrading as to ensure that it would be the option of last resort. Menial and dangerous labour, the resources of charity or of sorely strapped families, survival by one's wits on the street if need be, these were all to be tried before the state was turned to. In this way, all but the "truly needy" would be discouraged.

The legacy of the English Poor Law tradition bulks large in the recent

Reprinted from *Development: Seeds of Change*, Vol. 2, 1982, pp. 57-62 (journal of the Society for International Development).

history of the American welfare state. The general principle is the same: so long as the spur of economic insecurity was needed to ensure a willing and pliant labour force, relief could be made a feasible option to work only under conditions of duress. Recently this principle has received support from another quarter. Faced with a growing fiscal crisis (O'Conner, 1975), the state has had to make every effort to curtail wasteful (i.e. non-productive) expenditures, such as welfare. But needy populations are not necessarily passive ones. The combined power of the poor law tradition and the fiscal crisis is opposed and offset by a third factor, which, historically has been the locus of the leverage of the poor. For what has determined the level of resources devoted to the support of dependent or "disadvantaged" populations is the level of civil "disorder"—ranging from electoral defections, to crime in the streets, to rioting and organized protest—they have generated in response. Not need but demand; not suffering but the unwillingness to endure it any longer; not the deserving but the unruly poor—historically, these have proven the decisive factors in liberalizing welfare measures. Put simply, the benefits of relief have been extended only when the costs of not doing so have proven—or are likely to prove—prohibitive (Piven and Cloward, 1971).

No less an authority than the Supreme Court has recognized the operation of this principle in practice. Writing for the Court in *Goldberg v. Kelly* (1969), Justice Brennan observed: "Welfare, by meeting the basic demands of subsistence, can help bring within the reach of the poor the same opportunities that are available to others to participate meaningfully in the life of the community. At the same time, welfare guards against the societal malaise that may flow from a widespread sense of unjustified frustration and security."

Historically, what has been distinctive about the dependent group we are here concerned with, the homeless poor, has been their inability to tender their demands in the public arena, let alone give them persuasive force. Nor has the "societal malaise" that might have accompanied their emergence assumed anything other than vest-pocket proportions, confined primarily to isolated instances of outrage at so visible an injustice. Indeed, the actual threat the homeless pose, directly or indirectly, is small. Inured by time against the rage they may have once felt against a society which has so easily ignored them; more often than not resigned to a fate for which they hold no one accountable; poorly organized; scattered; often transient; and invariably victims of popular misconceptions about who they are and why they're on the street—the homeless poor have proven ineffective as a constituency of demand. By default, it almost seems, legal channels have become the preferred mode of redressing their grievances.

Litigation as a Tool of Advocacy

In New York City, litigation has proven to be a uniquely effective tool in promoting the cause of homeless men and women. Since 1979, when a lawsuit was filed on behalf of homeless men against New York State and New York City, a court order has been entered recognising the right of the homeless to shelter, establishing quantitative standards which must be met in public shelters and providing advocates for the homeless with extensive access to those shelters for the purpose of monitoring compliance with the court order. Practically speaking, since the litigation began, the number of shelter beds for homeless men has increased from 1,700 beds to 3,700 beds and for homeless women from 48 beds to nearly 400 beds. While conditions in public shelters have improved considerably in the wake of the litigation, shelter accommodations remain desolate and barren if, in the main, minimally clean and secure.

In addition to winning for the homeless an enforceable entitlement to shelter, the New York litigation has served as a focal point for public scrutiny of the government's policies toward the homeless. The litigation has received continuing coverage from the New York media, and both the City and State governments have been called on repeatedly by the press, by legislative bodies, and by a growing cross section of the citizenry, to improve their care of the homeless.

Origins

In late 1978, Robert M. Hayes, a young New York lawyer in private corporate practice, began investigating the plight of homeless adults in New York City. The lawyer visited the City's Men's Shelter, a processing center near New York's Bowery where homeless men applied for bed and board. From the Men's Shelter the homeless were then sent to one of two places: a Bowery lodging house which provided the men a bunk in unspeakably filthy and dangerous dormitories or cubicles, or at Camp LaGuardia, a derelict women's prison in the Catskills, sixty miles from the city, which served as a shelter for about 1,000 homeless men. Once the Bowery hotels and Camp LaGuardia were filled—as they invariably were in cold weather—the remaining applicants for shelter were either offered space on the floor of the Men's Shelter with several hundred other men or were simply turned back into the streets.

After witnessing conditions at the Men's Shelter and the bowery hotels, Hayes began—in his spare time—to interview the homeless he found living in the City streets. Almost unanimously the homeless men told Hayes they had stayed on one occasion or another at the city's shelter but that they found the streets and the subways less dangerous and less degrading. In short, the homeless convinced the lawyer that from their perspective the streets were the preferred option to the city shelter—not because the streets were desirable but only because conditions at the city shelters were so abominable.[1]

The lawyer began making the rounds of religious and charitable organizations which worked with the homeless. Again and again the same point was emphasized: there was a growing gulf between the need for shelter beds and the supply. Further, the demand for shelter beds was far lower than the true need since conditions at the municipal shelters were so bad that the shelter effectively deterred many of the homeless from even seeking assistance. Most agencies working with the homeless told the lawyer that the City would refuse to either expand or improve its assistance to the homeless.

As it turned out these agencies were right. Hayes began meeting with city employees who ran the municipal shelters. Repeatedly, these employees told him of their inability to get needed staff or supplies from the City administration. They told the lawyer that getting a new shelter was a pipe dream. The director of the Men's Shelter, a civil service employee, conceded that if he were homeless he would stay on the streets. The lawyer went to meet with the city commissioner in charge of shelters.

The commissioner conceded that it was City policy to keep the shelters forbidding. Otherwise, the commissioner said, the homeless would not feel compelled to make other arrangements for themselves. The lawyer recalls the commissioner shrugging his shoulders when it was suggested that the only other "arrangements" available were the streets. The commissioner said his aim was to keep existing services for the homeless afloat. The community surrounding the Men's Shelter was clamouring for its closure, the commissioner said. And besides, said the commissioner, New York's fiscal crisis was not yet over.

The lawyer began researching the law, looking for a legal basis to obtain judicial relief for the homeless.

Legal Theories

During the 1970's, as the appointments to the Supreme Court by President Nixon began to form a majority voice for the court, lower federal courts became increasingly reluctant to intervene on behalf of individual plaintiffs aggrieved by government malfeasance or nonfeasance. As the Supreme Court articulated a judicial deference, first to states' rights and then to the discretion of public administrators, so called public interest lawyers began shying away from the federal courts as the preferred forum for advancing the rights of minorities and the poor. This was a radical change from the strategies of the 1950's when the federal courts—shaped largely by the activist doctrines of Chief Justice Earl Warren—were in the forefront of defining and enforcing individual liberties and individual entitlements.

With that backdrop, the lawyer began researching ways to bring a "right to shelter" suit in the state courts. The first thread of a legal right was discovered in the New York Constitution which provides:

> The aid, care and support of the needy are public concerns and shall be provided by the state . . . as the legislative may from time to time determine.

The general language seemed to suggest that, at a minimum, the bare necessities for survival—like shelter—"shall be provided." But most of the case law interpreting the constitutional provision found it to be largely advisory, setting out an ideal social policy without imposing on the goverment an affirmative obligation. None of the cases previously decided, however, had considered the address delivered by the proponent of that constitutional provision as he introduced it at the 1938 New York constitutional convention, a convention held during the depths of the Great Depression. The proponent's stirring words were found deep in the recesses of a university's law library:

> Here are the words which set forth a definite policy of government, a concrete social obligation which no court may ever misread. By this section, the committee hopes to achieve two purposes. First: to remove from the area of constitutional doubt the responsibility of the State to those who must look to society for the bare necessities of life; and secondly, to set down explicitly in our basic law a much needed definition of the relationship of the people to their government.

At a minimum, the proposed right to shelter had a legitimate grounding in the state constitution.

Further research turned up additional bases for arguing the existence of a right to shelter under both State law and City law. The New York State Social Services law provides, rather bluntly, that:

> Each public welfare district (county) shall be responsible for the assistance and care of any person who resides or is found in its territory and who is in need of public assistance and care which he is unable to provide for himself.

The New York City Municipal Code was even more direct:

> It shall be the duty of the commissioner of, or the superintendent of, any municipal lodging house acting under him, to provide for any applicants for shelter who, in his judgement, may properly be received, plain and wholesome food and lodging for a night, free of charge, and also to cause such applicants to be bathed on admission and their clothing to be steamed and disinfected.

For good measure, an additional legal theory based on the equal protection clauses of both the state and federal constitutions was advanced. Equal protection means, in substance, that the government may not make irrational distinctions in the way it treats classes of people who are basically similarly situated. Counsel reasoned that it was indeed irrational for the state to provide public assistance to poor people who have homes while denying any assistance at all to even poorer people who are homeless. This theory, while logically attractive, was without precedent and lacked the comparative specificity of the other constitutional and statutory theories.

The Litigation

The fall of 1979 began ominously for the homeless men in New York. Several Bowery lodging houses had closed during the summer and, as a result of conversions of cheap hotels to higher priced accommodations, it was apparent that many more people were newly homeless. The City had fewer beds available to it in Bowery hotels and, as the autumn began, had made no provisions to increase the amount of space available to shelter the homeless. It was at this point that Hayes was completing his legal research and began looking for homeless men willing and able to represent a class of homeless men in a lawsuit against the Governor and the Mayor.

Finding named plaintiffs was a simple matter. At the Holy Name Center for Homeless Men, a Catholic day center on the Bowery, the lawyer met Robert Callahan, a 53-year-old Irishman who loved a good scrap. He was scared away from the Men's Shelter the first time he went there when at age 49, he found himself homeless for the first time. The second time back Mr. Callahan was given floor space at the Men's Shelter. He was attacked before the night was over. Mr. Callahan felt he had a score to settle with the Mayor. He was the first plaintiff recruited.

Mr. Callahan scouted the streets and found two more plaintiffs: one, a 31-year-old Manhattan College dropout; the other, a 46-year-old devotee of politics and opera. Each of the named plaintiffs met the criteria for representative parties in a class action lawsuit: they were atypically resourceful and aware, they were clients of the Men's Shelter, and they felt compelled to join a cause to improve the lot of their fellow travellers—and fellow sufferers.

In October 1979 the shelter lawsuit, *Callahan v. Carey*, was filed citing, at the onset of the litigation, the need for emergency relief. The State and City responded with voluminous papers challenging the asserted legal entitlements to shelter and arguing that the performance of the executive branch of government in providing for the homeless was not, in any event, the business of the court. In legal parlance, the defendants claimed the controversy brought to court by the homeless men was not "justiciable." Neither the State nor the City disputed plaintiffs' contention that there would be men turned away from the Men's Shelter during the coming winter. The court heard arguments in late October and promised a speedy decision.

In early December 1979, in a landmark decision, the New York Supreme Court granted the homeless men a preliminary injunction requiring the City to provide sufficient beds for the homeless men who applied for shelter. The Court grounded its decision on its recognition of a legal right to shelter citing provisions of the New York Constitution, the State Social Services Law and the City's Administrative Code. The Court, having concluded that state law mandated the provision of shelter, did not need to consider plaintiff's argument that they were entitled to shelter under the equal protection clause of the United States Constitution. On Christmas Eve, 1979 the Court entered a temporary order requiring the State and City to: provide shelter (including clean bedding, wholesome board and adequate security and supervision) to any person who applies for shelter at the Men's Shelter.

The immediate result of this decision was the rapid opening by the City of a shelter for homeless men in a deserted psychiatric hospital building on Wards Island, located in the East River. Homeless men were taken by bus from the Men's Shelter near the Bowery to the new shelter, called the Keener Building. Quite rapidly the building filled, first to capacity, then to overflowing. In a building originally certified to hold 180, upwards of 625 men were being sheltered in the early months of 1980. The City failed to put any professional staff into the shelter, operating it entirely with so-called "institutional aides" who lacked the training and the skills to manage, not to speak of caring for, the homeless. Soon, violence and neglect characterized the Keener Shelter.

Again, litigation played a role in improving conditions at that shelter. In April 1980 a new action was brought by Hayes on behalf of a group of men being sheltered at Keener. The basis of this action was a contract between the State of New York (owner of the Keener Building) and the City of New York (the operator of the shelter). The State agreed in that contract to permit the City rent-free use of the building; the City, in turn, agreed to limit the capacity of the shelter and to provide psychiatric, medical and social services sufficient to meet the needs of the shelter residents. Again, plaintiffs sought preliminary relief from the Court before a trial. The Court denied emergency relief, but ordered an immediate trial stating that the "health and safety of homeless men must not be jeopardized by judicial delay." On the eve of trial in August 1980 the City agreed to triple its funding for the shelter and to provide professional social workers as well as medical and psychiatric resources at the facility. The lawsuit was then dropped, subject to being recommenced upon abdication by the City of its commitment.

Meanwhile, the *Callahan* case had finally reached the trial stage. In early January 1981 the homeless men began to call witnesses to prove their case. During two weeks of trial the case seemed to seesaw with the judge appearing impressed with plaintiffs' case one day, unimpressed the next. At least another full month of trial loomed when plaintiffs' counsel suggested a possible settlement of the case.

Hayes proposed, in the judge's chambers, that if the City were to agree to recognize its obligation to shelter the homeless in minimally decent quarters, plaintiffs would withdraw their demand that the shelters be "community-based." This proved to be the basis for a settlement, a settlement negotiated among the plaintiffs, State and City over the next six months. During the course of those negotiations Justice Richard Wallach, an extraordinarily able trial judge, succeeded in cajoling major concessions time and time again from all parties concerned. In August 1981 a final judgement was entered in the Callahan case setting forth in the form of a Consent Decree, the terms and conditions under which shelter is to be offered to homeless men and (the City later agreed), to homeless women as well. Of particular import, was the recognition with the force of law of a right to shelter. Beyond that, certain qualitative standards for the provision of shelter extended and gave specificity to Justice Tyler's original order of Christmas Eve 1979. The decree stipulated exactly what would count as "decent bedding" and "adequate security and supervision"; it set minimal staffing levels, recognized that arrangements must be made for storage of clients' belongings, and provided for regular monitoring of the City's compliance by outside observers.

The Callahan final judgement did not rest quietly for long. In October, just six weeks after the decree's signing, the City acknowledged that it had run out of beds for homeless men. With colder weather approaching, plaintiffs' counsel hauled the City back into court for a proceeding to enforce the terms of the decree. On October 20, 1981 the City told the Court it had no facilities which could be used to shelter the homeless. The Court responded that the City was under order to provide those beds, and gave the City 24 hours to open 400 new beds for homeless men. The City complied, making an abandoned public school in Brooklyn available as an emergency shelter the next day.

Within a month the new 400-bed shelter was filled to capacity. Again, the City was brought back to court. The City's lawyer, in court, announced that the City was opening a new shelter (in a State Armory) that same night. Just two weeks later, as the Court continued to demand from the City a plan to meet the growing demand for shelter, the City opened an additional shelter (again making use of a State Armory).

Nine months after the entry of the final judgement in Callahan the City is faithfully meeting its obligation to provide shelter to homeless men who apply for it. However, the shelter system, by and large, does not meet the qualitative standards set forth in the decree. Some sites would be considered objectionable by any standard of decency. Only two of the ten shelter options used by the City would meet Callahan standards. The remaining sites fail to comply because of overcrowding, insufficient shower and toilet facilities, inadequate staffing and security, and/or the absence of other program amenities. As a result, the shelters remain dangerous and forbidding, continuing to deter many homeless men from coming off the streets. Further proceedings to enforce the Callahan decree are expected.

Limitations of the Approach

Certain limitations are inherent in any attempt to use the court as a forcing-house for redressing civil grievances. Given the current federal administration's cutbacks in public service projects, the most obvious of these is a shortage of the legal service resources needed to mount effective litigation. Trial preparations and court proceedings are costly, time-consuming affairs. Advocates may soon find themselves in short supply of the needed expertise and logistical support needed to conduct civil actions. Without public support, reliance on the *pro bono* activities of private attorneys, or the support of charitable or philanthropic organizations, may prove to be a haphazard recourse at best.

Second, the judiciary as a rule is most reluctant to enter into domain of concern which may be claimed by a coordinate branch of government. It takes a gross violation of a clearly delineated right to ensure the court's willingness to intervene—an unfortunate condition, since it is rare that a "right to shelter" will be forthrightly espoused in any jurisdiction. Instead, the more probable course would be one which would require creative interpretation of more general statutory and constitutional language to arrive at an enforceable entitlement. And while such a course proved successful in New York a growing judicial conservatism will make additional right to shelter arguments increasingly risky ventures.

The nature of the legal process itself contains a third limitation: time. Litigation is invariably a protracted affair. For advocates seeking creation of shelter—affirmative relief rather than a curtailment, say, of unfair discrimination against applicants for shelter—the most likely speedy outcome to a lawsuit will be dismissal of plaintiffs' claims. Rarely will quick remedial action, such as the opening of public buildings as emergency shelter, be possible. And for the homeless, a loss of time may well mean the loss of lives.

Impact litigation seeks relief in the form of institutional reform, rather than individual damages. This peculiarity introduces a fourth class of limitations: the hazards of implementation (*Harvard Law Review*, 1977). In deciding such cases, the courts must go beyond their traditional domains of jurisdiction and enter the worlds of social service and management. Judges are thus cast in the role of at least part-time administrators burdened with the task of moving often unwieldy bureaucracies in the desired directions of reform. Several difficulties immediately arise.

In the first place, courts are notably reluctant to engage in any "finetuning" of the relief ordered, even when it's clear that in matters of administrative policy, the details of implementation may well determine the success of relief. Matters are further complicated by the fact that in such cases plaintiffs may lack the necessary resources and expertise to devise feasible programs, and defendants may be less than enthusiastic about offering their cooperation (Cf. Rhoden, forthcoming). The requisite cooperation is further jeopardized by the adversarial nature of the proceedings, a *de facto*, if not insurmountable, hurdle to collaborative attempts to arrive at feasible means of implementing relief. Finally, it often happens that responsibility for administering and regulating social services is so fragmented that no one defendant is capable of seeing the order through to completion. And while this circumstance may provide opportunities for unexpected alliances between plaintiffs and one or another defendant, it also imperils the often cumbersome process of interagency collaboration.

In litigation seeking relief for the homeless, courts may well be disposed to order a defendant to provide shelter, but unwilling to specify further the terms and conditions of shelter. Where it is located, what the entry requirements are, and what it looks like will normally be left to the discretion of the defendants—not altogether dissimilar to letting the fox supervise construction of the chicken coop.

Interestingly, as noted earlier, the Callahan decree was fairly specific in its definition of what would constitute acceptable shelter. This development may be attributed to unusually detailed state regulations governing the provision of shelter. Callahan plaintiffs did not need to ask the court to establish standards; they merely requested that the court enforce standards which were already a matter of record. This is not likely to be a typical situation.

In another matter, the outcome in implementation was less than satisfactory. In the provision of shelter, a key element to use is accessibility. The Callahan order permits the City to locate shelters in sites of its own choosing, provided the City transports applicants from central intake centers. By January 1982 (a scant five months after the signing of the decree) the City—true to its avowed policy of favouring large and remote shelters—was spending at a rate of 1.5 million dollars annually simply to transport the homeless through the shelter system. Still, the relative inaccessibility of the sites has deterred many from making use of them.

Lack of governmental cooperation in abiding by the court order is also apparent. In particular, the City has proven intransigent to going beyond the merest letter of the law, making for a shelter system which, in the words of a *New York Times* columnist "lurches from court order to court order." Nor is its compliance with even the narrow terms of its own construction of the order assured. After final judgement in *Callahan* plaintiffs were forced to return repeatedly to court in order to win, what still remains, incomplete compliance with the order.

The drain such maneuverings place on the invariably limited legal resources for the homeless can be considerable. And the ill will which inevitably develops during prolonged litigation between advocates for the homeless and public officials charged with their care will likely endanger much-needed cooperative efforts on behalf of the homeless.

Conclusion

In October 1979, when the *Callahan* complaint was filed in State Supreme Court, 1,000 emergency shelters beds were available to homeless men and women in New York City. Four times that number were provided throughout this past winter. Without question, litigation has proved to be an effective means of securing emergency relief. But with thousands upon thousands of destitute city dwellers without homes, mass provision of minimally humane asylum for the homeless poor is but part of the solution—a necessary, palliative first-step. And while the courts do provide a forum for redressing the grievances of the disenfranchised, they may under certain circumstances serve a larger purpose as well. Specifically the court can become an independent means of catalyzing broad-based popular support for reform. For this reason, litigation as an advocacy tool should be viewed within the context of an overall strategy for social change.

Economically, the homeless poor represent but one form of parasitism—an unfortunate by-product of an allegedly well functioning social system. In the teeth of a seemingly relentless recession, of course, that claim is increasingly difficult to uphold, as economic hardship strikes an ever-increasing section of the population. Ultimately, the task of advocacy is to make common cause with this larger constituency of grievance. With respect to the homeless poor, the more immediate goal is simpler: to protest the justice of an algebra of relief which reduces human suffering to the abstract dimensions of a public nuisance.

In certifying the legitimacy of such a protest, the court has proven an unexpected ally. The crucial transformation appears to be the reversal of what had been, to date, commonly accepted as fair policy: that the claim of the homeless poor on public resources had no legitimacy other than that gratuitously extended by officials of the state. What was popularly and officially perceived as a plea became, through the agency of the court, endowed with the dignity and power of a right.

The court action and attendant media coverage proved the dramatic vehicle for forcing a general re-examination of the issue of homelessness. The court had sanctioned the legitimacy of an unmet need, reclaiming silent suffering as the public disgrace it properly represents. In so doing, the court challenged the legitimacy of established state policy toward one disenfranchised group. It shook public complacency with "the way things have always been done." And it is this legacy, a public newly awakened to its own complicity in a set of questionable practices, that may prove the most enduring feature of the *Callahan* action.

NOTES

[1] This impressionistic conclusion was later confirmed by research conducted during the course of the shelter litigation. (See Baxter and Hopper, 1981.)

REFERENCES

Ackley, S. "A Right to Subsistence." *Social Policy* 8 (5): 3-1, 1978.
Baxter E. and Hopper, K. *Private Lives/ Public Spaces: Homeless Adults on the Streets of New York City.* New York Community Service Society, 1981.
Harvard Law Review. "Mental Health Litigation: Implementing Institutional Reform." *Mental Disability Law Reporter* 2: 221-233, 1977.
O'Connor, J. *The Fiscal Crisis of the State.* New York: St. Martin's Press, 1975.
Piven, F. and Cloward, R. *Regulating the Poor.* New York: Pantheon, 1971.
Rhoden, N. "The Limits of Liberty: Deinstitutionalization, Homelessness and Libertarian Theory." *Emory University Law Review.* Forthcoming.
Ringenback, P. *Tramps and Reformers, 1873-1916.* Westport, Conn., Greenwood Press, 1973.

23

Federal Housing Programs and Their Impact on Homelessness

Roger Sanjek

"No one is living on the streets."

—Philip Abrams, Deputy Assistant Director for Housing for the U.S. Department of Housing and Urban Development. In a speech in Boston, June 16, 1982.

L AST NOVEMBER, Dorothy Lykes called the New York Gray Panthers office seeking our assistance. She knew of nowhere else to turn. Mrs. Lykes is 78, is terminally ill with cancer and weighs seventy pounds. Her husband is terminally ill as well. Most of their Social Security is going for his bills in the hospital. The City has taken possession of their home—which they bought in the 1940's—because they cannot pay the property taxes. Nor can they pay the $300 a month rent that the City is demanding for living in their own house. Mrs. Lykes asked me if her next step would be to move to Penn Station where the homeless women live.

I referred her to the local public legal services project. I don't know how successful they were in saving her home.

It is the case of Mrs. Lykes and others like her that colors how I view public policy in housing—especially how public policies can help prevent homelessness.[1]

Reprinted by permission of the Coalition for the Homeless, 105 E. 22nd Street, New York, New York 10010.

There are three aspects of federal housing policy I wish to consider:

1. the social structure of housing subsidies;
2. whether changes in regulations in current federal low income housing programs can help those now homeless; [and]
3. prospects for the prevention of homelessness.

First, let me sketch briefly the general context of housing today.

We need about 2 million new units per year to replace dilapidated dwellings and to take care of population increase. In 1981, we built about 1 million units. Experts and activists all recognize that it is no longer profitable to build housing that low- and moderate-income owners and renters can afford. New homes (median price around $72,000) and new apartments (averaging $1,800 per month rent in New York City) are mainly for households with $40,000+ annual incomes—the upper 17 percent of the population. There is some "trickling down" of housing as a result of new construction, but the overall picture for moderate-income families, and even more so for low-income renters, is one of shortage of affordable units. At the same time, competition, crowding, and rents are all on the rise. Ever greater percentages of income are going for shelter.[2] High interest rates and shortage of mortgage funds make it difficult financially to preserve existing low- or moderate-rent housing. The increasing volume of low-to-high rent conversions (often with encouragement by local tax policies), and landlord abandonment of buildings exacerbate the shortage of low-rent housing. (One hundred apartment units a day are abandoned in New York City.) Unemployment rates above 10 percent make meeting the rent even harder for low-income households. Federal low-income housing programs—public housing, Section 8 rent subsidies, Section 202 loans to non-profits for housing for the elderly and disabled—operate within this context of increasing scarcity of low rent accommodations.

The roots of homelessness in this situation are the familiar ones: unaffordable rent increases; escape from deteriorating and dangerous buildings being undermaintained or cleared for conversions; domestic violence or psychological distress in overcrowded, economically pressed, pressure-cooker situations.

The Social Structure of Housing Subsidies

There is no residential housing constructed today without a federal subsidy. All American housing is subsidized in one way or another. And, contrary to popular opinion, the wealthy have greater access to housing subsidies than the poor. The richer you are, the greater the federal housing subsidy you receive. Tax rates more favorable to capital gains than to earned income, depreciation deductions, developer subsidies and abatements, homeowner deductions, and participation in real estate tax shelter syndications all operate to subsidize the wealthy real estate owner or investor.[3] It is only the homeless—the poorest of the poor—for whom no categorical federal housing subsidy program exists.

The largest federal housing program is homeowner income tax deductions for property taxes and mortgage interest payments. This subsidy—and we should call it that—costs the federal treasury $30 billion in 1981, four times what was spent that year on all low-income housing programs. The following year (1982), the homeowner subsidy amounted to $39 billion in lost taxes—an amount larger than the entire HUD budget for the year. It should be stressed that the subsidy is an entitlement: no eligibility other than homeownership is needed. First, second, and vacation homes are all equally eligible for federal aid. Virtually all (92%) those with annual incomes of $100,000 or more benefit. They receive an average of $5,500 a year in federal housing assistance from this program. By contrast, only 17 percent of Americans with incomes below $30,000 get such federal housing assistance. Overall, less than half of all homeowners (46%), the wealthier ones, take advantage of this entitlement.[4]

Federal housing subsidies for low-income people are much less widely distributed. They are not entitlements; only 9 percent of those eligible for Section 8 rental subsidies receive them. (Most potential recipients do not benefit because sufficient funds have not been appropriated by Congress.) The waiting-list time for public housing in New York City is now 18 years. The Section 202 units for the elderly and disabled meet only a small part of the need recognized by the 1961, 1971 and 1981 White House Conferences on Aging. No federal subsidies exist for sheltering those in greatest need—the homeless.

The structure of federal subsidies—with the lion's share going into tax benefits for developers and the wealthier homeowners—shapes the entire stock of available housing. The Congressional Budget Office finds that the homeowner deduction program has shifted housing investment from rental apartments to single-family homes. Moreover, it has encouraged construction of large expensive houses rather than providing for the needs of low- and moderate-income people, or for the increasing numbers of elderly Americans and single-person households. Such people cannot afford nor do they require large, single-family homes.

Americans get what they pay for. And they don't get what they don't pay for. The structure of federal housing subsidies does not match the structure of housing need. In 1981 we had a half-million empty new homes, too expensive to be sold. The least goes to those in most severe housing circumstances.

Can Changes in Regulations in Current
Federal Programs Help Those Now Homeless?

Whether because the bureaucratic maze overwhelms them, or eligibility standards exclude them, homeless people on their own are not able to take advantage of federal low-income subsidized housing programs. With supportive social and health services, some persons now homeless might be able to move into public housing or 202 and Section 8 units. Others simply could not—even if such units were available, and the low priority assigned single, non-elderly persons was not a barrier. Tier 1 and 2 shelters (emergency shelters and transitional accommodations) are essential. But the creation of permanent housing—whether it be safe, supportive SRO dwellings or novel congregate living arrangements (tier 3)—will remain a key housing target for advocates for the homeless.[5]

The question arises next of whether existing federal subsidy programs could be used to support tier 1, 2 or 3 shelters. Section 8, especially in the proposed voucher form, is the one possibility.[6] But the use of Section 8 in this way would require changes in regulations defining acceptable housing standards. Such changes would shift standards downward. Let me explain.

The call for deregulation along these lines is already in the air—in both the recommendations of the President's Housing Commission and from HUD officials. In 1981 Federal Housing Commissioner Philip Winn made speeches calling for "deregulation" to permit existing homes and apartments to be split up into smaller units; to allow the use of cheaper building materials; and to reduce required building amenities. In 1982 the final report of the President's Housing Commission reiterated this call for deregulation, and Reagan administration steps to implement these recommendations are under way.

While such deregulation might allow Section 8 subsidies to be used in constructing permanent residences for the homeless, it would pose a threat to existing housing standards for those now housed and receiving (or eligible for) federal assistance. If lower federal housing standards become generally acceptable, the pressure to apply them universally would lead to poorer quality housing for millions of Americans who, however poorly housed, are not homeless—but only poor or elderly or disabled. A Pandora's box could be opened. It is not farfetched to imagine that lower standards would make it profitable for developers to build the lowest acceptable SRO-type housing. (Think of the growth of the proprietary nursing home industry following Medicaid.) Section 8 voucher holders would have no alternative but to accept such housing. If "prior homelessness" were an eligibility requirement, would we find such a policy encouraging people with intolerable rents and accommodations to "become homeless" in order to qualify for places in federally subsidized housing?

Advocates for the homeless do not favor repeating the history of 100 years ago, when slap-dash poor quality housing was put up to house the poor and turn handsome profits at the same time.

An alternative and preferable mode for federal shelter support was contained in proposed legislation passed by the House Banking committee earlier this year—H.R. 6296, the omnibus Housing and Urban/Rural Recovery Act of 1982. An amendment to the bill proposed that $50 million from the Multifamily Construction Stimulus Program for low-income housing be made available to non-profit organizations in rehabilitation and operating funds for shelters for the homeless. (Although the HURRA package was three times greater than the housing allocations in the President's Budget Resolution, and the bill was pulled from the House calendar as too expensive, components of it could still be included in bills reported by the House Appropriations Committee.)

This method of federal support for tier 1 (and possibly tier 2) shelters addresses the most immediate need. It also funds the production of new beds, new units of housing for the homeless. It expands housing alternatives, rather than forcing homeless people to compete with other poor people also in need of federal housing aid. Such categorical funding for shelters meets our broader housing needs better than would regulatory changes in existing housing programs.

Prevention of Homelessness

Advocates for the homeless recognize two goals: immediate shelter for those now homeless, and the prevention of homelessness among those now housed, however precariously. No one is born homeless. People become homeless when their housing conditions become intolerable, or when they are displaced. General economic conditions, and state and local policies, have much to do with producing or alleviating homelessness. But, there are at least seven areas where federal policy could help to prevent more homelessness in the future.[7] I list them in ascending order, from the feasible to the visionary.

1. Preservation of rent control. Federal policy to deny funds to localities with rent controls will increase, not prevent, homelessness.[8]
2. A moratorium on—or, at the least, increased tenant protection in the face of—cooperative and condominium conversions.

3. Housing production programs and / or mortgage subsidy efforts for new or rehabilitated low-and moderate-rent housing.
4. Policies that prevent landlord abandonment of buildings. Federal regulations could encourage localities to formulate such programs.[9]
5. Preservation of SRO housing through tax incentives and direct subsidies.[10]
6. Tax policy reversing the trend of a decreasing proportion of taxes paid by business. The present policy shifts the burden of higher property taxes to homeowners, and makes it difficult for low-income homeowners to maintain and stay in their homes.[11]
7. National credit allocation policy ensuring a percentage of available credit to housing needs, at affordable interest rates. This may seem visionary to us, but it is not visionary at all in Western European countries. And it is within the present powers of the Federal Reserve Board.[12]

NOTES

[1] Muchas gracias à Kim Hopper and Cille Kennedy for their suggested improvements to this paper.

[2] Fully 53 percent of the nation's renters spent more than a quarter of their income for housing in 1980; a decade ago that figure was 40 percent. Today, more than a third spend at least 35 percent of their income for shelter. See Peter Dreier, "The Housing Crisis: Dreams and Nightmares." *The Nation*, August 21-28, 1982.

[3] For a broader, impassioned discussion, see Peter Hawley, *Housing in the Public Domain: The Only Solution*, 1978, Metropolitan Council on Housing, 137 Fifth Avenue, New York, New York 10010.

[4] The background, operations, and fiscal impact of the homeowner deductions are analyzed in the Congressional Budget Office study, *The Tax Treatment of Homeownership: Issues and Options*, 1981, U.S. Government Printing Office, Washington, D.C. 20402.

[5] For a fuller discussion of the three-tier concept, see Kim Hopper, Ellen Baxter, Stuart Cox and Laurence Klein, *One Year Later: The Homeless Poor in New York City, 1982*, 1982, Community Service Society, Institute for Social Welfare Research, 105 East 22nd Street, New York, N.Y. 10010.

[6] On the Reagan administration's voucher proposal and its likely consequences, see Frank DeGiovanni and Mary Brooks, *Impact of a Housing Voucher Program on New York City's Population*, 1982, Pratt Institute Center for Community and Environmental Development, 275 Washington Avenue, Brooklyn, New York 11205.

[7] Local-level steps to prevent homelessness by fighting displacement, and innovative state and local financing schemes for low- and moderate-income housing—all without new federal intervention—are also important. See Richard LeGates and Chester Hartman, "Displacement," *Clearinghouse Review* 15(3)207-249, July 1981, National Clearinghouse for Legal Services, 500 North Michigan Avenue, Suite 1940,

Chicago Ill. 60611; Hartman, Dennis Keating, and LeGates, *Displacement: How to Fight It*, 1982, National Housing Law Project, 2150 Shattuck Avenue, Berkeley, Calif. 94704; Ruth Messinger and the Municipal Research Institute, *Revitalizing New York City's Economy: The Role of Public Pension Funds*, 1980 Conference on Alternative State and Local Policies, 2000 Florida Avenue, N.W., Washington, D.C. 20009; Robert Schur and Marilyn Phelan, *The Housing Crisis: A Strategy for Public Pension Funds*, 1981, Conference on Alternative State and Local Policies; *Can You Have a Balanced Economy if All Your Eggs Are Going Into One Basket: Building a New City Housing and Development Policy*, 1982, New Yorkers for Equitable Growth (NYFED), 424 West 33rd Street, New York, New York 10001.

8   John Gilderbloom, *Moderate Rent Control: The Experiences of U.S. Cities*, 1980, Conference on Alternative State and Local Policies; Gilderbloom and Friends, *Rent Control: A Sourcebook*, Foundation for National Progress, Housing Information Center, P.O. Box 3396, Santa Barbara, CA 93105.

9   Peter Marcuse, *Housing Abandonment: Does Rent Control Make a Difference?*, 1981, Conference on Alternative State and Local Policies; *Housing Abandonment in New York City*, 1979, Homefront, 56 West 22nd Street, New York, N.Y. 10010.

10   Bradford Paul, *Rehabilitating Residential Hotels*, 1981, National Trust for Historic Preservation, 1785 Massachusetts Avenue, N.W., Washington, D.C. 20036; Frances Werner and David Bryson, "A Guide to the Preservation and Maintenance of Single Room Occupancy (SRO) Housing," *Clearinghouse Review* 15 (12):999-1009, 16 (1):1-25, April and May 1982.

11   Robert Kuttner and David Kelston, *The Shifting Property Tax Burden: The Untold Cause of the Tax Revolt*, 1979, Conference on Alternative State and Local Policies: Michael Kieschnick, *Taxes and Growth: Business Incentives and Economic Development*, 1981, Council of State Planning Agencies, Hall of the States, 400 North Capitol Street, Washington, D.C. 20001.

12   On credit allocations see Robert Lekachman, *Greed is Not Enough: Reaganomics*, 1982, Pantheon Books, especially chapter 9.

24

A Model of Services to Homeless Families in Shelters

Michael H. Phillips, Daniel Kronenfeld, and Verona Jeter

D ESPITE A CURRENT FOCUS on the homeless, the problem has been with us for a long time. The Urban Family Center (U.F.C.) has been serving homeless families since 1972. The shelter, a part of Henry Street Settlement, was set up in response to the recognition in the early 70's that housing families in welfare hotels was both expensive and damaging to family life. Henry Street Settlement proposed to the city of New York that if given a building and paid the same reimbursement rate as welfare hotels it could operate a facility which provided not only adequate shelter but social service support for the families as well. An arrangement was made under which Henry Street Settlement leased an old housing project for $1.00 per year. The shelter, called The Urban Family Center, currently houses ninety homeless families, has social service staff available on a 24-hour-a-day basis (provided partially by staff who live permanently at the residence), an educational program for children, and a program to help families seek alternate housing. Due to its large size and the nature of the population served, the U.F.C. has an extensive staff including three administrators, three clerical workers, six social workers, three youth workers, two teachers (who conduct an alternative school on the premises), two nursery school staff, nine maintenance staff, four guards, one driver, and two housing specialists (who are outstationed at the shelter by the New York City Housing Authority and the New York City Department of Social Services).

This chapter will review what has been learned at the Urban Family Center about homeless families, the way services should be delivered to this popula-

Reprinted by permission of the authors. A draft of this paper was presented at the 1985 Annual Conference of the American Orthopsychiatric Association.

tion, and some details about the economics of such a shelter. It is important to begin by noting that while homelessness has existed over the years, the population served has changed. In the 1970's the population served by shelters was far smaller than it is today. During the last four to five years, the number of homeless have grown dramatically. All are familiar with the growing number of single individuals who are living on the streets. What people are less aware of is the diverse background of these homeless individuals. Included in the group are deinstitutionalized mental patients, persons who have been pushed out of single-room-occupancy hotels, persons out of work, and persons whose families have disintegrated. In New York City single-room-occupancy hotels (SRO's) have been given tax breaks to convert to apartments, effectively putting the marginal population who used to reside in such housing out on the street.

A less visible population are the many families who are homeless. This group, of whom about ninety percent are single, female-headed households, are often cared for by relatives, somewhat less frequently live in abandoned buildings, and reside in city shelters and welfare hotels. In New York City there were about 2,300 homeless families who received shelter in January 1984.

As with homeless individuals, a major reason for homelessness among families is the lack of affordable adequate permanent housing. The economics of housing and the limited welfare housing allowance not only lead to increasing numbers of homeless but also cause a problem for the shelters who must force families to leave and return to inadequate housing. The reality is that for poor people in New York City adequate housing is extremely difficult to find.

While the deterioration of the housing stock is a primary cause of homelessness we do not want to suggest that homeless families do not have other problems. About 90 percent of the families who come to U.F.C. are most aptly described as multi-problem families. Included in the remaining ten percent are families who were just overwhelmed with temporary stresses and a small group where the woman is psychotic. This latter group is rare, probably because the family has already disintegrated and the women are found among the single homeless population. The range of problems the majority of the homeless have are extensive; moreover, the homeless are hard to engage in a treatment process. Most of the homeless women at U.F.C. have problems in their own functioning, have a history of economic problems, their housing problems have been chronic in nature, and the functioning of the children is problematic. In a study of U.F.C. families it was found that 31 percent of the families had been evicted from their previous housing, 20 percent had to move out of an apartment where they had temporarily doubled up with relatives, and 18 percent had to move because their previous housing had been inadequate. Furthermore, a third had experienced two or more moves before coming to U.F.C. Not only had these families had housing difficulties but they had also been subjected to high levels of stress during the year prior to coming to U.F.C. Thirty percent had a serious illness in the family, 25 percent had a close family member die, 62 percent had a decline in their economic circumstances, and 31 percent had experienced a separation.

The homeless who come to U.F.C. are generally black or Hispanic, relatively young (mean age—29), and tend to have more children than the average family. Sixty-six percent have three or more children. Sixty-five percent had given birth to their first child before the age of twenty and for half, one or more of their children had lived away from home for some period of time. One third of the women reported having been treated for mental illness or "a problem with their nerves." Possibly due to the stresses the families experienced the level of child care was low, with two-thirds of the women providing what was judged to be marginal or inadequate child care.

The profile for the children was similar with twenty-six percent having academic difficulty in school, twelve percent having a physical disability, 18 percent fighting a lot with brothers and sisters, and 15 percent having temper tantrums.

Although the overall picture of these families looks discouraging, closer analysis shows that they have strengths that are often overlooked in the mass of problems. The fact that they have held their families together under adverse circumstances, that they want to change their circumstance, that children, albeit inappropriately, carry major responsibilities, should all be seen as strengths to build on.

Initially U.F.C. staff tried to make up for the many losses the families had suffered. But no matter how much the staff gave it never seemed to be enough. The lines between staff and clients became blurred. Staff was having some successes but it was not clear why. As a treatment approach evolved it became clear that if the staff tried to meet every client need, clients would not have the opportunity to do things for themselves and would not develop coping skills. Furthermore it was clear that the families needed help in developing priorities. They had the tendency to run from crisis to crisis without ever solving any. If the worker helped the client focus and helped them work on reality-based service issues, changes were possible. However, if he or she merely focused on intrapsychic or interpersonal issues in the family, the family soon labeled the treatment process as "just talk" having no meaning to their circumstances. Staff came to realize that they needed to see the work not just as providing shelter and social services but as a residential approach to services.

What has developed is a model for treatment which includes elements of three diverse approaches: crisis intervention, task centered practice, and life space interviewing.

Crisis Intervention

The crisis intervention approach to practice is the first model of practice that U.F.C. staff found of value. Lydia Rapoport has defined a crisis as an upset in a steady state which occurs in four stages: 1. a specific and identifiable stressful event, 2. the perception of that event as meaningful and threatening, 3. feelings of shock followed by anxiety or grief, [and] 4. a response to that event in which the client mobilizes his or her adaptive resources. The coping methods used may represent a successful or unsuccessful adaptation. For most who come to U.F.C. the fact that they are in the position of having to come to a shelter reflects an unsuccessful adaptation. Given the crisis of coming to a shelter and the previous unsuccessful adaptation the client is open to a redevelopment of basic coping patterns.

It is important to place the general crisis model within a larger context to understand the model's relevance to the work at U.F.C. Marc Fried considers the general crisis model relevant for acute stress but insufficient in dealing with the area of endemic stress. He defines endemic stress in terms of ongoing scarcity or environmental deprivation that results "in subtle, ominous, sub-clinical manifestations of apathy, alienation, withdrawal, affective denial, decreased productivity and resignation, all examples of pervasive reduction in role." (Marc Fried, "Endemic Stress: The Psychology of Resignation and the Politics of Scarcity," *American Journal of Orthopsychiatry*, vol. 52, January 1982, p.6). The resignation serves to mask a lowered self-concept as well as underlying anger and resentment. It is important to recognize that the families who come to us at U.F.C. have been living under endemic stress. They have responded to the constant stresses they experienced with the reduction in activity suggested by Fried. By the time they come to us their typical response to the world is one of apathy and hopelessness.

The acute housing crisis has challenged the families' adaptative withdrawal, and if workers move quickly they can help develop new coping patterns. Quick intervention is important because as families settle in they see the shelter as the solution to their problems and often try to deny the breadth of their problems. They lose their initial desire to do something about their situation and become increasingly complacent. They withdraw from workers to avoid shaking the boat. This return to the pattern of constricted role behavior hinders their ability to fight the injustices they and their families are subjected to on a daily basis. Workers must look with the family at the meaning of the "precipitating event(s)" leading to the families' current crises. Families must recognize what part if any, their own behavior played in their situation. Usually the tendency of many of the families is to act only when a situation becomes so acute as to break through their role constriction. This pattern has usually played a part in the development of the families' current situation. In focusing on the realities leading up to the current housing crisis and the way it can be coped with, workers are recognizing that the family is more accessible to treatment because its sense of equilibrium has been disrupted. In clarifying the problem(s) the worker focuses on what concrete actions the client can take and how to demonstrate the value of these actions to the client. Reality-based actions designed to help the family cope rather than giving psychodynamic interpretation demonstrate caring and can give the family the sense of hope necessary to fight the ineffective behavior patterns developed to sustain the family against endemic stress. Focusing on actions which will address the clients' environmental problems makes, in time, the client more open to interventions in other, more-sensitive areas such as the emotional care provided the children. Thus the housing crisis can become a vehicle for important change, and the provision of shelter can set the stage for further work with the client.

Task-Centered Practice

The second approach which has been found useful by U.F.C. staff is task-centered practice. Task-centered practice is a short-term model of practice designed to resolve specific problems of individuals and families. The model was an outgrowth of experimentation with methods of planned brief treatment and of work on interventions organized around helping clients define and carry out tasks. It also drew upon Helen Perlman's formulation of social treatment as a problem-solving process. The client is seen as having a right to define the problem. The worker aids in that process. The problem which the client is most anxious to resolve is seen as the primary target of intervention. Once the worker helps to clarify the problem, there should be a mutual agreement to begin work. After the problem is defined, goals are set and a written record of the goals is kept.

The goals define what the client wishes to achieve within a given period of time (usually 3 months). The process of goal-setting involves helping the client establish and focus priorities. It encourages a recognition of the self-defeating aspects of moving from crisis to crisis.

After the goals have been developed the worker and client define the specific steps they will each take to achieve the goal. The worker must pay special attention to the fact that while the steps (called tasks) must be jointly agreed upon, the worker must see to it that the tasks the client have are manageable. The client must succeed if hope is to be developed. This means setting very small tasks initially. The worker must also be sure that in the hurry to help the client . . . he or she does not do so much for the client that it encourages dependency rather than reinforcing coping. Each task represents both an immediate goal that the client will pursue with the worker's support as well as a means of achieving the larger problem-solving goal. This model of practice allows the client to take an active part in the problem-solving process from beginning to end. At U.F.C. goal and task sheets are kept by both worker and client and are used to maintain the focus of their work together. Plans are not modified unless an emergency (a life-threatening event) occurs. The U.F.C. experience is that when the worker helps the client remain focused, the need to add additional goals is rare.

To investigate the foci of treatment we did an analysis of the goals listed on client goal sheets. The analysis showed that 37 percent of all goals centered on the problem of housing (this goal in fact existed for all families). Fourteen percent of the goals dealt with welfare issues, 15 percent with their relationship with some other formal group such as a school or agency. In the psychodynamic areas 13 percent of the goals dealt with a change the mother wanted to make in her functioning, 5 percent around the child's functioning, 5 percent around family relationships, 6 percent around household management, and 6 percent around child-care issues: Interestingly, measurement of client changes have shown significant changes in the area of the emotional care given the children, despite the fact that the majority of goals focused on reality-based issues.

In summary the task-centered model is an ego-supportive model of intervention with the primary objective of improving and enhancing the client's general functioning without specifically focusing on intra-psychic awareness. The model assumes that self-esteem and self-respect are improved and sustained by being able to cope with inter-personal relationships and role task if only in a small part, while in the crisis situation.

The Urban Family Center staff was able to provide services to individuals and families on a short-term basis and to give insight by using the day-to-day behaviors as a way of looking at how families might handle a given situation.

The task-centered problem solving model adapted by U.F.C. emphasized the following:

1. That the given in each human being is a desire to be active in exercising meaningful control of one's life.

2. That the client has a right to his or her definition of the problem.
3. That the target problem must be specified.
4. That there must be an explicit agreement between worker and client on what, when, and how problems will be solved.
5. That the identification of client strengths and a thorough history of survival and coping skills be an initial part of the assessment process.
6. That workers should look to the environment as well as the client for the possible cause of the client's problems.
7. That task and method of solution should be tailored to the individual client's capacity to accomplish goals that have been set.
8. That work with clients is time-limited and all contacts are meaningful.

Case Example

Ms. C. and her four children were referred to the Urban Family Center because the family was undomiciled due to eviction (children's ages: R-11, L-10, J-8 and H-6).

Intake Interview

At U.F.C. the intake interview is done when the family first arrives at the center. Basic information is gotten from the family, documents are signed, and the agency program is briefly explained before the family is shown to their apartment.

Ms. C. arrived at 9:00 P.M. with a male friend, without her children. She was appropriately dressed but smelled of alcohol.

She told her friend to wait outside during the interview, even though the worker gave her the opportunity to bring him in. Ms. C. signed the required documents, such as the license agreement. She stated that she had been evicted, her children were at a friend's and would join her tomorrow. She was told about the program and given general information about the neighborhood. She said that she would stop by the office tomorrow to meet her worker and set up a time for the initial interview.

Initial Interview

The initial interview is an opportunity for the assigned worker to begin to get a better understanding of the family's concerns and also to let the family know what the program is about and what can be expected of the worker. Ms. C. and her family participated in the initial interview. The children seemed surprised that they were being included, but welcomed the opportunity. The worker used this session as a get-acquainted time by clarifying the program objective, her role as the worker, how we work here with the entire family, and the fact that the entire family takes part in the problem-solving process. The family shared some of their concerns about the shelter and why they had to come. An appointment was made for school registration.

The family was given the task of thinking about things that they would like to change and bringing that list to the next session. It was agreed that the family would meet with the worker in their apartment the following week.

Ongoing Work

The following session was spent on the family's list of concerns. The list was long; however, the family agreed to start with two concerns and recognized the need to begin small. The two concerns were housing and budgeting. These concerns were changed to goals and placed on the goal sheet.

It was agreed to have weekly family meetings to work on the budgeting, and weekly individual sessions with Ms. C. would be used to work on housing and welfare problems around getting the check and food stamps. The family worked well together during the first four-month period around budgeting. The budgeting problem was identified by the children as having to beg or borrow food money from friends and relatives on a regular basis. They also mentioned having inadequate clothes and Ms. C.'s partying with friends.

The early work involved trying to insure that the checks and food stamps would come on schedule, that a list which included snacks would be prepared from the planned menu, and a budget would be developed with guidelines for expenditures in each grouping.

The family was found ineligible for public housing, and the ineligibility was successfully appealed.

The worker identified Ms. C.'s drinking problem as a concern. This behavior was observed by staff, as Ms. C. was one of the people who drank frequently at night parties that were often disruptive. Ms. C. was not convinced that this was affecting her functioning. However, this was added to the goals sheet later.

Dealing with the budgeting concerns helped the family to become more organized. They realized that this problem was related to their total functioning such as scheduled mealtime, planned snacks, cleaning of the kitchen and bedrooms, getting to school on time, and playtime. Most of the family work was spent on establishing daily routines for the entire family.

At the end of the three-month period, goals were reassessed and it was agreed to continue to work on the same ones, including controlling the drinking.

Termination

The family moved to public housing after six months at the center. The family felt that they had reached some of their goals. They were moving to public housing and they did not have to go hungry or begging for food.

The family needed additional supportive services to try and stabilize the gains while adjusting to their new home and community. The after-care plan was for the worker to help the family to make connections with resources in the community.

The above described model is not without problems. Given the basic disorganization of the clients, broken appointments and failure to follow [up] on assigned tasks are problems. Workers must follow up by going to the families' apartments. It is important to help the clients escape from their pattern of acting only on crisis. If the workers do not follow up it is easy for them to be caught in the pattern of moving with the family from crisis to crisis. When this happens the workers become overwhelmed and feel impotent. We have found that with consistent follow-up and repeated demonstration of the worker's willingness to provide support to clients in meeting their daily needs, productive treatment relationships can be established.

Life-Space Interviewing

The third approach which has been found useful by U.F.C. staff is the life-space interview approach initially developed by Fitz Redl and David Wineman in their work with troubled adolescents. Basically, the approach rests on the belief that the client's ongoing life experience can be used for therapeutic gain. While in more classical approaches, a client may share in therapeutic sessions the nature of their experiences, these experiences are overlaid with the patient's impressions and beliefs. At the U.F.C., workers have the opportunity to intercede in an immediate way with a client's coping. Their presence when a mother handles a child inappropriately, gets in a fight with another resident, keeps her children home from school, etc., enables the worker to use that event as a learning opportunity.

It is important to make a distinction between life-space interviewing and residential treatment. In residential treatment, one systematically manipulates the environment in such a way as to create a context within which a client will make progress. In the Urban Family Center, it is not possible to systematically modify the client's environment. There are basically three reasons for this:

1. The setting is too large with too small a staff to exert that degree of control over clients' lives.
2. The Urban Family Center is an open setting where clients live in their own apartments and as such, there is not the control that exists in a more communal living setting.
3. The residents at Urban Family Center are free to leave at any time. Their length of stay has largely to do with when they find an apartment and not with treatment considerations.

Life-space interviewing is different from residential treatment in that a worker uses "what is" as the basis for their interventive strategies. This is not to suggest that life-space interviewing deals only with discussing the client's overt actions. The social workers must decide, in every incident, the degree to which they will intercede. Thus, the life-space interview requires a high degree of diagnostic judgement. In every incident, the worker must first decide whether the behavior of a family is the result of the stress all these families are under or if the behavior of the client reflects underlying pathology. If it is the former, the focus of the worker will be upon giving the client "emotional first aid." They will provide help to the client in decision making. They will strengthen reality testing and help the client see that their behavior, while possibly dysfunctional, is due to a stress overload. This will, of course, strengthen the client's self-image. If the social worker, in working with the client, sees the problem as more than an overload of stress, the worker must decide whether he/she wishes to go beyond the provision of "first aid" and use the event as an opportunity for client insight. This insight happens in a variety of ways including helping a client increase self-observation skills, clarifying the chain of events which led to the behavior, defining the boundary of self and others, and exploring how such situations might be coped with in the future.

This emphasis on using things that occur in a worker's presence fits well with the Urban Family Center approach because it focuses upon coping. Work with multi-problem families must emphasize coping and *their* reality. Only as reality pressures are coped with will there be an opportunity for more in-depth change. In-depth change is possible at moments in which the client's reality is confronted by the worker and client together.

To use an example, Mrs. X. tended to appear late in the morning, and while she went through the motions of trying to handle her circumstances, little progress was being made. Her worker went to her apartment about a welfare issue and the children told the worker she was sleeping. When the worker insisted, the children stepped aside. On entering the bedroom the worker discovered a room filled with empty bottles. It was clear that Mrs. X. stayed up late drinking every night. This served as an opportunity to discuss the problem caused by her drinking as well as an opportunity to discuss the nature of her relationship with the worker.

Similarly, the presence of school-age children in the buildings during school hours offers the opportunity for staff to take the children to their mothers and discuss the issues involved in keeping kids out of school. Mothers can be helped to see the inappropriateness of "keeping the kids out of school to do things for her."

Such events often occur in the presence of persons other than the client's worker. Since life-space interviewing is not designed to delve deeply into intrapsychic issues, but rather, is directed toward ego development and coping, any staff person can and should use such techniques with any resident. The staff later communicate the event to the client's worker for further action. Needless to say, the twenty-four hour coverage at the Urban Family Center provides many opportunities to intercede in ways which can help the client cope.

In the process of evolving the service model used at U.F.C. repeated attempts have been made to engage families by group methods. By and large, groups have been unsuccessful at the Urban Family Center. Groups have only worked in those instances when they focus on the reality needs of the clients. Similarly, efforts to establish after-care services have been unsuccessful at U.F.C. despite the fact that clients may remain connected to the agency in others ways (such as receiving mail at U.F.C. long after they leave).

To fully understand the changes that can take place in families while they are at U.F.C. it is important to realize that significant work is also done with the children. There is a nursery which helps the children with their developmental lags and there are both an afterschool program and an alternative school program on site. Though in all programs attendance can be a problem if there is not consistent follow-up, the children who attend the educational program regularly make significant progress. We feel child-focused programs are important in shelters because the child is often neglected despite the fact that they too have gone through a crisis involving a loss of friends, neighborhood, and school.

Finances

An often-asked question is "How much does a program for the homeless cost to run?" It is our view that to be cost-effective a program [must] be of large size. Small facilities will not be able to afford sufficient staff and will need to depend on volunteers. On the other hand, the larger the facility the more sense of distance between staff and resident. Even at U.F.C. size (90) there is a need for extra maintenance staff to keep down damage. If one ignores damage the facility deteriorates rapidly through escalating levels of damage. It is our impression that a facility larger than 100 units loses its treatment focus and that facilities under 30 units are not economically viable given the level of emergency funding available. Even at thirty units one must assume that the facility is owned by the persons running it. Below is detailed a sample budget for a thirty-unit facility. The budget assumes that five apartment units are being used for offices and staff.

Personnel

Director	$ 30,000
Social Service Director	25,000
Social Worker	18,000
3 Security Guards	24,000
3 Program Aides	36,000
Weekend Coverage S.W.	5,000
Clerk/Receptionist	12,000
Secretary/Manager	14,000
Maintenance (2)	27,000
Housing Specialist p/t	7,500
Fringe 24%	$ 47,640
Total: Personnel	$246,140

[Other Direct Costs]	
Utilities	$ 30,000
Telephone	3,600
Maintenance/Supplies	15,000
Replacement of Furniture	10,000
Insurance (reg. & lib.)	10,000
Legal Expenses	2,000
Office Supplies	10,000
Equipment Rental	10,000
Miscellaneous	5,000
[Other Direct Costs: Total]	$ 95,600
GRAND TOTAL	$341,740

As the reader will note the program is expensive but it is, at least in New York City, far less expensive than providing foster care for the children of these families. Assuming a 90 percent occupancy rate with an average family size of two children in each of the 25 units, providing for these children in foster care at $40.00-a-day-board rate would cost $647,000 in contrast to the $341,740 listed above.

REFERENCES

Fried, Marc. "Endemic Stress: The Psychology of Resignation and The Politics of Scarcity." *American Journal of Orthopsychiatry*, Vol. 52, No. 1 (Jan. 1982).

Perlman, Helen. *Social Casework: A Problem-Solving Process*. Chicago: University of Chicago Press, 1957.

Rapoport, Lydia. "The State of Crisis: Some Theoretical Considerations" in Howard J. Parad, editor, *Crisis Intervention: Selected Readings*. New York: Family Service Association of America, 1965.

Redl, Fritz. "Strategy and Technique of Life Space Interviewing." *American Journal of Orthopsychiatry*, Vol. 28, No. 1 (Jan. 1959).

25

Homelessness: A Comprehensive Policy Approach

Nancy K. Kaufman

Introduction

THE PROBLEM of homelessness is not a new phenomenon. As the numbers of homeless men, women and children grow, however, the problem is becoming more visible and is receiving increased public attention through the media and the political process. This chapter reviews the recent efforts of one state that has identified homelessness as a major social welfare concern. It considers how Massachusetts has attempted to address the causes and effects of homelessness in as comprehensive a manner as possible.

The purpose of this article is to define the problem and causes of homelessness, to suggest a comprehensive policy approach, and to discuss the implementation underway in Massachusetts. Obviously, any truly useful evaluation of these efforts would be impossible at this early date. The approach is based on the belief that the problem of homelessness represents a multidimensional human services issue which touches many facets of the modern social welfare system. It requires, therefore, a review of the present successes and failures of key components of that system before any new initiatives are established. However, before attempting this, it is worthwhile to consider the assumptions regarding homelessness under which the administration operates.

From *Urban and Social Change Review*, Vol. 17, Winter 1984, pp. 21-26. Reprinted by permission of *Urban and Social Change Review*.

Definition of the Problem

For the purpose of this article, homelessness is defined as a condition wherein an individual on a given night has no place to sleep and is forced to be on the street or seek shelter in a temporary facility.

Homelessness is seen as a problem which has a variety of causes and includes a mix of people with differing needs. The stereotype of a homeless person has been the skid-row alcoholic or bag-lady living on the street. While "bag-ladies" and "alcoholics" do make up part of the homeless population, they represent only a fraction of the total population. Despite beliefs to the contrary, it is increasingly evident that when offered shelter these people readily accept a warm place to sleep.

Other homeless people include: battered women; low-income families who have been evicted for non-payment of rent; people displaced by condominium conversion, urban renewal, or gentrification; mentally ill people who have, "fallen out" of the system because of inadequate after-care following deinstitutionalization or inability to be hospitalized because of commitment laws and overcrowded hospitals; the unemployed; and those who have been cut off of federal programs and cannot find affordable housing.

Reports from cities across the country indicate an increasing homeless problem with very similar population breakdowns. In Detroit and Philadelphia, it is estimated that 8,000 people are homeless. Chicago estimates anywhere from 1,000 to 200,000 depending on how one counts. New York estimates between 10,000 and 75,000 and Los Angeles estimates 1,000-8,500 (Hombs and Snyder, 1983). The numbers differ depending on the methodology used to count homeless people. The City of Boston recently completed a one-night census which indicated 2,700 people homeless on an October night in Boston (Kaufman and Harris, 1983).

Homelessness is not a new social problem. It represents the culmination of many social problems which have not been adequately dealt with over the years by federal, state, local housing and social welfare policies. While some people are quick to blame "deinstitutionalization" of the mentally ill and retarded for the problem, others are just as quick to say that it is exclusively related to the serious shortage of affordable housing. The reality is that both of these and other causes as well are all important, and solutions will require an honest acknowledgment of those policies and programs which have either failed, or have never been adequately supported and implemented.

In the case of "deinstitutionalization," for example, it is true, as recent studies have pointed out (UCPC/MAMH, 1983), that among the homeless are many people with chronic mental illness who have been patients in state mental hospitals. This does not mean necessarily that deinstitutionalization has failed and that we can or should return to the pre-60's days of large, underfunded, inadequate institutions for the care of the mentally ill. It only means that the implementation of many support services has been less than adequate. What we must now do is reexamine the weaknesses in the system and address those weaknesses, *not* turn the clock back twenty years.

The problem at the state level has clearly been exacerbated by the federal government's withdrawal of a commitment to a national mental health policy. With the advent of block grants, the federal government has abdicated its role as a leader in community mental health policy and funding, forcing community-based mental health centers to seek non-public dollars to carry out their mental health plans. This abdication left responsibility for the overall system to the individual state which now has fewer dollars to meet the needs of its people. The result, in some areas, has been a service shift away from the poorest clients to the middle-class who have private insurance to pay for services. Homelessness has, too frequently, been a by-product of these mental health system problems. This is not to suggest that all homeless people are, or need to be, mental health clients. As mentioned before, there are numerous causes of homelessness.

The homelessness problem is further exacerbated by the fact that there is a serious housing shortage in this state and in this country. The reality is that while we have come to accept this phenomenon as a fact of life, it has been brought on by a concerted effort in Washington *not* to have a national policy which guarantees a decent home for all people. Thus, whether a person has special needs or not, the fact is for people with little or no income, housing is not available. In urban areas the problem has been further exacerbated by condominium conversions and gentrification. Public Housing Authorities across the state report a three to four year waiting list with thousands of names of people seeking subsidized housing. Recently, the Executive Office of Communities and Development opened up its Section 8 subsidized housing program in Greater Boston and received 20,000 applications for 1,000 certificates. This demand clearly exceeds the supply of affordable housing. The situation has been exacerbated by the fact that rental housing production has lagged behind by 20,000-30,000 units per year in terms of what is necessary to keep up with the market demand.

A Continuum of Services

Given these harsh realities, what is the most appropriate public policy response at the state level? In Massachusetts, a comprehensive policy approach is based on two important assumptions:

1. Solutions must come from the local level with policy and program support from the state.
2. The federal government must become more involved in supporting state and local efforts.

[Exhibit 25-1] suggests a continuum of services which are necessary in order to develop long-term solutions to the problem of homelessness. The diagram acknowledges the crisis nature of the problem in the short-term, while pointing to the need for long-term, permanent solutions.

The model lists the components necessary for a comprehensive approach to the problem. The critical link is "case management/advocacy." Case management is the glue which holds the continuum together. Without it, a person could easily fall back into the homeless cycle. It is, however, the most difficult part to define and implement. First, what is case management and how does it work?

The social welfare system is a complex maze of policies and programs. It is difficult to understand even when one is not in crisis. Imagine not knowing where you were to sleep tonight, being responsible for hungry children, facing inclement weather, and having no knowledge of how to access the service providers who might help you re-stabilize. A case manager is someone who guides a person in crisis to the appropriate services to address the immediate emergency and prevent future crisis.

Exhibit 25-1
Homelessness: A Continuum of Services

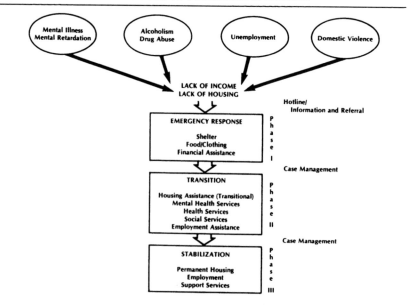

By definition, homelessness is a crisis that would confuse and disorient even the healthiest person or family. When the crisis is further complicated by emotional problems, alcohol, or drug abuse it is particularly difficult and frightening. A case manager can mobilize the resources necessary to assist a person out of the crisis and on the road to stabilization. Naturally, the extent of intervention by the case manager depends on the resourcefulness of the client to share the task of finding transitional and/or permanent housing and other necessary services. For some clients, homelessness is a cause and consequence of severe emotional debilitation and mental health services may be necessary to help the client help him or herself.

In this model, it is assumed that all attempts will be made to *prevent* homelessness in the first instance. Homelessness, ultimately, is very costly both in personal and public terms. There are a variety of policy changes which have been instituted recently to prevent homelessness. For example, if an AFDC family has fallen behind on their rent and is in danger of being evicted from their home, emergency assistance is now available to pay back rent and utility bills. To further assist welfare clients in preventing a homeless situation from occurring, the Welfare Department has established a client services number. This is designed to apprise recipients of options available to them in order to avoid becoming homeless.

Intervention Phase I: Emergency Response

Once a family or individual is homeless, emergency food and shelter are necessary first steps. Massachusetts is fortunate to have a well-organized food network. Project Bread and the Boston Food Bank in the greater Boston area provide emergency food to individuals and support local feeding and shelter programs. The new Administration, through the Department of Public Welfare, has also created thirteen new community-based shelters. These are in addition to the state's ongoing support of the acclaimed Pine Street Inn, which shelters 300-600 persons per night, and the Shattuck Hospital which shelters 50-100, and Long Island Hospital which shelters 100 persons per night.

The new shelters have been designed with the concept of stability in mind. They are small (20-35 beds) and are required to provide case management and day services. They provide homeless people with a bed and support services and they do not require people to line up each night. In this way, they are designed to interrupt the cycle of homelessness which has many people wandering from shelter to shelter night after night. In no way are these shelters seen as a solution to homelessness. Solutions will only be successful if they attack the root causes of homelessness which include inadequate income, inadequate housing, and inadequate social and mental health services.

Transitional Phase (II)

Once a person is temporarily stabilized in a community shelter, the other necessary basic needs of life can be organized to assist the person in need. The new shelter model provides a case advocate to assist the person during the day. Such assistance includes identifying appropriate public assistance benefits and accessing those benefits. Many shelters which are not state-funded do not have the resources to provide these services. For people in those shelters, services must be provided by state workers from the Departments of Mental Health, Welfare and Social Services. The Homeless Bill recently signed into law in our state mandates mental health and social services for homeless people. Until recently, a homeless person found it difficult to access benefits because, in the case of General Relief, a permanent address was required. As a result of passage of the Homeless Bill, a permanent address is no longer required and a shelter can now be used as an address. This is important in order for someone to get enough income to use to secure permanent housing.

Once income and shelter are secured, people can then begin the search for permanent housing. They often need assistance in negotiating the complex maze of housing programs. A person may have a Section 8 certificate, but may need assistance in identifying a landlord who will accept the certificate. The person may be on a waiting list for public housing and, depending on the local housing authority, may be viewed as a priority for a unit. The difficulty is if no housing is available for the person, or if the person needs special supportive services. To deal with this problem, a housing counseling program has been proposed. This program would be administered by the Executive Office of Communities and Development under contract with regional, non-profit agencies. It would provide the necessary link between people who are homeless or threatened with homelessness, and the public and private housing market.

In this second phase, other services must also be made available if needed. Social, mental health, employment, and health services are often available through traditional state and private service providers. The case manager working in conjunction with the homeless person can help match needs to appropriate services. More money and new programs will not solve the problem unless existing services are refocused on meeting the needs of the poorest and most vulnerable people.

Stabilization: The Third Phase

The third phase in the process of breaking the homeless cycle is stabilization. It is at this point that a person, hopefully, has been assisted in putting together a service package which will provide ongoing stability. This package will be different for different people. For an AFDC mother with two young children, it may require employment, training and day care as well as ongoing social services and, of course, a permanent place to live. For a chronically, mentally ill person it may mean a supervised or cooperative apartment. For an elderly, single person it may mean congregate living with access to medical services, or a single residence occupancy unit (SRO).

Whatever the situation, it is important to acknowledge the need for a variety of housing options. The Massachusetts Legislature recently passed and Governor Michael S. Dukakis signed into law a comprehensive housing package that will add 4-5,000 additional units of low- and moderate-income housing. These units vary from scattered-site family housing to special housing for handicapped people, to congregate arrangements for the elderly, to subsidized rental units in lodging houses and multi-family dwellings.

The Massachusetts Mental Health Center, for example, has developed a continuum of housing services for its client population. The ultimate goal in such a system is a permanent home in the community with ongoing supportive services. On a recent visit to the Center, I was convinced such a system could work when I visited a woman in her Section 8 apartment who was living alone and participated in an ongoing support group at the center. This woman had formerly been a patient in a state hospital for 15 years. Her situation was an excellent example of what could be if the right individualized services were provided. Certainly, if more such housing, linked with services, was available, we would not have people warehoused in large shelters in New York or sleeping on the floor in the Pine Street Inn in Boston.

For the mentally ill or alcoholic, the housing continuum may begin with a "dormitory" which is a safe, secure place for people who have been discharged from an inpatient unit and have no housing. Other possibilities include a quarterway house, nursing homes, family care homes, supervised apartments, and independent living apartments. All of these are supported by two day treatment programs and an extensive after-care staff.

In a recent *Globe* article, Eileen McNamara (1983) suggests that "the emphasis should be on integrating the people on the streets into existing programs for alcoholics, the mentally ill and the drug addicted instead of treating the issue as a new phenomenon." Massachusetts, in contrast to New York, is trying to take exactly such an approach. It is attempting to push the problem back to the appropriate agencies for alternative solutions. In many cases, it is the inadequate funding or insufficient implementation of social welfare programs that have contributed to the problem. Before "new" solutions are developed, it is essential that we understand why current programs have failed so many people in need.

In his article "The Homeless of New York," Thomas J. Main further emphasizes this point. While Mr. Main's article shows a basic misunderstanding of the complex nature of the homeless problem and tends to blame the victim, I do agree with his statement that:

> The shelters should operate as bases from which the homeless are reintegrated into the appropriate social service programs. Whether these programs are treatment for mental illness, day care for working mothers, or affordable housing it is true that the skeletons of such programs do exist. Unfortunately, they have been so fragmented and underfunded for so long that they can no longer provide the extent of services which are necessary for people in need.

The approach in Exhibit 25-1 acknowledges the necessary interdependence of these services. If shelter, income, and food provide the necessary ingredients of an emergency response, housing assistance, supportive services and employment assistance provide the second phase response. Taken together they can lead a person to the third phase: permanent housing, employment and/or adequate income and supportive services. What is important is that different people need different services, but *all* people need income, food and shelter.

Housing is a problem which can be solved, but only with the combined resources of local, state and federal government and the commitment of the private sector to help. There is a national housing crisis which must be redirected toward all populations of people who find themselves closed out of the housing market. This is not a problem which can be solved quickly, but it is one which must be addressed if permanent solutions to homelessness are to be put in place.

Policy Implementation

The Governor's Office of Human Resources has been charged by the Governor with the overall coordination of the homeless initiative. The approach has been to work through the line agencies to develop policies which build on agency mandates and programs. An Interagency Homeless Planning Group has been organized with representatives from: Executive Office of Human Services, Executive Office of Communities and Development, Department of Public Welfare, Department of Mental Health, Department of Social Services, Department of Public Health, Massachusetts Rehabilitation Commission, Department of Elder Affairs, the Lt. Governor's Office and the Executive Office of Administration and Finance. This group is a key feature in the attempt to analyze where state policies have not produced desired results. By not categorizing homelessness as an isolated problem, there is the opportunity to redirect existing resources toward solving it.

This planning group has been working together to develop interagency programs and budget proposals. It has served as a problem-solving body for recommending changes in those policies which perpetuate rather than prevent homelessness. The group also receives input from a special Governor's Advisory Committee on Homelessness (through its Planning Committee) and the network of convener agencies which operate at the local level. The Governor's Advisory Committee is comprised of a cross-section of advocacy, provider, and private sector community representatives. Its Planning Committee meets regularly with representatives of the Office of Human Resources to advise on policy and program directions.

A unique feature of the overall policy approach is the network of "convener agencies." The conveners are agencies at the local level who have agreed to serve as local coordinators of groups working with homeless people. A majority of the convener agencies are Community Action Programs (CAPs) who have a mandate to work on the elimination and/or alleviation of poverty. Since most homeless people live in poverty or on the edge of poverty, it is very appropriate for the CAPs to be involved in developing a coordinated local response. Other convener agencies include: local governments, local coalitions and the Salvation Army. Their primary role has been to hold meetings at the local level, to assess the homeless problem, and to advise the Office of Human Resources on local needs and possible programmatic and policy approaches.

This network of agencies has proven to be an invaluable resource in ensuring that the approaches to solving the homeless problem build on the uniqueness of local needs and resources. It was this group of agencies that was asked to develop local plans for the distribution of the federal emergency aid for the homeless. Each convener area identified an applicant to receive the funds and sub-applicant through which the funds would be distributed. Applications were reviewed by the Planning Committee of the Governor's Advisory Committee. Through this process over a million dollars was allocated through 24 recipient agencies to 175 sub-applicants and ultimately to an estimated 5,000 homeless people.

While this inter-agency, decentralized approach may appear cumbersome, it ensures that the state's response to homelessness will be built on the special characteristics of each geographic area of the state. The fact remains that the nature and extent of the homeless problem in Pittsfield is vastly different than it is in Boston or Lowell. There is not one "right" response, but a variety of responses depending on the extent of the problem and the adequacy of existing resources.

The State sees its role as developing policies which assist local communities in filling the gaps as they appear at the local level. While the state has a critical role to play in filling the gaps, there are also roles for local government, United Ways, churches and synagogues. The problem of homelessness is too complex for any one group to solve on its own. Community responses have been most successful where the public and private sectors have joined together to tackle the problem and develop a coordinated approach to solving it. A missing piece in this policy approach is a more pronounced federal role. While the federal government did include an emergency food and shelter program as part of the Jobs Partnership Bill signed into law last spring, they have yet to address the root causes of the problem. The emergency assistance was important and certainly needed, but in the face of continued cutbacks in public assistance and social programs, including housing programs, the response is not enough.

In an effort to develop a policy statement for the National Governor's Association last June a group of people representing 20 states gathered in New York. Rather than create new programs to respond to homelessness, the group advocated to review and strengthen existing programs funded by the federal government. These were identified to include: housing, mental health, public assistance, social services, alcohol and drug assistance. If all the policies currently advocated by the National Governor's Association were being adequately funded and implemented, it was suggested, there would be a marked decrease in the homeless problem.

Conclusion

Homelessness is a costly social problem. It is only costly, however, if we allow it to continue to expand and increase in scope. New York City is an example of what can happen when the focus is on short-term solutions. As reported in *The New York Times* (10/2/83), New York has gone from an annual budget for homeless programs of $18 million in 1978 to $135 million in 1983. What is sad to note is that the problem has not been solved even with that kind of money. In fact, for every emergency shelter bed opened, another homeless person appears. This indicates the extent of the problem and the need to deal with both short and long-term solutions.

Money will help only if it is focused on the causes of homelessness and long-term solutions. While short-term responses are necessary, we must also work on ensuring adequate income and focusing on a better organization and delivery of existing services. If the homeless person can move from worrying about a bed for the night to looking for permanent housing and a job or appropriate supportive services, then we will have accomplished a great deal. The dilemma is, of course, that unless and until we can provide people with jobs and permanent housing, shelters and short-term programs are necessary. As Kim Hopper and Ellen Baxter (1983) recently expressed in a response to Thomas Main's article:

Adequate shelter is but a first—absolutely essential—step. Good jobs and decent housing are needed, emphatically so, if the much lamented cycle of dependency is to be broken. But when work is scarce, skills lacking, and housing unavailable, justice no less than compassion demands those requesting shelter be given it unconditionally. The indignity of having to ask is sufficient proof of their worthiness.

REFERENCES

Hombs, M. and M. Snyder. (1983) *Homelessness in America: A Forced March to Nowhere.* Washington, D.C.: Community for Creative Non-Violence.
Homelessness: Organizing a Community Response. (1983) Boston: Massachusetts Association for Mental Health and United Community Planning Corporation.
Hopper, K. and E. Baxter. (1983) "A Rejoinder to Thomas Main." Unpublished paper.
Kaufman, N. and J. Harris. (1983) "Profile of Homeless in Massachusetts." Boston: Governor's Office of Human Resources.
Main, Thomas J. (1983) "The Homeless of New York." *Public Interest 72.*
McNamara, Eileen. (1983) *Boston Globe,* 6 November.

VI

Resources

26

New Jersey Housing Assistance Program for the Homeless

Demonstration Program Design

New Jersey Department of Community Affairs

Purpose

THE PURPOSE of the Housing Assistance Program for the Homeless demonstration is threefold:

- To prevent displacement of individuals and families who are presently homeless or in imminent danger of becoming homeless by reason of their inability to pay rent or mortgage payments.
- To provide housing assistance and referral services to individuals and families who are presently without housing by reason of their inability to pay rent or to locate suitable, affordable rental housing.
- To analyze the problems of providing housing assistance to the homeless, including its costs, impact on communities and households or single individuals, and potential long-range implications.

Definition of Terms

Housing Assistance—Assisting the homeless with their efforts to locate suitable housing, referring eligible homeless to subsidized housing, disbursing temporary supplemental rent payments to property owners on behalf of

From "A Report on the Homeless Pilot Improvement Program," November 1984. Reprinted· by permission of the New Jersey Department of Community Affairs.

families and individuals, or loans to homeowners for the purpose of supplementing mortgage payments.

Referral Services—Establishment of linkage between homeless families and individuals with public, private and voluntary service agencies to provide support services including health, educational, and social welfare benefits.

Homeless—Low- and moderate-income families and individuals having no identifiable or available place of residence.

Inability to Pay—Lack of financial assets, income or eligibility and entitlement for all types of assistance to the extent that rent or mortgage payments are not totally affordable.

Imminent Danger—Individuals or families who have been ordered by the courts to vacate their present housing by Judgement for Possession notice, or who have received notice of Judgement of Foreclosure because of the inability to pay for housing costs.

Outreach—(1) Before application intake is initiated contact will be made with appropriate public and private agencies. These will include, but not be limited to, CEAS committee-established and other agencies in each county to assist the Homeless, Welfare Agencies, Salvation Army, Catholic Charities, United Way Agencies, etc.

Determination of Eligibility

Each person or family applying for housing assistance will complete a brief application form which surveys family composition including number of family members, ages and sexes, social security numbers, present income and assets, and most recent address. Information will be used to help determine eligibility and housing requirements for each applicant.

Eligibility Requirements

Families and individuals who are defined as low- or moderate-income families whose income levels do not exceed 80 percent of the median income for their localities and who are homeless or in imminent danger of becoming homeless (as described above) will be eligible for selection.

Program Funding Allocations by Applicant Type

Funding will be allocated to assure that assistance will be available for the most needy applicants. The following distribution of funding will be established initially, but may be reallocated based on needs demonstrated in the outreach process:

Applicants Presently Without Housing

Zero Income Applicants (no income or assets)	35%
Very Low Income Applicants (income does not exceed 50% of the median)	25%
Low and Moderate Income Applicants (income does not exceed 80% of median)	10%
Applicants in Imminent Danger of Eviction	20%
Applicants in Imminent Danger of Mortgage Foreclosure	10%

The following are examples of income levels for each distribution:

Family Income		Newark	Camden
Very Low Income	1 Person	$11,450	$ 9,850
(not exceeding 50%	2 Persons	13,100	11,300
of the median)	3 Persons	14,700	12,700
	4 Persons	16,350	14,100
Low and Moderate Income			
(51% to 80% of the	1 Person	$17,650	$15,250
Median)	2 Persons	20,150	17,400
	3 Persons	22,700	19,600
	4 Persons	25,200	21,750

Note: Income levels set by the U.S. Department of Housing and Urban Development for all low-income public housing authorities and all Section 8 housing programs have been incorporated into the Homeless Housing Assistance Program.

Selection Priorities

Applications will be screened by the Housing Assistance Program to determine eligibility and to assign them to selection categories.

Applicants will be selected on the basis of the following priorities:

1. Households including at least one member who is elderly and handicapped or disabled.
2. Households including at least one member who is handicapped or disabled.

3. Families in danger of breaking up.
4. Single-parent households including children.
5. Other households including children.
6. Handicapped or disabled individuals.
7. Elderly individuals.
8. Non-elderly individuals.
9. Households without children.

Selection of Housing

The Housing Assistance Program staff will assess the housing needs of participants and refer them to appropriate housing.

The program will maintain in cooperation with the Comprehensive Emergency Assistance Service a current inventory of available subsidized housing vacancies in addition to other housing assistance programs including federal, state, and local program availability, and available housing in the private rental market.

Subsidized Housing—Wherever possible the program will obtain housing in buildings already receiving public subsidies.

Federal Housing Assistance Programs—The program will utilize certificates available through the Section 8 Existing and Section 8 Moderate Rehabilitation Programs which are administered by local, county, and state public housing agencies. Priority consideration will be given to eligible homeless over the established waiting lists for subsidies.

Privately Owned Rental Housing—The program will negotiate supplemental rent payments with owners of rental housing properties for suitable housing. Guidelines established by the federal government or as amended by the local, county, and state assessments of up to 120 percent of current Fair Market Rental prices for each locality will be used to determine the acceptable cost level of selected privately owned housing including mobile homes, boarding homes, and group homes, rooming houses, hotels and motels, as well as conventional housing units.

Housing Standards

Selection of housing for families and individuals receiving rental subsidies from the programs will be limited to decent, safe, and sanitary dwellings. The program will use the U.S. Department of Housing and Urban Development's Housing Quality Standards, which regulate the selection of housing for the

Section 8 Existing and Moderate Rehabilitation programs, as a guideline for acceptable housing.

Since it is a program objective to transfer assisted families and individuals to the federally assisted housing programs when available, utilization of the federal housing standards would greatly facilitate the transition and help to assure uninterrupted rental assistance.

State and local housing ordinances would not be affected and would continue to function normally.

Housing Location Assistance

Families and individuals who are homeless because of their inability to locate suitable rental housing and who can afford to rent at fair market levels, will be assisted in their effort to locate housing by the program field staff.

Loans for Security Deposits

Families and individuals who are presently unable to obtain rental housing because of the inability to pay the total initial security deposits, will be granted loans for the supplemental amount. Fair market rental guidelines will be used to determine acceptable levels of rental costs.

Loans for Delinquency Payments

Families and individuals who are presently in imminent danger of eviction because they are unable to make total delinquent rent payments, but who are able to afford current monthly rent payments, will be granted loans for the supplemental amount of the back rent which is owed. Loans will not exceed the supplemental rent due for a three-month period.

Housing Assistance Payments

Families and individuals who are selected for rental subsidies will be required to pay 30 percent of their gross monthly income toward their monthly rent. The program will pay the remainder of the rent directly to the owner of the rental property. A contract would be executed between the program and the owner to provide supplemental rent payments on a month-to-month basis. Fair market rentals for each locality will be used to determine acceptable housing costs.

Mortgage Payment Loans

Families and individuals who are in imminent danger of becoming homeless because of their inability to make total mortgage payments due to a temporary reduction of income will be granted loans for the supplemental amount of mortgage payments required. Only those applicants who have acquired equity in their homes which is sufficient to repay the loans will be eligible for the loans. Applicants must agree to place the home on sale. However, loans may be repaid without selling the homes if resources become available within the contract period.

Applicants who have insufficient equity will not be eligible for loans, but will be eligible for rental assistance payments.

Applicant Intake Procedure

The Program will distribute application forms to all county welfare offices and to community agencies most likely to come into contact with the homeless in the provision of social, health and welfare services.

Data sheets describing the requirements, procedures, and benefits of the Homeless Housing Assistance Program will be provided to all participating agencies.

Families and individuals will be directed to county welfare offices in order to complete applications for housing assistance benefits. The Program will assign field staff to county welfare office locations as needed in order to screen applications and to provide additional program information as required.

After applications have been screened by the field staff and assigned to selection priority categories, the Program Supervisor will review the applications and assign them to field staff for housing assistance.

Program field staff will contact families and individuals directly or through the referring agencies in order to begin service delivery.

When it is apparent that a sufficient number of applications have been received to utilize available funding, the program will terminate the intake process and publicly announce the closing date for acceptance of applications.

27

City of Chicago Model Zoning, Building, and Shelter Standards

Task Force on Emergency Shelter

A COMMITTEE of the Task Force was formed to examine the range of issues related to standards for shelter operation which would insure that shelter guests be treated with dignity, provided a sanitary, healthy and safe environment, and take into account the varying types and sizes of shelter program operations.

Existing standards from other cities, as well as organizations involved with the provisions of shelter services, were compiled and reviewed. The City of Chicago Building and Zoning Codes were also reviewed for provisions relating to fire, health and safety standards for shelter buildings.

The results of this review indicated that there are currently no uniform, agreed-upon standards governing the operation of shelter facilities. In addition, there are no direct provisions in the current city building and zoning codes governing the operation of shelters for the homeless.

Following this review, the committee began to identify the basic elements which any standards should contain, and developed the following proposed operational standards for shelters. The Task Force is recommending that these standards be incorporated into the existing zoning and building codes to assure the safety and welfare of guests in all shelter facilities. To achieve this goal, current building and zoning code provisions should be suspended for a one-year period pending revision of the codes to create sections specifically regulating emergency shelters, and to allow for the implementation of the new standards for shelter operation.[1] During the interim period, all shelters

From *Homelessness in Chicago*, October 1983. (Prepared by the Task Force on Emergency Shelter in cooperation with the Social Services Task Force, Department of Human Services, City of Chicago.) Reprinted with permission.

should be required to meet the minimum health, safety and operational standards.

A. Operational Standards for Shelters

The following major principles should govern shelter operation:

1. Shelters should be operated in a manner which insures that all guests are treated with dignity, and provided a sanitary, healthy, and safe environment.
2. Shelters should be neighborhood-based. The main group of people to be served should be from the surrounding community. In addition, the group operating the shelter should be based in the community.
3. Shelters should be limited in size if possible. If there is a great need, then several sites should be considered. It is not desirable to have shelters where capacity is over 60 in one site. However, this goal has to be weighed against the need.
4. The board that governs the shelter should be reflective of groups and persons interested in shelter and the community where possible—for example, supportive community activists, religious groups, churches, business people and homeowners.
5. Shelters should operate with a minimum of bureaucratic procedures.
6. Shelters must be linked in some way with other services (food, day care, medical counseling, clothing). If the community has many services, a system of referral and information sharing must be created. If essential services are not available, the shelter may have to provide them (soup kitchen, clothing, pantry, drop-in center, etc.).

B. Proposed Standards for Overnight Shelters

1. Building Standards—Location of the shelter(s) should be in buildings that meet minimum fire, health and safety standards as defined by the proposed "Environmental Standards" which may be found in the next section of the report.

- Open and easy access for entrance and exit
- Diagram with exit routes posted in visible location
- Shelters with capacity of 30 or more must have access to a shower
- Separate sleeping areas for men, women, and families

- Separate and supervised smoking area; no smoking in sleeping area
- Maintained in a clean and sanitary manner

2. Staffing Standards—In shelters with a capacity of 100 or less, there must be a minimum of one trained staff person per 20 people on duty; in shelters with more than 100 guests, a minimum of six trained staff on duty during operating hours.

- At least one staff member must be awake at all times during hours of shelter operation.
- Shelter shall have a staff manual identifying established procedures for evacuation and medical emergencies
- All staff will be trained in the prescribed emergency evacuation and medical procedures.
- Staff will be responsible for referrals and security of persons and the building.

Based on a thorough review of the current zoning and building codes, and available alternatives, the Task Force developed the following report and recommendations.

Format: Section A—Rationale and Recommendations
      Section B—Definitions of "Transitional" and "Overnight" Shelters
        —Proposed Building Code Revisions for Transitional Shelters
        —Proposed "Environment Standards" (related to the current building code) for overnight shelters
      Section C—Proposed changes in the Zoning Code for Transitional and Overnight Shelters

Section A

Rationale

1. An emergency shortage of low-income housing and the incidence of homeless people in the City of Chicago continue to increase.
2. The onset of winter makes it difficult to survive in this city without a warm shelter in which to sleep.

3. Many churches and not-for-profit community organizations have offered to provide temporary shelter to homeless people.
4. No adequate alternative is immediately available.

Recommendations

1. Amend existing building and zoning codes in the City of Chicago to make legal provision for Residential Shelter Homes (Transitional Shelters), defined below.
2. Amend the Chicago Zoning Ordinance to make legal provision for Temporary Overnight Shelters, as defined below.
3. Suspend enforcement of existing building code provisions, and zoning regulations if necessary, on an experimental·one-year basis, for Temporary Overnight Shelters. Enforce substitute Environmental Standards for Temporary Shelters outlined below.
4. Enact a procedure to administer these Environmental Standards. This procedure may emulate the licensing procedure for Day Care Centers in Chicago. An application to operate such a Temporary Shelter would be submitted to the City of Chicago (e.g. Department of Human Services) with a plan of the proposed facility to be reviewed by an architect in the employ of the City. An inspection of the site would be undertaken by an inspection Task Force, to include representatives of the Bureau of Fire Prevention, Department of Inspectional Services, Department of Housing, and Department of Health if scheduled meals are to be served on the premises.
5. For Shelters that are in operation before the effective date of the implementation of the Standards, a six-month period shall be granted to allow upgrading of existing facilities to conform to these Standards.

Section B

Residential Shelter Home (Transitional Shelter)

1. *Definition*: A Residential Shelter Home (Transitional Shelter)—A private boarding home, institution, building, residence, or other place

occupied not-for-profit, which through its ownership or management provides temporary residence not to exceed 120 consecutive days, but no medical or health-related care on the premises, to three or more persons who are not related to the applicants or owner by blood or marriage.

2. *Zoning*: For purposes of administering Chapter 194A of the Municipal code of Chicago, the Chicago Zoning Ordinance, a Residential Shelter Home shall be a Permitted Use in areas designated R-3 and higher, and wherever else Lodging Rooms are permitted. No separate "Innkeeper's Apartment" shall be required. However, all other regulations that apply to Lodging Rooms shall apply to this use.

3. *Building Code*: For purposes of administering the Chicago Building Code, a Residential Shelter Home shall be classified as Class A-2, Multiple Dwellings, and shall be included among those occupancies listed in Section 48-2.2 of the Code. Regulations and requirements applicable to this use shall be only those regulations and requirements that apply to Rooming Houses or Lodging Houses.

Temporary Overnight Shelter

1. *Definition*: A Temporary Overnight Shelter—A building or part thereof occupied not-for-profit, which through its ownership or management provides sleeping accommodations for a period of time not to exceed 12 hours every 24 hours to three or more persons who are not related to the applicants or owner by blood or marriage.

2. The following standards shall apply to Temporary Overnight Shelters.

Environmental Standards for Temporary Overnight Shelters

1. A Temporary Overnight Shelter shall be considered a Permitted Use in areas designated R-4 and higher, and all Business, Manufacturing and Commercial Districts.

2. No Temporary Overnight Shelter shall be permitted in a Type IV, wood-frame building.

3. Maximum permitted occupancy shall be determined on the basis of allowing 45 to 50 square feet per occupant, including staff and registered guests. In situations of high need (extreme weather or emergency) a 20% overage of maximum capacity will be allowed.

4. To determine required separation from other occupancies in a building of mixed occupancy, a Temporary Overnight Shelter shall be classified as C-2, Small Assembly (Section 48-12.5), except that openings in such separations shall be protected by Class "B" label doors, frames, and closers.

5. The facility shall be maintained in a good state of repair and sanitation at all times.

6. Smoke detectors of a type approved by the Chicago Building Code shall be located in each sleeping area, in corridors at a minimum 40 feet on center, at the ceiling of each stairwell and open shaft, and in each room used for active or inactive storage.

7. A Class 1 fire alarm system shall be required in all shelters with more than forty occupants. The fire system shall be supervised by a central station service (Chapter 91—Building Code).

8. An automatic sprinkler system conforming to the requirements of Chapter 91 of the Chicago Building Code shall be required in all buildings of Type III construction greater than two stories in height used as a Temporary Overnight Shelter.

9. Fire separations as required in Chapter 62 of the Code shall be required throughout the area designated Temporary Overnight Shelter. The standards specific to C-2, Small Assembly, shall apply.

10. There shall not be less than two exits from every building, floor, space, or room used as sleeping accommodations in a temporary Overnight Shelter. Exit requirements as contained in Chapter 67 of the Chicago Code shall apply.

11. Illuminated exit and directional signs in conformance with Section 67-18.2 through 67-18.5 of the Chicago Code shall be located to mark all ways of egress.

12. Emergency lighting in accordance with the requirements of Chapter 88 of the Code shall be provided. A system 2 shall be required (Sec. 88-700.5).

13. Fire extinguishers which meet National Fire Prevention Association standards and which are appropriate for the type of fire which may occur at the site of the facility shall be:
    a. placed at accessible location on each floor,
    b. wall hung, and
    c. properly charged and checked.

14. Electrical wiring and equipment shall be maintained and protected to prevent it from becoming a fire hazard or a source of ignition for combustible materials.

15. Plumbing fixtures shall be provided in accordance with the requirements of Section 82-153 of the Chicago Code, except that a Tempo-

rary Overnight Shelter shall have a minimum of one toilet per 15 persons.

16. Ventilation shall be provided as required in Table A, Section 81-7 of the Chicago Code, for "Sleeping Stall rooms."

17. The Heating Provisions of Chapter 80 shall apply to Temporary Overnight Shelters.

Section C

Zoning Recommendations for Shelters for the Homeless

1. Residential Shelter Homes should be a Permitted Use in all residential districts designated R-3 and higher.

2. Temporary Overnight Shelters should be a Permitted Use in all residential districts zoned R-4 and higher.

3. Both types of shelter should be permitted in any Business, Commercial or Manufacturing District. The use of first-floor space in commercial buildings should also be permitted.

4. Given the desire of many non-profit groups in various Chicago neighborhoods to provide shelter locally, existing churches, schools, convents, monasteries, community centers and public use and recreational buildings should be available to them, regardless of where they are situated.

To accomplish these goals, the following specific amendments should be made to the Chicago Zoning Ordinance:
Add the words:
"and Residential Shelter Homes" at 7.3-3 (2);
"and Temporary Overnight Shelters" at 7.3-4 (7);
"except Residential Shelter Homes and Temporary Overnight Shelters" after the words "below the second floor" at the following places:

8.3-1.A (1)	8.3-6.A (1)
8.3-2.A (1)	8.3-7.A (1)
8.3-3.A (1)	9.3-1 (1)
8.3-4.A (1)	9.3-2 (1)
8.3-5.A (1)	9.3-3 (1)

"and temporary Overnight Shelter" at 9.3-4 (10).

At 7.31 add:

(16) Residential Shelter Homes and Temporary Overnight Shelters in existing, lawful churches, convents, monasteries, schools, community centers, public use and recreational buildings.

NOTE

[1] The City of Minneapolis, Minnesota, has also used this approach. . . .

28

Comparative Shelter Construction and Operation Cost Estimates

Alice Callahan, Jeff Dietrich, and Gary Blaise

Summary

THERE are over 25,000 Los Angeles County residents living on our streets. This is a fact known to our City Councils, Board of Supervisors, and Courts. Our policy makers are aware of the crisis of homelessness, know of its implications for public health and crime and have sympathy for the human misery experienced daily by the homeless. What our policy makers need is a clear vision of how to attack this most difficult problem.

This proposal provides two simple and effective strategies for housing the homeless:

1. Conversion of existing surplus or underutilized buildings to housing; and
2. Factory-built emergency housing developed on either public or private land.

Each strategy is outlined with alternatives for greater or lesser government involvement in development and management, and each includes an option model for private financing and tax shelter investment.

In addition to the physical shelter, we propose an implementing vehicle—a Special Purpose Organization that will develop and manage emergency hous-

From *Homelessness Report: Strategy for Survival*, February 1984. Prepared for Los Angeles Catholic Worker. Reprinted with permission.

ing throughout the county. The Special Purpose Organization will be a business designed to circumvent the costly and ineffective bureaucracy that is now struggling with the crisis of homelessness.

This is not a research paper; it is a development proposal. As a development proposal it does not provide elaborate documentation of the problem of homelessness. . . .

County Resource Request

This proposal calls for three levels of County participation:

1. Grants of surplus government property, either buildings for conversion to housing, or land for placement of modular housing; .
2. Financing assistance, either in a grant context, or in [the] form of low-cost loan[s] and guarantees of loans made by private lenders; and
3. Decentralized processing of homeless people through direct contracts with the shelter on a beds-filled basis.

The proposal considers two approaches to County support of emergency housing: The first (Public Sector Model) pays for the shelter up-front through capital grants; the second approach (Private Sector Model) considers each shelter as a business with surplus revenues that can be applied to amortization of loans, and loans rather than grants are used to cover the cost of the shelters. The loans can be made directly by the County, or the County can guarantee loans made by private lenders.

Below are listed the specific resources and their costs that the Proposal asks the County to contribute toward housing the homeless. A distinction is made both between costs attributed under the Public Sector Model and the Private Sector Model, and between costs associated with modular housing. Exhibit 28-1 enables comparison of both housing types under each funding strategy. While the development pro forma in the proposal considers 250-bed facilities, the proposal calls for an initial commitment from the County for 1,000 beds, and the following assessment of resource requirements is based on that larger commitment.

The Homeless Problem

While it is difficult to count the number of homeless people in metropolitan

Los Angeles, the United Way estimates that there are 25,000 homeless people, and the Department of Mental Health estimates between 30,000 and 50,000 people. In all of Los Angeles County there are 217 publicly funded shelter beds—enough to shelter less than one percent of the community's homeless people. According to a United Way survey, private shelter facilities are limited to only an additional 1,500 beds in 23 emergency shelters, most of them religious missions. Virtually all private-sector shelter-providers report

Exhibit 28-1
Resources Requested From the County by Building and Funding Type

	Building Conversion		Modular Conversion	
	Private Sector	Public Sector	Private Sector	Public Sector
1. SURPLUS PROPERTY GRANTS				
A. Land for Modular Housing	-0-	-0-	***	$1,400,000
B. Buildings for Conversion	-0-	$1,648,000	-0-	-0-
2. FINANCING				
A. Grants	-0-	$1,500,000	-0-	$1,416,000
B. Loans	-0-	-0-	$ 288,000	-0-
C. Loan Guarantees*	$2,800,000	-0-	$2,248,000	-0-
3. DIRECT CONTRACTS				
Contracts between shelter provider and County $3,000/yr. x 1,000 persons**	$3,000,000	$3,000,000	$3,000,000	$3,000,000
TOTAL RESOURCE REQUEST	$3,000,000	$6,148,000	$3,288,000	5,816,000

* Guarantees not figured in total.
** Based on current expenditures by County @ $8.00/bed per night.
***Temporary use of surplus land would reduce costs by $1.4 million.

their resources to be strained to the breaking—most turn away more people per night than they are able to house. In greater Los Angeles the situation is no better. There is one 75-bed shelter in Long Beach and one 12-bed facility in the San Fernando Valley.

The homeless population has shifted dramatically in the past decade. A UCLA study is indicating that the homeless today are substantially younger and better educated than at any time in the past. Many of these "new homeless" are recently unemployed, including whole homeless families. A subset of the homeless population is severely mentally ill, put out of State mental hospitals because of budget cuts and given no recourse but the streets. According to the City of Los Angeles Community Redevelopment Agency, only 30 percent of the Skid Row population are chronic substance-abusers. The homeless Angeleno today does not fit any old stereotypes of "wino" and "derelict"; the common denominators instead are unemployment or under-employment and inability to pay Los Angeles's high rents.

The fate of a homeless person in Los Angeles is grim, sometimes deadly. A nationally known expert in emergency medicine reports that more cases of hypothermia are treated at Los Angeles County/USC Medical Center than at Bellevue Hospital, the equivalent facility in New York. Rape and battery are daily tragedies, especially for homeless women. In addition, there is the more subtle but no less debilitating grinding of constant cold, hunger, and humiliation which disables the people of the streets.

While emergency shelter is only a provisional solution to deeper social and personal problems, it at least sets at bay the imminent threats to life and health which daily confront the homeless person in our County.[1]

Housing the Homeless: The Mandate

By law the mandate to assist the indigent devolves upon the County. Section 17000 of the State Welfare and Institutions Code requires that the County "relieve and support all incompetent, poor and indigent persons. . . lawfully resident therein." Traditionally Los Angeles County has complied with this law through its General Relief program, which supplies housing through an inefficient and overburdened system of voucher payments to single-room-occupancy hotels. The supply of SRO hotels is dwindling in Los Angeles as more and more are condemned. In any case they are an expensive and unpleasant way to shelter large numbers of people. The supply of voucher hotels does not come near to meeting the housing needs of the thousands of homeless people seeking shelter today.

The County Supervisors have authorized an expenditure of $8.00 per bed per night for these vouchers, and in most places this full amount is being spent by the General Relief program. What follows is a cost-effective alternative which will [house] people in safe, clean dwellings for the same $8.00 per night and provide two meals per day.

Shelter Development Proposal

Following are pro forma and analyses of two strategies to quickly expand the supply of shelter available to the homeless. The strategies are: 1. the conversion of existing buildings to housing, and 2. factory construction of new housing. While to facilitate cost comparisons each pro forma considers a 250-person facility, a minimum of 1,000 beds would constitute the first step in a substantive shelter plan. Operations assume private-sector management, two meals per day, and minimal social services.

Selection of one development strategy over the other will depend upon cost factors, desire for flexibility, and the availability of surplus or underutilized buildings. The pros and cons of each strategy are outlined following the pro forma.

Two approaches to financing are included in each Development Strategy pro forma. The first assumes a standard public grant approach to developing emergency housing. The second pro forma assumes a private-sector development model that approaches emergency shelter as a business involving long-term borrowing and private tax-shelter investment. Both of these approaches utilize assistance paid per resident by the County.

While the private sector model is more complex, it has the potential for substantial savings. It is based on the assumption that either directly from their own pockets, or indirectly through the welfare system, the homeless can pay for room and board. At $8.00 per night, a 250-bed facility could conceivably generate a monthly income of $60,000. Transition House, run by the Skid Row Development Corp., runs an intensive shelter and social support system on Skid Row for $7.50 per night. The Union Rescue Mission has a more skeletal program with a base cost of $1.92 per night. Conservative estimates of expenses show that such a shelter could realize a net income of $10,000 per month. Under these assumptions, an emergency shelter should be able to operate as any other business enterprise and use its incomes to borrow development capital. Given the unusual nature of the business, private lenders would require loan guarantees—probably from local government—but the actual funds need not come from public coffers.

Moreover, with guarantees in place, shelter operations could joint-venture with a general partner and raise capital through tax shelter syndications. The private-sector financing model utilizes both private lending and syndications as an alternative or supplement to public grants.

A key characteristic of emergency shelter is that bureaucratic barriers be removed. Currently the homeless must wait for hours or days to receive a voucher through the Department of Public Social Services and often leave the DPSS office with no shelter at all. If we are serious about getting the homeless population off of our streets and out of our back yards, we must make shelter easy to obtain. This means that County processing must be done by the shelter operators at the shelter site. The Homeless will be immediately housed. Only then should they enter the more difficult process of seeking permanent housing, employment or General Relief. Application for, qualification for, or receipt of General Relief should not be tied to an individual's receiving emergency shelter in the proposed facilities.

Implementation Vehicle

Addressing the Continuum of Shelter Needs

The major issue confronting us is not so much the creation of physical structures for housing as it is the development of tools that will give us a handle on the complete problem of homelessness. We urge the County to take a bold and innovative step outside traditional boundaries of the bureaucratic mindset and create a private non-profit corporation, a special-purpose organization, whose sole mandate is to address the entire spectrum of the homelessness issue. It will develop and manage emergency shelters, rehabilitate marginal single-room-occupancy hotels, and create new, permanent, low-cost housing.

The advantages of such an approach are numerous and apparent. Such entities have demonstrated the ability to attract the kind of significant and varied resources that have eluded more traditional social service agencies and government bureaucracies. Through a combination of private investment capital, foundation grants, state and federal monies, as well as donations of time, money, and creative energies from individuals, community groups, and churches, the special-purpose organization is able to leverage its investments many times over. Here in Los Angeles, the Community Redevelopment Agency (CRA) has used this approach with considerable success with the creation of the Skid Row Development Corporation. For a relatively small annual investment of $300,000, a total of over $8 million was channeled into this underdeveloped area of the city through the efforts of the Development Corporation. The CRA has been so satisfied with this prototype that it has created another non-profit entity, SRO Inc., to deal with the rehabilitating of single-room-occupancy hotels in Skid Row.

The key to a successful special-purpose entity is the provision of a relatively small, stable, ongoing source of income, which in this case could be made available through a County contract to provide shelter. Also important is the moral support of the County in attracting to the board of directors substantial community leaders in the social services and business communities.

Threefold Continuum

Based on the highly successful Burnside Housing Consortium in Portland, Oregon, a "County-wide Shelter Consortium" could begin immediately to address homelessness in a three-phase continuum.

Phase I—Shelters

With 25,000 to 50,000 homeless, the corporation's first job is to provide emergency shelter. The immediate goal is the development and management of four 250-bed shelters providing two daily meals, minimal counseling, and referral services.

Phase II—SRO

The most inexpensive form of housing in the County is the single-room occupancy hotel. These hotels are the homes of the marginal people, the elderly, the handicapped, the indigent. In recent years, thousands of SRO's throughout the County will become subject to tougher seismic ordinances, requiring substantial improvements, and causing many to be declared an economic loss and demolished. The continued loss of SRO's can only exacerbate the homelessness problem. It is essential that the special purpose organization work to save this significant stock of low cost housing on a County-wide basis just as SRO Inc. is about to do for the Skid Row area.

Phase III—Permanent Low-Cost Housing

Eventually the corporation must explore creative options for developing and building truly low-cost housing and thereby addressing the root cause of homelessness. It is indeed a difficult and challenging task, but special-purpose organizations throughout the country have in many cases demonstrated the ability to leverage not only capital, but creativity as well.

Emergency Shelter Strategy 1

Conversion of Existing Buildings

The most common strategy for housing the homeless is the conversion of existing, usually commercial or industrial, buildings to dormatory-type facilities with basic shower and dining facilities. This strategy is particularly cost-effective in situations in which there exist public facilities, or in which privately owned, but outmoded facilities can be purchased at relatively low cost.

The pro forma below considers the conversion of a hypothetical 18,750 square foot facility adequate to house 250 persons in a dormitory setting. In addition to acquisition, the costs of development are for a steel-reinforced concrete structure (low seismic requirements) to be renovated to include dormatories, offices, a dining room, no kitchen (meals are catered), and a toilet/shower room. The dorm areas would allow 50 gross square feet per bed, there would be 1,000 feet attributed to offices, 1,000 to showers, 2,500 to the dining/common room, and 1,750 to circulation and unuseable space [see Exhibit 28-2].

Emergency Shelter Strategy 2

Factory-Built Housing

An innovative alternative to sheltering the homeless in dormatories in converted buildings is factory construction of motel-like portable emergency housing. Factory-built modules can be developed on surplus public land or on low-cost properties bought for emergency housing purposes.

While many configurations are possible, the pro forma below considers a 250-person facility comprised of 25 portable modules housing ten persons each, plus factory-built common facilities. Each module is 12-feet wide by 40-feet long, and contains five double-occupancy rooms. The 8 foot by 12 foot rooms could also accommodate two parents and a child. Each room has a door that exits directly to an outdoor commons. The sleeping rooms do not contain bathrooms. Common facilities include a 1,000 square-foot toilet/-

Exhibit 28-2
Building Conversion Pro Forma

	250 BEDS	1000 BEDS
DEVELOPMENT COSTS		
Building Acquisition	$412,000	$1,648,000
250 beds x 75'/bed=18,750'x $22		
Renovation		
@$20/ft.	375,000	1,500,000
TOTAL DEVELOPMENT COSTS	$787,000	$3,148,000
MONTHLY INCOME		
Food/Rent: $8.00/day x 250	$ 60,000	
Operating Subsidy	-0-	
TOTAL INCOME	$ 60,000	$ 240,000
MONTHLY EXPENSES*		
Salaries & Fringe	25,000	
Operating: utilities, temporary		
help, linen, supplies, phone	11,000	
Food—2 meals	10,000	
Insurance	2,000	
TOTAL EXPENSES	$ 48,000	$ 192,000
*Based on Skid Row Development Corp.		
Transition House		
MONTHLY OPERATION SURPLUS		
(DEFICIT)	$ 12,000	
A) FINANCING PUBLIC SECTOR MODEL		
Government Cash Grant	$375,000	$1,500,000
Building Donation (or $1 lease)	412,000	1,648,000
TOTAL FINANCING	$692,000	$2,768,000
B) FINANCING PRIVATE SECTOR MODEL		
Debt Service (op. surplus/1.10)	$ 10,900	
Mortgage 14%, 10 yrs.		
(w/government guarantee)	$700,000	$2,800,000
Private Investment		
20% of $450,000 basis	90,000	360,000
Deferred Loan from government	-0-	
TOTAL FINANCING	$790,000	$3,160,000

shower, no kitchen (meals are catered) and a 2,000-square-foot office and dining building. There would also be outdoor space available for dining and other activities.

A key feature of factory-built housing is its cost. The sleeping rooms set in place will cost about $12 per square foot. The bathing and dining facilities will cost about $30 and $50 per foot. These costs are for facilities that are of quality construction and which meet minimum housing codes. Development time for the first project is about 120 days. After factory engineering and state review requirements have been met on the first project, subsequent shelters can go up in 60 days.

While this pro forma assumes the purchase of land at market prices ($10/ft.) for marginal industrial areas, the small size of individual housing modules allows flexibility in site design that can accommodate narrow strips of unuseable publicly owned land. Moreover, their portability allows temporary placements of housing modules on sites being held for future development [see Exhibit 28-3].

Pros and Cons

Conversion Versus Factory-Built Housing

There are at least five factors to be considered in evaluating the benefits of converting an existing building to housing as compared to building new housing in a factory. They are:

- Cost
- Quality of Living Environment
- Time for Development
- Flexibility
- Ability to Finance

Cost

Cost depends upon the availability of public buildings that can be had at no cost, the availability of public land, the cost of existing buildings, the cost of privately held land, and the cost of renovating existing buildings. Absent the existence of a free building, or of a privately held building that can be bought at low cost and which requires minor renovation, factory-built housing will be

Exhibit 28-3
Factory-Built Housing Pro Forma

	250 BEDS	1000 BEDS
DEVELOPMENT COSTS		
Land Acquisition 35,000' @ $10/ft	$350,000	$1,400,000
Site Improvements	100,000	
Sleeping Facilities	144,000	
25 5-room, 10-bed modules @ $12/ft		1,416,000
Bathing Facility 1,000' @ $50/ft	50,000	
Dining Facility w/office 2,000' @ $30	60,000	
TOTAL DEVELOPMENT COSTS	$704,000	$2,816,000
MONTHLY INCOME		
Food/Rent: $8.00/day x 250	$ 60,000	
Operating Subsidy	-0-	
TOTAL INCOME	$ 60,000	$ 240,000
MONTHLY EXPENSES*		
Salaries & Fringe	25,000	
Operating: utilities, temporary		
help, linen, supplies, phone	11,000	
Food—2 meals	10,000	
Insurance	2,000	
TOTAL EXPENSES	$ 48,000	$ 192,000
*Based on Skid Row Development Corp. Transition House		
MONTHLY OPERATION SURPLUS (DEFICIT)	$ 12,000	
A) FINANCING PUBLIC SECTOR MODEL		
Government Cash Grant	$354,000	$1,416,000
Land Donation (or $1 lease)	350,000	1,400,000
TOTAL FINANCING	$704,000	$2,816,000
B) FINANCING PRIVATE SECTOR MODEL		
Debt Service (op. surplus/1.10)	$ 10,900	
Mortgage 14%, 10 yrs. (for land)** ds=4347	$280,000	$1,120,000
Mortgage 14%, 5 yrs. (for housing)** ds=6552	282,000	1,128,000
Private Investment		
20% of $354,000 basis	70,000	280,000
Deferred Loan from government	72,000	288,000
TOTAL FINANCING	$704,000	$2,816,000

**Portability necessitates separate financing or building lease.

more cost-effective. But with a free public building that requires little earth-quake reinforcement, conversion is more cost-effective.

Quality of Living Environment

Because factory-built housing provides semi-private rooms and can easily accommodate families, it will result in a living environment superior to the more dormatory-like housing of converted buildings. The outdoor common areas are also superior to interior spaces of converted buildings when recreation and children are taken into consideration. The more home-like environment of the modular housing is more conducive than dormatories to transitions to standard housing.

Time for Development

Factory-built housing can be put in place four months after the decision is made to build. Most conversions will have extensive engineering and regulatory requirements that extend development time . . . As a result the average conversion will take 18 months, while a modular project should take no more than four or five months.

Flexibility

A clear advantage of modular housing is its flexibility. Given the availability of land, modular projects can be almost any size. In addition, the housing modules can be moved to another location at minimal cost. Conversions, on the other hand, are restricted to available buildings, and to the configuration of individual buildings that weren't designed for housing.

Ability to Finance

Because modular housing will not in most cases be tied to the ground, and due to its specialized use, modular housing may be more difficult to finance. Existing buildings are tied to the land and will be perceived by lenders to be more solid collateral than the modules. The reverse is true, however, in the case of unreinforced masonry buildings, which are spurned by lenders.

NOTE

[1] Los Angeles County at present is housing many of the homeless in jails and hospitals at substantially higher cost than more reasonable shelter. Pine Street Inn, a shelter in Boston, was established after it was demonstrated that it was much less expensive to house people in shelters than in jails and hospitals.

29

Community Relations Strategies

Rose Anello and Tillie Shuster

Understanding the Concerns of a Community

COMMUNITY OPPOSITION to residences for the homeless stems from a variety of fears and misconceptions. In many cases, a well-planned strategy can overcome community resistance. However, an agency's sensitivity to community concerns is necessary to achieve the desired outcome. Interests relative to a particular community's needs, hidden agendas, or the demographics of a community can also come into play. A planner's analytical, strategic, political, and interpersonal skills will all be called upon. The following are a sample of concerns found to be common in most communities.

"Not In My Neighborhood"

Because Community Boards in New York City are not required to accept a certain number of homeless facilities, nor is there a limit to the number of such facilities which can be established in any one Community Board, communities often claim to be "dumped on" or "over-saturated." This refers to a community's fear that it is being forced to accept shelters while other communities are not.

There are reasons particular communities have a disproportionate number

From *Community Relations Strategies: A Handbook for Sponsors of Community-Based Programs for the Homeless* (New York: Community Service Society of New York), January 1985, pp.18-33. Reprinted with permission.

of facilities. Foremost is the nature of the housing stock. Where property values are high, the development of shelters is too costly. Not-for-profit agencies find themselves competing with real estate developers for scarce properties. In impoverished communities, the housing stock is more affordable and it is usually these communities that feel they are a dumping ground for shelters and other residential-treatment programs. Organizations that are not indigenous to the community in which they are planning a shelter should be wary of this issue.

Some communities that have accepted facilities for the homeless are viewed as "liberal." Their tolerant attitude, however, can become less so as new sponsors seek additional approvals.

A Community's Interest Versus Outside Interest

If the prospective site had previously been identified by a community-based organization for another purpose, it is likely that the planner proposing a shelter will experience opposition. When city-owned property is involved, community-based groups and agencies extrinsic to the community can find themselves competing for site control of the same building.

In most cases a more sophisticated planning agency will be better able to deal with proposal writing, architectural design, legal, and financial matters than a grassroots community-based organization. Planners should be cognizant of prior plans the community may have for the prospective site. In one Manhattan Community Board, local leaders mobilized an effort to prohibit a shelter from entering the community. The community resented the new agency that had been successful in gaining site control of a building that they wanted to use as a senior center. The planners of this shelter might have been able to avoid the ensuing community resistance and hostilities if they had known of the community's own plans for the site. Although the community was viewed as resisting a shelter for the homeless, in reality it may have been an act of transference from the real issue: an outside interest versus the community's interest.

Property Values

The fear of a decline in property values often leads a neighborhood to mobilize against the planned residence. When the problem of homelessness is evident in a community, this fear is misguided. A shelter housing people who would otherwise be loitering in doorways and alleys can only increase the value of property in that community.

In neighborhoods where homelessness is not so prevalent (usually those that are not accessible by public transportation), residents will invariably believe that the opening of a shelter will cause a decline in property values. Although research does not verify this point of view, neighborhood groups and block associations can become animated by this issue. . . .[1]

Concern About Crime

Communities often fear that the opening of a shelter for the homeless will cause an increase in crime. Although the reverse usually occurs, planners must allay fears around this issue.

Shelters in which inadequate supervision is provided can be ominous neighbors. Large municipal shelters usually have poor staff-to-client ratios as well as unstructured programs. Residents of these shelters are faced with many idle hours, and they are perceived in the community as intimidating figures. On the other hand, programs which employ adequate management can enhance the safety of a community. Additional neighborhood security is usually a by-product of a well-planned community-based residence.

Community-based organizations that have experience running residential programs can draw upon their reputation for managing well-supervised programs. . . .

Communities may also be concerned with the proximity of a proposed shelter to a school or day-care center. Researching the makeup of the surrounding neighborhood before investing a lot of time and money can help planners avoid neighborhoods in which community opposition might be too great.

Community Acceptance Strategies

The beginning steps of a community relations strategy should be the formation of a working committee which will be responsible for the planning and execution of a well-thought-out plan. Before deciding on an appropriate community relations strategy, agencies should conduct as thorough an assessment as possible of their strengths and weaknesses as well as an assessment of the unique qualities of the target community. Readers may want to refer to Exhibit 29-1 for an overview of the steps involved in a community relations campaign.

Choosing an Appropriate Community Relations Strategy

Successful residential programs have used either a high-profile or a low-profile approach (though often these are mixed during the course of the project).

Deciding which approach is best is an individual decision, based on an assessment of the unique strengths of the agency, matched against the anticipated support or resistance to the shelter.

In sum, there is no one best strategy. Each group must make its own decision, based on its own assessment.

The Low Profile Approach

A low profile approach can be chosen if:

- the community assessment reveals a plethora of other political and social issues in the targeted area. By becoming highly visible, the planning group may become involved in issues beyond its immediate concern (i.e., asking for formal Community Board support if there is no legislative mandate to do so could force an agency to seek support from political factions the agency may not want to be indebted to. . . .)
- the community is highly mobile and heterogenous; its members may not feel the long-term effects of the proposed facility, nor organize against it.
- the planning agency feels it does not have the strength and support in the community to maintain a high profile.
- neither staff nor time is available to maintain high profile (i.e., access to the media, money for promotional displays, etc.).
- the issue has a past history of opposition in the host community (i.e., if the City has opened large armory-style facilities and the community has mobilized against these).
- the agency is not locally based, or if the City is providing major funding for the project.

While choosing a low-profile approach means less visibility, it does not require less effort or contact with the community. A community relations campaign must still start as early as possible in the planning process. Also, groups should be aware that there will be times of increased visibility when events go beyond the agency's control.

Exhibit 29-1
Strategic Steps: Planning and Development Timetable

Action	1	2	3	4	5	6	7	8	9	10	11	12
						Months						
1. Obtain approval from your Agency's Board of Directors to pursue proposed project.	x	x										
2. Form a working committee composed of Board members and / or community residents to develop and implement community relations strategies.	x	x	x	x	x	x	x	x		x	x	x
3. Conduct a community needs assessment.	x	x	x									
4. Obtain community input into site selection by meeting with community Board or neighborhood groups, local and city housing agencies, private real estate developers, and community-based organizations.				x	x	x	x	x				
5. Develop community education campaigns (i.e., brochures, mini proposals, slide show presentation).						x	x	x	x		x	x
6. Presentation of proposed shelter.						x	x	x	x		x	x
7. Research zoning and legal issues.						x	x	x	x	x		
8. Identify and meet with the formal power structure in the community (e.g. representatives of State Legislature, City Council members, the Mayor) to generate support.						x	x	x	x		x	x
9. Identify and meet with the informal power structure in the community (community leaders) to generate support.	x	x	x	x	x	x	x	x		x	x	x
10. Reassess initial strategy. Based on feedback from the community, you may need to restructure the												

Exhibit 29-1 (continued)

Action	Months
	1 2 3 4 5 6 7 8 9 10 11 12
program, taking into account your agency's mandate (e.g., residents and staff of shelter will be drawn from the community).	x x x x x x
11. Following key meeting and reassessment, send follow-up letters. Maintain these contacts throughout development and implementation phases.	x x x

Notes:

1. It should be noted that this timeline is a theoretical model and may not be realistic for each community to follow. An agency's resources will determine the planning and development phase. As the degree of difficulty encountered in given communities will vary, so will the time needed to pursue a community's relations strategy.

2. Community relations strategies should continue throughout the planning and development phase as well as the start-up and implementation phases of the shelter. The working committee formed in Step 2 can be broadened during the start-up phase to serve as a liaison council or the board of directors of the facility.

3. Another variable to consider is city-owned versus privately owned properties. City approval is required when an agency intends to buy a city-owned property. Consequently, a transaction between your Agency and a private owner may allow for a lower profile in the community.

The High-Profile Approach

A planning group may choose a high-profile approach if:

- they are locally based, with a long, strong history of providing needed, good services to the community. The program can be seen as simply an extension of what is already in place.

- their agency has maintained a broad base of support from local politicians and community leaders and can use this support to counter adverse arguments.
- the agency has the staff time and money to maintain an active, sustained community-relations campaign.
- the influx of services outweighs any possible negative social impacts (i.e., in a distressed neighborhood, the potential for new jobs and housing may overshadow any negative aspects).
- the site being acquired is city-owned. A high-profile approach may be necessary because of the need for Community Board approval.

Needs Assessment: A Strategy for Gaining Support

When planning a community-based shelter, research the characteristics and size of the indigenous homeless population. Before deciding upon the targeted population (youth, families, elderly) and type of facility (emergency, transitional or permanent), it is important to elicit the community's perceptions of their homeless population. This tactic allows for community input into the planning of the shelter. It also provides validation of the need for such a facility.

While undertaking a needs assessment, the planning group can often gain the support of local human-service providers. During the process, these local providers often become interested in the shelter as a potential source for their housing-placement referrals. Hospitals, social service agencies and welfare centers have difficulty finding decent, affordable housing for their homeless clients. They will be eager to support a solution to this problem.

A needs assessment is not necessarily a complicated and sophisticated research undertaking. The planning group can administer brief questionnaires through face-to-face or telephone interviews. This technique can stimulate those interviewed to lend support as well as collect the pertinent data.

Unanticipated benefits can result. Respondents may be willing to provide the planning agency with letters of recommendation, positive representation in their professional network or neighborhood, money, assistance with screening prospective residents for the shelter, staff services or help finding appropriate sites.

The dialogue between each interviewer and human service provider will provide the data for an exploratory study. It will not only conceptualize what the ideal shelter should look like, but will also provide a census of problems regarded as urgent by all those involved. The data collected will also be useful in documenting that the need for a shelter exists in that community.

Offering Incentives to the Community

There are a variety of incentives a proposed program can offer to a community to overcome initial opposition, but also encourage eventual integration into community life.

Examples of possible incentives include:

- locating the residence where there is an obvious need (e.g., rehabilitate the only vacant site on an otherwise stable block).
- offering housing/services to community persons (e.g., the homeless who live in local business doorways, etc.).
- where possible, hiring local staff persons. Employment of community members increases both acceptance and visibility of the program.
- using local builders and services to renovate the facility.
- offering local service agencies access to resources (beds) in return for the use of their services (e.g., a local mental health clinic), as well as their support.
- the provision of a needed community service (e.g., young-adult residents can renovate other community sites as part of a training program).
- staffing a facility on a twenty-four-hour basis. This can increase security on the host block.
- offering local residents the use of the facility for public meetings, etc.
- enabling shelter residents to volunteer their time to the community (e.g., organize a community garden, start a block "clean-up" day once a month, etc.).
- leveraging public and/or private funds which will be spent in the host community.

Using Your Local Power Brokers

By knowing both the formal and informal power structures within the community, planners can improve the chances of gaining community acceptance. In New York City, a planner's focus is usually on the formal structure of the Community Board and the local block association. However, informal power structures operate within both entities.

A community-based organization interested in purchasing city-owned property must present the proposed use of the property to the local Community Planning Board. Without the Board's approval, the community-based organization is stymied.[2] *Formal* presentation to the Community Board should therefore take place in the latter stages of the community acceptance campaign. It is the informal power structures in most New York City communities that initially need attention, as it is often through leveraging support of these power brokers that Community Board approval is won.

Identifying the Informal Power Brokers

> It is important to identify the well-known neighborhood persons (i.e., heads of local homeowner or block associations, leaders in neighborhood improvement groups, religious leaders, influential local business persons), and to learn where the focus of power is in the community. A very effective approach is to identify a community member who is especially well regarded and respected by his peers, and is willing to serve as an advocate and interpreter of the residence program to others.[3]

Usually a by-product of the needs assessment is the identification of people with clout who live and/or work in the community. Respondents to the survey are quick to point out who might help your agency's efforts, as well as those whom the planning agency will need to reckon with.

The latter group should not be taken lightly. A respected businessman, minister, or homeowner can be instrumental in organizing a neighborhood to petition against the opening of a shelter on their block.

These same people are often respected by the formal decision-makers, as they act as "informants" to the Community Board. The Board relies on them for a reading of the community. Oftentimes, if a Community Board is approached at the onset of the community-relations campaign, the Board will advise that the planners meet with the informal power brokers prior to a Board decision. This deference is often necessary in order for the formal decisions made by the Board to be respected and carried out in the community.

There are two main issues that should be stressed when resistance to a proposed shelter is encountered. Planners need to inform members of the community that:

- a community-based shelter operated by a not-for-profit organization is an alternative to the large-scale shelters developed by the municipal shelter system. The warehousing of people in armories and schools is an inhumane approach to homelessness. A community-based shelter insures supervision and dignity. It is the best option for the community and the homeless themselves.

- the data received from the needs-assessment survey proves there are, indeed, homeless in the community. Pointing out this information can persuade the more reluctant of the need for a shelter.

Identifying the Formal Power Brokers

Planners should be cognizant of the formal power brokers within New York City communities: the Community Board and local political officials.

As already mentioned, Community Board approval is necessary in order for an organization to acquire city-owned property. A vote in favor of the proposed use of a piece of property is a pivotal point in the community acceptance campaign. Following are three situations in which attaining Community Board approval is either required or in the project's best interest:

1. Approval by the Community Board is required when the sale of property must pass through the Uniform Land Use Review Process. Although the Board of Estimate has the power to override the Community Board's decision, this is rarely done. A veto of the Community Board's decision is politically uncomfortable for the respective Borough President.
2. While Community Board approval is not required when a transaction involving the sale of a privately owned property to a community-based organization takes place, it is recommended if a city contract covering program costs is anticipated. . . . Hence, every effort was made to gain a unanimous vote in favor of a project. The City may have been reluctant to participate in this not-for-profit's venture if the Community Board opposed it.
3. Although Community Board approval is oftentimes not a prerequisite of a potential funding source, it positively influences the outcome. Funding sources, both private and public, are unwilling to provide financing to a project that has been formally rejected by a community. When Community Board approval is omitted, the funding source may fear the proposal has hidden problems. Proposals are more likely to be awarded funds if they have the support of the formal local leadership.

In some communities, influential political figures are contacted immediately to engender support. Local and State officials can exercise a good deal of influence and their constituents often endorse their views. And whether an agency chooses to do this at the onset and sees it as a primary tool . . . or uses it only occasionally when particularly difficult occasions arise . . . it would appear that at some point during the development, implementation or operation of the program, a group will need to rally political support. An accurate assessment of the political actors in the target community is crucial.

How to Present the Shelter

It is important for planners to realize the impact on a community that the name and initial presentation of the shelter will have. It is advisable to leave out the word "shelter" entirely. Too often "shelter" connotes a large-scale facility with a lack of supervision and structure for those warehoused within. Because large municipal shelters are prevalent in New York City, it is the characteristics of these facilities which come to mind when "shelter" is mentioned.

Communities, therefore, must be approached with non-threatening words and descriptions, when presenting their proposal to the community. . . .

A variety of implements can be used to present proposals for community-based shelters to the Community Board and to other parties whose support (either material or conceptual) is necessary. . . .

Community Education Strategies

The objectives of a public education campaign should be to raise the consciousness of the community at large and encourage members to take ownership of the homeless situation within their midst. With these goals achieved, planners can more easily introduce their proposed shelter as a solution to the community's social quandary.

In New York City, a minimal amount of community education seems to be necessary. Most people living in this city acknowledge the extent of the problem and the need for solutions. (In the outer-boroughs, however, where homelessness is not as visible, this may not be as true.) More often, the focus is placed on the presentation of proposals to Community Board committees or block associations. The experience of shelter developers has been that as neighborhoods vary, so does the amount of time and effort one needs to put into an education campaign.

Community education can be facilitated by calling upon the expertise and resources of advocacy agencies. Often these agencies are willing to prepare statistical data, lend slide and film shows, or assist in the formation of a speakers' bureau. An initial inquiry about resources available can prevent planners from reinventing the wheel. . . .

. . . Since many providers are in need of housing or shelter for their homeless clients, they may be anxious to have such a proposal accepted in the community.

A community education campaign should be tailored to respond to a community's specific concerns, sophistication, and needs. The tools an agency chooses to employ in the program should reflect the capacity and time the committee has to devote to the campaign. . . .

Knowing Zoning Issues and Department Regulations

Because there are a myriad of state regulations and local zoning issues surrounding shelters and residences for the homeless, sponsors are advised to enlist the technical assistance of specialized professionals.

By adhering to New York State regulations governing adult residential-care facilities and shelters for the homeless as well as local building codes, sponsors can mitigate the concerns of a community. A well-thought-out and researched plan will gain approval from the Community Board while a proposal that is open to criticism due to lack of compliance with local codes and state regulations will not.

A good resource for sponsors to have is:

Building and Zoning Regulations: A Guide for Sponsors of Shelters and Housing for the Homeless in NYC, prepared by the Shelter Development Project of the Community Service Society.

This guide summarizes some of the more important zoning regulations relevant to the shelter development process in New York City. For information regarding State regulations governing facilities for homeless, sponsors are advised to contact:

New York State Department of Social Services
Bureau of Shelter and Supported Housing
2 World Trade Center, Room 2986
New York, New York 10048

NOTES

[1] A national study by the Washington D.C. Department of Corrections noted no significant decrease in the price of homes following the opening of a halfway house. A

second study carried out by the Green Bay Plan Commission in Green Bay, Wisconsin, found no appreciable decline in purchase price or assessed value of homes, within a two-block radius of a Community Residential Facility, over a four-year period of its operation.

[2] The approval of the Board is necessary in order for the Uniform Land Use Review Process (ULURP) to be completed.

[3] *Gaining Community Acceptance: A Handbook for Community Residence Planners.* Community Residence Information Services Program, 1981.

30

Program Design and Management

U.S. Department of Health and Human Services

THE LACK of a permanent residence is the only general characteristic shared by homeless persons. Otherwise, they are a diverse aggregate of individuals with needs and characteristics that mirror—although not proportionately—the needs and characteristics of the larger society. Homeless persons are men, women, children and families; homeless persons are young, middle-aged, and old; and homeless persons are skilled craftsworkers, homemakers and untrained individuals. Moreover, homeless persons' needs can range from the basics of a bed and meal to functional life skills to physical or mental health assistance.

Such diversity poses major problems for designing and managing effective housing projects that serve the homeless. Administrators must design, plan and implement programs that meet the diverse needs of homeless persons. Staff must provide appropriate services to people with very different needs. The program must be stable in order to facilitate stability in the lives of homeless clients. Moreover, these activities must be accomplished in a situation characterized by limited funding, paucity of information about successful projects and a demand for services that exceeds the supply of services. As a result, programming decisions often are made without information about questions such as:

- What areas of consistency exist among successful programs with regard to their philosophy, goals and objectives?
- What types of services, arranged in what order, constitute a viable

Reprinted from *Helping the Homeless: A Resource Guide*, U.S. Department of Health and Human Services, Washington, D.C., 1984.

continuum of services to meet the needs of guests/clients of housing programs?

- What skills, responsibilities and allocations of time define the job of program administrator in successful housing programs?
- What roles do/can volunteers play in effective programs?
- What communication patterns and techniques help define effective shelter programs?
- What organizational/management/administrative structures facilitate program implementation?

The answers to each of these questions hold value for persons who are starting programs as well as for staff of programs that may be interested in modifying or upgrading operations. There seems to be consistency across programs that suggests guidelines for future action. Each of the issues is addressed in turn throughout the remainder of this section.

Philosophy, Goals, and Program Purposes

The explicit goal of each shelter program is the survival of homeless guests in need of the facility's services. Yet neither simple survival nor continuation of the status quo best characterizes the focus of successful programs. Rather, the focus is a belief in the importance of each individual coupled with a determination to provide an opportunity, a stimulus and a support in assisting each homeless person to "take hold" of his or her life and begin to change it.

Programs vary in their determination to change the lives of guests; however, each clearly expresses the philosophy of respecting the dignity of each homeless guest. Most programs use specific procedures to express this concern for the dignity of homeless people. For example, most programs no longer call the homeless persons they serve "clients"; instead, most programs employ the term "guests" and accept the connotations and denotations that accompany the term. In some programs, the Pine Street Inn for example, each guest is regularly addressed by name as "Mr.__" or "Ms.__." Further, staff members routinely try to converse with each guest daily about their day, health, feelings and plans for tomorrow. Other programs, like the St. Louis Salvation Army's Transitional Housing Project , have extended their concern to the development of group counseling and formal peer support groups to encourage additional feelings of self-esteem. Still other programs, like the Committee for Dignity and Fairness, incorporate the philosophy into their name, their charter and all of their descriptive materials.

The program philosophy of treating each individual with respect and dignity underlies and directs the goals and purposes of successful programs. Additionally, a consistent pattern of goals, purposes and missions exists for most programs along with the underlying philosophy. Programs have a clear and definitive sense of mission grounded in the determination to provide services to their client population. Moreover, this mission is translated as a clear and logical pattern of services that establishes program identity for every project.

The sense of mission and identity is not stagnant; rather, it is an evolving identity which adapts as the need for services expands, as the programs grow, and as service providers gain a better understanding of the client population. Consistently, programs begin with an intention to provide for emergency survival needs such as "a hot and cot" for the night. However, over time many programs have come to believe that emergency treatment by itself is simply not sufficient because it does nothing to break the patterns or causes of homelessness. More importantly, many programs have come to believe that emergency services by themselves function to perpetuate the status quo—they do not empower or encourage homeless people to change their lives.

Therefore, many programs have added to their objective of providing emergency services other objectives to provide for more comprehensive services. First the emergency needs such as immediate food and housing are cared for; then services associated with advocacy are provided to stabilize the guests' situation and assist them in overcoming the cause of the homelessness. Finally, training and support services are provided in order to help individuals gain control over their lives and start anew.

Many programs are good examples of this growth. Take for example the Seattle Emergency Housing Services Program. Originally an emergency overnight shelter, program administrators soon came to realize that the needs of their guests extended beyond a bed for a night. They expanded their mission and services to provide not only emergency overnight shelter, but also longer-term transitional housing, advocacy and training services, and outreach services to other programs. Based on these goals, the program provides referral to other agencies, employment assistance, counseling, instruction in life skills and relocation service. The program also offers housing resource programs to improve housing opportunities and to promote self-sufficiency. The thrust is to generate and enable a new start.

Other programs also focus on initiating change. For example, the St. Louis Transitional Housing Project offers many of the opportunities of the Seattle program and adds the opportunity for limited vocational and employability training as well as self-help peer support groups for guests. The clear expectation and goal is self-sufficiency; the individual must participate and make a positive effort to meet the program's requirements and goals.

This individual effort is the last consistent element of goals and missions of successful programs. Increasingly, programs demand "from and of" guests something in the way of effort or contribution. Effort means that the guest makes a positive attempt to begin to resolve his or her problems quickly. For example, at Jessie's House a guest's stay beyond a week is contingent on evidence that the guest is beginning (and continuing) to work to resolve problems. Contribution means giving something back to the program or "investing" in the program. Sometimes this means contributing time and skills to the program operation such as preparing meals, cleaning up, and performing maintenance, as at Jessie's House; sometimes it means providing a partial financial payback such as a nominal apartment rent or utility payment, as in the Seattle Emergency Housing Services or the St. Louis Transitional Housing Projects, respectively. Whatever the contribution, achievement of the goals depends on moving a homeless person toward self-control and personal action.

Continuum of Services

Housing programs basically provide shelter to homeless people. However, relatively few successful programs provide only shelter; rather, many successful programs have grown to expand services to meet a wide range of basic needs for their guests. Typically services provided by many shelters include referral, food, transportation and clothing in addition to shelter. Moreover, a number of shelters recently have expanded their services even beyond these services to offer shelter-based medical services, rehabilitation services, skills training, outreach and prevention services.

Taken together, these efforts to meet guest needs are a continuum of services that reflect logical strategies for achieving the goals and objectives of programs. For purposes of this report, services have been grouped into four categories: (1) basic services; (2) stabilization services; (3) development or growth services; and (4) preventive services. As a continuum, these services include the entire range of assistance and training that logically could enable a homeless person to move back into typical social roles.

Basic services are those services that meet the survival needs of homeless guests. For housing programs, regardless of whether it is emergency, transitional or long-term housing, these basic services include food and shelter. Differences in the way housing services are provided reside in the period of time for services, intake, and the specific program design of the project. For example, emergency shelters tend to serve people on a one-night-at-a-time basis; transitional housing programs tend to offer shelter for six to twelve week periods; long-term housing programs tend to offer shelter indefinitely. Intake differs between emergency housing and the other two types. In general, emergency housing programs serve anyone who presents himself or herself to the program and who abides by the house rules. Transitional and long-term housing programs tend to serve those guests who abide by the rules and who either are referred to them or those guests who pass their screening requirements. Moreover, emergency and long-term housing programs often serve individuals and may be age or gender specific; transitional housing programs may serve families or individuals.

Food services vary across programs on relatively minor points like the number of people served, mealtime, and source of food. These are relatively inconsequential differences. The important points are (1) that food is a basic service of most successful shelter programs and (2) that volunteers often make a major contribution to the food program, either through donating food or through donating time.

Stabilization services grew from the recognition that providing only basic services tended to perpetuate the status quo; by themselves, survival or basic services do not terminate homelessness. Stabilization services begin to build structure, purpose and routine back into the lives of homeless persons by addressing a wider range of problems any homeless person might have. Among the services that perform this stabilization function are: transportation, laundry, showers, clothing, medical care, mental health services, recreation, dependency control, advocacy, and referral. While some of these services, such as clothing (in some seasons) or medical treatment (in some cases), may be more a basic service than a stabilization service, the overall function of the service is to begin to address individual problems of homeless people.

While the exact means of providing stabilization services varies across programs, depending upon program design, most successful programs now offer several of these services directly or through a network arrangement with other agencies or organizations. Each service is an opportunity to meet an individual's needs by adjusting or focusing mechanisms within the existing social service system on the individual need. Referral and advocacy services are especially important in this regard. Each emphasizes getting the system to offer support to homeless individuals in order for the individual to receive those services to which he/she is entitled. Program staff negotiate or help negotiate the system to secure entitlements such as Social Security, veterans benefits, Medicare, Medicaid, public health, Aid to Families with Dependent Children, food stamps and other similar programs whose purpose is to help people straighten out their lives. The limitation of stabilization services is that the emphasis is on manipulating the system for or on behalf of the individual homeless person rather than on providing homeless people with the individual skills they need to end personal causes that contributed to their homeless situation.

Developmental or growth services are an attempt to provide skills and enable individuals to overcome the personal limitations that contributed to their homelessness. A relatively new effort in many programs, developmental services include: assigning guests to a caseworker; providing peer and group counseling, child care, work experience, vocational rehabilitiation and employability and adult functional skill training; assisting guests to find jobs, housing and obtain financial support; and exposing guests (often for the first time) to the concepts of having their own space, engaging in individual contracts and observing house and program rules. Each of these services directly involves homeless people in the effort to gain control of their own lives; each provides the homeless person with skills, attitudes and knowledge necessary to function effectively in the larger society; and each requires the individual to exert personal effort and responsibility for his or her own life and well-being.

Typically, these services begin with the program staff assuming major responsibility for interacting with homeless individuals. However, as the relationship is built and as the homeless person gains skills and self-confidence, more and more of the responsibility for the activity is shifted to the homeless individual. The staff person's role continues to be one of providing training and opportunities, but focuses increasingly on reinforcing, supporting and calling attention to especially pertinent activity for the guest. For example, initially the staff counselor and guest may draw up an individual case plan for the guest in which together they plan the guest's activities for three months. The activities may be focused on acquiring skills, seeking employment, finding housing, and interacting with others. Initially the counselor may have to encourage—even force—the guest to keep his or her commitments; further, the counselor may have to provide (or arrange for) skills training so the guest can carry out the activity. Then, as the guest begins to acquire skills, and reinforce those skills through activity, the counselor may emphasize reinforcing appropriate behavior, shift responsibility to the guest for continued action, and point out to the guest that the guest is, in fact, controlling his or her own life as he/she functions successfully and appropriately in society.

Even as simple a service as providing personal space for individual belongings can help in this process because it calls attention to the fact that each individual is a somebody with belongings and personal space. Moreover, it provides a relatively simple task such as storing and retrieving belongings with which the guest can experience success.

Programs are experiencing notable success by using several of these services. For example, the Seattle Emergency Housing Service, the St. Louis Salvation Army Transitional Housing Project and the Memphis Interfaith Association Project each use some form of housing search and financial assistance services. In each instance, project staff work with the guest and with community agencies to secure a permanent housing location. Then, working with the guest through community organizations, the guest can borrow enough money to pay the security deposit and set up housekeeping. Project staff help to secure the loan and provide training to the guest about how to deal with banks, how to budget money, and how to pay off debts. As the guest learns the skills and pays off the loan, not only does the guest acquire skills and use the money to reestablish him/herself, but also the guest establishes a viable credit history.

Other programs, such as the Catholic Charities Parish Shelter Program, Transition House, and the Committee for Dignity and Fairness have had great success in drawing up individual "behavioral contracts" with guests. Here, a staff counselor works with each guest to set, commit to writing and sign individual goals and specific activities for that guest. Goals and activities teach individual planning skills and place responsibility on the guest to perform. Among typical activities covered in the contract are statements about the contribution the guest will make to the program (for example, hours a week helping with maintenance), the actions the guest will take regarding treatment or skills training (for example, joining and participating in AA), the steps the guest will take toward securing employment or housing, and the timeframe when activities will take place. The counselor or caseworker then meets with the guest every few days to monitor activity, offer assistance and provide encouragement and reinforcement.

The Burnside Community Council, the Pine Street Inn, and the Charles H. Gay Shelter have had success with providing yet another developmental skill, employment experience. In these programs, guest can acquire employment skills and experience by securing paid staff positions with the program. While on the job, they earn a wage as they acquire skills and confidence that can be used in employment settings beyond the program.

The St. Louis Salvation Army Transitional Housing Project has extended the idea of guests assuming responsibility for their own destiny to a peer counseling and support program. Here, guests help each other acquire courage, self-confidence and social skills. Guests draw on each other's experience and ideas to summon courage and develop strategeies to deal with problems that each may be experiencing.

Recently several programs have begun services that can only be described as preventive services. These services differ from developmental services because rather than concentrating on remediating individual causes that contribute to persons being homeless, they work to remove or overcome the societal causes that contribute to homelessness. Among such services are mortgage and low-income energy assistance programs, community education efforts, outreach programs, and family share programs.

For example, the mortgage and low-income energy assistance programs of the St. Louis Salvation Army Transitional Housing Project and the Burnside Community Council head off homelessness by providing temporary relief from two major financial pressures—rent and utilities—that can drive homeowners into foreclosure and homelessness. In addition, each program will provide skills training and/or employment seeking assistance to their client to help them earn and/or manage their money effectively and thus avert the problem in the future.

The Burnside Council, the St. Louis Transitional Housing Project and the Housing Development Support Program of Worcester, Massachusetts take the community education beyond the individual client. They also work in their communities to make businesses, landlords and organizational members more knowledgeable about and aware of their programs' clients and benefits. For example, the Housing Development Program conducts workshops and services where they teach landlords about program clients, program services, and the benefits (such as tax and loan support) that can accrue to the landlord by participating in the program.

The Committee for Dignity and Fairness takes the community education aspect in a different direction by providing outreach to potential guests. With their van, staff members seek out those homeless persons who need the program. They then offer emergency assistance and information about the program. If the guest responds positively, the guest begins to develop a self-help relationship with the program.

Administrator Skills and Time Use

The skills and responsibilities of program administrators are factors that contribute to the development and implementation of successful programs. Adminstrator responsibilities comprise four sets of activities: (1) administrative, (2) client/guest services, (3) community and public relations, and (4) program design. Administrative activities include responsibilities like resolving staffing and personnel issues, preparing and monitoring budgets, collecting data, and making decisions. Responsibilities like providing guest counseling, directing self-help training and offering referral assistance are among client/guest service activities. Seeking funding and resources, working with boards of directors and advisory committees, establishing a niche for the program within the network of community services, and working with the power brokers within the community are among the community and public relations activities and responsibilities. Program design responsibilities include activities like establishing need for the program and for specific services within the program, establishing program goals and objectives, and creating the continuum-of-services design.

The importance of each of the four sets of responsibilities seems to be related to the size and maturity of the program. For example, in smaller and newer programs, administrators seem to provide more direct services to guests than do administrators in larger and more mature programs; conversely, in larger and more mature programs, administrators deal more exclusively with administrative, design and community public relations functions. Further, in very large programs, many administrative functions are delegated to assistants in order to allow the chief administrator to devote full-time to community/public relations and program design activities. Additionally, in smaller and newer programs administrators seem more likely to maintain their residence and/or office at the program site; when this happens, the probability of the administrator providing direct services increases.

A third relationship of program size and maturity to administrator responsibility exists in the area of formalized job description and division of labor. In newer and smaller programs, administrators are less likely to work from formalized job descriptions or to have formal division of labor within the program staff for administrative activities; most often expectations are not institutionalized and personnel function as generalists. Conversely, in more mature and often in larger programs, formal job descriptions reflect high degrees of task specialization.

Given their varied responsibilities, administrators of successful programs exhibit a consistent set of skills and characteristics. These skills include at least the following items:

1. writing and verbal communication skills;
2. community and public relations experience;
3. experience/training in working with the program's guests;
4. organizational skills and experience;
5. staff management skills;
6. fiscal management skills;
7. fundraising skills and experience;
8. social service delivery system experience;
9. program planning skills and training; and
10. board development/management skills.

In terms of characteristics, three items seem to distinguish administrators of successful programs. First, they have a fierce commitment or loyalty to the issue of serving homeless people. Often this is reflected in their willingness to accept large amounts of responsibility as well as in their determination to operate programs with very few resources and comparatively poor individual remuneration for the time and energy they expend. Second, administrators share an ability to recognize the inherent potential opportunities and resources in many situations; more specifically, they seem to be able to spot materials they can restore and use among surplus and discarded products in much the same way that they spot and develop potential among the guests they serve. Third, administrators share a mind-set that enables them to create and implement an image or vision of the future for their program. They have a dream of what the program can look like and what it can accomplish. It serves as a blueprint that provides programmatic direction as it is translated into day-to-day activities. When coupled with an administrator's ability to get maximum return from few resources, this image of the future may be the most distinguishing characteristic of administrators of successful programs.

Role of Volunteers

The majority of successful programs use the time, skills and services of volunteers in one or more of a number of ways. For example, depending upon the specific program design, volunteers prepare meals, furnish facilities and materials, offer referral information, operate commissaries and stores, provide company and assistance, maintain the grounds and building, and serve on policy-making boards. Their roles are limited by the design, location and services provided by the program. For example, a geographically isolated program like New York's Charles H. Gay Shelter or a program that provides highly specialized training like the St. Louis Transitional Housing Project uses few volunteers in the role of providing direct services to guests. However, they do use volunteers to help secure adequate resources for the project.

Perhaps the Pine Street Inn of Boston makes as extensive use of volunteers as any program in the United States. There, volunteers provide services valued at over $2,000,000 per year to the operation of the program. Among the services volunteers provide are: (1) evening meals each night; (2) clothing; (3) furnishings; (4) nursing and health care; (5) guest visitation; (6) information referral; (7) ministry; (8) donation screening and distribution; (9) staff and guest training; and (10) policy suggestions.

Pine Street, like a number of other successful programs, has a fairly formal procedure for involving volunteers. A paid staff person called a volunteer coordinator secures and orchestrates the activities of volunteers in order to derive maximum benefit from their contribution. Often such activities include recruiting and providing general information to potential volunteers, scheduling volunteer time, screening volunteers before their participation to be sure they will "fit" with program needs, providing orientation to volunteers about the program and expectations for their participation, and thanking and recognizing volunteers after their contribution.

Each of these activities is relatively critical to the success of the effort. For example, if the scheduling is not efficient, a program may find volunteers wasting time (and good will) by having too little to do or having skills duplicated on the same afternoon, while at other times no one will be available to help. Similarly, if volunteers are not thanked or their efforts not recognized, then they may not be willing to help in the future. Likewise, if they are not provided an orientation to the program and clients, their efforts may be unfocused. Among the materials and activities that are useful in orientations are discussions of the program's philosophy; coverage of program rules and expectations for guest, staff, and volunteer behavior; directions for providing services; and suggestions about where to turn for assistance.

Programs are consistent in their sources of volunteers. Most are drawn from churches, colleges, civic organizations, and local businesses. Initial contact can come either from the volunteer or from the program. Whichever the source of contact, the critical point seems to be the ability within the program to find a fairly immediate opportunity for the volunteer group or individual to participate. Both the opportunity to serve and the fact of need appear to be substantial stimuli to encourage volunteer efforts.

Just as the need for orientation and recognition and the need for immediacy in offering an opportunity are important considerations in using volunteers, so too is the necessity of realizing that volunteers can not be expected to perform too many tasks or to perform their tasks for too long. Their commitment is that of a volunteer, not that of a professional in a paid staff position.

Communication Patterns

Successful housing programs are characterized by effective communication practices at each of three levels: (1) interaction with and among guests, (2) interaction between the program and the community, and (3) interaction among and between staff. Each level features combinations of formal and informal channels for communication. Further, within each level, interaction is regular and frequent.

Interaction with and among guests is critical to housing program success because it is a tool through which guests gain information, develop self-esteem and begin to exercise control over their lives. Within successful programs, great care and attention is focused on developing these particular patterns of interaction. For example, as mentioned earlier, the Pine Street Inn insists that each guest be welcomed by name each day as "Mr.___" or "Mrs.___" or "Miss___." Further, they train and encourage staff and volunteers to try to spend time each day with each guest talking about how that guest passed the day and his or her plans for tomorrow. The idea is to let the guests know that someone does care; further, it is a subtle way of encouraging guests to think constructively about tomorrow and to begin to gain control of their lives by planning their activities for the next day.

Many programs, including Jessie's House and Transition House, require guests to make a contribution of time and effort in support of the program. Toward that end, such programs hold at least a weekly meeting among staff and guests to discuss work and work suggestions. These meetings also serve as a forum for volunteering for or assigning responsibilities, making announcements, and explaining how to perform certain tasks.

Every successful program has a set of "house rules" or expectations for guest and staff behavior. These rules usually are posted in written form; further, they are the topic of individual and group meetings between guests and staff in most programs. The idea is to establish clear expectations for individual behavior and to help guests understand that they are responsible for and can control both their own behavior and that of other guests. This contributes to positive self-control and self-confidence, as well as developing a sense of responsibility for and about others.

Many programs have regular and frequent interactions between each guest and a service counselor. In some programs like Jessie's House and the Committee for Dignity and Fairness, this interaction must begin within a week of entry into the program or a guest forefeits his or her opportunity to remain with the program. Further, the interaction must continue and show progress as the guest and counselor or case worker work to resolve the guest's problems, to find permanent housing, and to develop self-confidence within the guest.

Lastly, every program tries to stimulate guest-to-guest interaction as well as guest-to-staff interaction. Some programs encourage interaction by providing structured time and facilities like a covered porch or a T.V. common area. Other programs, like the St. Louis Transitional Housing Project, provide a structured task and sometimes a facilitator to stimulate interaction. In the St. Louis program, peer support, peer counseling and some skill training take place in such groups. The peer support program is especially noteworthy in that it enables guests to share their triumphs and concerns with others going through the same process as they move to permanent housing, seek and find employment and reestablish control over their lives.

The communication efforts within programs seem to focus on establishing or stimulating three outcomes among clients. First, the programs seem to concentrate on overcoming the poverty and type of relationships that typically are associated with homelessness. Communication helps stabilize the guest and establish a lasting and trusting relationship between the guest and staff or other guests. Second, communication efforts seem to concentrate on providing an opportunity for guests to learn and practice interaction and self-help skills and thus become more confident in their ability to carry on similar interaction on their own. Third, communication efforts focus on demonstrating that interaction is a very effective tool for controlling one's own life and for establishing expectations with others.

The second level of interaction occurs between the program and the community. Here again, the main purpose of interaction between the program and the community seems to be to establish program stability. It is to the program's benefit to ensure that the community knows not only what the program needs, but also that the program can be counted on in the long-term for providing certain services or meeting certain needs.

Within most programs, communication with the community can be characterized as frequent, intentional, purposive and informal. It is frequent in that most programs recognize that community support—both good will and resources—often depends on informing the community about program services and successes as well as describing program needs and the opportunities for service. In large and more mature programs, administrators often spend the majority of their time each day involved in such contacts. Likewise, contacts initiated by the volunteer coordinator occur every day as he/she orchestrates volunteer efforts, arranges schedules and thanks volunteers for their contributions.

Typical community contacts also are intentional and purposive. Whether initiated by the program or the community, usually there is a very specific purpose for the contact. Often, if the contact is from the community, the purpose is to offer assistance or to discuss the program. If contact is initiated by the program, the reasons for the communication are varied, but usually fall within one of five categories:

1. educating/informing community organizations about the program and/or guest population;
2. explaining how the program services and supports various community groups and efforts;
3. offering an opportunity for service to the program;
4. asking for assistance or resources as well as explaining program needs; and
5. expressing appreciation for prior assistance provided to the program.

Sometimes the contacts will be with individuals and other times it will be through the media.

Most community contacts are informal. Formal contacts seem to be reserved for important but less frequent occurrences like preparing proposals and zoning petitions or appeals, and for recruiting members for the board of directors. Board membership is a particularly important contact because it involves community members directly in making program policy and because it generates many contacts for the program.

Of particular importance are community contacts that (1) offer members of the community an opportunity to serve, and (2) that explain the value of the program for the community itself. For example, the SRO Housing Programs of Portland and Los Angeles have developed business education programs that demonstrate the economic and social returns of their programs to the business community as a strategy for developing direct support for these programs. Returns are noted in terms of increases in property values and business sales as well as decreases in the need for current and additional tax dollars.

Communication with staff is a third important communication area. Successful programs are characterized by regular and frequent, formal and informal interaction among staff and between staff and administrators. Most programs hold at least one weekly staff meeting to conduct business. Many hold a brief meeting each day at the beginning of each shift. Further, most programs have frequent informal and social contact among staff throughout any given day or week.

Organizational, Management, and Administrative Structures

Successful programs created to serve homeless people share similar organizational, management, and administrative schemes in the areas of corporate structure; administrative structure; reporting procedures; orientation and training efforts; and staffing patterns. For example, in terms of corporate structure, most successful programs are organized as formal, nonprofit corporations. They have charters and/or articles of incorporation, by-laws and boards of directors that represent the community. Further, they have applied or are qualified for Federal, state and local tax-exempt status.

Successful housing programs also are similar in terms of administrative structure in that the programs have a formal structure; that is, programs have carefully drawn lines of authority, responsibility and behavioral expectations. In most cases, lines of authority are set forth in organizational charts that indicate the relative position, authority and accountability of each administrative and staff job within the organization. Even more important, most housing programs also have formulated job descriptions for administrative and staff positions. These job descriptions typically indicate the expected qualifications of the staff member together with a list of tasks that the worker must perform. Some job descriptions even include statements of expected outcomes or standards of performance for each position. Further, many programs expand on the organizational chart and job description with a procedures manual that explains in detail the behavioral expectations for staff and administrative positions.

Perhaps the most comprehensive example of this formal structure is the Procedures Manual of the Burnside Consortium. The document not only describes the program, but locates each staff and administrative position within the program in terms of its relationship with other positions, its responsibility and its authority. Further, the manual explains, through example and description, exactly what actions (and reactions) are expected of staff and administrators in a wide array of situations. The SRO Housing Corporation plans to develop a similar manual reflecting differences in tenant-landlord law, code enforcement practices, social service provision policy and other areas.

Reporting procedures is a third area of organizational similarity among successful housing programs. Most programs collect information about the guests they serve, the services they provide and the resources they use. This information falls into three categories: (1) planning information; (2) activity information; and (3) outcomes information. The planning information usually is needs-assessment data about who and how many people need services, what services are available, and how a particular program's services will meet the need. Activity information is routinely collected by resources. Among the information collected in this phase of activity are accounts of donations or contributions received, records of expenditures, indications of time spent on tasks by staff, and counts of homeless people and their characteristics as served in each aspect of the program. This information is used both for tax accounting and for examining operating efficiency.

Outcomes information is critical supporting evidence for continued or expanded funding and operations. Successful programs routinely collect and generate information like the cost per bed per night of operation; the number of guests who acquire skills, secure permanent housing, and find jobs; and the cost efficiency of selected program services.

The need for planning and accountability data is recognized as so essential to many successful programs that they even commission evaluation studies to examine effectiveness. For example, the St. Louis Salvation Army Transitional Housing Project has undertaken a three-year study to examine, document and improve program effectiveness. The study traces a group of guests through program services and into a year-long follow-up after they have begun to live on their own. The findings not only demonstrate the effectiveness of the program, but also indicate areas for program revision that could make it even more effective.

Successful programs have orientation and training programs for new staff and volunteers. Typically, such training provides an overview of program facilities and services, plus information about other services in the community and how to refer guests to the services; an explanation of typical guest needs; and both explanation and practice in carrying out expected procedures. Duration of training ranges from eight to 40 hours depending on program and job complexity. Further, many programs, such as The House of Ruth, supplement initial training with a regular series of staff development workshops and seminars on topics of continuing interest including new treatment strategies, communication skills, and self-defense.

Training and orientation are especially important for volunteers because the degree to which volunteers understand expectations is directly proportional to how well they do their job and how long they remain committed to the program.

Staffing is the last area of organizational structure in which successful programs are very similar. Successful programs often have differentiated staffing, especially in larger and more mature programs. That is, staff have special areas for which they alone are responsible. For example, many programs have a property manager who is responsible for maintaining all program facilities. Likewise, most programs have a formally designated volunteer coordinator who organizes, orchestrates and thanks volunteers for their efforts. Moreover, all successful programs have counselors or case-workers who work directly with guests to provide stabilization, development, and preventive services.

The specialized staff services usually require personnel with formal specialized training. Many programs also have some general staff positions that require training, but not formal training or certification. Often these paid and sometimes live-in positions are filled by former guests who now are functioning again in the mainstream of society. Often they are interim or training positions for moving on to other jobs. Almost always such positions provide both role models for other homeless persons as well as staff who have great sympathy for the guests' situations.

Resource Development

Facilities, funding, staff, supplies, services—the interplay of these resources determines the scope and breadth of housing programs. Most housing programs start with the recognition that the needs and numbers of homeless people are great; that it is virtually impossible to serve all of the needs of all of the homeless in their localities; and that, due to the nature of housing programs, some capital investment for facilities, staffing and/or supplies most likely will be required. Therefore, in the planning stages of most housing programs, decisions are made regarding the population to be served, the types of services to be provided and the amount of capital and personnel investment required to start the program.

The amount of pre-planning among programs varies greatly. Whereas some programs start rather spontaneously with limited resources and less planning, others take the time to assess and evaluate program needs, making a long-term commitment to program implementation. Some programs begin their activities in hopes that eventually the program will be taken over by the public sector, while others start with the purpose of coordinating and taking over public sector services. Other programs are designed as private, nonprofit ongoing corporations.

Regardless of these differences, all programs ultimately tap the same types of sources and use similar approaches for obtaining resources. The sources include private individuals, community groups and institutions. Private sources of funding and supplies include private donations of facilities, money, time and supplies by individuals, churches, businesses, civic groups and charitable organizations, as well as money obtained through grant applications to private foundations. Public sources, which supply grants of money and facilities and supplies (foodstuffs), as well as services, consist of local, state and Federal agencies including: local tax increment funds; state and Federal block grants; U.S. Departments of Defense, Agriculture, Housing and Urban Development goods, facilities, and supplies; and Federal Emergency Management Agency (FEMA) monies.

Approaches to Resource Development

Most programs start with private monies obtained through donations and grants and the hard work and dedication of their founders. However, as they become established, they all seek to obtain local, state and/or Federal support. The majority of programs receive partial funding and/or support from the public sector.

In spite of the fact that programs approach different groups, they all face the task of educating people about the homeless and asking for all types of assistance. While the larger programs, sponsored by the Salvation Army and Catholic Charities, do not face the same fundraising requirements (many aspects of their housing programs are self-financed) that groups like the Committee for Fairness and Dignity face, most programs start with at least six months of seed money. Many programs have evolved in a way that they now require guests to contribute in some way to the well-being of the program. These contributions are usually in the form of volunteer services to the running of the organization.

As programs become more established they begin to seek public monies. It is generally agreed that it takes more time and effort to obtain these monies and requires a great deal of planning and administrative time. Nevertheless, once programs obtain public sector support, they become more stable and resource development activities become more routine. Rather than constantly searching for new funding sources, they are able to focus on maintaining the ones they have while working to improve the quality of the program. Some of the specific approaches used by different programs are discussed next.

Individuals

Individuals generally are approached for contributions of time, money, food and clothing. They are asked to participate in fundraising telethons and walkathons and are usually tapped by a sponsoring organization to which they belong. One example is Jessie's House, which uses approximately 400 hours per month of volunteer time to run its program. Volunteers are recruited from local colleges and church groups. Another example is The House of Ruth, which has hired a volunteer coordinator who trains 30 volunteers to work on a regular basis. Volunteers are recruited from the local volunteer clearinghouse, the Junior League, and local colleges.

Group Sponsorship

Many programs contact churches and civic groups to sponsor fundraising or donation activities for them. These organizations then use their resources to obtain community support for the program. Activities include drives for food, clothing, furniture, and other supplies needed by the program, as well as fundraising drives.

For example, the Memphis Interfaith Association uses local church groups to provide sponsorship for the houses in their program. At the Pine Street Inn, the evening meals are donated and served every night by members of different churches.

Business Donations

Donations of money are the most common contributions made by local businesses. Many businesses have funds set aside for community projects and are generally interested in supporting programs for housing the homeless. Depending on the type of business, supplies are also donated. In addition, local businesses support housing programs through provision of actual locations for rent. For instance, the Housing Development Support Program works closely with landlords and real estate associations to obtain apartments for their clients. The SRO Housing Corporation, a membership organization that includes business/community organizations and individuals, draws upon its members to provide technical assistance, support and resources.

Foundations and Charities

Local and national foundations and charities are another source of financial support for programs. Grant applications are made according to individual funding cycles. The Seattle Emergency Services Program and Jessie's House receive a portion of their funding from the United Way. The House of Ruth also receives partial funding from D.C.-based foundations.

State and Local Assistance

Many programs obtain funding from state and local government through block grants and matching funds. For example, the Pine Street Inn receives $2 million per year (half of its operating costs) from the Commonwealth of Massachusetts. The Charles H. Gay Shelter, run by Volunteers of America, is totally funded by the City of New York.

Federal Assistance

Most programs initially stay away from Federal programs because of a fear of red tape. However, programs do access Federal monies and support through the Section 8 housing subsidies, by leasing HUD-owned houses, and through applying for grants. The houses used in the Memphis Interfaith Program, for example, are leased from the U.S. Department of Housing and Urban Development, while surplus food from the U.S. Department of Agriculture is used by the Transition House in Los Angeles.

As mentioned earlier, many programs obtain in-kind contributions from guests who are required to help with the running of the program. Several programs have taken this concept a step further and actually generate additional revenue. Note the Seattle Emergency Housing Service Program, which requires families to pay a minimal amount of rent while they search for permanent housing. This money helps to defray program costs.

Guests at the Burnside Consortium also contribute to the program's continuation by collecting cans, bottles and newspapers which are recycled. Part of the money goes to the guest and part to the program.

By obtaining their own facilities (or having private groups purchase them) and taking advantage of creative financing, programs have been able to maintain, and in some cases expand, program activities. The housing program of the Burnside Consortium in Portland, Oregon provides a good example. There, staff obtained partial financing through the Historic Preservation Fund to purchase one of its buildings. The SRO Housing Corporation in Los Angeles, building on the Portland experience, also is exploring innovative financing. The facility used by Jessie's House was donated by a private citizen. The Skid Row Development Corporation purchased and renovated an old warehouse for its transitional housing program. Many of the houses used in the Seattle Emergency Housing Service Program were donated by local churches. Although the churches maintain ownership, property management is the responsibility of the program.

31

Summary of Major Federal Programs Assisting the Homeless

U.S. General Accounting Office

Agency	Service/Activity or Program	Objectives/ Accomplishments	Funds Budgeted for the Homeless
Federal Emergency Management Agency (FEMA)	To provide funding for emergency food and shelter	Funds provided to all states and over 3,650 voluntary organizations.	$140 million appropriated through November 1983. An additional $70 million appropriated in August 1984 extending the program through fiscal year 1985.
Department of Housing and Urban Development (HUD)	Community Development Block Grant (CDBG)	Facilitating provision of shelters.	In January 1985 HUD reported that $53 million in CDBG funds had been spent over the past 2 years to help the homeless.

Reprinted from *Homelessness: A Complex Problem and the Federal Response*, U.S. General Accounting Office, Washington, D.C., 1985.

Agency	Service/Activity or Program	Objectives/ Accomplishments	Funds Budgeted for the Homeless
Department of Defense (DOD)	Renovate Facilities on Military Installations for Shelter	$900,000 of the 1984 appropriation was obligated to make renovations for two shelters; an additional four shelters have been opened at DOD facilities using local community and base funds.	In fiscal year 1984 $8 million was made available; $900,000 was obligated. In fiscal year 1985 $500,000 was budgeted; DOD has reported that it will spend whatever is necessary above that amount, if needed for shelter renovations.
Department of Health and Human Services (HHS)	Federal Interagency Task Force	Broker with public sector to make facilities or other resources available for the homeless.	No funds specifically appropriated.
	Social Security Outreach Program	Outreach program in New York City with regional HHS staff and city officials to help individuals in shelters obtain HHS benefits; in October 1984, program offered in other communities.	No funds specifically appropriated.

Agency	Service/Activity or Program	Objectives/ Accomplishments	Funds Budgeted for the Homeless
Department of Health and Human Services (HHS) (continued)	Model Shelter	In November 1984 HHS agreed to help renovate a building in Washington, D.C., for use as an 800- to 1,000- bed model shelter.	Up to $5 million to be spent over 3 years.
	Community Services Block Grant (CSBG)	Funds can be used for a range of antipoverty programs, including emergency food and shelter.	
	Social Services Block Grant	Can provide funds for counseling programs for the homeless.	Total funds spent for the homeless from these three block grants cannot be identified. HHS reported that $65 million of fiscal year 1983 CSBG funds were budgeted for emergency service which could include efforts to help the homeless.
	Alcohol, Drug Abuse, and Mental Health Block Grant	Can provide funds for community mental health centers and other community-based mental health services to all persons, including the homeless.	

Agency	Service/ Activity or Program	Objectives/ Accomplishments	Funds Budgeted for the Homeless
Veteran's Administration (VA)	Outreach Program	To visit shelters in New York City to identify and accept applications from homeless veterans for VA disability benefits. VA is considering expanding this program to other cities.	Unknown
ACTION	VISTA (Volunteers in Service to America)	By the end of 1984, 194 volunteers were working on 42 projects for the homeless.	Unknown
Department of Agriculture (USDA)	Food Stamps; Surplus Commodities	Food Stamps available to the homeless. No fixed length-of-time-in-residence requirement. Surplus food made available to nonprofit institutions, including soup kitchens and shelters.	Unknown

Bibliography

Adams, G.R. "Runaway Youth Projects: Comments on Care Programs for Runaways and Throwaways," *Journal of Adolescence*, vol. 3 (December 1980), 321-324.

Alter, Jonathan, et al. "Homeless in America," *Newsweek* (January 2, 1984) 20-29.

Anderson, Nels. *The Hobo: The Sociology of the Homeless Man* (Chicago: University of Chicago Press, 1923).

———. *Men on the Move* (Chicago: University of Chicago Press, 1940).

Bahr, Howard M. "The Gradual Disappearance of Skid Row," *Social Problems*, vol. 15 (Summer 1967) 41-45.

———. *Homelessness and Disaffiliation* (New York: Columbia University Press, 1969).

———. *Disaffiliated Man: Essays and Bibliography on Skid Row, Vagrancy and Outsiders* (Toronto: University of Toronto Press, 1970).

———. *Skid Row: An Introduction to Disaffiliation* (New York: Oxford University Press, 1973).

——— and Garrett, Gerald. "Women on Skid Row," *Quarterly Journal of Studies on Alcohol*, vol. 34 (1973) 1228-1245.

———. *Women Alone: The Disaffiliation of Urban Females* (Lexington, MA: D.C. Heath, 1976).

Baker, Patricia and Ferrer, Barbara. *Down and Out: A Manual on Basic Rights and Benefits for the Homeless in Massachusetts* (Boston: Massachusetts Law Reform Institute and the Coalition for the Homeless, 1984).

Baldwin, Susan. "Salvaging SRO Housing," *City Limits* (April 1978).

Bassuk, Ellen. "The Homelessness Problem," *Scientific American*, vol. 251 (1984) 40-45.

Baxter, Ellen L. "Troubled on the Streets: The Mentally Disabled Homeless Poor," in John Talbott (ed.), *The Chronic Mental Patient: Five Years Later* (New York: Grune and Stratton, 1984).

———, and Hopper, Kim. *Private Lives/Public Spaces* (New York: Community Service Society, 1981).

———. "The New Mendicancy: Homeless in New York City," *American Journal of Orthopsychiatry*, vol. 52 (July 1982) 393-408.

Bedinarzik, Robert, "Lay-offs and Permanent Job Losses: Worker's Traits and Cyclical Patterns," *Monthly Labor Review* (September 1983) 3-11.

Beller, Janet. *Street People* (New York: Macmillan, 1980).

Benalcazar, B. "Study of Fifteen Runaway Patients," *Adolescence*, vol. 17 (1982) 553-566.

Bendiner, Elmer. *The Bowery Man* (New York: Thomas Nelson, 1961).

Birkenshaw, P. "Homelessness and the Law—The Effects of Legislation," *Urban Law and Policy*, vol. 5 (1982) 255-295.

Blumberg, Leonard. "The Skid Row Man and the Skid Row Status Community," *Quarterly Journal of Studies on Alcohol*, vol. 32 (1971) 909-941.

———— et al. *Skid Row and Its Alternatives* (Philadelphia: Temple University Press, 1973).

————. *Liquor and Poverty: Skid Row as a Human Condition* (New Brunswick, NJ: Rutgers Center of Alcohol Studies, 1978).

Bogue, Donald. *Skid Row in American Cities* (Chicago: University of Chicago Press, 1963).

————. "A Theory of Why Skid Row Exists," in R.A. Decritler (ed.), *Major American Social Problems* (Chicago: Rand-McNally, 1967).

Brantley, Carlotta. *New York City's Services to Homeless Families: A Report to the Mayor* (New York: Health and Hospitals Corporation, 1983).

Bruns, Roger. *Knights of the Road* (New York: Methuen, 1980).

————. "Hobo," *American History* (January 1982).

Buff, D.; Kenney, J.; and Light, D. "Health Problems of Residents in Single-Room Occupancy Hotels," *New York State Journal of Medicine*, vol. 80 (December 1980) 2000-2005.

Chaze, William L. "Street People: Adrift and Alone in America," *U.S. News and World Report*, March 8, 1982.

Citizens' Committee for Children. *No One's in Charge: Homeless Families with Children in Temporary Shelter* (New York, 1983).

————. *7000 Homeless Children: The Crisis Continues* (New York, 1984).

———— and Coalition for the Homeless. *Homeless Youth in New York City: Nowhere to Turn* (New York, 1983).

City of Chicago. *The Homeless Man on Skid Row* (Chicago: Tenant Relocation Bureau, 1961).

————. Report of the Mayor's Task Force on the Homeless (Chicago, 1984).

Coalition for the Homeless. *Cruel Brinksmanship: Planning for the Homeless—1983* (New York, August 1982).

————. *Single Room Occupancy Hotels: Standing in the Way of the Gentry* (New York, March 1985).

Cohen, Carl I. and Sokolovsky, Jay. "Toward a Concept of Homelessness Among Aged Men," *Journal of Gerontology*, vol. 38 (1983) 81-89.

Coleman, John. "Diary of a Homeless Man," *New York*, vol. 16 (February 21, 1983) 26-35.

Collier, Barney. "Down and Out in the Bowery: How it Feels," *New York*, May 12, 1969.

Collin, R.W. "Homelessness: The Policy and the Law," *Urban Lawyer*, vol. 16 (1984), 317-329.

Crystal, Stephen. "Homeless Men and Homeless Women: The Gender Gap," *Urban and Social Change Review*, vol. 17 (Summer 1984) 2-6.

_____ et al. *Chronic and Situational Dependency: Long-Term Residents in a Shelter for Men* (New York: New York City Human Resources Administration, 1982).

Cuomo, Mario. *1933/1983: Never Again. A Report to the National Governors' Association Task Force on the Homeless* (Albany, NY: State of New York, 1983).

Dunham, H. Warren. *Homeless Men and Their Habitats* (Detroit: Wayne State University, 1953).

Fabricant, Michael and Epstein, Irwin. "Legal and Welfare Rights Advocacy: Complementary Approaches in Organizing on Behalf of the Homeless," *Urban and Social Change Review*, vol. 17 (Winter 1984) 15-20.

Friedman, E. "On the Street: Hospitals Wrestle with the Problem of Homeless Patients," *Hospitals*, vol. 57 (August 16, 1984) 97-98, 102, 105.

Hacker, Andrew. "The Lower Depths," *New York Review of Books*, vol. 29 (August 12, 1982) 15-20.

Hackman, Theodore G. *Homeless Youth in New York City: A Field Study* (New York: Community Service Society, 1977).

Hartman, Chester (ed.). *America's Housing Crisis: What is to be Done* (Boston: Rutledge & Kegan Paul, 1983).

Hoch, Charles and Cibulskis, Ann. "Planning for the Homeless," a paper to the 1985 Conference of the American Planning Association in Montreal, Canada.

Hombs, Mary Ellen and Snyder, Mitch. *Homelessness in America: A Forced March to Nowhere* (Washington, D.C.: Community for Creative Non-Violence, 1982).

_____. *Homelessness in America: One Year Later* (Washington, D.C.: Community for Creative Non-Violence, 1983).

Hopper, Kim. "Homelessness: Reducing the Distance," *New England Journal of Human Services* (Fall 1983) 30-47.

_____. "Whose Lives Are These Anyway," *Urban and Social Change Review*, vol. 17 (Summer, 1984) 12-13.

_____, and Cox, Stuart. "Litigation in Advocacy for the Homeless: The Case of New York City," *Development: Seeds of Change*, vol. 2 (1982) 57-62.

_____, and Baxter, Ellen. *Not Making It Crazy: Some Remarks on the Young*

Homeless Patients in New York City (New York: Community Service Society, 1981).

_____, and Klein, Lawrence. *One Year Later: The Homeless Poor in New York City 1982* (New York: Community Service Society, 1982).

Hopper, Kim, and Hamberg, Jill. *The Making of America's Homeless: From Skid Row to New Poor 1945-1984* (New York: Community Service Society, 1984).

Hope, Marjorie and Young, James. "From Back Wards to Back Alleys: Deinstitutionalization and the Homeless," *Urban and Social Change Review*, vol. 17 (Summer 1984), 7-11.

_____. "The Politics of Displacement: Sinking into Homelessness," *Commonweal*, vol. 3 (June 15, 1984) 368-371.

Hospital and Community Psychiatry, vol. 39 (1984). (Special Issue devoted to homelessness).

Kasinitz, Philip. "Gentrification and Homelessness: The Single Room Occupant and the Inner City Revival," *Urban and Social Change Review*, vol. 17 (Winter 1984) 9-14.

Kaufman, Nancy. "Homelessness: A Comprehensive Policy Approach," *Urban and Social Change Review*, vol. 17 (Winter 1984) 21-26.

_____, and Harris, Janet. *Profile of the Homeless in Massachusetts* (Boston: Governor's Office of Human Resources, 1983).

Lamb, H. Richard (ed.), *The Homeless Mentally Ill* (Washington, D.C.: American Psychiatric Association, 1984).

Leepson, Marc. "The Homeless: A Growing National Problem," *Editorial Research Reports* (October 29, 1982) 795-812.

Lipton, F.; Sabtini, A; and Katz, R. "Down and Out in the City: The Homeless Mentally Ill," *Hospital and Community Psychiatry*, vol. 34 (November 1983).

Los Angeles Catholic Worker. *Homeless Report: Strategy for Survival*, February 1984.

McGerigle, Paul and Lauriat, Alison. *More Than Shelter: A Community Response to Homelessness* (Boston: United Community Planning and Massachusetts Association for Mental Health, 1984).

McSheehy, W. *Skid Row* (Cambridge, MA: Shenkman, 1979).

Main, Thomas J. "The Homeless of New York," *The Public Interest*, vol. 72 (Summer 1983) 3-28.

Maitra, A.K. "Dealing with the Disadvantaged—Single Homeless: Are We Doing Enough?" Public Health, vol. 96 (May 1982) 141-144.

Majority Report, vol. 4 (October 17, 1974). (Special Issue devoted to homelessness).

Malone, Mark. "Homelessness in a Modern Urban Setting," *Fordham Urban Law Journal*, vol. 10 (Fall 1981) 749-841.

Maurer, Harry. *Not Working* (New York: Holt, Rinehart and Winston, 1979).

Miller, Ronald. *The Demolition of Skid Row* (Lexington, MA: Lexington Books, 1982).

Mort, Geoffrey. "Establishing A Right to Shelter for the Homeless," *Brooklyn Law Review*, vol. 50 (1984) 944-994.

Murray, Harry. "Time in the Streets," *Human Organization*, vol. 43 (Summer 1984) 154-161.

Nash, George. *The Habitats of Homeless Men in Manhattan* (New York: Columbia University, Bureau of Applied Social Research, 1964).

National Coalition for the Homeless. *Downward Spiral: The Homeless in New Jersey* (New York, 1983).

_____. *The Homeless and the Economic Recovery* (New York, 1983).

_____. *The Homeless and the Economic Recovery: One Year Later* (New York, 1984).

Nelson, Marcia Z. "Street People," *Progressive*, vol. 49 (March 1984) 24-29.

New Jersey. Report of the Governor's Task Force on the Homeless (Trenton, NJ: Department of Human Services, October 7, 1983).

New York City. City Council. Office of the President. *Fron Country Asylums to City Streets: The Contradictions Between Deinstitutionalization and State Mental Health Funding Priorities* (New York: Office of the President of the City Council, June 1979).

New York City. Human Resources Administration. *Deinstitutionalization and the Mentally Ill* (New York: Human Resources Administration, Bureau of Management Systems, 1982).

_____. *New York City Plan for Homeless Adults* (New York: Human Resources Administration, April 1984).

New York City. Office of the Comptroller. *Report on the Problems of and Services Available to the Homeless in New York City* (New York: Office of the Comptroller, 1982).

_____. *Soldiers of Misfortune: Homeless Veterans in New York City* (New York: Office of the Comptroller, November 11, 1982).

New York State. Department of Social Services. *Homeless Housing and Assistance Program: Report to the Governor and the Legislature*, 1983-1984 Final Report (Albany, NY: Department of Social Services, July, 1984).

_____. *Homelessness in New York State: A Report to the Governor and the Legislature* (Albany, NY: Department of Social Services, October, 1984).

New York State. Legislative Commission on Expenditure Review. *Runaway and Homeless Youth* (Albany, NY: Legislative Commission on Expenditure Review, July 1981).

New York State. Legislature. Assembly. Committee on Mental Health. *From* the Back Wards to the Back Alleys: A Report on Community Mental Health Care in New York State (Albany, New York: Committee on Mental Health, 1978).

New York State. Legislature. Senate. Mental Hygiene and Addiction Control Committee. Single Room Occupancy Hotels: A Dead End in the Human Services Delivery System (Albany, NY: Committee on Mental Hygiene, January 1980).

New York State. Office of Mental Health. Who Are the Homeless? (New York: Office of Mental Health, May 1982).

Orwell, George. Down and Out in Paris and London (New York: Harcourt, Brace and Co., 1950).

Patterson, Kenneth J., "Shelters and Statistics: A New Face to An Old Problem," Urban and Social Change Review, vol. 17 (Summer 1984), 14-17.

Paul, Brad. Rehabilitating Residential Hotels (Washington, D.C.: National Trust for Historic Preservation, 1981).

Phillips, Michael H.; Kronenfeld, Daniel; and Jeter, Verona. "A Model of Services to Homeless Families in Shelters," a paper presented at the 1985 Annual Conference of the American Orthopsychiatric Association.

Reich, Robert and Siegel, Lloyd. "The Emergence of the Bowery as a Psychiatric Dumping Ground," Psychiatric Quarterly, vol. 50 (Fall 1978) 191-201.

Rhoden, N.K. "The Limits of Liberty: Deinstitutionalization, Homelessness, and Libertarian Theory," Emory Law Journal, vol. 31 (1982) 375-440.

Ribton-Turner, C.J. A History of Vagrants and Vagrancy (Montclair, N.J: Patterson-Smith, 1972).

Roberts, A.R. "Adolescent Runaways in Suburbia: A New Typology," Adolescence, vol. 17 (Summer 1982) 387-396.

Robinson, Gail. "The Squatters, Desperate for Housing, Homeless People Are Risking Arrest to Occupy Abandoned Buildings," Environmental Action, vol. 24 (September 1982) 15-17.

Rooney, James F. "Organizational Success Through Program Failure: Skid Row Rescue Mission," Social Forces, vol. 58 (March 1980) 904-924.

Rousseau, Ann Marie. Shopping Bag Ladies: Homeless Women Speak About Their Lives (New York: Pilgrim Press, 1982).

Ryan, P.E. Migration and Social Welfare (New York: Russell Sage Foundation, 1940).

Salerno, Dan; Hopper, Kim; and Baxter, Ellen. Hardship in the Heartland: Homelessness in Eight U.S. Cities (New York: Community Services Society, 1984).

Sanjek, Roger. Federal Housing Programs and Their Impact on Homelessness (New York: Coalition for the Homeless, 1982).

Schneider, John C. "Skid Row as an Urban Neighborhood, 1880-1960," *Urbanism Past and Present*, vol. 9 (Winter/Spring 1984) 10-19.

Schoonmaker, Mary Ellen. "Hope for the Homeless," *Progressive*, vol. 46 (December 1982) 20-21.

Scully, Michael. "The Bombayization of New York," *National Review*, vol. 35 (August 19, 1983) 1020.

Segal, Steven and Specht, Harry. "A Poorhouse in California, 1983: Oddity or Prelude?" *Social Work*, vol. 28 (July 1983) 319-323.

Seldon, Paul and Jones, Margot. *Moving On: Making Room for the Homeless* (New York, United Church of Christ, 1982).

Sexton, Patricia Cayo. "The Life of the Homeless," *Dissent*, vol. 30 (Winter 1983) 79-84.

Simpson, John and Kilduff, Margaret. *Homelessness in Newark: A Report on the Trailer People* (Newark: Newark Committee on the Homeless, 1984).

Siegal, Harvey A. *Outposts of the Forgotten* (New Brunswick, NJ: Transaction Books, 1978).

_____ and Inciardi, James A. "The Demise of Skid Row," *Society*, vol. 19 (January-February 1982) 39-45.

Slavinsky, A.T. and Cousins, A. "Homeless Women," *Nursing Outlook*, vol. 30 (June 1982) 358-362.

Sloss, Michael. "The Crisis of Homelessness: Its Dimensions and Solutions," *Urban and Social Change Review*, vol. 17 (Summer 1984), 18-20.

Stern, Mark. "The Emergence of the Homeless as a Public Problem," *Social Service Review*, vol. 58 (June 1984) 291-301.

Stoil, Julie. "Women on the Street," *Working Women*, vol. 8 (April 1983) 84.

Stoner, Madeleine. "The Plight of Homeless Women," *Social Service Review*, vol. 57 (December 1983) 565-581.

_____. "An Analysis of Public and Private Sector Provisions for Homeless People," *Urban and Social Change Review*, vol. 17 (Winter, 1984).

Task Force on Emergency Shelter. *Homelessness in Chicago* (Chicago, October 1983).

United States Conference of Mayors. *Homelessness in America's Cities: Ten ·Case Studies* (Washington, D.C.: June 1984).

United States. Congress. House. Committee on Banking, Finance and Urban Affairs, Subcommittee on Housing and Community Development, *Hearing on Shelter for the Homeless* (Washington, D.C.: U.S. Government Printing Office, December 1982).

_____. *Hearing on Homeless in America* (Washington, D.C.: U.S. Government Printing Office, January 1984).

_____. *Homelessness in America II* (Washington, D.C.: U.S. Government Printing Office, 1984).

———. *HUD Report on Homelessness* (Washington, D.C.: U.S. Government Printing Office, May 24, 1984).

United States. Congress. House. Select Committee on Aging. Subcommittee on Housing and Consumer Interest. *Homeless Older Americans* (Washington, D.C.: U.S. Government Printing Office, May 2, 1984).

United States. Congress. Senate. Committee on Appropriations. *Street People: Hearing*, 98th Congress, 1st session, January 24, 1983 (Washington, D.C.: U.S. Government Printing Office, 1983).

United States. Congress. Senate. Committee on the Judiciary. *Homeless Youth: The Saga of "Pushouts" and "Throwaways" in America*. Committee Print, 96th Congress, 2nd session, December 1980 (Washington, D.C.: U.S. Government Printing Office, 1980).

———. *Problems of the Runaway Youth: Hearing*, 97th Congress, 2nd Session, July 22, 1982 (Washington, D.C.: U.S. Government Printing Office, 1982).

United States. Congress. Senate. Special Committee on Aging. *Single Room Occupancy: A Need for National Concern*. Committee Print, 95th Congress, 2nd Session, June 1978 (Washington, D.C.: U.S. Government Printing Office, 1978).

United States Department of Health and Human Services. *Helping the Homeless: A Resource Guide* (Washington, D.C.: U.S. Government Printing Office, Summer 1984).

United States Department of Housing and Urban Development. *A Report to the Secretary on the Homeless and Emergency Shelters* (Washington, D.C.: U.S. Government Printing Office, 1984).

United States General Accounting Office. *Homelessness: A Complex Problem and the Federal Response* (Washington, D.C.: U.S. Government Printing Office, April 9, 1985).

Wallace, S.E. *Skid Row as a Way of Life* (Totowa, NJ: Bedminster Press, 1965).

Walsh, Brendan and Davenport, D. *The Long Loneliness in Baltimore: A Study of Homeless Women* (Baltimore, 1981).

Werner, Frances. "On the Streets: A Look at Homelessness and What is Being Done About It." *Housing Law Bulletin*, vol. 13 (September-October 1983), 1-6.

———. "Homelessness: A Litigation Roundup," *Housing Law Bulletin*, vol. 14 (November-December, 1984) 1-14.

Winograd, Kenneth. *Street People and Other Homeless — A Pittsburgh Study* (Pittsburgh: Emergency Shelter Task Force, 1983).

"Women Who Died in a Box," *Hastings Center Report*, vol. 12 (June 1982) 18-19.

Young, Randy. "The Homeless: Shame of the City," *New York*, vol. 14 (December 21, 1981) 26-32.

Index

CPSIA information can be obtained at www.ICGtesting.com
Printed in the USA
BVOW011626180412

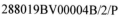

9 781412 847681